Money, Mania and Markets

To my mother and late father

Money, Mania and Markets

Investment, Company Formation
and the Stock Exchange
in Nineteenth-Century Scotland

R. C. MICHIE

Department of Economic History
University of Durham

JOHN DONALD PUBLISHERS LTD
EDINBURGH

ISBN 0 85976 070 7

Printed in Great Britain by Bell & Bain Ltd., Glasgow

Preface

THIS book required not only original research but also the culling of the work of others, especially in the twin fields of Scottish economic history and the literature of finance. Without the prior effort of many others, a book on a theme such as investment, with its many ramifications, would have been impossible. The notes indicate the specific debts owed, as well as suggesting that the points made are not merely the impressions of superficial observation, but the considered opinions of those who have studied the topics in depth.

Many colleagues at Aberdeen and Durham Universities have assisted in formulating the ideas contained in this book, none more so than Professor P. L. Payne, who supervised the original thesis, and Professor A. K. Cairncross, who examined it. I also owe a debt of gratitude to the Scottish stockbroking profession who, unreservedly, opened up their records to me. These were both the records of the various Scottish stock exchanges, still held in their regional centres, and of a number of Scottish stockbroking firms, especially Bell, Laurie, Robertson & Co. in Edinburgh and Parsons & Co. in Glasgow.

Naturally, any researcher owes much to the librarians and archivists of the institutions housing the essential primary material, while, without a research studentship from the S.S.R.C., this work would never have been begun, and without a lectureship at the University of Durham, who also contributed to the expenses of travel and typing, the book would never have been completed. Finally, I must thank Miss D. A. Brooks who did more than one expects from a typist. In addition, the substance of the chapter entitled 'Prelude to Specialisation, 1700-1820', originally appeared in *Business History,* and I am grateful for permission to reproduce it.

R. C. Michie

Contents

Tables

Figure

Abbreviations

(see also Sections B, C and D of Bibliography)

A.H.R.	*Agricultural History Review*
A.Ec.H.R.	*Australian Economic History Review*
B.H.	*Business History*
B.E.M.	*Blackwoods Edinburgh Magazine*
B.P.P.	*British Parliamentary Papers*
E.B.H.C.P.	*Ealing Business History Conference Paper*
E.H.	*Economic History*
Ec.H.R.	*Economic History Review*
Econ.	*Economist*
E.E.H.	*Explorations in Entrepreneurial Economic History*
J.Ec.H.	*Journal of Economic History*
J. of T.H.	*Journal of Transport History*
J.R.S.S.	*Journal of the Royal Statistical Society*
J.W. S.I. & S.I.	*Journal of the West of Scotland Iron & Steel Institute*
I.L.N.	*Illustrated London News*
O.E.P.	*Oxford Economic Papers*
P.R.P.S.G.	*Proceedings of the Royal Philosophical Society of Glasgow*
Q.J.E.	*Quarterly Journal of Economics*
R.M.	*Railway Magazine*
S.C.R.O.	*Scottish Companies Registration Office*
S.J.P.E.	*Scottish Journal of Political Economy*
T.A.P.S.	*Transactions of the Aberdeen Philosophical Society*
T.B.R.	*Three Banks Review*
T.H.	*Transport History*
T.H. & A.S.	*Transactions of the Highland and Agricultural Society*

INTRODUCTION

... there is, perhaps, no science in which the state of things at a given moment, however accurately delineated, is of less value than in economics, unless it be accompanied by a knowledge of the earlier conditions out of which the state of things has developed.
E. T. Powell, *The Mechanism of the City* (Lon. 1910) p. 74.

Because a stock exchange is a medium through which so many savings and investment decisions gain expression, its role can only be properly interpreted when its history is firmly imbedded in the economy of which it is a part.
A. R. Hall, *The Stock Exchange of Melbourne and the Victorian Economy, 1852-1900* (Canberra 1968) vii.

The stock market is the great governor of values, and the determinant of the relationship between production and consumption, — the guide which points the finger as to where capital is needed and where it has ceased to be needed.
C. A. Conant, *Wall Street and the Country: A Study of Recent Financial Tendencies* (New York 1904) p. 95.

Introduction

THE published financial history of nineteenth-century Scotland reveals strange discrepancies. Certain areas have been studied in considerable depth, with many articles, monographs, and general studies devoted to them. In particular, the history of Scottish banking possesses a large and worthy literature, including contributions from some of Scotland's foremost economic historians. Scottish overseas investment has also been the subject of considerable research, especially investment in the Western United States. Yet, other financial topics of no less importance have been virtually ignored. Almost nothing is known about the Scottish insurance companies, despite the substantial international role that they played. More is known concerning the stock exchanges, but it is insufficient to provide more than a surface sketch which is often inaccurate with regard to dates, emphasis and role. Consequently, one of the aims of this book is partially to rectify a major imbalance in Scottish economic history by giving a detailed description of the development of the Scottish share market up to 1900.

However, this book attempts more than that. The appearance of stockbrokers and the establishment of stock exchanges in Scotland was a product of the growth of indigenous joint-stock enterprise. Without the securities issued by these concerns, there would have been no need for a Scottish share market. Thus, the book traces the history of the joint-stock company in Scotland during the nineteenth century. The fluctuating fortunes and changing composition of these companies had a major and growing influence upon the investor, but the securities they issued were not the only openings available for savings, nor were stocks and shares consistently popular. Therefore, the book examines the nature of investment in general, and the varied factors that determined the investor's decisions of when to invest, where to invest, and in what to invest.

In order to achieve these objectives it was necessary to go beyond the study of the stock exchanges themselves and the records that they possessed. The minutes, correspondence, lists and recorded transactions of the stock exchanges did provide invaluable information, but they also hinted at an even more interesting and important financial world outside the confines of their institutional walls. It was only by consulting a wide range of other contemporary material, supplemented by secondary and often unpublished accounts, that the complex and inter-related activities of stock exchanges, stockbrokers, joint-stock companies and investors could be properly understood. Even the stock exchange records that were of great use had to be processed before their secrets were revealed. In the case of the transactions of the Aberdeen Stock Exchange, it was only by the classification of the companies being traded and the measurement of the value of business in each category from month to month, that an accurate picture of the changing nature and value of turnover could be discovered. Without adopting this methodology it would have been impossible to study either the changes in stock exchange business or the forces affecting investment.

Also, it was considered important to assess the relative significance of stockbrokers and stock exchanges and to understand the functions which they performed. The period before either appeared was studied so as to permit an evaluation of the novelty of the contribution made by the new profession and its institutions. Contemporary economic conditions, especially current trends in investment, were investigated in order to place the activities of both stockbrokers and stock exchanges in perspective, rather than leave them isolated from their historical context. Finally, the specific contributions of the stockbroker and the stock exchange to investment were examined, as well as the contribution of the share market as a whole. This investigation reveals the central role played by the stockbroker rather than the stock exchange, and serves to justify the function of the much maligned secondary market as opposed to the raising of primary capital.

In short, the aim of the book was to study the evolution of a major Scottish financial institution within the national and international environment in which it operated.

PART I:

BIRTH OF THE PROFESSION, 1700-1830

There is, perhaps, no legitimate business which holds more fascination for the general public than that of stock and share-broker, and yet, comparatively, is so little understood.
J. E. Day, *Stockbrokers' Office Organisation, Management and Accounts* (London 1911) p. 1.

For, as the wealth of this nation depends largely on the efficiency of its industrial production, so does that efficiency depend largely upon wise choice between the many possible investment opportunities open to the small supply of resources available for investment.
R. F. Henderson, *The New Issue Market and the Finance of Industry* (Cambridge 1951) p. 14.

1

Prelude to Specialisation, 1700-1820

CONVENTIONALLY, the beginning of the stock or share market in any country is dated from the foundation of the first stock exchange or possibly the appearance of the first stock or share brokers. However, the need for such an institution or such specialists existed long before their actual appearance. In Scotland companies with transferable shares were first formed in the seventeenth century,[1] but it was not until 1824 that the first share brokers appear, and 1844 when the first stock exchange was founded. Dealing certainly took place in the shares of those concerns and in the increasing number of other joint-stock ventures formed in the eighteenth and early nineteenth centuries.[2]

There were three main forms of joint-stock enterprise in eighteenth-century Scotland. The most numerous were those concerns formed under a contract of copartnery, which bound those participating to observe the regulations of the company and to unite it providing the necessary capital. A common feature in the contracts of the larger concerns was a clause giving the share-holder the right to transfer his shares at will, or with only minimal hindrance. The Dundee Assurance Company, formed in 1783, allowed '... every partner during the subsistence of this contract to sell or otherwise dispose of his share or shares of the stock of the company ...'[3] Larger concerns, such as the Royal Bank of Scotland, the British Linen Company, and the Forth and Clyde Canal, were formed under government charter, which usually included a clause giving shareholders the freedom to sell their shares. In the charter of the British Linen Company it was stated that '... the particular share of every member in the capital or joint-stock of the said corporation, hereby established, from time to time shall be transferable, assignable and divisible ...' and the company opened transfer books to record transactions in the shares.[4] The tontine societies, first established in 1781 in Scotland, also had their capital in the form of equal transferable shares. These ventures were mainly engaged in the ownership of property, particularly coffee-houses, hotels, and streets of houses and shops.[5] Thus there existed in eighteenth-century Scotland a growing number of companies whose capital was in the form of transferable shares.

The oldest method by which shares were bought and sold was through direct negotiation between vendor and purchaser. This appears to have been the main method used for the transfer of shares in the New Mills Cloth Manufactory over the 1701-03 period.[6] Direct private transfer was facilitated in the eighteenth century by the contemporary organisation of joint-stock enterprise and the very nature of Scottish society and business life. Shares were normally of high denomination and value as, for example, amongst banks. In the 1760s the Perth United Banking Company issued £100 shares, the Dundee Banking Company issued £200 shares, while those of the Banking Company in Aberdeen were £500 each. If the company was successful the actual value of the share could be much higher, for a £100 Royal Bank of Scotland share was worth £161 in 1774 and £269 in 1788.[7] Shares of those values tended to be traded singly, making the matching of numbers of shares offered and required a simple matter.

Though joint-stock concerns did grow in number in the eighteenth century they were by no means numerous, being confined to one or a few banks, insurance companies, tontine societies, and a small number of industrial and shipping ventures, in the larger cities and towns. This curtailed the varieties of opportunity for investment in shares and so made it likely that a share for sale was in a company that a prospective purchaser was acquainted with and interested in buying into. What made this even more likely was that the share-holders in any one company were not drawn from Scotland as a whole but normally from the particular area of Scotland in which the concern was founded and operated. The investors in the Aberdeen Whale Fishing Company of 1754, and the Banking Company in Aberdeen of 1767, were overwhelmingly from the Aberdeen area while the investors in the Dundee Assurance Co. came almost entirely from Dundee and its vicinity. Only six per cent of the shareholders in Aberdeen's Banking Company and five per cent of the shareholders in Dundee's Insurance Company were not local.[8] Therefore, the range of companies available to the investors in any one area was indeed restricted, easing the matching of bargains.

The number of investors involved in the shares of joint-stock companies was also small though it did grow progressively in the eighteenth century. In the 1730s, the Royal Bank of Scotland had an average of 115 shareholders, the British Linen Company had 126 by 1751, only 89 people subscribed to the Forth and Clyde Canal in 1768, while the Aberdeen Whaling and Banking ventures attracted 99 and 109 investors respectively.[9] These shareholders were normally composed of the landed interest, merchants, or professional people such as lawyers, physicians, or ministers.[10] Consequently, those interested in shares were not only a fairly small group in society but one restricted to certain economic or social classes and divided up by location. At the same time general conditions in eighteenth-century Scotland were conducive to private deals between those holding or interested in shares. Edinburgh, Scotland's largest town, was still on the scale of a small market town in which people knew each other by sight, and business was conducted on the open street or in adjacent coffee-houses or taverns.[11] In Glasgow and other Scottish cities and towns, the same situation also prevailed; in Aberdeen, a ready market appeared to exist for shares in the coffee-houses of the town.[12] Overall, there was very little division between social and business intercourse, making contact between the varied groups interested in shares fairly easy. The early commercial exchanges, for example, were no more than regular meeting places for those with business of any kind to transact or for acquaintances to meet.

By the early nineteenth century, the growth of population, the expanding size of towns, and the increasing separation of social and business life, were increasingly restricting the individual's range of contact. One account of Edinburgh in 1816 reported that: 'The time was when scarcely any business was transacted except in a tavern; but as this practice is now greatly laid aside, such places are less frequented than they were formerly.'[13] Within business itself, the general exchanges and markets were becoming more specialised, confining themselves to certain activities and a certain clientele. Shops were replacing markets while professions and businesses clustered in their own specific areas rather than being all intermingled.[14] At the same time rising numbers of shares, companies and investors magnified the problems of matching deals. The Edinburgh and Glasgow Union Canal had 540 shareholders in 1817, for example, and they came not just from Edinburgh or Glasgow but from such towns as Linlithgow, Falkirk and Crieff.[15] In addition to these growing difficulties private share transfers had inherent problems which were not altogether out-weighed by the negligible cost of arranging the deal. Chance played a major role in whether a buyer met a compatible purchaser, as coverage and contract were never complete and largely non-existent between towns. Also, as deals were strictly private there was little opportunity for information to circulate concerning companies, available shares, and current prices, all of which were essential if a ready market was to be established. These problems and difficulties were serious enough to lead eighteenth-century investors to adopt additional means in order to arrange transfers.

One of the oldest devices used in Scotland in order to facilitate the transfer of shares was the auction or roup, a traditional means of disposing of goods or property. As early as 1703 it was employed for the transfer of a share in the New Mills Cloth Manufactory from Patrick Stiell, an Edinburgh wine merchant, to Robert Blackwood, an Edinburgh baillie.[16] It was also the method used in 1727 by Archibald, the first Earl of Rosebery, to sell twenty Bank of Scotland shares,[17] and by Laurence Hill, in 1818 and 1819, to dispose of a number of shares in the Glasgow Assembly & Concert Rooms venture on behalf of clients.[18] Joint-stock companies frequently included a clause in their contract of copartnery which gave them the right to sell shares by public roup if they happened to acquire any, such as by forfeiture. Such was the case for the Edinburgh Dutch Shipping Company in 1751.[19] At first the venue for a public roup of shares was the offices of the company, with the proceedings handled by the clerk of company who afterwards entered the change in the transfer book.[20] However, in the course of the eighteenth century more public places were resorted to as locations for auctions, especially coffee-houses. The roup of Lord Rosebery's Bank of Scotland shares was, for example, held in 'John's', an Edinburgh coffee-house.[21] Auctions were also increasingly publicised by an advertisement placed in a local newspaper well in advance: 'To be exposed to sale by voluntary roup, on Wednesday next, the 16th inst. at the Exchange coffee house betwixt 12 and 1 Forenoon, one, two, or three shares in the Bank of Scotland. Any person that inclines to purchase may enquire for the seller at the House.'[22] That advertisement was inserted in the *Caledonian Mercury,* an Edinburgh newspaper, in 1744, and was fairly typical of any to be found in Scottish newspapers in the eighteenth century. Though in most cases shares were auctioned alone, in a number of instances they were included with other forms of property. The *Edinburgh Advertiser* of 1778 contained the following advertisement: 'Household Furniture, and two shares in the East Lothian and Merse Whale-Fishing Company to be sold, by public roup, within the dwelling-house of Robert Macklish, brewer in Dunbar, on Wednesday the 16th day of September instant.' In 1817, two shares in the Edinburgh, Leith and Hull Shipping Company were included in an auction along with '. . . twenty-four 6 pounder carronades, with their carriages and other apparatus . . .'[23] There was little differentiation between shares and any other form of property.

Despite the obvious popularity of the auction as a means of transferring shares, as judged by newspaper advertisements, it did suffer from a number of important disadvantages. An auction with its need for prior advertising, the services of an auctioneer and possibly a legal agent, and the let of a room, was an expensive way of selling property. One estimate for 1835 put the cost of the auction itself at five per cent of the price of each share, ignoring incidental expenditures.[24] Most of these costs had to be incurred whether a sale was made or not, and that could not always be guaranteed. Over the period 1800-02, at least five different public roups were held to dispose of the shares in Carron Company held by Francis Garbett and Charles Gascoigne. The only reported sale was in January 1801 when twelve shares were sold.[25] With large holdings and high share values such costs and risks could be endured, but they would be prohibitive for the investor of lesser means with only a small holding. The effectiveness of an auction was also limited, as the knowledge of its taking place was largely confined to those reading the advertisement, while the physical presence of a potential purchaser was also required. These were not serious defects as long as shareholdings remained geographically restricted. More serious was the fact that the roup was a one-way market, being initiated by, and for, the vendor of the shares. No general attempt was made to spread information about the current prices obtained for shares when auctioned so as to encourage potential sellers and purchasers to act. It was only infrequently that advertisements for roups included expected prices or the newspapers themselves reported prices obtained.[26] Regular auctions of shares were not organised until the 1820s.

These deficiencies encouraged some shareholders to by-pass the auction and to advertise directly shares for sale or wanted: 'To be sold, £300 capital stock of the Royal Bank of Scotland. Apply to James Beveridge, writer in Edinburgh.'[27] Advertisements of that kind appeared in all Scottish newspapers in increasing numbers over the years 1700 to 1820. Another, from the *Aberdeen Chronicle* of 1816, is the following: 'For sale, two shares of the Greenland Whale Fishing Company. Also one share of the Aberdeen, Leith, and Clyde Shipping Company. Apply to James Johnston, Gallowgate.'[28] Advertisements listing shares wanted were not common but a few did appear, such as in 1783, when the following was inserted in the *Edinburgh Advertiser:* 'Wanted to purchase, some shares of the Stock of the Bank of Scotland. Apply to publisher.'[29] The success of advertising as a medium of transfer was very dependent upon the circulation and readership of the newspapers. Prior to 1800, newspapers were concentrated in the main Scottish cities, but by 1820 most towns were served by at least one local newspaper.[30] However, a newspaper was an expensive item, with the average price rising from 3d. per copy in 1761 to 7d. in 1815, mainly as a result of heavy government taxation.[31] This restricted readership, though it is likely that all who could afford to purchase shares could also afford newspapers, yet they would be unlikely to buy more than one.

As with other forms of transfer, newspaper advertisements had serious disadvantages. They were sufficiently expensive to inhibit their use, for the cost had to be borne irrespective of whether a sale was made or not.[32] With the rapidly expanding number of individual newspapers, from the late eighteenth century onwards, it also became increasingly difficult and costly to ensure adequate coverage for an advertisement among the required geographic, social and business groupings who might be potential purchasers. '... Advertising in a greater number of newspapers tends greatly to increase the expense, without completely attaining the object in view' was the view of an article in the *Aberdeen Journal* in 1823, and the same article summarised the other inadequacies of advertising: 'The circulation of an advertisement in a newspaper may be considered as limited, in point of time, to the day on which it is published, and, in point of extent, to the range of circulation which the newspaper possesses ...'[33] Though newspaper advertising was a popular means by which to arrange share deals, it could be costly and success was not guaranteed, while the market was fragmented by the existence of many newspapers. In addition there was little publicity given in advertisements to current prices, which hindered future pricing and curtailed response to a changing situation.

Notwithstanding the use made of direct methods for transferring shares, an early recourse was had to intermediaries to handle the business. The obvious choice for such a role were the members of the Scottish legal profession, to be found under such titles as advocate, solicitor, writer or clerk to the signet. In addition to purely legal business they handled, from at least the seventeenth century, such activities as estate management, arranging loans, and handling investments.[34] 'We trust ... our fortune ... to the lawyer and attorney' was the view of Adam Smith.[35] The social and family connections of the legal profession also made them suitable for arranging the sale and purchase of shares. Socially they were one of the most respected and influential professional groups, while their family relationships were among the very people who were likely to be involved in joint-stock concerns. In a survey of the fathers of 300 writers to the signet, over the 1690-1829 period, it was found that the most popular parental occupations were those of landowner, merchant, minister, physician, army or naval officer, government official, or lawyer itself. The foundation of a successful legal business rested largely on a wide range of influential friends, relatives, and acquaintances, and on performing varied services for them.[36]

Most of the newspaper advertisements offering shares for sale were inserted by lawyers and they also arranged many of the auctions of shares. These were the public manifestations of legal involvement, for deals could also be handled without recourse to either advertisement or auction. Advertising was merely a means by which the lawyer extended his contacts and brought the shares to the notice of potential purchasers who were not among his own range of acquaintances. If a share could be placed among the existing contacts at a fair price, an advertisement, or roup, could be replaced by private negotiation.[37] In 1814, Mitchell, Grahame and Mitchell, writers in Glasgow, arranged the transfer of Robert Liddell's shares in the Edinburgh and Leith Shipping Co. to Joseph Adams in Glasgöw and Colin MacNab in Glasgow, and the transaction was completely private.[38] However, with the large number of lawyers operating in Scotland, there being 600 writers to the signet in Edinburgh alone around 1800,[39] and nearly all of them prepared to sell or purchase shares on behalf of their clients, the market for shares without advertising was exceedingly fragmented. This had become so acute by the early nineteenth century that a number of attempts were made to remedy the situation. In 1816, James Taylor Smith and Company of Edinburgh established a 'General Newspaper and Advertising Office', one of whose functions was to make available all the newspapers to the legal profession so that the advertisements inserted by others could be perused.[40] Another attempt, made in 1823, was to publish and circulate to Scottish lawyers a newspaper entitled *The Money Register* which would '. . . report as to the state of the Money Market in Scotland, the selling prices of Feu duties, ground rents, etc., and of the stocks of the various Banks, Insurance and Shipping Companies, etc.'[41] Neither of these remedies was successful in overcoming the problems of communication between the many and varied members of the legal profession.

Although members of the legal profession were by far the most important intermediaries in share-dealing, they were not alone. Occasionally an auctioneer, or the clerk to a joint-stock company, acted independently in arranging transfers. Simpson, the Cashier of the Royal Bank of Scotland, often found buyers for the stock of that Company, if requested to do so, in the late eighteenth century.[42] These instances were rare, however. More common were the growing number of accountants in Scotland, whose business of handling books and accounts, and managing bankrupt estates, easily led them into shares. By the late eighteenth century, accountants can be noted handling share transfers for clients, initially in conjunction with a member of the legal profession. Walter Hogg, an accountant in Edinburgh, was associated with Andrew MacWhinnie, an Edinburgh writer, in disposing of some Carron Company stock in 1795.[43] Increasingly, the accountants acted alone in share deals, challenging the dominance of the lawyer.[44] A variety of personnel in other professions also dabbled in share-dealing. Insurance brokers were one such group; in Aberdeen in 1816, James Petrie and William White conducted a limited share business in addition to arranging insurance and selling ships.[45] Bank agents were another group who also appeared from time to time as intermediaries in share transfers, such as John Matthew, an Aberdeen banker, and Mr. Mitchell, the agent of the British Linen Company's bank in Tain.[46] Even merchants became involved, such as John Robertson, a Leith wine merchant in 1815, and William Clark, an Aberdeen general merchant.[47]

Over the course of the eighteenth and early nineteenth centuries virtually anybody who acted in a responsible capacity for the monied people in Scottish society was called upon to handle transactions in shares in the same way as he arranged the sale of some other forms of property, the obtaining of loans or insurance, or the purchase of wine or other commodities. This proliferation of individuals who were engaged in the share business on an intermittent basis fragmented the market and made it difficult for those interested in shares to identify the people who were active intermediaries — any lawyer, accountant, banker, insurance broker, or even merchant, might be the person to approach. All these people suffered from the same basic deficiency with regard to share transfers, in that shares were only a minor adjunct to their main business. Even if a lawyer neglected his legal activities and concentrated upon financial affairs, it was the disposal of land, farms, estates, houses, etc. that dominated his time and effort, not the sale of a few shares from time to time. Samuel Mitchelson, for example, an Edinburgh clerk to the signet who handled transactions in shares in the 1770s-80s, was more interested in the sale of houses and annuities than shares.[48] The same was true of those accountants, insurance brokers, merchants or bankers who were also involved in share business.[49] The result was that all those engaged in share-transfer had a low involvement in it and a low commitment to it, but naturally charged the specialist fees that their knowledge and training allowed them to charge for other aspects of their business. This meant that the use of these intermediaries for share-transfer was expensive, and it was made more expensive by the cost of advertisements and possibly of auctions to reach the potential market. In return, the seller or purchaser of shares did not receive the specialist service required for shares.

The transfer of shares did not require the expertise that the other forms of property needed. Shares did not fit comfortably into the property market in general in which items of property had a unique price depending upon condition, location, and other factors. Land, for example, could not command a uniform price per acre, as this comment from a traveller in Scotland in 1767 indicates:

> Land lets here for various prices, according to its situation and goodness, and indeed it is very hard to ascertain the real price of any land in Scotland, because in a hollow or valley, perhaps a farm may let at twenty shillings an acre, and on high land not for fourpence an acre.[50]

Pricing of this type of property required the attention of a skilled and practised expert and the consequent high fee demanded could be borne by the large value of the property involved. In contrast, all the shares in a joint-stock company had exactly the same value and would all fetch the same price. The shares in a joint-stock company of equal standing would also fetch similar prices. Thus the expertise of those skilled in the disposal of land, houses, or ships was not required for the far less complicated business of pricing and transferring shares. What the seller or purchaser of shares required were regular lists of current prices of shares and these were not provided until the emergence of specialist share brokers in Scotland in the mid-1820s.

After this brief description of the various means by which shares were transferred in eighteenth-century Scotland, what can be concluded about the state of the market? Throughout the eighteenth and early nineteenth centuries an increasingly sophisticated and well-used mechanism for the buying and selling of shares was developed. It centred mainly around the members of the Scottish legal profession and was largely dependent upon advertising in the local press for successful contact with potential buyers. In normal circumstances few problems existed for the seller of shares in a popular concern. From 1748 to 1775 there were 141 separate transfers in the shares of the British Linen Company, excluding changes of ownership through death and bequest, and this involved stock to the value of £92,657. In the twenty-eight year period there were only three years in which no such transfers took place, indicating a regular turnover of shares averaging five transactions a year and £3,309 worth of stock in each.[51] Difficulty could be encountered in disposing of a substantial number of shares in a less popular venture. The stock of the Carron Company became unsaleable in 1773, when the concern was passing through a period of great difficulty, but no such problems were encountered in the case of the British Linen Company. Between 1763 and 1774 no dividend was paid and there was a possibility of the company being wound up, but trading in the shares was very active.[52] Generally, it was fairly easy to dispose of shares, and the time involved could be no more than that taken to insert an advertisement in a newspaper and contact to be made. For example, Captain Leslie of Aberdeen held shares in the Banking Company in Aberdeen and regarded them, in 1801, as '. . . at all times saleable . . .'[53] A holder of stock in a Scottish joint-stock company could speedily and economically convert it into cash. Potential buyers contacted, though, were rarely all those who were interested in the shares on offer.

It was less easy to buy shares, unless the purchaser was willing to accept the type and number on offer. Apart from the very occasional advertisement for shares wanted, the means to encourage holders to part with shares were limited without current price lists to bring out investors attracted by capital gains. However, the means of transfer in existence did create changing share prices and these do appear to have obtained a degree of circulation. The Edinburgh bookseller, Creech, writing in 1792, was in a position to comment:

> In 1763 — the Royal Bank Stock sold at the rate of £160 per cent — In 1791, Royal Bank New Stock sold at £240 per cent — The original shares of Bank of Scotland, or Old Bank, of £83. 6s. 8d., sold in 1763, at £119, in 1791, at £80. The British Linen Company's stock, in 1763, and for many years later, sold at £40 per cent below par. In 1792 — £336 of this stock sold for £545, that is £162. 4s. 1½d. per cent.[54]

Other contemporaries were also able to refer to current share prices for banks, canals or even tontine societies,[55] implying a reasonable awareness from those interested concerning activity in shares.

These prices were also responsive to changes in the fortunes of the company involved and to the general economic climate. The prices of the shares of the Scottish canal companies, for example, were directly related to their success, or otherwise, in overcoming problems during construction and, later, to the dividends paid. Following the full opening of the Monkland Canal in 1792, its prospects were so unfavourable that the £100 shares fell to between five and seven pounds each but, with later success, they rose to £3,200 each. On the declaration of a 25 per cent dividend in March 1816, the shares of the Forth and Clyde Canal rose quickly to £500 each.[56] The response of share prices to changing situations was also sufficiently fast to allow speculation in the shares of the Forth and Clyde Canal in 1817,[57] while the price of the shares in one company was related to those in other companies. A good indication of this was the yield on shares. As early as 1757 the current prices of Bank of Scotland and Royal Bank of Scotland stock were such as to give a yield of between three and a half and four per cent on each, despite differing original prices and dividends.[58] These prices were also related to the current economic situation and responded to it with, for example, Royal Bank shares rising in price when the American War of Independence released Scottish capital from trade and made it available for temporary investment.[59]

There existed in eighteenth and early nineteenth-century Scotland recognised means for buying and selling shares and the prices obtained for these shares were related to company and general economic performance. These prices also obtained a degree of circulation and responded to change reasonably quickly. Hugh Hutcheon, the Aberdeen advocate who was handling Captain Leslie's affairs, wrote to him in October 1801 that:

> With respect to your Bank shares, the market price of a share has lately risen from £400 to £435; and as there is a probability of their still rising higher, I think they should not be sold hastily: at least so long as your other funds will answer, which I hope they will at present.[60]

Even before the appearance of stock or share brokers, let alone stock exchanges, there did exist something of a ready market for shares in Scotland. It was not perfect but, considering the small number of investors, the few joint-stock companies and the limited number of transfers, it was adequate for the times, though any increase in companies, investors, or transfers would place severe strains on the system. This share market was not, in any way, separate from the market for property in general. Shares were regarded no differently from houses, land, or ships, and the same personnel and the same methods were utilised in their disposal. The merit of this situation was that from an early stage joint-stock securities had a well-developed market available to them, but for them it was an unnecessarily expensive market and one that was geared to the sale of unique items of property in local or regional markets. However, as long as joint-stock companies and their shares remained a very small item of property, there was little prospect of their peculiar needs being catered for.

NOTES

1. See W. R. Scott, *The Constitution and Finance of English, Scottish and Irish Joint-Stock Companies to 1720* (Cam. 1910-12) I, pp. 300-1, 327, 333-4.

2. Scott, op. cit., III, p. 274; W. R. Scott (ed.), *Records of a Scottish Cloth Manufactory at New Mills, Haddingtonshire, 1681-1703* (Edin. 1905) — See Minutes of 16 July 1701, 1 April 1702, 22 July 1702,

etc.; W. Graham, *The One Pound Note in the History of Banking in Great Britain* (Edin. 1911, 2nd edn.) p. 140; J. Lindsay, *The Canals of Scotland* (Newton Abbot 1968) pp. 57-9; R. H. Campbell, *Carron Company* (Edin. 1961) pp. 177-9; *Edinburgh Sugar House Company* — Minute book, 10 September 1753, 29 November 1753, 25 November 1754, etc.

3. *Contract of Copartnery — Dundee Assurance Company* (Dundee 1783). See also R. H. Campbell, 'The Law and the joint stock company in Scotland' in P. L. Payne (ed.), *Studies in Scottish Business History* (Lon. 1967) p. 143; C. W. Munn, The Scottish Provincial Banking Companies, 1747-1864 (Ph.D. Glasgow Univ. 1976) p. 260.

4. *Charter of the British Linen Company* (Edin. 1746).

5. 'Tontines and the Royal Bank' in *Three Banks Review*, No. 57, 1963, pp. 29, 35; J. Cleland, *The Rise and Progress of the City of Glasgow* (Glasgow 1820), pp. 123-4. For a description of the organisation of the first Glasgow Tontine see J. Denholm, *An Historical Account of the City of Glasgow* (Glasgow 1797) p. 107.

6. Scott (ed.), loc. cit.

7. S. G. Checkland, *Scottish Banking: a History 1695-1973* (Glasgow 1975) p. 160.

8. *Banking Company in Aberdeen — Contract of Copartnery* (Abdn. 1767); *List of Subscribers to the Aberdeen Whale Fishing Company* (Abdn. 1754); *Contract of Copartnery — Dundee Assurance Company* (Dundee 1783).

9. Checkland, op. cit., pp. 65, 112; C. A. Malcolm, *The History of the British Linen Bank* (Edin. 1950) p. 234; *List of Subscribers*, op. cit.; *Banking Co. in Aberdeen*, op. cit.; J. Hopkirk, *Account of the Forth and Clyde Navigation — From its origin to the present time* (Glasgow 1816) p. 16; A. Durie — Personal communication regarding British Linen Company (18 August 1977); cf. Munn, op. cit., pp. 247-252 for a selection of Banking Companies.

10. See, for example, *Contract of Copartnery — Dundee Assurance Co.* and *Banking Co. in Aberdeen; List of Subscribers to the Edinburgh and Glasgow Union Canal* (Edin. 1817); Munn, loc. cit.; etc. In 1696 there were 1,317 investors in the Darien Company while Sinclair estimated the 'monied interest' at '2,000 souls' in the 1790s. See Scott, op. cit., III, pp. 478-9 and J. Sinclair, *Analysis of the Statistical Account of Scotland* (Edin. 1825), Part I, pp. 210-11.

11. A. J. Youngson, *The Making of Classical Edinburgh, 1750-1840* (Edin. 1966) pp. 53, 58-9, 236; A. Kincaid, *The History of Edinburgh* (Edin. 1787) p. 153; H. Cockburn, *Memorials of His Time* (Edin. 1856) p. 169; *S.M.*, IV, 1742 p. 75.

12. R. N. Forbes, 'Early Banking Excursions', *Three Banks Review*, No. 102, 1974, p. 555; W. J. Couper, 'Old Glasgow Coffee-Houses' in *Old Glasgow Club*, March 1911, pp. 4-5, 10; *The Picture of Glasgow* (Glasgow 1812) p. 116; *Memoirs & Portraits of One Hundred Glasgow Men* (Glasgow 1886) I, p. 108; *Banking Co. in Aberdeen*, op. cit.

13. *The New Picture of Edinburgh* (Edin. 1816) p. 215.

14. Youngson, op. cit., p. 236; W. H. Marwick, 'Shops in 18th and 19th Century Edinburgh' in *Book of the Old Edinburgh Club*, vol. 30, 1959, p. 127; L . J. Saunders, *Scottish Democracy*, 1815-1840 (Edin. 1950) p. 110; two letters written in 1799 comparing Dundee in 1746 and 1799 reprinted in *The History of Dundee* (Dundee 1847) p. 180.

15. *List of Subscribers to the Edinburgh and Glasgow Union Canal*, op. cit.

16. Scott (ed.), op. cit., Minutes, 13 January 1703.

17. J. M. Forbes, 'John's. A Famous Edinburgh Coffee House', *Scottish Bankers Magazine*, I, 1909-10, p. 265.

18. Memoranda: Hill & Hogan, Writers, Glasgow 14 October 1818, 4 May 1819.

19. *Contract of Copartnery — Edinburgh Dutch Shipping Company* (Edin. 1751).

20. Scott (ed.), loc. cit.; *Edinburgh Sugar House Co.* Minutes, 25 November 1754.

21. J. M. Forbes, loc. cit.

22. *Caledonian Mercury* 10 May 1744.

23. *E.A.*, 8 September 1778, 18 July 1817.

24. *G.H.*, 29 June 1835.

25. *E.W.J.*, 26 November 1800, 28 January 1801, 4 March 1801, 16 December 1801, 24 March 1802, 14 January 1801.

26. For some examples see *E.E.C.*, 24 December 1795; *E.W.J.*, 14 January 1801.

27. *E.A.*, 27 October 1778.

28. *A.C.*, 13 January 1816.

29. *E.A.*, 11 March 1783.

30. See R. M. W. Cowan, *The Newspaper in Scotland* (Glasgow 1946) p. 7.

31. J. Grant, *The Newspaper Press* (Lon. 1871 & 1872), I, pp. 99, 173, 221, 223; Cowan, op. cit., pp. 23, 163.

32. W. Creech, *Edinburgh Fugitive Pieces* (Edin. 1792, repr. 1815) p. 76; Grant, op. cit., p. 300.

33. *A.J.*, 14 May 1823. See also *The Periodical Press of Great Britain and Ireland* (Lon. 1824) p. 57 for a similar view.

34. A. R. B. Haldane, *New Ways through the Glens* (Lon. 1962) p. 41; T. C. Smout, *A History of the Scottish People, 1560-1830* (Lon. 1969) p. 363.

35. Adam Smith, *An Inquiry into the Nature and Cause of the Wealth of Nations* (Lon. 1789, 5th edn.) I, p. 160.

36. Smout, op. cit., p. 375; Haldane, op. cit., p. 42; See also B. L. Anderson, 'Law, Finance and economic growth in England: some long term influence', in B. M. Radcliffe (ed.), *Great Britain and her world* (Manchester 1975) pp. 110-11.

37. See, for example, *A.C.* 29 March 1817, advertisement by John Smith, advocate; and *Dundee, Perth and Cupar Advertiser* 6 February 1823, advertisement by James Hunter, writer.

38. Mitchell, Grahame & Mitchell: Transfer documents 24 February 1814.

39. Haldane, op. cit., p. 41.

40. *A.C.* 27 April 1816.

41. *A.J.* 14 May 1823.

42. Checkland, op. cit., p. 159.

43. *E.E.C.* 29 January 1795.

44. See *G.H.* 1824, especially 30 July and 29 November.

45. *A.C.* 17 February 1816, 24 February 1816, 28 December 1816.

46. *A.C.* 29 September 1821; *I.J.* 4 July 1823.

47. *Memorandum prepared by John H. Robertson,* 7 April 1927; *A.C.* 6 January 1816, 2 March 1816, 27 April 1816.

48. *E.A.* 29 September 1778, 29 December 1778, 26 January 1779, 27 July 1781 etc.

49. For accountants see *A History of the Chartered Accountants of Scotland* (Edin. 1954) pp. 11, 12, 16 — Reprints of advertisements and circulars of chartered accountants; R. Brown, *A History of Accounting and Accountants* (Edin. 1905) p. 321.

50. D. Varley, *The Unfortunate Husbandman* (1768, repr. Lon. 1964) p. 84.

51. *British Linen Company: Stock Transfers, 1748-1775.* Annual figures compiled by A. Durie. See also *List of Subscribers to the Aberdeen Whale Fishing Company* (Abdn. 1754 and 1755); Lindsay, op. cit., p. 57.

52. H. Hamilton, *The Industrial Revolution in Scotland* (Oxf. 1932) p. 161; Durie, op. cit.

53. A. Leslie to H. Hutcheon, 10 January 1801.

54. Creech, op. cit., p. 82.

55. See Adam Smith, op. cit., III, p. 149; Cleland, op. cit., p. 118; Denholm, op. cit., p. 107.

56. See E. A. Pratt, *Scottish Canals and Waterways* (Lon. 1922) pp. 56, 117, 148; J. Hopkirk, *Account of the Forth and Clyde Canal Navigation — From its Origin to the Present Time* (Glasgow 1816) p. 26.

57. *Papers written in opposition to the Union canal* (Leith 1817) p. 6.

58. M. Postlethwayt, *Universal Dictionary of Trade and Commerce* (2nd ed., Lon. 1757) II, p. 667.

59. D. MacPherson, *Annals of Commerce* (Lon. 1805) p. 593.

60. H. Hutcheon to A. Leslie, 1 October 1801.

2
Consequences of War, 1790-1820

THE appearance of stockbrokers in Scotland was much later than in comparable parts of England, with large English provincial towns, such as Bristol or Liverpool, possessing stockbrokers in the 1790s,[1] whereas these did not begin to operate in Edinburgh and Glasgow until the 1820s. It was during the rash of joint-stock canal company flotations between 1789 and 1797, and the accompanying speculation in their shares, that sufficient business was generated in England, outside London, to warrant the establishment of specialist brokers. In contrast, however, Scotland had few joint-stock canal companies compared to the network of waterways in the English Midlands or Lancashire and Yorkshire.[2] Many canal schemes were put forward in Scotland in the late eighteenth century but few were eventually promoted and almost none implemented compared to England,[3] partly because Scottish terrain and economic conditions meant high capital costs and less prospects of remunerative traffic.[4] Also, though the development in both countries was similar, Scotland was a much poorer region of the United Kingdom and thus had less capital available for investment.[5]

What wealth there was in Scotland continued to be channelled into traditional areas of more immediate need, especially building and land. Both Edinburgh and Glasgow experienced building booms in the 1780s and 1790s.[6] Therefore there was little extra business which would warrant someone setting up as a specialist broker of shares in Scotland in the 1790s. Such conditions were not to appear until 30 years later.

The French Revolutionary and Napoleonic wars made a substantial impact upon the Scottish economy both through the commitment of resources to waging war and distortions to normal peacetime activity. At the peak of hostilities around 500,000 men, or 10% of the British labour force, were engaged in the armed services and their auxiliaries, and they had to be provisioned, equipped, and serviced.[7] Government expenditure rose almost sixfold between 1793 and 1815 in order to finance the war.[8] This rapid growth in government spending, combined with uncontrolled civilian demand and the withdrawal of a substantial segment of the labour force, led to rapid price rises and general inflation, as demand outstripped the supply of most commodities, manufactures and services. Existing banks expanded their business and many new ones were established, with 12 provincial banking companies being formed between 1802 and 1810 in Scotland, and all issued notes.[9]

Wartime inflation and demand brought prosperity to many branches of the Scottish economy. Not only did those industries directly involved in the

17

production of war material benefit, such as iron, coal or lead, but so did those concerned in the production of everyday items of consumption such as candles, beer, glass, fish and agricultural products.[10]

However, this prosperity was not shared equally amongst all. Wages rose between 1790 and 1815, but less so than prices. In agriculture, while the prices for most agricultural products doubled from 1790 to 1812, wages rose only half as much.[11] Judging from the available fragmentary evidence, and the demand for such consumer goods as beer, whisky, and candles, wages in Scotland expanded rapidly for the first ten years of the war, and then tended to fall behind the increase in prices.[12] It was those who owned or controlled the assets and resources of the Scottish economy that benefited most during these inflationary times. The value of land rose greatly, as did the profits to be made in agriculture, fishing, trade or industry.[13] Profits made by such concerns as the Stevenston Colliery in Ayrshire, the Dumbarton Glass Company, or the Carron Iron works all rose greatly.[14] The removal of such competitors as France, Holland or Spain meant a great boost for Scottish trade and shipping as Britain, during the course of the war, acquired and maintained almost a monopoly of the world's commerce. The Scottish whaling industry underwent a wartime transformation with the disappearance of rival whaling fleets, such as the Dutch, while the demand for oil continued, producing 'windfall' profits.[15] Altogether, the consequence of the war was that

> ... money was drawn up into great masses, in the hands of saving persons of the trading and farming classes.[16]

It was, of course, precisely those groups in society who had been inclined to invest in the shares of Scottish joint-stock companies before the war. Consequently, such conditions would suggest increased opportunities for joint-stock enterprise and encourage the appearance of stockbrokers.

However, not all the increased income of these people was available for investment in shares, as the activities producing the enhanced profits also required further investment, in order to increase output and reap even greater profits in the face of ever rising prices and demand. In particular, farmers and landowners utilised substantial amounts of their increased income in bringing new land into cultivation, and increasing production on the old in response to wartime food shortages. Coal, iron, glass, and textiles all required substantial capital, obtained from ploughed back profits. North-East Scotland's investment in whale fishing rose from a mere £15,000 in 1793 to £170,000 by 1815, for example.[17] Alexander Johnson, a merchant and manufacturer in Elgin, sold his banking and insurance shares in 1812, in order to meet the financial needs of his ventures into local textiles, shipping, and iron founding.[18] According to Purves, writing in 1817,

> The additional capital employed in cultivating new, and improving old land, in agricultural and manufacturing machinery, etc., in buildings, in shipping, in canals, and roads, and by insurance, banking, and other companies, etc. is astonishing.[19]

At the same time, heavier taxation to finance increased government spending took its share of the increased incomes with the new income tax, for example, raising an extra £137m in revenue between 1798 and 1815.[20]

Savings did remain once the direct requirements of business and government had been met. However, most of this did not flow into Scottish joint-stock enterprise as the growing funded and unfunded debt of the government offered attractive yields and absorbed a large amount of the money available for investment. Government debt rose from £243m in 1793 to £745m in 1815, and came to occupy a growing proportion of British income-producing wealth.[21] Whereas before the Napoleonic Wars the holders of government securities were largely confined to London and vicinity, by the end of the war they were to be found throughout Britain.[22] Substantial Scottish investors became important holders of government stock at this time, especially those with London connections, such as financial institutions or wealthy landowners. By 1810, every Scottish bank of any size had large investments in the funds, while the New Club of Edinburgh purchased stock to the value of £3,490 in February 1803. Francis Russell, a Kincardineshire landowner, and Patrick Sellar, a Sutherland sheep farmer, both invested their wartime profits from agriculture in government securities.[23]

Government stock had an increasingly national appeal and its purchase and sale were catered for by specialists and institutions concentrated in London. It was in London that a ready market existed with the most competitive prices, and it was to London that provincial buying and selling was orientated. Consequently, the investment by Scottish institutions and individuals in government securities was channelled through London stockbrokers and facilities, and did not stimulate the development of such specialist services in Scotland.[24] The orientation of investment towards government stock jeopardised the growing Scottish market for transferable securities. If the government had continued to increase its funded borrowings, it is possible that little in the way of a market for stocks and shares would have come into existence outside London.

However, even during the war, government borrowing did not absorb all investment. A few joint-stock companies with substantial capitals and numerous shareholders were begun. There occurred a rash of flotations in the period 1807 to 1810, when there was a slight lull in the government's financial demands.[25] Three insurance companies were formed in Scotland, namely the Caledonian in 1805, and the Hercules and the North British in 1809. In 1810, a number of large banking companies were organised, including the Commercial Bank of Scotland. This company had a paid-up capital of £600,000 and 673 shareholders by 1815.[26] Other important joint-stock ventures were proposed at this time, such as the railways from Kelso to Berwick, Glasgow to Berwick, and Edinburgh to Dalkeith, but they failed to find sufficient financial support to get them under way. The same fate befell the project to complete the Edinburgh to Glasgow canal link.[27] Despite the establishment of a small number of substantial joint-stock enterprises during the wartime period, they were sufficiently few in number not to force any fundamental change in the existing methods of share transfer. The buying and selling of shares could still be accommodated within the general property market, and it was not of sufficient importance to warrant separate treatment.

The termination of the war, in 1815, itself had a major impact upon the British economy. Soldiers and sailors were quickly demobilised, while government spending was severely cut back, falling from its wartime peak of £113m in 1815 to £58m by 1819.[28] The situation was aggravated by the collapse of a number of banks and the contraction in credit and banknote circulation in those that remained. Bank failures were relatively few in Scotland compared to England, but the Falkirk Union Bank ceased business in 1816, while the East Lothian Bank collapsed in 1822, with severe economic consequences for that area.[29] This contraction of government spending, credit, and money supply resulted in a severe slump in domestic demand. National Income, for example, fell from £27 per head in 1812, to £20 per head in 1822 in money terms.[30] At the same time, many industries had been over-expanded, and this became apparent when they faced renewed European competition. Hamilton, writing in Glasgow, in 1822, noted,

> the check which our manufactures met with, upon the return of peace, on account of other nations being relieved from the necessity which they had been under during the war, of purchasing British goods, their advancement in the mechanic arts, enabling them in some measure, to supply their own wants, and the low state of their finances, which, like our own, had been much exhausted by the late expensive war, compelling them to it.[31]

European countries were too impoverished to be good markets and their main concern was to keep out British manufactures in order to provide prosperity and employment for their own industries.[32]

Scotland's foreign trade and shipping were depressed in the immediate post-war years, as were agriculture and major industries such as cotton, linen textiles, and distilling.[33] The village of Stanley, near Perth, fell from a state of great prosperity during the war to almost desolation and ruin soon after the war's end, with the collapse of the cotton-spinning mills in the area.[34] Many linen textile villages in Fife were similarly afflicted[35] and large cities such as Edinburgh and Aberdeen were also depressed. Aberdeen, for instance, had started an ambitious civic building programme during the war, the costs of which it was unable to meet when wartime prosperity ended. As a consequence, the city was declared bankrupt in 1817.[36]

Although the year 1816 was probably the most depressed post-war year, the economic problems of the dislocation continued until the early 1820s. Both Craig in Edinburgh, in 1821, and Hamilton in Glasgow, in 1822, continued to observe the effects caused by wartime distortion.[37] Craig noted that

> The last war being unexampled in duration, extent, and exertion, it might have been expected, when peace at last arrived, that the derangement of what had become the established course of trade would be greater than had formerly been experienced, and probably of somewhat longer continuance. But there seemed no reason to anticipate so universal a depression of wages and profits, or to such a degree, or for so long a time.[38]

Wages, prices, and profits all fell in post-war years, with the decline in profits being the most dramatic, caught between labour resistance to cuts in wages and falling demand leading to lower prices.[39] In line with these lower profits was a decline in wartime demand for capital. Taxation was reduced, with Income Tax being abolished in 1817. However, Government borrowing did not begin to decline until after 1819, while foreigners gradually unloaded their considerable holdings of government stock on the British market between 1817 and 1824.[40] Thus, the government's funded debt still represented a substantial drain upon available savings.

Funds for investment were available, but in the light of the depressed state of the British and international economies, the main objective in placing these savings was security.[41] The rate of return was of less significance:

> Every person entitled to credit, it is well known, can easily procure sufficient funds for his ordinary trade, or even for extensive occasional speculations; and no sooner is any adventure believed to yield profit, than there is a rush of capital towards it, by which, in a very short time, the market is over-stocked.

This was Craig's observation in 1821.[42]

It was not so much the absolute shortage of capital for investment that inhibited joint-stock developments in the immediate post-war years, but the lack of confidence by potential investors, faced with falling prices and weak demand both at home and abroad. However, the growth in popularity of interest-paying government stock which, in the course of the war, called forth '. . . money that has lain dormant or inactive, for want of the proper means of employing it, . . .' ensured that the holders of idle funds would not be content until a return was being obtained.[43]

Land and property continued to attract substantial investment. Kirkman Finlay, the Glasgow-based India merchant, enjoyed an income of £5-6,000 in 1819, and devoted £14,000 to buy and improve a house and estate.[44] The war had brought much private building work to an end and so there was considerable scope for investment in the construction of houses for let.[45]

However, in Scotland, an even more convenient alternative to the funds existed. Increasingly, from the 1780s onwards, the Scottish banks paid interest on bank deposits, reflecting the shortage of capital in the Scottish economy and the means taken to mobilise what was available.[46] In the post-war period, especially after 1817, many Scottish investors were selling their holdings of government securities at a profit, and depositing the proceeds in the Scottish banks for the higher rate of interest they would bring.[47] As early as 1817, the Scottish banks were receiving more money on deposit than they could comfortably cope with, and this brought about a reduction in the rate of interest paid, from 4% to 3%. Only the Commercial Bank left its rate unaltered, at the higher level, and, by 1821, it had received so much extra money on deposit, by clients switching their savings to it from other banks, that it was forced to reduce its interest to the level offered by its competitors.[48] Investment funds were definitely available, but good security, reasonable yield, a minimum of trouble, and liquidity were demanded if they were to be made available to borrowers.

Certain types of joint-stock companies offered a sufficient combination of these attributes to be attractive to investors. Joint-stock companies demanded nothing more of their shareholders than their capital, in return for which they usually paid better than government stock, property, or bank deposits. The yield on bank shares, for example, was generally higher than on the funds or other alternative investments,[49] while shares could be readily sold if cash was required.

The joint-stock companies that were promoted in Scotland in the depressed post-war era were mainly of three types. There was the implementation of a small number of projects whose necessity had long been realised, but conditions had never quite justified the outlay. Hugh Baird, a civil engineer, had reported in 1812 that

> A communication, by navigable canals, between the cities of Edinburgh and Glasgow, has appeared at different periods to be so much wanted, that a great sum of money has been spent in making surveys and plans; the cause of failure in accomplishing this object can only be attributed to the expense.[50]

Edinburgh had suffered a shortage of coal from at least 1790 and the completion of a direct canal linking Edinburgh with the Lanarkshire coal field had long been considered essential to alleviate the situation.[51] In 1817, such a project got under way with the successful promotion of the Edinburgh and Glasgow Union Canal. The Company attracted 540 subscribers for its shares, who were mainly Edinburgh trades people and merchants, and so could expect to benefit from a more reliable supply of cheaper coal. Financially, the canal was not a success, but £0.6m had been spent on it by 1826.[52]

Edinburgh had also suffered from an inadequate supply of pure water, especially when compared to Glasgow with its two water companies, formed in 1806 and 1808 respectively. Consequently, the Edinburgh Water Company was promoted in 1819. Despite the obvious utility of the project, the company found it extremely difficult to raise the necessary capital, and only £75,000 was subscribed out of the required £105,000. The remainder had to be taken up, in 1821, by the existing shareholders in order to complete the scheme.[53] Conditions could not yet support many large-scale projects aimed at improving the infrastructure of economic life, but yielding small financial returns.

The other kind of joint-stock company being promoted was that designed to utilise a new technology, such as gas lighting or steam shipping. These developments were considered to be profitable — whatever the economic climate — as they could create a new market for themselves. The Glasgow and Edinburgh Gas Light Companies were both promoted in 1817, but no others appeared until the mid-1820s.[54] The Edinburgh Gas Light Company attracted a total of 284 investors, nearly all from Edinburgh and area, and consisting largely of tradespeople, manufacturers, merchants and the professions. These were the very people who were to be consumers of gas.[55]

Numerous small steam shipping companies appeared in Scotland in the post-war years. They concentrated on coastal and short-distance transportation. Most of the companies were owned and financed by shareholders living in the localities to which the vessels plied and who were likely to benefit from the improved transportation. The Dumbarton Steam Boat Company was founded, in 1815, to undertake the Dumbarton to Glasgow run, and its capital was provided by 16 Dumbarton merchants and tradesmen, who expected the venture to aid the locality's prosperity, including their own.[56]

Finally, the post-war depression itself encouraged the establishment of joint-stock companies. Trading interests, for example, faced with depression and increased competition, banded together with the object of sharing the risks and costs of opening up the routes, and the markets, that would bring new business. Prime amongst these was the Australian Company, formed in Edinburgh in 1822, whose aim was to establish trading and shipping links between Scotland and Australia. It had a capital of £55,000, mainly subscribed by Edinburgh and Leith merchants.[57]

In the immediate post-war years, as during the war, there was a continuing formation of joint-stock companies in Scotland. Some had substantial capitals and large shareholdings, yet the actual number formed remained low for this whole thirty-year period, 1790-1820. Almost all of those established rested heavily upon the support of investors, not merely from a single locality, but often with a strong direct interest in the successful working of the company. They were investing not so much for the return, but as an extension of their main business. Consequently, they were not readily inclined to switch investments in response to differing yields or changing prospects. As a result of this the turnover of shares was low.

This was even true in banking companies which had minimal restrictions on the transfer of shares and a larger proportion of investors seeking a good yield alone.[58] Certainly concerns such as the Commercial Bank and the Union Canal, with shareholders numbering over 500 in each, were putting a strain on the share market mechanism. This was especially so in Edinburgh, where the greatest number of these enterprises were based, and where their shareholders resided. However, there was little sign of any fundamental change in the personnel and means of share transfers. The share market continued to remain an integral part of the general property market, utilising auctions, advertisements and intermediaries such as lawyers and accountants in order to arrange transfers. In 1820, regular buying and selling of shares continued to take place under this system without any indication that it was to be challenged by a new profession specialising in such a business.[59]

NOTES

1. C. Hadfield, *British Canals* (London 1950) p. 99; A. Burton, *The Canal Builders* (London 1972) pp. 38, 62-3, 66; E. T. Barnes, *History of the Commerce and Town of Liverpool* (London 1852) p. 488.

2. B. F. Duckham, *A History of the Scottish Coal Industry, 1700-1815* (Newton Abbot 1970) p. 217.

3. S. G. E. Lythe, 'The Canal Mania in East Scotland', *S.M.* 33 (1940) p. 125; R. N. Millman, *The Making of the Scottish Landscape* (London 1975) p. 180; cf. J. Lindsay *The Canals of Scotland* (Newton Abbot 1968).

4. Millman, op. cit., p. 180.

5. R. H. Campbell, *Scotland since 1707: The Rise of an Industrial Society* (Oxford 1965) p. 83; A. K. Cairncross & B. Weber, 'Fluctuations in Building in Great Britain, 1785-1849', *Ec.H.R.* 9 (1957) p. 286.

6. A. J. Youngson, *The Making of Classical Edinburgh, 1750-1840* (Edin. 1966) p. 100; J. C. Logan, The Dumbarton Glass Work Company c.1777-c.1850 (M. Litt. Strathclyde University 1970) p. 144.

7. P. Colquhoun, *A Treatise on the Wealth, Power, and Resources of the British Empire* (London 1815) p. 423; cf. G. Hueckel, 'War and the British Economy, 1793-1815: A General Equilibrium Analysis', *E.E.H.* 10 (1973); J. L. Anderson, 'Aspects of the Effects on the British Economy of the Wars against France, 1793-1815', *A.Ec.H.R.* 12 (1972).

8. B. R. Mitchell, *Abstract of British Historical Statistics* (Cam. 1962) pp. 391, 396.

9. Mitchell, op. cit., pp. 442-3; L. S. Pressnell, 'Public Monies and the Development of English Banking', *Ec.H.R.* 1S (1952) pp. 378, 384; C. W. Munn, The Scottish Provincial Banking Companies, 1747-1864 (Ph.D. Glasgow University 1976) pp. 93, 104.

10. I. F. Gibson, The Economic History of the Scottish Iron and Steel Industry (Ph.D. London University 1955) pp. 85-8; C. A. Whatley, The Process of Industrialisation in Ayrshire, c.1707-1871 (Ph.D. Strathclyde Univ. 1975); Logan, op. cit., p. 18; I. Donnachie, *A History of the Brewing Industry in Scotland* (Edin. 1979) p. 29; M. S. Cotterill, The Scottish Gas Industry up to 1914 (Ph.D. Strathclyde Univ. 1976) pp. 1, 353; M. Gray, *The Fishing Industries of Scotland, 1790-1914: A Study in Regional Adaptation* (Abdn. 1978) p. 35; B. Duckham, *A History of the Scottish Coal Industry, 1700-1815* (Newton Abbot 1970) p. 193; T. C. Smout, 'Lead Mining in Scotland, 1650-1850' in Payne (ed.) op. cit., p. 106.

11. T. C. Smout, *A History of the Scottish People, 1560-1830* (London 1970) pp. 318, 399; M. Gray, 'The Kelp Industry in the Highlands and Islands', *Ec.H.R.* 4 (1951-2) pp. 198-203.

12. B. Lenman, *An Economic History of Modern Scotland, 1660-1976* (Lon. 1977) p. 132; R. B. Weir, The Distilling Industry in Scotland in the Nineteenth and early Twentieth Centuries (Ph.D. Edin. Univ. 1974) p. 108; Donnachie, loc. cit.; Duckham, op. cit., p. 272.

13. R. Hamilton, *Observations upon the Causes of Distress in the Country* (Glasgow 1822) p. 26.

14. Whatley, op. cit., p. 138; Logan, op. cit., p. 136; A. Birch, 'Carron Company, 1784-1822: The Profits of Industry during the Industrial Revolution', *E.E.H.* 8 (1955-6) p. 73.

15. Hamilton, op. cit., p. 28; J. Craig, *Remarks on some Fundamental Doctrines in Political Economy illustrated by a Brief Inquiry into the Commercial State of Britain since the Year 1815* (Edin. 1821) p. 169; S. G. Checkland, 'Finance for the West Indies, 1780-1815', *Ec.H.R.* 10 (1957-8) p. 461; R. C. Michie, 'North-East Scotland and the Northern Whale Fishing, 1752-1893', *N.S.* 3 (1977-8) pp. 68-9.

16. T. Doubleday, *A Financial, Monetary and Statistical History of England from the Revolution of 1688* (Lon. 1859) pp. 200-1.

17. F. Crouzet (ed.), *Capital Formation in the Industrial Revolution* (Lon. 1972) p. 31; I. F. Grant, 'The Social Effects of the Agricultural Reforms and Enclosure Movement in Aberdeenshire', *Ec.H.R.* 1 (1926-9) p. 109; Craig, op. cit., p. 167; Whatley, op. cit., pp. 144-216, 326; Logan, op. cit., p. 46; Gray (1978), op. cit., p. 35; Duckham, op. cit., p. 193; Michie, op. cit., p. 67.

18. C. Gulvin, *The Tweedmakers: A History of the Scottish Fancy Woollen Industry, 1600-1914* (Newton Abbot 1973) pp. 58, 62.

19. G. Purves, *All Classes Productive of National Wealth* (Lon. 1817) p. 182.

20. Mitchell, op. cit., p. 427.

21. Mitchell, op. cit., p. 402; P. K. O'Brien, 'British Incomes and Property in the early 19th Century', *Ec.H.R.* 12 (1959-60) p. 262.

22. J. Lowe, *The Present State of England in regard to Agriculture, Trade and Finance* (Lon. 1823) p. 364; A. D. Gayer, W. W. Rostow & A. J. Schwartz, *The Growth and Fluctuation of the British Economy, 1790-1850* (Oxf. 1953) I, p. 376.

23. S. G. Checkland, *Scottish Banking: A History, 1695-1973* (Glasgow 1975) pp. 194, 216, 285; *A History of the New Club, Edinburgh, 1797-1937* (Lon. 1938) p. 198; Law Case between Archibald Farquharson of Finzean and Miss Francis Barstow, residing in Aberdeen (House of Lords, May 1826); E. S. Richards, 'Structural Change in a Regional Economy: Sutherland in the Industrial Revolution, 1780-1830', *Ec.H.R.* 26 (1973) p.69.

24. Munn, op. cit., p. 207.

25. T. Tooke, *A History of Prices* (Lon. 1838), I, pp. 277-8; W. W. Rostow, *British Economy of the Nineteenth Century* (Oxf. 1948) p. 16.

26. *The New Picture of Edinburgh* (Edin. 1816) pp. 134-6; J. L. Anderson, *The Story of the Commercial Bank of Scotland (1810-1910)* (Edin. 1910) pp. 3, 31; Munn, op. cit., p. 95; Checkland (Banking), op. cit., pp. 287, 292, 377.

27. *Report by Mr. John Rennie respecting the proposed Railway from Kelso to Berwick* (Kelso 1810); *Report by Mr. Telford relative to the proposed Railway from Glasgow to Berwick-upon-Tweed* (Edin. 1810); H. Baird, *Report on the proposed Edinburgh and Glasgow Union Canal* (Edin. 1813); J. A. Hassan The Development of the Coal Industry in Mid and West Lothian, 1815-1873 (Ph.D. Strathclyde Univ. 1976) p. 18.

28. W. Smart, *Economic Annals of the Nineteenth Century* (Lon. 1910 & 1917); Mitchell, op. cit., p. 396.

29. Pressnell, op. cit., p. 392; Mitchell, op. cit., p. 443; J. Miller, *The History of Dunbar* (Dunbar 1859) pp. 306-7; 'Banks of Issue (Scotland) — A Return, 1815-45' (B.P.P. 28 (1845)).

30. P. Deane, 'Contemporary Estimates of National Income in the first half of the Nineteenth Century', *Ec.H.R.* 8 (1956) p. 353.

31. Hamilton, op. cit., p. 23.

32. Smart, op. cit., p. 491.

33. D. S. MacMillan, *Scotland and Australia, 1788-1850: Emigration, Commerce and Investment* (Lon. 1967) pp. 27, 132; R. Wilson, *An Historical Account and Delineation of Aberdeen* (Abdn. 1822) p. 219; I. F. Grant, *The Economic History of Scotland* (Lon. 1934) p. 214; D. Chapman, 'The Establishment of the Jute Industry', *R. of E.S.* 6 (1938-9) p. 44; Munn, op. cit., p. 116; Weir, op. cit., pp. 129, 134, 137.

34. *S.M.* October 1825.

35. D. I. A. Steel, The Linen Industry of Fife in the Later Eighteenth and Nineteenth Centuries (Ph.D. St. Andrews Univ. 1975) p. 258.

36. H. Cockburn, *Memorials of His Time* (Edin. 1856) p. 306; Anon., *Archibald Simpson: Architect of Aberdeen 1790-1847* (Abdn. 1978) p. 7; *Sketch of the Affairs of the Treasury of Aberdeen under the Administration of the Trustees, by one of their number* (Abdn. 1817).

37. Craig, op. cit., pp. 161-2; Hamilton, op. cit., p. 2.

38. Craig, loc. cit.

39. A. Slaven, *The Development of the West of Scotland, 1750-1960* (Lon. 1975) pp. 156-7; T. R. Gourvish, 'The Cost of Living in Glasgow in the Early Nineteenth Century', *Ec.H.R.* 25 (1972) pp. 72-3; Michie, op. cit., p. 72.

40. Mitchell, op. cit., pp. 402, 427; A. H. Imlah, 'British Balance of Payments and Export of Capital, 1816-1913', *Ec.H.R.* 5 (1952-3) p. 227.

41. J. Anderson, 'A Measure of the Effects of British Public Finance, 1793-1815', *Ec.H.R.* 27 (1974) p. 617.

42. Craig, op. cit., pp. 211-2.

43. Sir John Sinclair, *The History of the Public Revenue of the British Empire* (Lon. 1803-4) p. 137; cf. Lowe pp. 364-6; Colquhoun, op. cit., p. 276; *Statistical Illustrations of the British Empire* (Lon. 1827) p. 128.

44. Anon., *James Finlay & Co. Ltd., 1750-1950* (Glasgow 1951) p. 126.

45. T. Binnie, *Memoir of Thomas Binnie, Builder in Glasgow, 1792-1867* (Glasgow 1882) p. 26; Archibald Simpson, op. cit., p. 15; John Niven to Wm. Leslie, 23 February 1818 (Leslie Correspondence).

46. C. W. Boase, *A Century of Banking in Dundee* (Edin. 1867) XXIX, p. 549; Munn, op. cit., p. 237.

47. Munn, op. cit., p. 115.

48. Boase, op. cit., p. 301; J. L. Anderson, op. cit., p. 33.

49. *A.C.* 6 January 1816; Munn, op. cit., pp. 183, 255.

50. Baird, op. cit., p. 13.

51. Hassan, op. cit., pp. 3, 16.

52. *List of subscribers to the Edinburgh and Glasgow Union Canal* (Edin. 1817); Hassan, op. cit., p. 38.

53. I. H. Adams, *The Making of Urban Scotland* (Lon. 1978) p. 135; J. Burnett, *History of the Water Supply to Glasgow* (Glasgow 1869) pp. 3-5; Cockburn, op. cit., p. 353; Edinburgh Water Company: *Prospectus* (Edin. 1819); *Statement by the Directors of the Edinburgh Joint Stock Water Company* (Edin. 1825) p. 8.

54. M. S. Cotterill, The Scottish Gas Industry up to 1914 (Ph.D. Strathclyde Univ. 1976) pp. 121-131; F. Accum, *Description of the Process of Manufacturing Coal Gas* (Lon. 1819) p. 11; G. MacGregor, *The History of Glasgow* (Glasgow 1881) p. 405; *E.A.* 21 March 1817, 8 April 1817.

55. List of Proprietors of the Edinburgh Gas Light Company, 1821; Cotterill, op. cit., pp. 205-6.

56. J. Williamson, *The Clyde Passenger Steamer: Its rise and progress during the Nineteenth Century* (Glasgow 1904) pp. 44, 263; B. Lenman, *From Esk to Tweed: Harbours, Ships and Men of the East Coast of Scotland* (Glasgow 1975) pp. 177-8; Logan, op. cit., pp. 102, 212.

57. D. S. MacMillan, 'Scottish Enterprise in Australia, 1798-1897', in Payne (ed.), op. cit., p. 328; Lenman, loc. cit.

58. Munn, op. cit., pp. 255, 260.

59. Cotterill, op. cit., p. 1115.

3

Speculative Mania, 1823-5

FUNDAMENTAL change came in the Scottish share market, not as the culmination of gradual growth but as a consequence of the mania for speculation in shares which occurred in the mid 1820s, and which affected most of Scotland. Numerous joint-stock companies were promoted and there was frantic trading in the shares of both old and new ventures. In the midst of this frenzy appeared the first recognised share brokers in Scotland, and the beginnings of an independent and separate Scottish share market. By the mid-1820s, the uncertainty that had discouraged investment and risk-taking was being dispelled. The British and world economies were entering a new phase of growth after the traumas of prolonged war and its aftermath; economic indicators in Scotland showed growing prosperity and confidence; brick production expanded steadily from 1820 onwards; and the number of bankruptcies declined every year, from 289 in 1819 to only 90 in 1825.[1]

This prosperity had both monetary and real causes. Excellent British harvests in the early 1820s reduced imports of wheat to almost negligible levels between 1821 and 1824. As a result food prices fell, leaving consumers with income to spend on manufactures or to save, while at the same time the growing population's demand for foodstuffs meant that the agricultural interest could remain reasonably prosperous through a higher volume of sales.[2] In addition, as these wheat imports were irregular purchases dependent upon the state of the British harvest, they were not balanced by exports and arranged through mercantile credit. They were paid for in bullion, which became released for other uses, especially as the succession of good harvests made it difficult for merchants to believe that it was necessary to hoard gold against the eventuality of a forced and large importation.[3] The mid-1820s also witnessed a gradual reflation, by the government and the Bank of England, of the British economy, which was apparent in Scotland.[4]

Since the early 1790s government stock had offered a profitable and secure home for surplus funds — either directly or through the banks. However, in the 1820s the government was actively reducing the size of its outstanding borrowings and so, between 1822 and 1824, some £10.5m from the sinking fund was applied to re-purchasing stock. A further £8.5m was paid out to holders who were unwilling to accept conversion of part of the debt to lower rates of interest. Those who continued to invest in government stock were faced with a falling yield as the price rose,[5] and this had a wide-ranging effect on Scotland.

Scottish bankers had tended to place their surplus funds either directly in government securities or with their London correspondents, who employed them

in commercial bills and other temporary investments. As a consequence of the
falling interest rates, Scottish banks not only suffered a declining return on this
capital but also found it difficult to place all the funds deposited with them
profitably.[6] In Edinburgh alone the banks held an estimated £5m on deposit, in
November 1824, for which they had no obvious use. The Scottish banks were
forced to reduce the interest paid on deposits from 3% to 2.5% in December 1824,
and restrict an individual's deposits to £5,000 — above which no interest at all was
to be paid.[7] Savings banks paid 4.5% per annum and they were besieged with
deposits until they, in turn, introduced restrictions.[8] Bank deposits were favourite
modes of investment in Scotland but the declining opportunities of applying
money profitably in London reduced their attractions for the Scottish investor.
The investor, and the banks themselves, had to seek alternatives if savings were to
earn any return.

Land, property and mortgages were traditional outlets for spare funds. 'Let
those . . ., who are not satisfied with Bank interest, invest their money in land or
substantial stone and lime, and not in bubbles ever ready to burst, . . .' was the
advice given by an Edinburgh inhabitant in 1824.[9] However, land for purchase
was becoming scarce in Scotland as entailing became more common.[10] There was a
growing inability in the land market to satisfy demand, with high prices and a
growing scarcity being reported generally.[11] A Fife correspondent of the *Scots
Magazine* reported, in May 1824, that

> . . ., in consequence of the rise in the funds, the demand for landed property had considerably
> increased, and . . ., particularly in this county, sales to a great extent, and at advantageous
> prices, had recently been made . . Generally, and we believe correctly speaking, thirty years
> purchase of the estimated value of the land has been given; and, upon the whole, we understand
> the purchasers are satisfied with these bargains. The demand, notwithstanding these
> investments, still continues, and it is highly probable that all the property for sale in Fife will
> soon be out of the market.[12]

Between March 1824 and March 1825, estates to the value of £633,650 were sold
in Fife.[13] A decline in the rents paid by tenants reduced the attractions of
purchasing house property for let, and falling mortgage rates discouraged lending
upon both urban and rural property.[14] Commercial firms with whom money was
left were also finding it difficult to employ all they had at their disposal. Thus, they
had to reduce the rate of interest paid and ask those lending the money to withdraw
some. An example was Colonel Forbes, an Aberdeenshire landowner who had
made his money in Indian military service. He had some £35,000 left in India with
Forbes & Co., a Bombay agency house, and they reduced their interest, from 5% to
4%, in May 1823, and to 3% in August 1824,

> In consequence of the continued stagnation of trade throughout India, and the insecurity and
> difficulty in employing money to any considerable extent, so as to yield returns adequate to the
> rate of interest we now allow to our constituents, . . .

Col. Forbes thus repatriated some of his Indian wealth and sought to employ it in
remunerative investments in Britain.[15] It is quite evident that by the mid-1820s

many of the traditional and more popular avenues of investment were either overstocked with funds or unattractive because of low yields.

The stock of foreign governments did represent to many such an alternative, as it offered the security of a state plus a higher return than consols. An estimated £50m was subscribed to foreign loans between 1822 and 1826.[16] For example, the Perth Banking Company invested £20,000 in French 5% Rentes in 1824.[17] However, most of the Scottish investing public were wary of investing in countries they knew little about and the security of whose government was suspect. This was especially true of the newly formed South American republics, which attempted to raise large sums in Britain in the mid-1820s.[18] Scotland's early experience with foreign investment was centred especially on the State of Poyais, an area in the north of Honduras, along the Mosquito shore.

A Scottish adventurer, Gregor MacGregor, had founded a settlement there in 1821. In 1822 he came to Britain and attempted to raise a loan of £200,000 at 6% for the development of the country. In addition, actual land was offered for sale at very low prices. The fact that MacGregor was a Scot attracted many Scottish investors,[19] and offices were set up in Edinburgh, Glasgow, Stirling and Inverness to handle sales of land. The Edinburgh office was reported to have sold 12,800 acres at one shilling an acre in a two-month period, from January to March 1822.[20] MacGregor's advertisements made the country appear most attractive:

> The Territory of Poyais (on the mountainous side of the Sea of Honduras) is distinguished by a climate which agrees admirably with the constitution of Europeans, and by a soil producing the necessaries of life almost without labour. The face of this very fine country is varied by Hills, Valleys, Savannahs and Plains, and Forests of the most valuable timber, such as Mahogany, Cedar, Santa Maria, Pitch Pine, Rose and Zebra Woods, and abundance of Dye Woods. Horses and Black Cattle are plentiful; also Deer, Wild Hogs, Poultry etc. — Rivers and streams of water are numerous. The lands for sale are subject to no tax or Impost whatever, except a very trifling feu duty. The price will shortly be advanced 25 or 50 per cent.[21]

A number of ships sailed from Leith to Poyais carrying Scottish emigrants. The paradise turned out to be a malarial swamp, most of the settlers died, and by the end of 1823 the fraud had been exposed. MacGregor was nowhere to be found.[22] The swindle left a legacy, as Scottish investors were disillusioned with foreign investment at an early stage of the mania. As early as December 1823 the *Aberdeen Journal* reported that they had '. . . got heart-sick of Foreign Speculation . . .'[23]

The only remaining investment outlet that offered the prospects of a reasonable return, along with some security and little personal involvement, was the shares of joint-stock companies. However, in the face of demand, share prices rose substantially and yields fell, so that by November 1824 the rate of return on the stock of the Royal Bank was only 2.9% per annum, and that of the Edinburgh Gas Company was little higher at 3.5% per annum.[24] It was possible to create additional joint-stock companies in order to obtain both a high yield and a capital gain. The price of the shares of both the North British and Hercules Insurance Companies had doubled between 1809 and 1824.[25] Therefore it was not long before numerous joint-stock enterprises were brought before the public by entrepreneurs who realised that the high share values and low yields of established companies offered opportunities for the successful promotion of alternative or additional concerns. The *Edinburgh Weekly Journal* reported, in November 1824, that

> Never was the capitalist so much at a loss how to turn his money to account, and live decently on the produce ... It is not to be wondered at, therefore, that undertakings of this description should be gone into.[26]

The speculative mania in Scotland in the mid-1820s was thus the outcome of a build-up of funds at a time of confidence in the economy, and an inability of traditional channels to absorb the savings being made. In fact, the re-distributive effect of the National Debt, in taking money from the poor and giving it to the rich via the tax system, meant that more and more was available for investment.[27]

The 1825 legislation, which allowed joint-stock companies to sue and be sued, removed a barrier to the establishment of joint-stock companies, and was contemporaneous with the mania. However, companies always had this power in Scotland. The preamble to the Act itself acknowledged the long duration of joint-stock enterprise in Scotland:

> ... the practice has prevailed in Scotland of instituting Societies possessing joint-stock, the shares of which are either conditionally or unconditionally transferable, for the purpose of carrying on banking and other commercial concerns, many of which have transacted business for a number of years to the great advantage of that country.[28]

Consequently, government legislation was irrelevant to company formation in Scotland.

Company organisation, based on the contract of copartnery, sufficed for all kinds of joint-stock enterprise. Most of the gas companies formed in Scotland, for example, relied on municipal sanction and Scots law.[29] Nor was the mania the result of technological change necessitating an immediate, large-scale outlay of capital for which only the joint-stock form of enterprise was suitable. Gas companies had been established as early as 1817, in Scotland, but even by the mid-1820s the technology they employed remained primitive.[30] Railway projects dated from even earlier, with the delay in their implementation being due not to technical problems, but to an inability to raise the necessary finance. The railway technology utilised in the mid-1820s was also primitive, while many of the routes had been suggested and surveyed in earlier years.[31] It was the changed circumstances of low interest rates and the ease of obtaining capital, allied to economic prosperity and a confidence in the future, that made joint-stock enterprise and its objectives attractive in the mid-1820s, and not before. A similar situation existed in England.[32]

The centre of the Scottish speculative mania was Edinburgh. It was there that the majority of joint-stock companies were promoted and the greatest excesses indulged in. This was only to be expected. Although Edinburgh was no longer Scotland's largest city, it remained the seat of a disproportionately large middle and upper class, attracted by its location, residential facilities and services.

Svendenstierna noted, in 1803, that 'The Scots are ... accustomed to say that one earns money in Glasgow and spends it in Edinburgh.'[33] In 1831, for example, Edinburgh possessed 7,463 inhabitants of the 'monied class' compared to Glasgow's 2,723.[34] Edinburgh was also the base for most of Scotland's financial institutions. The Edinburgh banks held 76% of Scottish bank deposits in 1825, drawing funds from the rest of the country through a network of branches.[35]

Contemporary opinion in Edinburgh dated the beginning of the mania as July 1824, when the Leith Docks Company was promoted. The improvement of the harbour at Leith had long been an Edinburgh project. By 1817 Edinburgh Town Council had spent £300,000 on the construction of Docks, leaving them with a considerable debt at high interest. In 1824 a scheme was devised whereby the Docks were to be acquired by a joint-stock company. This company would also take over the debt, which would be paid off by the profits arising from higher harbour charges, leaving a profitable harbour for the shareholders and the council free of debt.[36] In the prospectus of the Dock Company of Leith, issued in 1824, there was offered '... an immediate return to subscribers of more than can be obtained from investments in the public funds or in land, ...'[37] Interest from investors was limited until the Council guaranteed a return of 4% per annum during the early years of operation.[38] Although the Edinburgh Life Assurance Company had been formed in 1823, it was the Leith Docks promotion of 1824 that both emphasised the attractions of investments in joint-stock companies, and illustrated the quick gains to be made through trading in newly issued shares.[39] Anthony Romney, an Edinburgh resident, had observed that

> On the very morning after the subscription was completed, the Dock Scrip, as it may be termed, was in the market for sale. In the course of the day it bore a premium; it was transferred from one hand to another, and from that other to a third, at a considerable expense, ...So it went, till the idea was started by some prurient mind. Why direct all our speculations to this one thing? ... open the flood gates, open the flood gates, and let this high-toned enthusiasm expatiate in all the fanciful variety of curious and cunning projects![40]

The Leith Docks Company's success led to the immediate appearance of other schemes. Many of these had been promoted earlier but had been unsuccessful in finding support. Others had been in active preparation and were awaiting a favourable opportunity for raising capital. The Albyn Company, an Edinburgh property company, appeared originally in 1822 but was abandoned because of lack of interest. When the same company was floated in 1824, it was welcomed. The Scottish Union Banking Company was also promoted at the end of 1824, although its origins dated from 1823.[41]

However, many ventures were ill-thought-out and were ushered into the market only in order to take advantage of the easy conditions for raising finance.[42] Most of the newly promoted companies found no difficulty in getting sufficient investors to commit themselves for the sums required. The *Caledonian Mercury* reported, in 1824, that

> No sooner is any scheme announced for the joint investment of stock than the books are immediately filled, and enormous sums are engaged for, ...[43]

Altogether, at least 23 major joint-stock companies were promoted in Edinburgh during 1824-5, while their capital demands had reached £2.3m as early as November 1824.[44] Although the speculation began in Edinburgh and had its centre there, it eventually pervaded the whole of Scotland. Probably Glasgow participated least, relative to size, but, even there, an unusually large number of joint-stock companies were promoted.[45] An upsurge in both company promotion and speculation in shares was also noticeable in the other cities and towns of Scotland, especially Dundee, Aberdeen, and Inverness. Compared to Edinburgh, this was all on a fairly moderate scale, with attention being focused on a few companies reflecting local interest, and designed to meet significant deficiencies in the economy of the area.[46] When the Inverness Water and Gas Company was promoted, in December 1824, the local newspaper greeted its appearance with the statement, 'we are glad to perceive that the benefit of joint-stock companies is extending northwards, . . .' By February 1825 the whole of the required capital had been raised and local speculation had developed in the shares.[47] However, the excesses of Edinburgh and the variety of enterprises were missing in the rest of Scotland.

Most of the companies projected were in the traditional areas of joint-stock enterprise, notably providing the infrastructure of growth or high risk areas requiring collective action. Both banking and insurance attracted many potential new entrants, especially outside Edinburgh. There was considerable resentment in the rest of Scotland at the almost monopolistic position occupied by Edinburgh's financial institutions. In many towns merchants were keen to provide for their own credit or insurance requirements by the formation of local concerns, which would be more responsive to local needs and would operate an investment policy favouring the locality.[48] Thus, not only were large Edinburgh banks and insurance companies formed, such as the National Bank of Scotland or the Scottish Union Insurance Company, but also numerous provincial banks and insurance companies in such places as Aberdeen, Glasgow, Dundee, Perth and Arbroath.[49]

There had been many previous attempts to establish an insurance company in Glasgow but all had failed. However, in 1823 J. J. Duncan, a Glasgow accountant, successfully promoted the West of Scotland Fire Insurance Company with a nominal capital of £1m. A total of 989 shares were issued to friends and acquaintances of Duncan and £2,088 was paid-up. The same group formed the West of Scotland Life Assurance, Annuity and Endowment Company in 1825, while a rival group promoted the Glasgow Insurance Company, also in 1825.[50] In 1823, the Forfarshire Fire Insurance Company was established in Dundee and, in 1825, the Aberdeen Assurance Company appeared.[51]

Transport was also a favoured area of joint-stock enterprise dating from the canal era of the eighteenth century. However, in the mid-1820s it was centred on shipping and railways, especially the latter. Among the steamship companies promoted, for example, was one to operate a service between Greenock and Stornoway.[52] Even more numerous were the railway projects put up for consideration. In addition to revised or completely new projects, almost any route for which a canal had been once suggested now found itself being promoted as an attractive connection by rail.[53] Ian Anderson, an Edinburgh solicitor and Dumfriesshire landowner, actively contemplated forming, in 1824, a joint-stock company to construct a railway between Sanquhar and Dumfries.[54] The report by Charles Landale on the proposed Dundee to Newtyle railway summed up the prevailing attitude:

> There can be no doubt of the advantage which must arise to Dundee, and also to Strathmore, if the Railway be constructed. The only question is, whether there is sufficient prospect of success to warrant the investment of capital in the undertaking.[55]

Cheap money, prosperity and confidence in the mid-1820s made some of these railway projects appear both feasible and profitable. Jardine's report on the Edinburgh and Dalkeith Railway, for example, estimated the cost of construction at £70,125, producing an annual income of £8,490, which would create a return of 12% per annum for the shareholders.[56]

The continuing expansion of Scotland's urban population created a need for improved urban facilities, especially such essential services as gas and water. Additional gas and water companies were promoted in Glasgow and Edinburgh, while other large Scottish towns established their own facilities, such as a water company, in 1824, and a gas company, in 1825, in Greenock, or a water company in Paisley or a gas company in Dundee.[57] Despite the formation of a water company in Edinburgh, in 1819, the water supply remained inadequate and another company was promoted in 1825, while the existing concern increased its own capital by £118,000.[58]

Further gas companies were also formed, including the Edinburgh Oil Gas Co. An oil gas company was promoted in Glasgow as well. Both were failures, as animal or vegetable oil did not produce a sufficient level of light intensity. Over £61,000 had been spent on capital equipment by the Edinburgh Company.[59] Aberdeen's gas company was also to be an oil-based one, but it was quickly converted to the use of coal. The promotion was popular, for '. . . the requisite capital of £12,000 was raised in a few hours . . .', according to the *Aberdeen Journal* in January 1824. In contrast, the Aberdeen Water Company failed to raise the small sum of £20,000 needed to begin operations.[60] Altogether, though many of the projects to provide improved transport and urban and financial services came to nothing — especially the railways — a small number were formed and left a legacy of gas and water supply, banking and insurance facilities, or more efficient transportation links.

The mania of the mid-1820s also represented a partial departure from the areas in which joint-stock companies had traditionally been formed. This was not just the property or whale fishing companies, examples of which had appeared before. These types of companies were promoted in the mid-1820s, with Dundee and Edinburgh having one of each.[61] However, in Edinburgh, in particular, a large number of joint-stock industrial and commercial concerns were projected with substantial capitals. By late 1824, six industrial companies were actively seeking £600,000 of public capital in Edinburgh, their fields of operation ranging from textiles, paper, distilling and brewing to the manufacture of glass and iron. In addition, there were other concerns involved in the distribution of milk, wine, fish, and wool.[62]

During the eighteenth century there had been a few attempts to form a number of industrial joint-stock companies, but these had not been generally successful.[63] Certainly, industrial and commercial activities were being carried on with increasingly large capitals, and tied up the funds of those involved for a considerable period before a return was made. The capital required to put a paper mill into operation rose from £52,000 in 1800 to £125,000 in 1820. The Dumbarton Glass Company employed a capital of £98,000 by 1821.[64] Therefore, the funds required in many industrial enterprises were greater than most individuals could provide, and many depended upon the support of a number of partners. The Dysart Coal Co. had 20 partners in 1787, while Robert Tullis & Co., a Fife papermaker, had 10 in 1809.[65] It was only a short step from this kind of partnership to a joint-stock company with an extended shareholding.

Thus, a number of the industrial companies promoted in the mid-1820s were only conversions of established private firms. The New Shotts Iron Co., floated in 1824, intended initially to spend all its capital on purchasing the plant of the Shotts Iron Co., which had been established in 1801. Such was the enthusiasm amongst investors, however, that its nominal capital was raised from £40,000 to £100,000.[66] The Wilsontown Iron Works and Foundry Company and the Edinburgh, Glasgow, and Alloa Glass Company were also converted from established concerns into joint-stock ventures.[67] These conversions represented little in the way of an addition to the capital of the firms involved, but merely reflected the willingness of the public to invest in the shares of joint-stock companies, almost irrespective of their nature. Investors regarded industrial and commercial enterprises as involving a greater risk than companies that served the whole community from almost a monopolistic position, such as a bank or gas company, but they were willing to support them in the speculative conditions of the mid-1820s. The New Shotts Iron Co., for instance, had all its capital of £100,000 subscribed for by March 1825.[68]

Although the period 1822-6 was characterised by a very high volume of real investment in both property and machinery, and many of the new joint-stock companies were positive additions to the economy, an increasing number were little more than speculative counters.[69] Anthony Romney voiced the disquiet that was becoming evident by the end of 1824:

> . . . the ushering upon our little district of the world such a host of them at once, and several with a view to the very same objects, and then some of these so very visionary and chimerical, I confess this makes me jealous of the whole, and almost satisfies me that they are the illegitimate offspring of the wanton demon of speculation, and not the true wedlock children of an increased national capital, and an augmented commercial activity.[70]

The Thistle Insurance Company, for example, was begun solely with the intention of satisfying those investors who had been disappointed in obtaining shares in the previous insurance company formed in Edinburgh.[71] Investors were being attracted, not by the intrinsic merit of a company, but by the prospect of selling the shares subscribed for at a profit to others who had failed to obtain shares. Joint-stock companies were being formed neither because of legitimate need, nor because of cheap finance, but to create an opportunity for the promoters to make money by trading in their shares at a premium.

So, in order to enjoy the apparently easy gains to be made upon joint-stock company shares, capital was withdrawn from other areas of the economy. Colonel Forbes sold £1,000 worth of consols in October 1824 and invested the proceeds in the stock of the Edinburgh and Dalkeith Railway in January 1825, while the repatriated Indian funds went into the shares of the London-based Guardian Fire and Life Assurance Co. and the European Life Insurance.[72] Bank deposits, government stock, and the temporarily idle balances of merchants and industrialists, suffered most. Deposits with the Royal Bank of Scotland fell from £2.6m in September 1824 to £1.9m in September 1825, while loans and discounts rose from £2.2m to £3.1m.[73] Increased lending at a time of declining deposits could not be maintained indefinitely before the banks both cut back on credit and offered higher rates of interest so as to attract deposits.

Matters were brought to a head by the poor harvest of 1825, which necessitated a vast increase in the importation of foodstuffs from August onwards and the use of the funds that had been left idle in previous years.[74] The Bank of England began to restrict commercial accommodation, seriously, from November 1825, leading to a national credit squeeze.[75] Those who had bought stocks and shares for speculation, using borrowed funds, attempted to realise their profits, thus precipitating a decline in prices. Falling share price led others to try and sell before all gains were lost. This started a panic with rapidly dropping share prices and caused a glut of shares on the market. As a consequence, funds were either tied up in unsaleable shares, or only a fraction of the original value was recovered.

Six of the smaller Scottish banks collapsed between 1825 and 1829, including the Falkirk Banking Company, the Fife Banking Company, and the Stirling Banking Company, all in 1826.[76] Those that remained in business curtailed their lending.[77] Manufacturers, merchants and farmers made heavy use of bank credit in Scotland, and the ending of the period of liberality left many in a precarious position with unrealisable assets but heavy cash outgoings. The Scottish whisky distillers were left with unsold stocks as rising food prices cut consumption of other goods. Many of the newly founded distilleries collapsed in consequence. This was typical of the situation throughout Scotland.[78]

> . . . a considerable measure of distrust and want of confidence now pervade the mercantile circle in Scotland. Establishments of the first order, both in public estimation and mercantile confidence, have been obliged to yield to the storm,

reported the *Edinburgh Weekly Journal* in January 1826.[79] Signs of recovery were evident as early as 1827 but the confidence that had underpinned both the speculation and the company promotion had been shattered, and this was to take longer to mend.[80]

> When one is constantly meeting with people who are themselves filled with apprehension it is difficult to keep oneself entirely free from the feeling,

observed the *Banker's Circular* in November 1827. As late as April 1828 this unease still pervaded financial affairs.[81]

Not only did speculation and promotion virtually cease but the future of these companies actually formed was jeopardised. Financial stringency and the altered economic prospects led shareholders to refuse to pay calls on the shares for which they had subscribed. By June 1828 arrears on calls and interest amounted to £8,688 for the New Shotts Iron Co.[82] Both the Scottish Commercial Marine Insurance Co. and the West Lothian Railway were abandoned, while other prominent concerns also disappeared.[83] Even those companies that had raised all their capital encountered difficulties when they tried to obtain extra finance. Construction of the Dundee and Newtyle Railway had commenced in 1826, but by 1829 it was '. . . nearly at a stand owing to a want of funds; the expense having greatly exceeded the original estimate'. It was not until 1832 that the line was finished.[84]

Nevertheless, the mid-1820s mania had witnessed a fundamental increase in the number and importance of joint-stock companies in Scotland, their influence being, perhaps, of most significance in the provision of financial services and urban facilities.[85]

NOTES

1. Cairncross & Weber, op. cit., pp. 296-7; Boase, op. cit., p. 550.

2. J. Wilson, *Influences of the Corn Laws* (2nd ed. Lon. 1840) pp. 8, 11, 16-18; Rostow, op. cit., p. 51; H. J. Habakkuk, 'Fluctuations and Growth in the Nineteenth Century' in M. Kooy (ed.), *Studies in Economics and Economic History* (Lon. 1972) p. 261.

3. A. Mundell, *A Comparative View of the Industrial Situation of Great Britain (1775-1832)* (Lon. 1832) p. 44.

4. J. Clapham, *The Bank of England: A History* (Cam. 1944) pp. 93-4; M. J. Fenn, British Investment in South America and the Financial Crisis of 1825-6 (M.A. Univ. of Durham 1969) p. 40; Munn, op. cit., p. 119.

5. J. Exter, *Causes of the Present Depression in our Money Market* (Lon. 1825) pp. 3-8; Mitchell, op. cit., pp. 402, 455; Clapham, loc. cit.

6. Fenn, op. cit., pp. 35-6; Munn, op. cit., p. 311.

7. *E.W.J.* 17 Nov. 1824; Boase, op. cit., pp. 330, 343.

8. *E.W.J.* 5 May 1824.

9. *A Letter to the Inhabitants of Edinburgh on Joint-stock Companies by a Citizen* (Edin. 1824) p. 8.

10. J. R. McCulloch, *A Treatise on the Succession to Property* (Lon. 1848) pp. 52-6, 65.

11. *A.J.* 16 June 1824; *G.H.* 12 April 1824; *D.P. & C.A.* 13 February 1823.

12. *S.M.* May 1824.

13. *S.M.* March 1825.

14. Slaven, op. cit., p. 157; A. Jopp to W. Leslie 18 September 1824.

15. Forbes & Co., Circular, 31 May 1823; Forbes & Co. to D. Forbes 1 August 1824, 30 November 1824.

16. *Commerce in Consternation* (Lon. 1826) pp. 122-4; Exter, loc. cit.; Tooke, (II) p. 149; *Annual Register* (1824) p. 2.

17. Munn, op. cit., p. 216.

18. Fenn, op. cit., pp. 47, 60.

19. Fenn, op. cit., pp. 74-7, 165.

20. *I.J.* 15 March 1822, 12 July 1822, 1 November 1822, 7 February 1823.

21. *I.J.* 28 June 1822.

22. Fenn, loc. cit.

23. *A.J.* 24 December 1823.

24. *A.J.* 17 November 1824. Reprinted a table giving share yields of several Edinburgh joint-stock companies, according to their current prices and latest dividends.

25. *Proposals for a New Fire Insurance Company* (Edin., November 1824).

26. *E.W.J.* 17 November 1824.

27. Fenn, op. cit. IV.

28. Reprinted in R. Brown, 'The Genesis of Company Law in England and Scotland', *J.R.* 13 (1901-2) p. 191; cf. J. R. Christie, 'Joint-Stock Enterprise in Scotland before the Companies Acts', *J.R.* 21 (1909-10) p. 138.

29. Cotterill, op. cit., pp. 104, 895, 945.

30. Cotterill, op. cit., pp. 132-4.

31. N. Wood, *A Practical Treatise on Railroads* (Lon. 1825, repr. 1831) XII, pp. 7-8; M. Robbins, 'Sir Walter Scott and two Early Railway Schemes', *R.M.* February 1951, p. 89; Hassan, op. cit., pp. 18-20, 51.

32. *A.J.* 6 April 1825; J. Salt, 'The Pace and Progress of Port Investment in England, 1660-1830', *Y.B.Ec. & S.R.* XII (1960) p. 41; Crouzet, op. cit., p. 31.

33. E. T. Svendenstierna, *Svendenstierna's Tour of Great Britain, 1802-3* (Newton Abbot 1973) p. 157; Cockburn, op. cit., p. 264; B. Lenman, *An Economic History of Modern Scotland, 1660-1976* (Lon. 1977) p. 107.

34. L. J. Saunders, *Scottish Democracy, 1815-1840* (Edin. 1950) pp. 82, 388.

35. Checkland, op. cit., pp. 240, 424.

36. Lenman (1975) op. cit., pp. 66-8; Cockburn, op. cit., p. 429.

37. *E.W.J.* 21 July 1824.

38. *Edinburgh Journal*, 1823-1847 (Ms. — Edin. Central Library) June 1824, November 1824.

39. W. F. Gray, *A Brief Chronicle of the Scottish Union and National Insurance Co.*, 1824-1924 (Edin. 1924) p. 98.

40. A. Romney, *Three Letters on the Speculative Schemes of the Present Times and the Projected Banks* (Edin. 1825) p. 5.

41. *E.W.J.* 15 December 1824, 22 December 1824; *I.J.* 6 December 1822.

42. Romney, op. cit., p. 3; *A Letter*, op. cit., p. 6.

43. Repr. in *G.H.* 15 November 1824.

44. J. Anderson, *A History of Edinburgh* (Edin. 1856) p. 377; *A.J.* 17 November 1824, 24 November 1824.

45. G. Stewart, *Progress of Glasgow* (Glasgow 1883) p. 62.

46. G. Hay, *History of Arbroath* (Arbroath 1899) p. 389; R. Smith, *The History of Greenock* (Greenock 1921) pp. 42, 47; A. M'Kay, *The History of Kilmarnock* (Kilmarnock 1909) pp. 252, 361; Cockburn, op. cit., p. 432.

47. *I.J.* 17 December 1824, 11 February 1825; Cotterill, op. cit., p. 168.

48. Munn, op. cit., p. 76.

49. Munn, op. cit., p. 110; *Contract of Copartnery: Dundee Commercial Bank* (1825); *A.J.* 5 January 1825; Gray, op. cit., p. 135.

50. *Glasgow Delineated: A Description of the City, its Institutions, Manufactures and Commerce* (Glas. 1824) p. 66; *Salas 150: A History of the Scottish Amicable Life Assurance Society 1826-1976* (Glas. 1976) pp. 9-10; *G.H.* 7 January 1825, 18 January 1825.

51. *Contract of Copartnery: Forfarshire Fire Insurance Co.* (Dundee 1823); *Family Journal for the North of Scotland*, 18 September 1846.

52. *G.H.* 25 January 1825, 18 January 1825; *A.J.* 6 April 1825; *D.P. & C.A.* 6 January 1825; *I.J.* 1 December 1824, 18 March 1825; R. S. Craig, 'Some Aspects of Capital Formation in Shipping in the age of sail and steam', *E.B.H.C.P.* (1975) p. 7.

53. Carter, op. cit., pp. 18, 30-33; Lewin, op. cit., pp. 187-193; Hay, op. cit., pp. 388, 427; Hassan, op. cit., pp. 19-20, 51.

54. Weir, op. cit., pp. 185-6.

55. C. Landale, *Report on the Proposed Railway between the Valley of Strathmore and Dundee* (Sept. 1825) p. 9; *D.P. & C.A.* 18 November 1824, 5 January 1825, 27 January 1825, 27 January 1825, 31 March 1825, 5 May 1825, 14 July 1825; *E.W.J.* 17 November 1824.

56. J. A. Jardine, *Report to the Committee of the Edinburgh and Dalkeith Railway Co.*, February 1826.

57. D. Weir, *History of the Town of Greenock* (Greenock 1829) p. 1100; Cotterill, op. cit., pp. 121-131.

58. Cockburn, op. cit., p. 353; Youngson, op. cit., p. 241; *Statement by the Directors of the Edinburgh Joint Stock Water Co.* (Edin. 1825); *Address by the interim committee of the Edinburgh and Leith Water Company to the inhabitants of Edinburgh and Leith* (Edin. 1825); *Edinburgh and Leith Water Co.: A Prospectus* (Edin. 1825).

59. Cotterill, op. cit., pp. 414, 418, 426.

60. *Report on the Subject of Establishing a Gas Light Company in Aberdeen* (Abdn. 1824); *A.J.* 31 December 1823, 28 January 1824, 14 September 1825, 21 September 1825.

61. *D.P. & C.A.* 18 November 1824, 5 January 1825, 27 January 1825, 31 March 1825, 5 May 1825, 14 July 1825; *G.H.* 15 November 1824; *A.J.* 17 November 1824.

62. *G.H.* 15 November 1824; Anderson, op. cit., p. 377.

63. *Proposals for carrying on certain public works in the City of Edinburgh* (Edin. 1752) p. 21.

64. A. G. Thomson, *The Paper Industry in Scotland, 1590-1861* (Edin. 1974) p. 87; Logan, op. cit., p. 114.

65. Duckham, op. cit., p. 179; Steel, op. cit., p. 119.

66. A. M. C. MacEwan, The Shotts Iron Company, 1800-1805 (M. Litt. — Strathclyde Univ. 1972) p. 56; A. Muir, *The Story of Shotts* (Edin. 1961) pp. 1-5.

67. *G.H.* 21 January 1825; J. L. Carvel, *Alloa Glassworks* (Edin. 1953) p. 1.

68. MacEwan, op. cit., p. 56.

69. Cairncross & Weber, op. cit., p. 287; *S.M.* October 1825; *Glasgow Delineated*, op. cit., p. 75.

70. Romney, op. cit., p. 4, eg. *E.W.J.* 29 December 1824.

71. *E.W.J.* 5 January 1825.

72. Forbes & Co. to Col. Forbes, 17 May 1824, 30 December 1824, 5 October 1824, 4 January 1825.

73. Checkland, op. cit., pp. 408, 417; Anon., *Journal*, op. cit., 5 September 1825.

74. Wilson, op. cit., p. 11.

75. Fenn, op. cit., p. 150.

76. Banks of Issue (Scotland): A Return, 1815-1845, B.P.P., XXVIII (1845).

77. *Aberdeen Town and County Banking Co.: Sederunt Book of the Directors* 17 April 1826; J. Meetwell, *Incidents, Errors, and Experiences in the Life of a Scottish Merchant* (Edin. 1866) pp. 80-1, 89.

78. *B.C.* 28 August 1829; Anon., *Journal*, 4 March 1826; Stewart, op. cit., p. 62; W. E. K. Anderson (ed), *The Journal of Sir Walter Scott* (Oxford 1972) *14 December 1825; Meetwell, op. cit., p. 99; Weir, op. cit., p. 181.*

79. *E.W.J.* 31 January 1826.

80. R. C. O. Matthews, *A Study in Trade Cycle History: Economic Fluctuations in Great Britain, 1833-1842* (Cam. 1954) p. 2.

81. *B.C.* 23 November 1827, 27 July 1827, 3 April 1828.

82. MacEwan, op. cit., p. 56.

83. *Annual Register*, 1825, p. 97; *I.J.* 11 March 1825; *E.W.J.* 26 April 1826; Scottish Commercial Marine Insurance Co.: Letter to Shareholders, 30 May 1826; *The Scottish Railway Shareholders Manual* (Edin. 1849) p. 11.

84. *D.P. & C.A.* 18 June 1829; Lenman (1977) op. cit., p. 154.

85. *E.W.J.* 16 July 1826; Anon., *Journal*, op. cit., 4 March 1826; W. Chambers, *The Book of Scotland* (Edin. 1830) p. 338; B. C. Hunt, *The Development of the Business Corporation in England, 1800-1867* (Cam., Mass. 1936) p. 54.

4

Stockbroking in the 1820s

THE rapid growth in the number of joint-stock companies had a major impact on the market for shares in Scotland. By 1830 the paid-up capital of the Edinburgh-based companies was estimated as £15m. The variety of shares and the number of shareholders also expanded significantly. The nominal value of shares was increasingly pitched at around £20-£25, rather than £100 or £500, while the paid-up value was more often £10 and under. Thus, not only had price and company to be matched in any deal, but so had the number of shares involved, as transfers were no longer limited to single shares.[1]

The companies promoted in the mid-1820s had far more shareholders than previous concerns, reflecting the expansion in the size of the investing public. The National Bank of Scotland, formed in Edinburgh in 1825 with a paid-up capital of £0.5m, had 1,238 shareholders compared to the 521 of the Commercial Bank of Scotland, formed in 1810.[2] Banks formed outside Edinburgh also had numerous shareholders, with the Arbroath Banking Co. having 113, the Dundee Commercial Bank 198 and the Aberdeen Town and County Bank 446.[3] Insurance companies were popular investments and the Scottish Union Insurance Company had some 5,000 shareholders by 1830.[4] Gas and water companies found reasonable support, such as the Aberdeen Gas Co., which had 212 shareholders, compared to 172 in the Dundee Gas Co. and 124 in the speculative Edinburgh Portable Gas Co.[5] Those joint-stock enterprises that were the least favoured by investors in the 1820s were the railways and the industrial and commercial companies.

The Edinburgh and Dalkeith Railway obtained its capital of £56,150 from only 87 people. Other railways were even less popular, with the Dundee and Newtyle having only 18 shareholders, and the Ballochney only 14.[6] An industrial concern, such as the New Shotts Iron Co., had only 42 shareholders, although it had capital assets totalling £71,650 in 1826.[7] Investors preferred the security of infrastructure and services rather than trade and industry, and railroads were still too novel to attract much general support.

It was the deliberate policy of some joint-stock companies to attract as many shareholders as possible, for numerous shareholders increased the concern's likelihood of success, since those who invested in the company were likely to give it their custom. The Aberdeen Town and County Bank intended that its '... capital should be divided into small shares, to enable all classes of the community to participate in the benefits of the establishment; and by being widely diffused, to increase its credit and influence, and procure the patronage and support of the public'.[8] The Scottish Union Insurance Co. made each shareholder promise to take out an insurance policy, while the gas companies saw their shareholders as potential consumers.[9] Consequently, in 1824-5 there was a simultaneous increase in the number of joint-stock companies, the size of their paid-up capital, the amount of shares in existence, and the number of shareholders. That situation alone put extreme pressure upon the existing market, especially in Edinburgh, as 'By the ordinary causation of life and fortune . . . shares must progressively come into the market, . . .'[10]

Nevertheless, in many of the companies formed, the turnover of shares was low as a substantial proportion of the shareholders were interested in the concern's progress, not only as investors, but also as businessmen or consumers. Alexander Baird, for example, invested in the Glasgow and Garnkirk, and Monkland and Kirkintilloch Railways for the assistance they would give to his coal and iron interests. At least one third of those holding the shares of the Edinburgh and Dalkeith Railway were in the coal trade, and benefited from the improved transport provided by the line. There was a strong coincidence of consumers and shareholders in gas companies.

In the larger joint-stock concerns, with numerous shareholders, transfers were more common, for financial and other interests overlapped less.[11] However, during the mania not only were large numbers temporarily attracted to shares as investments, but also the turnover of shares was high, with speculators buying and selling for quick capital gains. The *Edinburgh Times* reported in February 1825 that

> The chief speculators are people who so far from having the power to pay up their shares if called on, could not by possibility obtain credit for a suit of clothes of their merchant-tailor. Having nothing to lose, they take the chance of the present mania; hoping that their stock may rise, and that, by selling out, they may clear a little money.[12]

Therefore, in addition to the expansion of companies, investors, and shares, there was a rapid increase in the number of transfers. The increased business meant not only a growth in activity for those already involved in the share business, and openings for others, but also created a new set of conditions. In order for the speculators to function, it was essential to have widely publicised lists showing the current prices of popular stocks and shares, and these prices had to alter quickly so as to reflect changing positions of supply and demand. Share transfers now required a greater knowledge of companies and market conditions from those handling the business, and thus a greater commitment from them than previously. Alterations in the share market were inevitable, but it was the speculation that determined that change would come in 1824-5.

The mania was not focused exclusively on shares but involved other forms of property, such as land. Therefore, there was ample justification and scope for improving the whole property market rather than just one small segment of it. It had long been considered a weakness that there was no central establishment through which all details of property wanted, or offered for sale or lease, could be made generally available. This remained, fragmentarily, in the hands of individual lawyers, local auctions and newspaper advertisements, and so, in November 1824,

James Taylor Smith & Co. attempted to rectify the omission by the formation of the 'Scottish Transfer and Property Record Office'. The office would record a description of every kind of property for sale, or in demand, throughout Scotland, and this information would then be circulated to all subscribers, especially the members of the legal profession. By these means the office would act as a passive intermediary in all property transactions, bringing buyer and seller together. Stocks and shares were to be an integral part of the office's operations:

> In the transference of stock, whether of Banks, or Canals, or any other public Joint Stock Companies, this office will afford a central market; and persons concerned may learn in it the current prices of the day, and where sales or purchases can with most advantage be effected.[13]

This grandiose scheme was doomed to failure, not only from the entrenched opposition of the powerful legal profession, who saw their privileges and monopolies threatened, but also because there was not a major need for a central institution catering for Scotland as a whole. The sales and purchase of property remained essentially local.

This was as true of the shares of joint-stock enterprises as of houses and land. The shareholders in any bank, railway, gas company or any other concern tended to be overwhelmingly from the area in which it operated. Almost all the shares of the Edinburgh and Dalkeith Railway were held by local residents. Only two of the 172 shareholders in the Dundee Gas Co. were non-local.[14]

At the same time, the mid-1820s speculation ensured that the activity and complexity of share business was reaching a level which would support the existence of specialists to handle its peculiar requirements. Speculation and the appearance of stockbrokers went hand-in-hand in 1824-5. According to Anthony Romney:

> There darted forth, . . ., as if from some hidden cavern, a race of men who proposed to act the part of golf-bearers, or bottle-holders, in this new game that was about to be played, under the designation of stockbrokers.[15]

Some of those who declared themselves to be sharebrokers had carried on the business to a limited extent beforehand. It was quite common for dealers or merchants to be involved in a variety of products and agencies.[16] John Robertson, an Edinburgh wine merchant, had arranged share transfers from about 1815 onwards, but, such was the expansion of business in the mid-1820s that he dropped the wine trade, took his son, an Edinburgh lawyer, into partnership, and publicised his capabilities as a sharebroker.[17] Gibson, an Edinburgh auctioneer, had handled the occasional sale of shares before, but by November 1824 he had found that '. . . the business of this description done in this quarter is greater than has been generally imagined, . . .' and, as a consequence, announced his attention '. . . to devote his exertions to this department more sedulously than he has hitherto done, . . .'[18] Although these individuals in Edinburgh had dabbled in stockbroking before 1824, it was in that year that it emerged as a distinct and recognised occupation.[19]

Stockbrokers also appeared in Glasgow in the mid-1820s. Wardlaw and Cunninghame, William Ewing, and Henry Paul all announced in December 1824 that they had commenced as agents or brokers for the sale and purchase of all kinds of stocks and shares, in order to remedy the deficiency of such a specialist service in Glasgow.[20] These early Glasgow stockbrokers were largely an offshoot of the Edinburgh speculation, for it was to that city that they looked for guidance in the companies to list and the current prices to quote. William Ewing publicised the fact that he was '. . . enabled to exhibit at the office, the value of the respective Joint Stocks in Edinburgh of the preceding day, having made the necessary arrangements for that purpose'.[21] The other brokers also relied upon prices obtained from Edinburgh.[22] Outside Glasgow, the rest of Scotland was even more dependent upon Edinburgh's lead, for independent sharebrokers did not even appear, only agents of Edinburgh stockbrokers. In Aberdeen the firm of Charles Fyfe & Co., snuff dealers and commission agents, acted for French & Co., prominent Edinburgh brokers. They exhibited '. . . the daily Prices of Shares in the various Joint Stock Companies in Scotland, and other Property, with the quantity and description of each for Sale or Purchase, . . .' and received orders for such on behalf of French & Co.[23]

In the realm of law Scotland was strongly orientated towards Edinburgh in the 1820s, with all the important law business of the country being transacted in the capital city. Edinburgh lawyers had agents throughout the country with whom they were in constant communication, and through them, as well, came much financial business, such as the sale and purchase of land and the lending and borrowing of money.[24] Col. Forbes, for example, purchased his shares in the Edinburgh and Dalkeith Railway through Charles Davidson, an Edinburgh lawyer and a friend.[25] However, as most investors in joint-stock enterprise were local there was no real necessity to channel transfers through Edinburgh, while Edinburgh brokers could hardly determine prices which accurately reflected current conditions in areas and companies of which they knew little.

Thus, outside Edinburgh, the transfer of shares continued to be done by traditional means, and this included Glasgow, for the brokers who had established themselves there soon disappeared.[26] In Aberdeen the legal profession continued to handle the transfer of shares in a local concern such as the Aberdeen Town and County Bank, whose clients involved in sales and purchases were almost wholly confined to people living in Aberdeen and its vicinity.[27] Transfers of gas company shares were still normally made through private bargains between friends and relatives living in the same locality.[28] Even in Edinburgh, auctions, advertisements and lawyers continued to play an important role in the share market in the mid-1820s.[29] So, although the first definite beginnings were made in 1824-5 for the establishment of a Scottish stockbroking profession, its only permanent manifestations were in Edinburgh. Outside that city, the business resumed its traditional pattern.

Stockbroking was one of the many professions that became established in the nineteenth century, even though their origins lay in the eighteenth, or even earlier.[30] Few regarded stockbroking as an honourable occupation, the typical opinion being that stockbrokers were parasites who were detrimental to all legitimate economic activity.[31] Observers in Scotland, in the 1820s, shared this general disapproval of stockbrokers, such as Romney or Cockburn.[32] Consequently, any Scottish entrant to the stockbroking profession was well aware of the poor opinion in which it was held, and of the uncertain future any new occupation had before it became established and accepted. Therefore, although the legal profession had dominated the Scottish share market before 1820, few lawyers became stockbrokers, for that would have involved both a loss of status and of security. Even without involvement in arranging share transfers, there existed ample opportunities for all members of the legal profession. Those people who did declare themselves as stockbrokers tended to be accountants, merchants, auctioneers, or agents of all descriptions. For them the transition was much less than for any member of the legal profession.[33]

John Robertson in Edinburgh, and Wardlaw and Cunninghame in Glasgow, had both been involved in the retail trade before becoming stockbrokers. Robertson had been a wine merchant, while Wardlaw and Cunninghame were booksellers and stationers.[34] These were areas of the retail trade which catered for the wealthy and their requirements, with many of those involved in the trade coming from well-off families themselves.[35] As a consequence, high-class shopkeepers were on familiar terms with their customers, were acquainted with their wants, and possessed the knowledge and contacts necessary to arrange share transfers and price according to current economic conditions. Wardlaw and Cunninghame, for example, had compiled a book in 1824 entitled *Glasgow Delineated — A Description of the City, its Institutions, Manufactures and Commerce*. Agents were already handling the requirements of the rich and it was a simple matter to extend the range into stocks and shares if the situation demanded it. James French & Co., for instance, were also house, estate and army agents, while John Hay was a general agent.[36] Circumstances were similar for auctioneers and accountants, such as Gibson in Edinburgh, an auctioneer, or Paul in Glasgow, an accountant.[37] Most of the stockbrokers continued to practise their previous occupation with stockbroking being added as an extra, often of only minor importance. John Robertson was the sole exception. When the mania was over many stockbrokers returned to their past profession full-time.[38] The early stockbroking profession in Scotland thus largely recruited its members from the ranks of associated activities; some had dabbled already in shares, while virtually none came from the legal profession though they did dominate the business. Robertson's son, who joined him in the family firm for a short period, was a rare exception.[39]

Amongst those who became stockbrokers in the mid-1820s there was not a unanimous view as to how business should be conducted, though most adopted the methods of the legal profession by handling transfers through private contact aided by newspaper advertisements. The stockbrokers perfected this latter procedure by publishing, regularly, lists offering shares for sale or wanted, as, for example, in this insertion by William Ewing in the *Glasgow Herald* in December 1824:[40]

For sale, a number of shares of the following Stocks.

West of Scotland Insurance Co.
Scottish Union Insurance Co.
Equitable Loan or Pawnbrokers Co.
Edinburgh and Leith Dock Co.
Edinburgh and Leith Glass Co.
Edinburgh Water Co.
North British Equitable Co.
Caledonian Foundry Co.
Edinburgh and Glasgow Railroad Co.
Midlothian Railroad Co.
Sea Insurance Co.
Edinburgh Coal Gas Co.
Edinburgh Oil Gas Co.

Wanted to Purchase

Union Canal Shares
Cranstonhill Water Shares

William Ewing
176, Trongate.

A few other brokers augmented these means by holding regular share auctions, such as Gibson and Lindsay & Co. in Edinburgh. Gibson advertised the fact that '. . . if sale cannot readily be effected privately, and holders become desirous to realize, the stock will be brought to sale, by Auction, at the Weekly Sale of such stock, . . .' and claimed that this method was a very effective way of disposing of securities for which there was only a limited market.[41] However, auctions were expensive and when, with the collapse of the mania, the turnover of shares, dropped greatly and interest almost disappeared, these regular auctions were discontinued.

Private contact and local newspaper advertisements constituted the mechanism of the share market in the 1820s, and this was perfectly adequate as the number of brokers were few, there being no more than three or four separate firms of acknowledged stockbrokers in Edinburgh. As there were so few brokers, each was in contact with a large proportion of those interested in the sale or purchase of shares. Each broker was a market for shares and these brokers all had their offices close to one another, making communication between brokers easy.[42] This ensured that the buying and selling of shares, and the settlement of bargains, was not confined to the clients of any single broker in any one case but involved the clients of them all, either directly or indirectly. In addition, for the first time, those who handled share transfers — though really only those in Edinburgh — were clearly recognised and designated, and so they were the natural focus for those wanting to buy or sell shares, either for themselves or on behalf of others. Chambers, writing in 1830, regarded it as automatic that anyone attempting to sell bank shares would employ a broker to handle the transaction.[43] Thus, despite the continued existence of alternative means and personnel, stockbrokers were increasingly the accepted intermediaries for share business in Edinburgh.

From mid-1824 onwards, a regular and separate market had been established in the shares of Scottish joint-stock companies. This market was largely an

Edinburgh creation, though it did have important Glasgow, Aberdeen and national manifestations and was active enough to produce frequently changing share prices. From December 1824 onwards, the Edinburgh newspapers included, as a weekly feature, a table entitled 'Prices of Edinburgh Stocks' which listed the shares being dealt in, and the current prices. This list was copied by newspapers in the rest of Scotland. After the collapse of the share boom the production and publication of these lists became more intermittent, but they did continue to be published and circulated.[44] French & Co. produced a regular monthly list giving the current prices of Scottish stocks and shares, especially those of the banks. This was copied by the London Stock Exchange and included in their own list from January 1827 onwards.[45] It was in Edinburgh that the prices of Scottish securities were made in the 1820s, indicating that London was not the only functioning share market at that time. An independent Scottish, or rather an Edinburgh share market, was in operation and continued to be so even after the end of the mania.[46]

The main activity in this market, both during the mania and afterwards, was dealing in the shares of Scottish banks, the largest joint-stock institutions at the time. The next in popularity were the shares of insurance, gas, water and canal companies, with shipping concerns, such as the Australian Company, experiencing sudden flurries of activity. Industrial and commercial enterprises were of only passing consequence for, once the speculation had died down, interest in their shares, in the market, rapidly faded. The same occurred with railway companies, with their shares being neglected by investor and speculator alike.

In the course of 1825 the securities of over 50 joint-stock companies were actively traded in the Edinburgh share market and these encompassed a wide range of economic activity including 5 banks, 10 insurance companies, 4 gas companies, 5 railways, 7 shipping companies, and 12 concerns involved in manufacturing, distribution, property or mining. Although, in the rest of Scotland, finance and utilities predominated, the mania did present the impression that the joint-stock form of enterprise was beginning to pervade all areas of the economy and to attract the investing public. However, once the boom collapsed investors tended to shun all but the shares of the local banks, insurance, gas and water companies, and it was transactions in these sectors that underpinned the market.[47]

Table 1

Joint-Stock Companies Known on the Edinburgh Market in 1825

I. Financial

Bank of Scotland	Caledonian Fire Insurance Co.
British Linen Co.	Edinburgh Friendly Insurance Co.
Commercial Bank of Scotland	Edinburgh Life Insurance Co.
National Bank of Scotland	Hercules Insurance Co.
Royal Bank of Scotland	Insurance Co. of Scotland
Equitable Loan Co.	London, Leith & Belfast Smack
	Insurance Co.

North British Equitable
 Loan Co.

North British Insurance Co.
Scottish Union Insurance Co.
Sea Insurance Co. of Scotland
West of Scotland Insurance Co.

II. Transport

Australian Co.
Brilliant Steam Yacht Co.
Hull & Leith Shipping Co.
Leith & Hamburgh Shipping Co.
London, Leith, Edinburgh &
 Glasgow Shipping Co.
London, Leith & Glasgow
 Shipping Co.
London & Leith Old Shipping Co.
Edinburgh & Leith Dock Co.

Berwick & Kelso Railroad
Edinburgh & Dalkeith Railroad
Edinburgh & Glasgow Railway
Edinburgh & Kelso Railway
Haddington & Dalkeith Railroad
Edinburgh & Glasgow Union Canal
Forth Clyde Canal Co.
Monkland Canal Co.

III. Urban Utilities

Edinburgh Coal Gas Co.
Edinburgh Portable Gas Co.
Edinburgh Oil Gas Co.
Leith Oil Gas Co.

Edinburgh Joint Stock Water Co.
New Town Water Co.
Edinburgh Southern Markets
New Town Market Co.
Waterloo Hotel & Tavern Co.

IV. Industrial & Commercial

British Distillery Co.
Caledonian Iron & Foundry Co.
Edinburgh, Glasgow & Alloa
 Glass Co.
Edinburgh & Leith Brewing Co.
Edinburgh & Leith Glass Co.
Scottish Porter Brewery Co.
New Shotts Iron & Foundry Co.

Edinburgh Dairy Co.
Canal Coal Co.

Sources: *E.W.J.* 22 December 1824, 5 January 1825, 12 January 1825
   S.M. August, October 1825

(Other companies were promoted but their shares do not appear to have been dealt in.)

NOTES

1. Chambers, op. cit., p. 36; *S.M.* August 1825.
2. Clapham, op. cit., p. 91.
3. Munn, op. cit., p. 110; Chambers, op. cit., p. 337.
4. Gray, op. cit., p. 135.
5. Cotterill, op. cit., pp. 431-2, 1391; Contract of Copartnery: Aberdeen Gas Light Co., 1824.
6. J. Priestly, *Historical Account of the Navigable Rivers, Canals, and Railways of Great Britain* (Lon. 1831) pp. 51-2, 214-6, 225-9; Lewin, op. cit., pp. 187-193; Carter, op. cit., pp. 20, 30-3.

7. MacEwan, op. cit., pp. 31, 252.

8. *A.J.* 5 January 1825.

9. Proposals for a New Fire Insurance Co., Edin. 1824; Cotterill, op. cit., p. 179.

10. Address, op. cit., p. 23.

11. R. D. Corrins, William Baird and Company: Coal and Iron Masters, 1830-1914 (Ph.D. Strathclyde Univ. 1974) p. 84; Hassan, op. cit., p. 19; Cotterill, op. cit., pp. 112, 176; MacEwan, op. cit., p. 30.

12. *E.T.* repr. in *D.P.* & *C.A.* 17 February 1825. cf. *E.W.J.* 29 December 1824.

13. *E.W.J.* 17 November 1824.

14. Hassan, op. cit., p. 19; Cotterill, op. cit., p. 1391.

15. Romney, op. cit., p. 5.

16. Weir, op. cit., pp. 41-2.

17. Memorandum prepared by John H. Robertson, 7 April 1927; *E.W.J.* 3 November 1824; *E.D.* 1825-6.

18. *E.W.J.* 3 November 1824.

19. *E.W.J.* 29 December 1824; Chambers, op. cit., p. 338.

20. *G.H.* 10 December 1824, 27 December 1824.

21. *G.H.* 27 December 1824.

22. *G.H.* 27 December 1824.

23. *A.J.* 2 March 1825.

24. J. Mitchell, *Reminiscences of my Life in the Highlands* (1883, repr. Newton Abbot 1971) II, pp. 18, 189, 309.

25. C. Davidson to Col. Forbes, 11 September 1826, 22 September 1826.

26. *G.D.* 1825-6; *G.H.* 30 July 1824, 29 November 1824 et seq.

27. Sederunt Book, op. cit., 1825-7, e.g. 26 June 1826, 26 August 1826, et seq.

28. Cotterill, op. cit., p. 176.

29. *E.W.J.* 7 January 1824, 3 November 1824, et seq.

30. A. M. Carr-Saunders & P. A. Wilson, *The Professions* (Oxf. 1933) pp. 295-6; R. Lewis & A. Maude, *Professional People* (Lon. 1952) pp. 23, 29.

31. *Thoughts on Trade and a Public Spirit* (Lon. 1716) p. 4; W. Gordon, *The Universal Accountant and Complete Merchant* (Edin. 1763) (I) p. 221; *Every Man his own Broker* (Lon. 1761) XIII: R. Price, *Observations on Revisionary Payments* (Lon. 1783) (I) p. 206.

32. Romney, op. cit., p. 5; Cockburn, op. cit., pp. 432-3.

33. *E.D.* 1824-6.

34. Memorandum, op. cit.; *G.D.* 1824-6.

35. W. H. Marwick, 'Shops in Eighteenth and Nineteenth Century Edinburgh', *Book of the Old Edinburgh Club* 30 (1959) p. 125.

36. *E.D.* 1824-6.

37. *E.D.* 1824-7; *G.H.* 27 December 1824; J. Mann, 'Glimpses of Early Accountancy in Glasgow', *A.M.* 58 (1954) p. 300.

38. *E.D.* 1824-7; *E.W.J.* 1 March 1826; *G.D.* 1824-8.

39. Memorandum, op. cit.

40. *G.H.* 27 December 1824.

41. *E.W.J.* 3 November 1824, 12 January 1825, 1 March 1826.

42. *E.D.* 1825-9.

43. Chambers, op. cit., p. 339.

44. *E.W.J.* December 1824 et seq.; *G.C.* 1 January 1825 et seq.

45. Chambers, op. cit., p. 338; H. C. Burdett, *Burdett's Official Intelligence* (Lon. 1882) XVI.

46. For a contrary view see B. L. Anderson, 'Law, finance and economic growth in England: Some Long-term Influences' in B. M. Radcliffe (ed.), *Great Britain and her World, 1750-1914* (Man. 1975) p. 113; M. C. Reed, 'Railways and the Growth of Capital Market' in M. C. Reed (ed.), *Railways in the Victorian Economy* (Newton Abbot 1969) p. 174.

47. *S.M.* 1824-8: the monthly list of shares and their prices gave an indication of active stocks; Chambers, op. cit., pp. 336-7.

PART II:

SPREAD OF THE MARKET, 1830-1840

It may be truly said that the capital now represented by joint-stock enterprise has become one of the great powers of the world. Joint-stock furnishes every civilized community with light, with water, with food and drink of many descriptions, and a thousand other articles indispensable to the wants of modern civilization; it multiplies the power of human labour by the production of coal and iron for the purposes of manufacture; it diffuses wealth to an immense extent in banks and credit institutions; it touches closely the hopes and fears of millions, and moderates even the terrors of death by vast insurance associations, firmly grounded on the law of probabilities; it launches fleets of steam-driven ships to interchange the produce of every clime and every nation; and lastly, and to crown all, it covers the whole earth with a wonderful network of railways, and girdles earth and ocean with a system of telegraph, destined, if anything made by human hands can do so, to raise mankind to higher moral and physical conditions than any yet attained in the course of history. *The Financial Register and Stock Manual* (London 1876) v.

5

The Consolidation of Joint-Stock Enterprise, 1830-1840

THE decade of the 1830s was one of substantial change in the Scottish economy as it responded to the market opportunities in England, and abroad, and the new developments in technology. Growing population and rising incomes, which arose from England's industrialisation, created an expanding demand for all types of products, especially agricultural produce.[1] Transportation improvements, which provided cheaper, faster and more reliable carriage, transmitted these demands to Scotland and stimulated fundamental responses. Prime among the transportation facilities developed in the 1830s was steam shipping, for this linked the coastal areas of Scotland with the main English maritime cities, and gave them an advantage over the landlocked English producers.[2] As early as 1834 it was noted that

> In consequence of the increase and improvements in navigation and the introduction of steam, the Scotch farmer now sends to London his livestock, fresh and salt meat, potatoes, butter, and other produce, at as little expense as the farmer who resides only 20 miles from the Metropolis but has to send his by land.[3]

Consequently, the 1830s were marked by improvements and expansion of Scottish agriculture as it strove to serve both its own growing urban markets and those in England.[4]

The invention and application of Nelson's hot blast, and the growing importance of the Scottish iron industry, typified the altered circumstances of Scotland. The industry's capacity rose from 45,000 tons in 1828, when it was producing 5 per cent of British pig iron, to 245,000 in 1840, when Scotland provided almost a quarter of British output and was serving markets in England, Wales, and abroad.[5] Coal and iron-ore were essential ingredients in the production of iron. These materials were obtainable in Scotland, and so led to the rapid expansion of mining. The cheap iron produced was an essential raw material for a growing number of industries as it supplemented, replaced and then extended the applications of wood. Much of this iron was utilised in Central Scotland, as the heavy engineering and shipbuilding industries were located there, in order to be near cheap sources of coal and mass-produced iron.[6] No longer was industrial development confined to textiles, for it was beginning to pervade other sectors, especially iron production and those activities linked to it, while agriculture was also being transformed in a less dramatic but still fundamental way as it sought to serve new and expanding markets.

These developments in agriculture, mining, and heavy industry all required substantial investment with the gross capital formation in iron manufacture rising from £1.8m in 1828 to £6.6m in 1840. Even a textile town, such as Dundee, had by 1835 an estimated £475,000 invested in buildings and machinery which employed steam power.[7] In agriculture, impressionistic evidence indicates investment on a large scale, taking the form of waste land under cultivation, wet areas drained, fields cleared of stones, walls built and buildings erected.[8] Until at least the late 1830s many of the wealthy in Scotland had their available funds largely committed to the further development of the resources that were producing their income. Landowners, farmers, manufacturers and mine owners utilised the increased returns being derived from these activities to finance further expansion, or to diversify into allied areas. The Bairds, for example, invested their profits from agriculture in coal and iron-mining, and then used the returns from that to finance the construction of extensive iron works. In 1830 they laid out £20,000 to commence iron production at Gartsherrie.[9] The Houldsworth family set up a successful cotton textile spinning enterprise in Glasgow in the early nineteenth century and, in 1837, used the proceeds from that venture to move into iron manufacture with the Coltness iron works. Further such examples are innumerable.[10]

There were, of course, many in Scottish society who were not in a position to invest their savings directly in industry, agriculture, mining, or commerce, or who did not want to tie up their funds in that way. Deposits in Scottish banks reached an estimated £24m by 1831, and this sum continued to grow in the 1830s.[11] 'There is perpetually a new accumulation of capital seeking advantageous investment, and it finds employment where profits are highest, . . .' was the view expressed by a writer in the *Scottish Monthly Magazine* in 1836.[12] People such as Thomas Binnie, a Glasgow builder, Wardlaw Ramsay, a Lothian landowner, Peter Brough, a Paisley draper, or those in the iron trade who were, according to Kirkman Finlay in 1836, '. . . making immense fortunes', were all in receipt of rising incomes and becoming wealthy.[13] One of the most profitable periods for the Shotts Iron Company was between 1834 and 1840, with gross profits reaching £20,264 in 1839.[14] However, by the late 1830s the heaviest investment phase was over for many Scottish industrial developments. Both the Scottish iron and textile industries were facing over-capacity with too many furnaces and mills in operation, thus reducing any incentive to reinvest in further facilities.[15]

In 1835 the Scottish banks paid 2% on the money deposited with them in Edinburgh, 2.5% in Glasgow and 3% in Dundee, reflecting the fact that Glasgow and Dundee were rapidly growing industrial centres, where capital was more in demand than elsewhere. However, by the end of the 1830s these regional differences in interest rates had largely disappeared, with the situation in Edinburgh determining the national pattern. This indicated a general abundance of capital, as there was now no differential between Edinburgh, where savings were traditionally plentiful, and the industrial areas.[16] The economic developments of the 1830s not only absorbed large amounts of capital, but also created new sources of wealth and income that were coming to fruition by the end of the decade.

Much of these savings was deposited with the Scottish banks, for they offered security, a reasonable rate of return, and an ease of withdrawal. Chambers observed in 1830 that

> By offering interest for money lodged with them, they are made the depositories of nearly all the money in the country not absolutely required to keep up the circulating medium. As soon as anyone accumulates ten pounds, which are not required for immediate use, they are dispatched to a bank . . . were it not for the interest and the security they offer in becoming the custodians of money, it is more than probable, that persons who were over-stocked with riches could not know where to place them in advance.[17]

The rate of interest paid by the Scottish banks, and their willingness to accept deposits, therefore played an important role in determining the choice and timing of alternative investments, as well as reflecting the abundance, or scarcity, of savings in Scotland.[18] From June 1828 to May 1834 the rate had remained unchanged at 3 per cent per annum, but in that month it was lowered to 2.5 per cent, at which level it remained until it was raised to 3 per cent in November 1836, and 3.5 per cent in November 1837.[19] By May 1836 the Glasgow merchant, Kirkman Finlay, was of the opinion that

> . . . capital has of late very much accumulated and increased, and at the present moment there appears to be not merely a sufficient, but a super-abundant capital for all operations of trade, and for all the enterprises that it is desirable should be accomplished for the benefit of the country.[20]

Gradual recovery from 1826 onwards, combined with a series of abundant harvests in the mid-1830s, had created conditions of confidence, wealth and prosperity akin to those of 1824-5.[21] Again, as in the mid-1820s, these circumstances led to a search for alternative, but more rewarding, investments. The decline in the interest obtained by Scottish banks in British government securities or through their London correspondents encouraged many of the banks to purchase foreign stocks. The Perth Banking Company diversified by buying into Dutch and then U.S. securities in 1837-8, while both the Paisley banks bought French and Dutch government bonds. However, the stock of other European governments also carried a low yield, while non-European investments continued to be risky affairs involving high losses.[22] The banks had little option but to pass on the lower yields to their customers, many of whom, in turn, sought more remunerative investments.[23] 'The banks having reduced interest to 2.5 per cent, I am very desirous to invest my money in railway shares, which, in the printed schemes, it is stated will yield a return of from 6.5 to 12.5 per cent . . .', was the view of one investor in 1835.[24] As in the 1820s, the stocks and shares of joint-stock companies were among the most attractive investments, and certainly the most available, with land still circumscribed by entail, and the amount of government stock declining in size.[25]

While in England a minor mania of speculation and company promotion developed in the mid-1830s, events in Scotland hardly took that form. The *Aberdeen Herald* estimated that 126 English joint-stock schemes had been projected in 1835, with a nominal capital of £57m, compared with the £1m required by the new Scottish ventures.[26] Numerous joint-stock enterprises were formed in Scotland in the 1830s, but their appearance was not concentrated by 1835 or 1836, for the whole decade witnessed a gradual build-up of company promotion from about 1834 onwards.[27] The bankruptcy of Edinburgh in 1833 affected confidence in Scotland and dampened down speculative activity.

After the failure of Edinburgh to shift the burden of debt it had incurred by improvements to Leith harbour through the formation of the Leith Docks Company, the Council was left owing £250,000 at high interest rates and, eventually, the city could not meet payments. The financial collapse brought down many who had lent money to the council and forced other leading investors to be wary of placing their available funds in any form of permanent investment.[28] Cockburn wrote in April 1835 that

> Edinburgh is at present almost a mass of insolvency. Trade, except in one or two branches, has left Leith, our port; its docks are bankrupt, our college has not a shilling; the writers to the signet are getting so destitute that it is not easy to see how they can maintain their library and general establishment; the Faculty of Advocates is in a similar condition, but further gone; most of our charities and other institutions are dying of hunger, . . . [29]

With Edinburgh, Scotland's financial capital and centre of wealth, in this state of affairs, it was only to be expected that the country's response to the conditions producing the speculative mania in England would be rather muted, especially since the nature of economic development left little capital free for placement in joint-stock enterprise until the later years of the decade.

Edinburgh's problems were reflected in the geographical distribution of company formation in the 1830s, when most of the developments took place in the rest of Scotland. According to Reid, an Edinburgh stockbroker, only 10 of the 52 principal joint-stock companies established in that decade were based in Edinburgh, compared with 16 in Glasgow, 12 in Aberdeen and 6 in Dundee. Edinburgh concerns took only £1.8m of the paid-up capital of these concerns, which amounted to £8.5m, and half of that sum was for the Edinburgh and Glasgow Railway Company which was not a purely Edinburgh venture. In contrast, Glasgow joint-stock enterprise absorbed £4.6m, Aberdeen £1m, and Dundee £0.8m. Thus, over half the paid-up capital and nearly a third of the companies originated in Glasgow, as compared with under a quarter of the capital and under a fifth of the number coming from Edinburgh. So, compared with the 1820s, the promotion of joint-stock companies was becoming more prevalent throughout Scotland rather than being concentrated in Edinburgh.

Growth in capital and numbers was most rapid in Glasgow but cities such as Aberdeen and Dundee became, also, relatively more important centres, while numerous small companies were formed in such towns as Inverness, Greenock or Dumfries.[30] This overshadowing of Edinburgh, especially by Glasgow, indicated the changing nature of the Scottish economy and the distribution of wealth, with the expansion of Glasgow's coal, iron and heavy industry, Dundee's textiles, and Aberdeen's agricultural hinterland; and it provided important additional sources of savings and finance.

E

The establishment of new joint-stock companies did not cease completely with the collapse of the mid-1820s mania. Yet it was greatly reduced, for economic development, population growth, and urbanisation combined to produce a growing need for the facilities provided by joint-stock enterprise. Numerous gas companies were set up in increasingly smaller towns, such as Dunfermline in 1828, or Elgin in 1830. Those who financed such projects were local people desiring a gas supply. The merchants of Glasgow, between December 1827 and September 1829, provided £49,434 through paying up shares of the Glasgow Royal Exchange, in order to construct an exchange building for themselves.[31] Coal owners also financed railway developments, in order to reduce the cost of transportation and so expand the market for coal and the profits they received because of increased sales. Both Alexander Baird, a Glasgow iron master, and Charles Tennant, a Glasgow chemical manufacturer, were instrumental in financing the Glasgow and Garnkirk Railway in 1826, as they believed it would be instrumental in assisting the progress of their own enterprises.[32] Railways such as the Ballochney, Glasgow and Garnkirk, and the Wishaw and Coltness, which were formed in the late 1820s, all relied upon the financial support of the people who could expect to benefit directly from cheaper coal, especially mine owners, iron masters, chemical manufacturers and coal merchants.[33]

Thus, when the investing public became more willing to finance ventures of this kind in the 1830s, as confidence returned and prosperity increased, more and more joint-stock companies were promoted which relied less and less upon the support of small groups of interested businessmen or consumers. The attempts by the Dundee Joint Stock Water Company to obtain sufficient capital epitomise the gradual increase in involvement of investors seeking a return upon their capital, rather than a direct benefit from the functioning of the concern. Dundee's water supply was acknowledged by all to be inadequate and a water company was formed in June 1833 to remedy the deficiency. However, the company failed to obtain the necessary support and lapsed until August 1834, when a fresh attempt was made to attract the necessary funds. This time the response was more promising, with many local investors taking the view of David Miln, a Dundee banker

> That water was required, no one would deny, and it was a matter of little consequence to him whether the want was supplied by a Joint Stock Company or by an assessment, . . . suppose no return at all, he did not think that the shareholders would be worse off than by assessment. If a person be assessed 5/- per year, it is just the same thing to him as though he were to lose his interest on a £5 share.[34]

Despite this sentiment insufficient local finance was obtained, but investors in other parts of Scotland, attracted by the prospects of the company, provided sufficient additional funds so that the work could be begun. In all, by March 1835, of the £30,000 promised by subscribers, one third was obtained from outside Dundee.[35] However, a new water company promoted in Glasgow in 1836, which hoped to raise £160,000, was abandoned because of only limited support, as was the Aberdeen Union Gas Light Company, also in 1836.

The urban utility joint-stock companies formed in the 1830s tended to be located in the smaller towns or suburbs which did not possess these facilities at all, rather than providing duplicate services in the large cities. Sixty-nine towns established gas companies during the 1830s, for example. Almost the only exception was the establishment of the Edinburgh and Leith Gas Company in 1838, and that itself was only an extension of the existing Leith Gas Company, which was a very small concern.[36] Thus, though passive investors became more important during the 1830s in the provision of urban utilities, for most of the decade it was local consumers who provided themselves with their own gas and water facilities.

According to Cockburn the company promotions of the 1830s were marked by '. . . a thirst for everything which tends to annihilate time and space, and to bring people, whether lovers or enemies, together; . . .'[37] The provision of transportation was certainly an obvious use for joint-stock enterprise as it involved substantial capital outlays and affected numerous people, whether it was a harbour, steamship or railway. In the course of the 1830s there was a spate of steamship companies formed to operate on the longer coastal routes, such as the City of Glasgow Steamship Company in 1831, the Dundee and Hull Steam Packet Company and the Aberdeen Steam Navigation Company in 1835, or the Edinburgh-based Forth Steam Navigation Company in 1836.[38] Steamship enterprise was not confined to the larger ports such as Glasgow, Dundee, Leith or Aberdeen, but affected much of the country as the inhabitants of the smaller harbours feared a loss of traffic if they did not have their own lines of steam-powered vessels. The prospectus of the Banffshire Steam Navigation Company, promoted in May 1836, voiced the concern of Scotland's numerous small harbours:

> It has been for some time predicted that the whole coasting trade of the Island will very soon be entirely conducted by means of steam-vessels, and every season is bringing the prediction nearer to fulfilment and there now can be no reasonable doubt, that every district, of the smallest importance, must have a steam conveyance to carry its produce to the all-consuming mart of London, . . . [39]

By the end of the 1830s joint-stock steamship companies were beginning to dominate regular coastal shipping services, driving the small independent sailing vessels out of business, and these lines operated increasingly out of the larger ports.[40] A number of joint-stock international shipping concerns were also established in Scotland during the 1830s, such as the British and North American Royal Mail Steam Navigation Company in 1839. This concern was largely formed and financed by a group of Glasgow businessmen.[41]

Despite the utility and popularity of steamship companies, it was railways that dominated joint-stock enterprise, in the field of transportation, in the 1830s. While steamshipping opened up new markets for the Scottish economy, the provision of improved land transport — through the construction of railways — allowed that economy, especially in the west of Scotland, to meet many of the new demands. However, the railways constructed in the 1830s remained largely tied to the coalfields and to finance from those expecting to benefit from the line.

Companies such as the Paisley and Renfrew and the Slamannan in 1835, the Glasgow, Paisley, Kilmarnock and Ayr, and the Glasgow and Greenock in 1837, all served the west of Scotland coalfield and its markets, and owed much of their funds and initiative to mine owners, manufacturers and merchants directly, or indirectly, involved in coal.[42] In fact, when the Glasgow, Paisley, Kilmarnock and Ayr Railway Company found itself with an uncompleted line and was unable to raise extra funds from the public in 1839, a number of Glasgow merchants and manufacturers rallied round to provide the additional finance required so that the project could go ahead.[43] The projects in Edinburgh such as the Edinburgh, Leith and Newhaven Railway in 1836, and the Edinburgh and Glasgow Railway in 1838, were also mainly for the carriage of coal. Dundee was the only major centre for railway enterprise outside the coalfields, with such companies as the Newtyle and Coupar Angus, the Newtyle and Glamis, the Arbroath and Forfar, and the Dundee and Arbroath, which were all promoted in 1835-6. The completion of the Dundee and Newtyle Railway in 1832, despite the technical and financial difficulties over the six years of construction, did create openings for additional lines in what was a rich agricultural and industrial region. Whereas there might not be sufficient traffic to justify the expense of the one single line, a small network could hope to generate enough traffic to keep all the lines employed, with each route creating business for another.[44] Altogether, between 1835 and 1838, ten Scottish railways were sanctioned by Parliament, with a total capital requirement of £3,117,430.[45]

However, far more railways than these were promoted but failed to obtain the necessary finance, such as the Forth and Tay, Glasgow and Carlisle, and Glasgow and Falkirk, all appearing in 1836.[46] In Aberdeen a short railway line between the harbour and the industrial suburb of Printfield was promoted in October 1835, with the aim of extending the route to Huntly, 30 miles from Aberdeen, shortly thereafter:

> It has occurred, that a Railway communication might, with great advantage, be opened between the extensive Manufactories at the Printfield, and the Harbour of Aberdeen, passing Old Aberdeen. In this age of improvement, when the system of Railroads has been so generally and thoroughly examined, and its advantages thereby known and acknowledged, it would be superfluous, in introducing the present plan, to expatiate upon the superiority of that system, over the present mode of conveyance.

Despite this appeal the project was shelved after a survey had been carried out and plans drawn up.[47] The required level of financial support was not forthcoming in Aberdeen and the North-East of Scotland for any of the proposed railway schemes in the area.

Many railway promotions represented the culmination of previous attempts to improve transportation, and were integrated parts of a local network, such as the Glasgow, Paisley, Kilmarnock and Ayr Railway or the Arbroath and Forfar Railway.[48] However, it was not technical improvements within the railways themselves that made their establishment possible now, but external conditions related to traffic prospects and, especially, the availability of finance.

Technological improvements did not suddenly make the railway a viable project where it had not been so before, nor did the success of an established company necessarily create additional lines, though it did open up opportunities in that direction. The Edinburgh and Dalkeith Railway was opened in 1831, having cost almost twice the original estimate of £57,700. However, the line soon became successful, with the average annual quantity of coal carried rising from 89,017 tons in 1832-5 to 116,141 in 1840-3, while an important passenger and general freight business developed. In 1843, 165,000 passengers were carried between Edinburgh and Dalkeith compared to 50,000 by omnibus. As a consequence, the company was producing a satisfactory revenue by 1837, and paying a reasonable dividend, but few further railways were successfully promoted in Edinburgh and its vicinity.[49] In contrast, Dundee's experience with railways had not been a happy one. As late as June 1833, the *Dundee Advertiser* admitted that:

> We are quite aware that owing to the immense expense which the Newtyle Railway has cost, and the present unprosperous aspect of the speculation this mode of iron communication is here, at this particular moment, a little out of fashion, but it is so nowhere else.[50]

A year later, however, the Dundee and Arbroath Railway was promoted and met with such an enthusiastic response that it was able to issue some shares at a premium.[51]

A railway from Edinburgh to Glasgow was a perennial project, and it was put forward many times during the 1830s by such wealthy and influential people as Charles Tennant, the chemical manufacturer; Andrew and Dugald Bannatyne and Laurence Hill, Glasgow lawyers; and John Leadbetter, a Glasgow merchant. Many of these had inspected similar English railways, such as the Liverpool and Manchester, and could see no reason why a commercial rail connection between Edinburgh and Glasgow should not be constructed. The prevailing view was, according to the Bankers' Circular, that

> ... Railroads between populous places or districts, where there exists a necessity for much personal communication, and the quick and frequent transmission of commodities, will be eminently successful.[52]

It was considered that the Edinburgh to Glasgow route met all these requirements, with the potential passenger traffic alone being sufficient to make it a paying proposition.[53] While in terms of technology and traffic the Edinburgh to Glasgow link was perfectly feasible at any time during the 1830s, it was a major financial undertaking compared to the short lines that were built and which could rely heavily for funds on a small number of interested entrepreneurs. The Edinburgh to Glasgow railway had to attract widespread public support if it was to be successful, and this it largely failed to do in the 1830s, as that type of finance was not available in the required amounts for what was, still, a fairly novel project. Scotland was still a relatively poor country with too many calls upon its available wealth to afford the luxury of an improved inter-city link, attractive and feasible though that was. When the company was, eventually, successfully promoted it was only through the assistance of the more numerous and affluent English investors, who could afford to be concerned solely with the financial return.[54]

Consequently, the major factor that made some railways viable projects in the 1830s was less the technology or the traffic, but more the availability of funds. As interest rates fell, the attraction of railway investments rose, and the companies were quick to point this out to investors, as did the Dundee and Arbroath Railway in July 1834:

> At a time like the present, when it is with the utmost difficulty (money being so plenty) that capital can be safely invested at more than 3 or 3.5 per cent, no more equitable nor promising investment exists at the present time than on that great invention which essentially belongs to the Nineteenth century, viz railroads.[55]

Scottish banks, for example, looked upon lending to railways as something to be done when the needs of all other prospective borrowers had been met, and funds still remained unemployed.[56] Although technological prospects had made railways feasible, and economic development was improving traffic prospects, railways remained heavily dependent upon the ability and willingness of the public to provide the necessary finance. The public were only willing to do this when capital was abundant and other avenues of investment were restricted, or offered a poor return. As it was, railway construction in Scotland in the 1830s was on a fairly limited scale and confined to short lines. Nevertheless, by December 1838 Scotland had 48.75 miles of railway track in operation compared with 496.5 in England, which was almost equality, in population terms, though grossly inadequate when compared to Scotland's geographic area.[57]

Rivalling railroads as a favourite form of joint-stock enterprise in the 1830s were banking companies, with 14 having been established by 1840.[58] Many of these banks were a direct outcome of developments in the Scottish economy and virtually all were located outside Edinburgh. At the beginning of the decade Edinburgh dominated Scottish banking, but it was outside Edinburgh that the greatest growth in demand for credit was taking place, and it was there that there was a need for understanding and sympathetic banks. Amongst the many important Glasgow banks formed were the Glasgow Union Bank in 1830, the Western Bank of Scotland in 1832, the Clydesdale Banking Company in 1838, the City of Glasgow Bank in 1839, and the Glasgow Joint Stock Bank in 1840. The towns around Glasgow, such as Ayr, Paisley and Greenock, also witnessed the formation of new banks, as did a number of other cities and towns in Scotland, including Aberdeen in 1836, and Dundee and Inverness in 1838. These new banks were generally formed to supplement the existing service provided either by local banks, or the branches of banks which were based in Edinburgh, Glasgow or Aberdeen. The Union Bank, for example, was unwilling to extend greatly its credit and this stimulated the foundation of the Western Bank of Scotland, which would have a more liberal lending policy. Similarly, the Caledonian Banking Company was formed in Inverness in 1838 with the object of catering for the needs of merchants in the northern counties of Scotland and employing local money in local industry, rather than being dependent upon the services of Edinburgh banks.[59]

The motivation behind the formation of these banks was aptly summarised in the prospectus of the North of Scotland Banking Company in 1836. Firstly the opportunities were sketched in:

> It is impossible to take into view the growing intelligence and enterprise of the North of Scotland — the wealth of its agricultural, manufacturing, and shipping interest — with the vast accumulations of unemployed capital, amply sufficient to supply a circulating medium of its own: and, at the same time, the fact that the whole Banking business in the North is conducted through Branches of Edinburgh Banks (with the exception of the two native establishments in Aberdeen) without being fully satisfied that a New Bank, upon an extended basis and liberal principles is called for.

Once that had been established, the inadequacies and iniquities of the existing system were exposed, with past economic problems being attributed to the selfish attitude of the Edinburgh banks:

> These establishments not only draw to a distance large sums of profit, arising from the business of our merchants and agriculturalists, but are objectionable in times of temporary embarrassment, when, from varying causes, the same steady and consistent relief cannot be secured through their operation, as the superior means of information of a local Banking Company enables them to extend to the public, and more particularly to their own partners, who, although under immediate pressure, may still be in a situation to give sufficient security for the accommodation required.[60]

Certainly, the Edinburgh banks tended to draw money to their head offices from the areas in which their branches operated and in crises they tended to safeguard their central business first, especially the interests of their shareholders as opposed to the needs of others. Local banks were much more willing to look to the interests of the area they operated in, as well as to accommodate their own shareholders.[61]

Despite the evident need for improved banking facilities, particularly outside Edinburgh, most concerns appeared in periods of easy money, when alternative investments were limited, illustrating again the importance of finance in the timing of joint-stock promotions. At the same time, not all new banking creations were taken up by the public. Both the Metropolitan Bank of Scotland, which appeared in Edinburgh in 1834, and the Banffshire Banking Company, projected in Banff in 1836, failed to attract sufficient financial support.[62] Those banks that were successfully established tended to be those that had been under consideration for some time, and were merely awaiting a favourable opportunity to approach the investing public.[63]

Though banking dominated financial promotions, insurance companies were also popular forms of joint-stock enterprise, with new fire and life concerns formed in Glasgow, Aberdeen and Edinburgh during the 1830s, while the relatively new field of marine insurance attracted considerable interest. Between 1836 and 1840, eight marine insurance companies were established, evenly divided between the four main Scottish cities. Until the late 1830s legislation had prevented insurance companies outside London from effecting marine cover, and the removal of this prohibition was followed by a spate of promotions of joint-stock marine insurance ventures to cater for the increased coastal and international traffic.[64]

Whereas in the mid-1820s joint-stock industrial and commercial companies were popular creations, in the 1830s few were promoted, and even fewer established. Both the Glasgow and Ayrshire Iron Company, formed in Glasgow in 1840, and the Edinburgh New Town Market Company, promoted in 1836, failed to find the finance required and so disappeared.[65] In Aberdeen a few concerns did become established, such as the Aberdeen Lime Company in 1837 and the Aberdeen Market Company in 1838, but most of the other promotions never reached fruition, including the Aberdeen Woollen and Hosiery Company in 1840. This was an attempt to resurrect a woollen mill that had recently failed with a loss of 300 jobs and so offered little prospect of success to intending investors, a fact implicitly admitted in the prospectus:

> This Company cannot pretend to offer so high returns for the capital invested as is to be had in the British Colonies, or in other countries; but they consider that they give an equivalent in the greater security of the capital invested in trade at home, less exposed to fluctuations and risks, and always within their immediate control.[66]

However, for those investors looking for a reasonable domestic return and security, there were ample openings in the shares of banks, gas companies, or even railways, without the need to accept the risks of a single industrial venture with a history of failure. At the same time the more promising industrial concerns had little need to tap the funds of investors, for they could raise sufficient finance from a small group of entrepreneurs and their connections. The Coltness Iron Company was established in 1836 with a capital of £80,000 in exactly that way.[67]

The major innovation in joint-stock enterprise in the 1830s was the formation of overseas investment companies specialising in Australia and the United States. However, these ventures were largely confined to Aberdeen, although attempts were made in other parts of Scotland to promote rival concerns, such as the Australasian Loan Company of Edinburgh in 1839, but they were almost all unsuccessful. One of the few that did attract support was the Glasgow-based Clyde Company in 1837, which had as its object the purchase of land in Australia, but its capital was a mere £8,600 and it was primarily a private venture.[68] The evident wealth of the region, stemming from the prosperous agriculture and the new southern markets, accounted for the Aberdeen area's propensity to become involved in overseas enterprises. At the same time there was only limited indigenous enterprise available to absorb the savings flowing from this prosperity, apart from banks, coastal shipping, and insurance companies, whose capital requirements were low. The region was basically rural, with the exception of Aberdeen itself, which was already well provided for, with gas and water facilities, and, unlike the coalfield areas of Central Scotland, or even the area around Dundee with its adjacent and important industrial towns such as Arbroath or Forfar, it offered few inducements for the construction of short railway lines. Any viable railway project in North-East Scotland would have to be a major one, linking Aberdeen with either Dundee to the south or Inverness to the north, and neither the finance nor the precedent for such lines was established in the 1830s.

Through strong overseas connections an outlet for spare savings was discovered. Emigrants from the area, who had settled in North America or Australia, were more than ready to relate to friends and relatives at home the opportunities that existed overseas for those with money to invest. 'I know ground bought four years ago for $1.25 now sells for $100 . . . so that you see what a chance there is of employing money profitably,' wrote one settler in Michigan in August 1835, while another in Upper Canada, in July 1836, claimed that:

> People possessed of surplus capital would here find a very profitable field for investment. Bank stock generally pays from 10 to 12 per cent and upwards; and loans, or mortgages on land, seven to eight per cent and upwards.[69]

With these attractive possibilities vouched for by the personal communication of friends, relatives or acquaintances, it was only a short step to arrange some means by which under-utilised savings in Aberdeen and its area could be gathered together and despatched to these areas and so earn a much higher return. Eventually, in 1837, the Illinois Investment Company was formed by a combination of Adam and Anderson, an Aberdeen legal firm who had promoted other companies, and George Smith, an Aberdeenshire man who had emigrated to Chicago in 1833, where he had successfully speculated in land and property and had seen the vast opportunities if only greater capital could be employed.[70] The Illinois Company had simple aims and simple means of effecting them, as its contract of copartnery indicated:

> . . ., considering the great returns obtained from the employment of capital in the United States of America, particularly in the State of Illinois, and the other Western States of America, as compared for it in Britain, . . . it will be for their mutual advantage to establish a joint stock company, for the purpose of raising a fund to be invested in the said United States of America, . . .[71]

Through Smith, the money obtained would be laid out in judicious investments in Illinois, a state Smith already knew well. Initially the shares were only slowly taken up, but, after declaration of two successive 15% dividends, all additional shares were easily disposed of, while four new concerns were promoted, three of which had much the same objects as the Illinois, namely the Michigan, the Aberdeen North American, and the North of Scotland North American. The other company, the Wisconsin Marine and Fire Insurance Company, was another of Smith's projects and stemmed from his intimate knowledge of where capital could be applied to advantage in the Western United States.[72] By 1840, these five companies had raised some £380,000 for transmission to North America.[73]

The success of the Illinois Investment Company encouraged not only imitations operating in the United States, but also two companies investing in Australia, namely the North British Australasian Loan and Investment Company in 1839, and the Scottish Australian Investment and Insurance Company in 1840. These companies were also formed by a combination of Aberdeen legal firms and Aberdonians who had settled in Australia.[74] In many ways both the Australian and North American companies were widening and formalising a practice that was already in existence, whereby private individuals in Scotland sent funds to connections overseas in order to obtain higher returns and capital gains. Other areas of Scotland had the necessary links, but only Aberdeen possessed the inclination and the potential to transform these informal connections into a means of channelling large sums into overseas investments.

Although the 1830s were marked by bouts of speculative promotions, as in the mid-1820s, they were characterised much more by a gradual build-up of joint-stock enterprise. Banking companies and railways were the most prominent features of company formation, although the usual range of gas, water, insurance and shipping ventures also appeared. Noteworthy, because of absence, were industrial and commercial enterprises, with few appealing for public support, and even fewer receiving it. Trade and industry were well able to finance themselves from reinvested profits or private means and there was no pressure from investors encouraging the formation of joint-stock companies in these fields, whether new, or conversions of existing firms. The only major departure was the formation of a number of investment companies which specialised in North America and Australia, but this development was largely confined to Aberdeen and did not represent a major Scottish trend. Overall, the decade witnessed a gradual consolidation of joint-stock enterprise in such major areas as financial services, transportation, and urban utilities, but no major extension into the primary or secondary areas of the economy. Joint-stock enterprise had threatened to invade manufacturing, industry and distribution in the mid-1820s, but in the 1830s these activities remained the unchallenged preserve of individuals, families or partnerships.

NOTES

1. R. H. Campbell, *Scotland since 1707* (Oxf. 1965) Chs. 6 & 7; J. MacKinnon, *The Social and Industrial History of Scotland* (Lon. 1921) Pt. II, Chs. 3, 4, 5.

2. R. C. Auld, *McCombie of Tillyfour and Old Cattle Markets* (Banff 1930); B. Lenman, *From Esk to Tweed* (Glasgow 1975) p. 179.

3. *A.H.* 8 February 1834. Cf. *A.H.* 11 January 1834, 4 June 1836, 30 July 1836, 20 July 1839, 27 February 1841, 22 May 1841.

4. I. F. Grant, *The Economic History of Scotland* (Lon. 1934) p. 214.

5. J. Butt, 'Capital and Enterprise in the Scottish Iron Industry, 1780-1840' in J. Butt & J. T. Ward, *Scottish Themes* (Edin. 1976) p. 73; I. F. Gibson, The Economic History of the Scottish Iron and Steel Industry (Ph.D. Univ. of London 1955) pp. 232, 285.

6. C. A. Whatley, The Process of Industrialisation in Ayrshire, c1707-1871 (Ph.D. Strathclyde Univ. 1975) c8; J. A. Hassan, The Development of the Coal Industry in Mid and West Lothian, 1815-73 (Ph.D. Strathclyde Univ. 1976) p. 45.

7. Butt, op. cit., p. 74; C. Mackie, *Historical Description of the Town of Dundee* (Glasgow 1846) p. 219.

8. H. Cockburn, *Journal of Henry Cockburn, 1831-54* (Edin. 1874) I, p. 172.

9. R. D. Corrins, *William Baird and Company: Coal and Iron Masters, 1830-1914* (Ph.D. Strathclyde Univ. 1974) pp. 6-17; *Memoirs & Portraits of One Hundred Glasgow Men* (Glasgow 1886) pp. 13-16.

10. *Memoirs*, op. cit., p. 165. Cf. Gibson, op. cit., p. 363; Whatley, op. cit., p. 242; Hassan, op. cit., pp. 134, 178; D. I. A. Steel, The Linen Industry of Fife in the later Eighteenth and Nineteenth Centuries (Ph.D. St. Andrews Univ. 1975) pp. 128, 131.

11. D. Hardcastle, *Banks and Bankers* (Lon. 1842) p. 344; R. H. I. Palgrave, *Notes on Banking* (Lon. 1873) p. 15; D. S. MacMillan, *Scotland and Australia, 1788-1850* (Lon. 1967) pp. 329-30; *Tait's Edinburgh Magazine* III (1836) p. 194.

12. *S.M.M.* I (1836) p. 515.

13. T. Binnie, *Memoir of Thomas Binnie, Builder in Glasgow, 1792-1867* (Glasgow 1882) p. 98; Hassan, op. cit., p. 140; *James Finlay & Company Ltd., 1750-1950* (Glasgow 1951) p. 140; J. B. Sturrock, *Peter Brough: A Paisley Philanthropist* (Paisley 1890) pp. 47, 57.

14. A. M. E. MacEwan, The Shotts Iron Company, 1800-1850 (M. Litt. Strathclyde Univ. 1972) pp. 240, 251.

15. MacEwan, op. cit., p. 213; C. W. Munn, The Scottish Provincial Banking Companies, 1747-1864 (Ph.D. Glasgow Univ. 1976) p. 155.

16. *B.C.* 18 December 1835; C. A. Malcolm, *The History of the British Linen Bank* (Edin. 1950) p. 115; A. Keith, *North of Scotland Bank Ltd., 1836-1936* (Abdn. 1936) p. 9; S. G. Checkland, *Scottish Banking: A History, 1695-1973* (Glasgow 1975) p. 392; 'The Glasgow Financial Scene in the early 19th century' *T.B.R.* 45 (1960) p. 35; Munn, op. cit., p. 193.

17. W. Chamber, *The Book of Scotland* (Edin. 1830) pp. 355-6.

18. *The Late Commercial Crisis; being a retrospect of the years 1836 to 1838, By a Glasgow Manufacturer* (Glasgow 1839) p. 52; W. H. Logan, *The Scottish Banker* (Edin. 1838 repr. 1844) p. 64.

19. C. W. Boase, *A Century of Banking in Dundee* (Edin. 1867) pp. 326-532.

20. Evidence by Kirkman Finlay in Report on the Law of Partnership, P.P. XLIV, (1837) pp. 49-50.

21. R. C. O. Matthews, *A Study in Trade-Cycle History: Economic Fluctuations in Great Britain 1833-1842* (Cam. 1953); L. Levi, *History of British Commerce, 1763-1870* (Lon. 1872); J. Wilson, *Influences of the Corn Laws* (Lon. 1840) p. 11; S. Fairlie, 'The Corn Laws and British Wheat Production, 1829-76' *Ec.H.R.* 12 (1969) pp. 98, 105; *B.C.* 4 January 1833, 11 April 1834, 13 March 1835.

22. Munn, op. cit., pp. 218-9, 220, 224.

23. J. Clapham, *The Bank of England: A History* (Cam. 1944) p. 150; Munn, op. cit., p. 243.

24. *D.P. & C.A.* 20 November 1835.

25. 'Joint-stock Banks and Companies' *E.R.* 63 (1836) p. 422.

26. *A.H.* 23 January 1836. Cf. Journal M.S. 1823-1847, 10 November 1835; Cockburn, op. cit., I, p. 115.

27. J. Reid, *Manual of the Scottish Stocks and British Funds* (Edin. 1842) pp. 172-7.

28. Lenman, op. cit., p. 68.

29. Cockburn, op. cit., I, p. 85.

30. Reid, loc. cit.

31. P. Chalmers, *Historical and Statistical Account of Dunfermline* (Edin. 1844) p. 393; *Russell's Morayshire Register for 1844;* (Elgin 1843) pp. 144, 188; M. S. Cotterill, The Scottish Gas Industry up to 1914 (Ph.D. Strathclyde Univ. 1976) pp. 121-131; C. C. Bewsher, *The Glasgow Royal Exchange: Centenary 1827-1927* (Glasgow 1927) pp. 11-23.

32. Corrins, op. cit., p. 84; N. Crathorne, *Tennants' Stalk: The Story of the Tennants of the Glen* (Lon. 1973) p. 91; *Memoirs*, op. cit., pp. 162-3.

33. D. O. Hill & G. Buchanan, *Views of the Opening of the Glasgow and Garnkirk Railway; Also an Account of that and other Railways in Lanarkshire* (Edin. 1832) pp. 4-10.

34. *D.P. & C.A.* 12 September 1834.

35. *Dundee Joint Stock Water Co.: Statement Relative to its Formation* (Dundee 1835); *D.P. & C.A.* 19 September 1834, 27 March 1835.

36. Cotterill, loc. cit.; J. Anderson, *A History of Edinburgh* (Edin. 1856) p. 467; J. Burnet, *History of the Water Supply to Glasgow* (Glasgow 1869) p. 9; *Aberdeen Union Gas Light Co.: Prospectus* (Abdn. 1836).

37. Cockburn, op. cit., I, p. 115; C. H. Lee, 'Some Aspects of the Coastal Shipping Trade: The Aberdeen Steam Navigation Company, 1835-1880' *J. of T.H.* (1975-6) 3, p. 94.

38. Lenman, op. cit., p. 180; *E.W.J.* 20 April 1836; *A.H.* 18 June 1836; *Memoirs*, op. cit., p. 64.

39. *A.H.* 28 May 1836.

40. *A.H.* 14 July 1838; Lenman, op. cit., p. 180.

41. G. Blake, *Down to the Sea: The Romance of the Clyde, its Ships and Shipbuilders* (Lon. 1937) p. 138; J. Shields, *Clyde Built: A History of Shipbuilding on the River Clyde* (Glasgow 1949) p. 46; *Memoirs*, op. cit., pp. 66-7; J. Napier, *Life of Robert Napier* (Edin. 1904) pp. 114, 139.

42. H. G. Lewin, *Early British Railways* (Lon. 1925) pp. 187-93; E. F. Carter, *An Historical Geography of the Railways of the British Isles* (Lon. 1959) pp. 54-7, 73; Hassan, op. cit., p. 50; Lenman, op. cit., (1977), p. 154.

43. Bannatyne, Kirkwood & France: Contract, July 1839.

44. Cf. note 42.

45. *The Scottish Railway Shareholder's Manual* (Edin. 1849) pp. 37-41.

46. *E.W.J.* 20 April 1836; G. Graham, *The Caledonian Railway* (Glasgow 1888) pp. 15-6; *G.H.* 22 April 1836.

47. *A.H.* 3 October 1835, 19 December 1835, 25 June 1836.

48. S. G. E. Lythe, 'The Early Days of the Arbroath and Forfar Railway' *R.M.* 99, (1953) p. 53.

49. Hassan, op. cit., pp. 42-4; A. Mitchell, *Political and Social Movements in Dalkeith, 1831-1882* (Dalkeith 1882) pp. 6, 41, 218.

50. *D.P. & C.A.* 21 June 1833.

51. *D.P. & C.A.* 11 July 1834, 23 October 1835, 30 October 1835.

52. *Memoirs*, op. cit., pp. 26, 162-3, 175-6; Crathorne, op. cit., pp. 92-3.

53. *B.C.* 8 October 1830, 21 January 1831; Hill & Buchanan, op. cit., p. 11.

54. W. Vamplew, 'Sources of Scottish Railway Capital before 1860' *S.J.P.E.* 17 (1970) p. 436; Hassan, op. cit., pp. 50-1.

55. *D.P. & C.A.* 11 July 1834.

56. 'Coronation Contrasts' *T.B.R.* June 1953, p. 39.

57. A. C. O'Dell, 'A Geographical Examination of the Development of Scottish Railways' *S.G.M.* 4 (1939) p. 131; M. C. Reed, *Investment in Railways in Britain, 1820-44: A Study in the Development of the Capital Market* (Oxf. 1975) p. 7; Lewin, op. cit., 59.

58. 'Banks of Issue (Scotland): A Return', P.P. (2) 1845.

59. 'Banks', op. cit.; Checkland, op. cit., pp. 326-7, 335, 337, 340, 347; J. Scott (Union Bank) to L. Houston 31 July 1832; A. T. Innes (ed.), *Report of the Petition of Wm Muir and Others for the Rectification of the list of contributories of the City of Glasgow Bank* (Edin. 1878) p. 6; *A.H.* 8 September 1838; Keith op. cit., pp. 10, 19.

60. *Prospectus of the North of Scotland Banking Company* (Abdn. 1836).

61. Munn, op. cit., pp. 184, 256.

62. *D.P. & C.A.* 7 November 1834; *A.J.* 7 December 1836.

63. A. W. Kerr, *History of Banking in Scotland* (Lon. 1918) p. 218.

64. Reid, op. cit., *A.H.* 23 April 1836, 8 June 1839; Keith, op. cit., pp. 14, 18.

65. *Glasgow and Ayrshire Iron Co.: Prospectus* (Glasgow 1840); *Edinburgh New Town Market Company: Prospectus* (Edin. 1836).

66. *Aberdeen Woollen and Hosiery Co.: Prospectus* (Abdn. 1840); *Aberdeen Market Co.: Prospectus* (Abdn. 1838); *Aberdeen Lime Co.: Prospectus* (Abdn. 1837); *A.H.* 7 November 1840, 30 January 1841.

67. J. L. Carvel, *The Coltness Iron Company* (Edin. 1848) p. 20; Butt, op. cit., p. 76.

68. *Australasian Loan Company of Scotland: Prospectus* (Edin. 1839); P. L. Brown (ed.), *Clyde Company Papers* (Lon. 1971) vii p.417.

69. *A.H.* 8 August 1835, 23 July 1836. Cf. *Counsel for Emigrants* (Abdn. 1834), *Sequel to the Counsel for Emigrants* (Abdn. 1834).

70. A. Johnston, *Sketch, . . . of the Illinois Investment Company* (Edin. 1857) p. 3; A. E. Smith, *George Smith's Money: A Scottish Investor in America* (Madison 1966) pp. 23-6; *A.H.* 4 February 1837, 21 July 1838.

71. *Contract of Copartnery of the Illinois Investment Company* (Abdn. 1837) p. 5.

72. Johnston, op. cit., pp. 5-7, 12, 77; Smith, op. cit., pp. 65, 67; *A.H.* 8 June 1839, 22 February 1840.

73. Reid, op. cit., pp. 172-7.

74. *A.H.* 5 January 1839, 26 September 1840, 9 January 1841; J. Anderson, *To the Shareholders of the North British Australasian Loan and Investment Company* (Ellon 1848); D. S. MacMillan, *The Debtor's War: Scottish Capitalists and the Economic Crisis in Australia* (Melbourne 1960); D. S. MacMillan, 'The Scottish Australian Company, 1840-50' *S.H.R.* 39 (1960); D. S. MacMillan, 'Scottish Enterprise in Australia, 1798-1879' in P. L. Payne (ed.), *Studies in Scottish Business History* (Lon. 1967); D. S. MacMillan, *Scotland and Australia, 1788-1850: Emigration, Commerce and Investment* (Lon. 1967).

6

Stockbroking in the 1830s

THE continuing formation of joint-stock companies in Scotland in the 1830s meant, for the Scottish share market, more companies, more shares, more shareholders, and more business. Outside Edinburgh, this put an added strain on the traditional means of arranging transfers. Banks had the most numerous shareholders with, in Glasgow, the Western Bank having a paid-up capital of £209,170 and 430 shareholders by 1833; the Union Bank having £0.5m paid-up and 517 shareholders by 1836; the City Bank having £656,250 paid-up and 779 shareholders in 1839; and the Clydesdale Bank having £0.5m paid-up and 776 shareholders by 1841.[1] Outside Glasgow the same situation prevailed with the Central Bank of Scotland, formed in Perth in 1834, having a paid-up capital of only £62,500 but 405 shareholders, while the North of Scotland Bank had nearly 1,600 shareholders and £250,000 paid-up by 1840.[2] Other financial institutions were also popular among investors, with the North of Scotland Insurance Company having nearly 1,000 shareholders, though its paid-up capital was only £50,000, while those of the Scottish Australian Company totalled 416.[3] Public utilities had considerable support as well, with the Glasgow Gas Company's shareholders numbering 331 by 1839.[4] Whereas in the 1820s railways had not attracted a large following in Scotland, this had changed by the late 1830s, with the Glasgow, Paisley & Greenock having 424 shareholders; the Glasgow, Paisley, Kilmarnock and Ayr having 335; the Arbroath and Forfar having 459; and the Edinburgh and Glasgow having 436.[5] For the first time in Scotland, railways were beginning to prove popular with investors, although they were still considered less attractive than banks or insurance companies. Altogether, judging by the aggregate number of partners in the various Scottish banks, there was an investing public of about 14,000 in Scotland by 1840, considerably more than had existed in 1830. Of these, some 30 per cent were to be found in Edinburgh, 24 per cent in Glasgow, 18 per cent in Aberdeen, and only 7 per cent in Dundee, with the remaining 21 per cent located largely in the smaller towns of Scotland, such as Inverness, Perth, Paisley, Dumfries or Arbroath.[6]

With these numbers of investors, traditional informal methods, even aided by advertising and auctions, would have found it difficult to cope with transfers, which were not only increasingly numerous but also more complex, with more people, companies and denominations of shares involved.[7] As shareholders tended to be located in the area in which the company operated and had its head office, obviously some form of facility for the local settling of transactions was required.[8] Of all the joint-stock companies in Scotland, only in railways was the participation of distant investors dominant, and then only for a few lines. The Glasgow, Paisley and Greenock Railway and the Arbroath and Forfar Railway both relied upon local support, but, in contrast, the shareholders of the Edinburgh and Glasgow Railway came largely from England, with only a third being Scottish.[9] Conversely, a certain amount of Scottish capital flowed into English railways in the 1830s. Upwards of £80,000 from the Glasgow region was subscribed to the London and Southampton Railway in the course of 1834, while another £27,650 was obtained in Edinburgh. The Aberdeenshire landowner, William Leslie, also held shares in the line by March 1836.[10]

However, Scottish holdings of English railway securities were a small proportion of the total capital of any line, such as the London and Southampton, and so the market for the shares remained in England. In contrast, such was the importance of the English shareholders in the Edinburgh and Glasgow Railway that much of the dealing in the stock of that line did not take place in Scotland but in Liverpool or Manchester, as the majority of the shareholders resided in Lancashire and Yorkshire. When Charles Davidson, an Edinburgh lawyer, bought shares in the Edinburgh and Glasgow Railway on behalf of a client in March 1836, he approached his Edinburgh contacts first but found the price too high, and so he then tried the Liverpool market where he obtained the shares more cheaply, as investors there were unacquainted with the latest developments.[11] Overall, though, the shares of Scottish joint-stock companies were held in Scotland, usually in specific regions, and so stimulated Scottish broking business.

Of course, for certain joint-stock companies the need for intermediaries to handle transfers was minimal. In 1841 Shotts Iron Company had only 42 shareholders, with many being related to each other, such as Archibald Bogle and his sons and daughters.[12] However, for the banks, railways, gas companies and other such concerns, with their large capitals and extended shareholdings, such specialists were essential. Stockbrokers re-appeared in Glasgow in 1830, when James Watson set up business, and Watson himself reminisced, in 1881, about his early beginnings:

> In 1830 there were not many joint-stock companies in and around Glasgow than you could have counted on your fingers. The Water and Gas Companies, the Forth and Clyde and the Monkland Canals, the Garnkirk and one or two mineral railways, the five Edinburgh banks, and one or two others, constituted the entire share list. Facilities were awanting for either acquiring or disposing of such stocks. Any transactions which took place were generally done through the secretary or manager of the Company, and no time could be fixed when such property could be realized. It might be weeks or months before any buyer could be found . . . During my first year there was no other broker. Subsequently, however, the business was taken up by my friends, Messrs. Buchanan & Aitken, followed by Messrs. MacEwan & Auld, Mr Peter White, and others. Our field of operations was extended by the establishing of the Union Bank in 1830, and the opening of those mineral railways in the Monklands which have done so much to enrich the district.[13]

By 1837 there were three acknowledged stockbroking firms operating in Glasgow, while brokers also appeared in Dundee in 1834, with D. B. Niven being the first, and in 1836 in Aberdeen, where William Gordon was the pioneer.[14] In Edinburgh itself, the number of stockbroking firms trebled, from three in 1833 to nine in 1839.[15]

Outside these cities stockbroking remained unrepresented, and business continued to be handled by any convenient agent, such as the local lawyer or banker. The legal firm of Aitken and Law in Cupar, Fife, handled many share transfers in such diverse companies as Scottish Union Insurance; National Bank of Scotland; Glasgow Union Bank; Perth Bank; Dundee, Perth and London Shipping; Kirkcaldy and London Shipping; Cupar Gas; and the Wine Co. of Scotland.[16] Within the main cities themselves, lawyers in particular continued to play a prominent role in sharebroking. Among the many who did so were John Sturrock, D. Rollo and Baxter & Miller in Dundee; Alexander Gordon and Blackie & Bannerman in Aberdeen; Rennie & Forbes, James Christie, and Alexander Morrison in Glasgow, and Charles Davidson in Edinburgh.[17] An impression of the commitment of these intermediaries to share business can be gauged from the advertisements inserted by Mitchell, Grahame, and Mitchell, a firm of Glasgow lawyers, in the local press between 1828 and 1841. Over that period 216 advertisements were placed and only 7 — or 3 per cent — related to the sale or purchase of stocks and shares. The overwhelming majority of the firm's activities were concerned with arranging the disposal of other forms of property, such as land and houses (53 per cent of advertisements) and such miscellaneous activities as arranging loans or acting as secretaries to a number of railway and canal companies, including the Wishaw & Coltness Railway and the Forth & Cart Junction Canal (44 per cent of advertisements). This was all in addition to the purely legal business the partners were presumably practising.[18]

The diversity of interests of legal firms was becoming a disadvantage with regard to share transfers, as the business grew in volume and complexity and required an increased awareness both of general market trends and of the particular circumstances of each company whose securities were being bought and sold. Logan, for example, writing in 1838, recommended all those who contemplated buying or selling shares, especially those of Scottish banks, to do so through brokers because of their expertise:

> It is always advisable when a sale or purchase of stock of whatever kind is required that the party should effect the transaction through the instrumentality of a stockbroker, as he will then be freed from all after reflections of the other party, should the stock eventually depreciate in value. He will also be able to prove the validity of a sale, and he will always get the current market price for his stock.[19]

Thus, in the large cities of Scotland the stockbroker increasingly encroached upon the preserve of the lawyer and came to take over part of his role in arranging share transfers. The legal firms' main function came to be in the promotion of joint-stock companies, with lawyers such as Alexander Anderson in Aberdeen or Laurence Hill in Glasgow being prominent creators of new concerns.[20]

The origins of the stockbrokers who appeared in Scotland in the 1830s were quite varied but were generally concentrated in the agency field, such as in insurance, accountancy, commissions etc. Before he became a stockbroker in Glasgow, James Watson had been a grain merchant, a bank official and an accountant, while both Andrew MacEwan and William Auld, a minister's son from Ayr, had trained as accountants with James McClelland, the leading accountant in the city.[21] Charles Blyth, who became an Edinburgh stockbroker, had been a metal merchant, while Samuel Clerk, another Edinburgh broker, had been an accountant and insurance agent.[22] D. B. Niven had begun as the Dundee agent of the Sun Fire and Life Insurance Co., while another Dundee broker, Andrew Ogilvie, was a commission and ship agent.[23] William Gordon in Aberdeen had previously operated as a commission agent while his partner, Robert Johnston, had been a stone merchant. Most other Aberdeen brokers had been either ship or insurance brokers.[24]

Altogether, most stockbrokers came from pursuits fairly closely allied with the business they were now entering, and from activities that were equally novel, with the great majority being agents or brokers of some kind previously. So for them it was an easy matter to enter this new field whenever the prospects appeared tempting, as they possessed both the necessary expertise and contacts. Henry Oswald, an Aberdeen ship and insurance broker, illustrates how simple the transition was, as he merely announced in the press in 1838 the addition of stockbroking to his established business:

> Henry C. Oswald begs respectfully to intimate that, in addition to his business as a Marine Insurance broker, he now carries on the business of a stockbroker, and will be glad to render his services to Purchasers and Disposers of stock of the various commercial and Banking Companies in this and other towns in Britain. As the want of a stockbroker in Aberdeen has long been complained of he feels convinced that his mode of conducting business will be found very advantageous to the proprietary etc. of this and the surrounding districts.[25]

By contrast with the previous decade, a few lawyers did become stockbrokers, most notably the Edinburgh solicitor Alexander Stevenson. Stockbroking was becoming a more acceptable and profitable occupation, while law was an overcrowded profession in the 1830s, especially in Edinburgh. Between 1798 and 1833 the number of law cases in that city fell by a third, yet the number of writers, solicitors and advocates had risen by 926. 'If this superabundance, or glut, of lawyers is not soon corrected, the result must prove most disastrous to that respectable class of men,' noted one observer in 1836. These conditions were sufficient to encourage a few members of the legal profession to concentrate fully upon stockbroking, but most lawyers continued to handle a little share business without becoming brokers.[26] In fact, most brokers did not abandon their original occupation: they usually retained it as an ancillary activity, as, for instance, Henry Oswald and Robert Johnston in Aberdeen or John Green and John Reid in Edinburgh.[27] Altogether, there appear to have been only nine individuals in Scotland who classified themselves as stock and share brokers by the end of the 1830s. In most cases it was broking that was a subsidiary activity for accountants, agents and solicitors.[28]

As there were so few stockbrokers in existence, each single broker was in receipt of a large proportion of the investing public's buying and selling orders, with even rival intermediaries utilising his services. John Robertson and Robert Allan, both Edinburgh stockbrokers, had lawyers and bankers as clients and regularly transacted business on their behalf.[29] Consequently, each stockbroker was in an excellent position to match sales and purchases without recourse to any other market mechanism. All that was required to complete the market was regular contact between brokers so that, indirectly, all investors could participate in influencing prices. In Edinburgh, where the number of brokers was the largest, the Royal Exchange became a regular meeting place for the profession. Much of John Robertson's business was done with other brokers.[30] Such was the degree of cohesion among the Edinburgh stockbrokers that they all agreed, in 1840, to abide by a common set of rates of commission to be charged, not only on share transfers but on all other business. English towns and cities without stock exchanges adopted the same practice, with the Newcastle stockbrokers regularly issuing a list of stocks traded and current prices.[31]

In order to supplement the private arrangement of transfers, and to stimulate business, stockbrokers regularly circulated clients with lists of current prices in favourite shares, and supplied such information to the newspapers: it became a regular feature not only in the *Edinburgh Press* but also in most other substantial Scottish newspapers. Robert Allan in Edinburgh, and James Watson in Glasgow, both published authoritative circulars assessing the current market, while Alexander Grey supplied the *Glasgow Herald* with the current prices of Scottish stocks from 1834 onwards.[32] In addition, the brokers paid for regular weekly advertisements in their local press, indicating shares in demand by their clients, or those they had available for purchase. Typical of the many inserted by Scottish stockbrokers is the following by Henry Oswald, which appeared in the *Aberdeen Herald* in December 1838:

> Wanted, 200 shares of the divided original stock of the Illinois Investment Company.
> For Sale,
> 250 shares of the Glasgow Fire & Life Insurance Co.
> 50 shares of the Aberdeen Fire & Life Insurance Co.
> 260 shares of the North of Scotland Fire & Life Insurance Co.
> 45 shares of the North of Scotland Bank
> 30 shares of the Town and County Bank
> 10 shares of the Peterhead Steam-Navigation Co.
> 15 shares of the Aberdeen Steam-Navigation Co.
> 13 shares of the Peterhead Gas-Light Co.
> 36 shares of the Aberdeen, Leith and Clyde Shipping Co.
> Apply to Henry C. Oswald, 45 Marischal St. Aberdeen
>   Dec. 1838[33]

Only where the shares of a company were difficult to sell would a specific advertisement be placed, or an auction arranged. John Robertson used both when trying to dispose of some Carron Company stock for a client in October 1834.[34]

The stockbrokers in the Scottish cities did not operate in isolation from each other but regularly corresponded and arranged business for each other. Aberdeen brokers, for example, were well aware of what was happening on the Edinburgh market, with the Edinburgh share list and current prices being regularly published in the Aberdeen newspapers. The two most important stockbrokers in

Edinburgh and Glasgow respectively, John Robertson and James Watson, had regular dealings with each other on behalf of their own clients.[35] Stockbrokers also handled business for distant customers, such as Reid & Nicholson in Edinburgh, but this was neither a common nor an altogether desirable practice. Charles Davidson, the Edinburgh lawyer, was rather wary of handling the share transactions of the Aberdeenshire landowner, Colonel Forbes, because he felt that '... you are at a distance and might not be readily disposed to rely on the judgement of agents for buying and selling'.[36] Overall, the clients of a stockbroker came overwhelmingly from the vicinity in which he operated. John Robertson drew his support from either Edinburgh itself, or such surrounding towns as Haddington and Leith, while James Watson depended upon the interest of investors in Glasgow or neighbouring areas, like Paisley. Both possessed clients from more remote areas, such as Dumfries, Ayr, Perth and Aberdeen in Scotland, or London, Birmingham, Preston or Bolton in England, but these were rare and single exceptions. Non-local transactions were largely channelled through inter-city stockbroking links, rather than on a personal basis.[37] These connections permitted the existence of not just a series of local share markets in Scotland by the end of the 1830s but of a national market, although one restricted to the cities and major towns.

Table 2
Joint-Stock Companies in Scotland c. 1840

Sector	Number	Per Cent	Capital	Per Cent
Railways	15	14	£2.9m	16
Canal	4	4	0.8	4
Shipping	6	6	0.3	2
Transport	25	24	4.0	22
Banking	25	24	10.2	55
Insurance	25	24	2.3	12
Investment	5	5	0.4	2
Financial	55	53	12.9	69
Gas	18	17	0.6	3
Water	3	3	0.4	2
Services	2	2	0.1	1
Utilities	23	22	1.1	6
Industrial	2	1	0.3	2
Government	1	1	0.3	2
Total	106		£18.6m	

Source: J. Reid, *Manual of the Scottish Stocks and British Funds* (Edin. 1842) pp. 172-7.

By 1840 there were some 100 major joint-stock companies in Scotland whose shares were regularly traded in, and they had a combined paid-up capital of almost £19m. The most important group, by far, were the joint-stock banking companies, as they provided 24 per cent of the number and 55 per cent of the capital. Insurance companies were as numerous as banks, but their capital comprised only 12 per cent, for much of it remained uncalled, as security for the business being carried out. Similarly, while many gas companies were in existence, most were small local concerns and their contribution to capital was limited, being only 3 per cent of the total. In the 1830s only railways approached the status of banks, providing 14 per cent of the numbers and 16 per cent of the capital of Scottish joint-stock enterprise. Regionally, there was little difference between the nature of joint-stock enterprise in each of the main cities, with the exception of Aberdeen's lack of railway companies and proliferation of overseas investment ventures.[38] In both Edinburgh and Glasgow, for example, banks dominated the paid-up capital of their joint-stock companies, with 59 per cent and 56 per cent respectively, in the mid-1830s.[39]

The business being done by the Scottish stockbrokers was not an exact reflection of the distribution of paid-up capital in joint-stock companies, but responded to the interest of investors and the relative turnover in each class of shares. Many Scottish railway shares were held outside Scotland and were traded in such cities as Manchester and Liverpool, while Scottish investors held either government stock or the shares of English concerns and utilised English brokers for buying and selling. Peter Brough, the Paisley draper, bought 50 shares in the Bank of Manchester in 1839, and did so through a Manchester stockbroker.[40] However, the business transacted by John Robertson & Co. of Edinburgh, probably the largest stockbrokers in Scotland in the 1830s, allows an accurate impression to be gained of both the size and composition of share turnover in Scotland for the mid-1830s.

Between January 1832 and April 1836, shares to the value of £0.5m were bought or sold through this firm. Two-thirds of all transactions, by value, were in bank shares, although over the years their importance was diminishing. In 1833 they comprised three-quarters of all business, but only just over half in 1836. Gas and water shares provided a fairly steady proportion of activity, averaging out at 16 per cent, while shipping companies, canals, and industrial and commercial ventures were of almost negligible importance, as was government stock.

The declining significance of banks was due to the simultaneous growth of insurance company shares on the one hand, rising from 2 per cent of transactions in 1833 to 12 per cent in 1836 and, on the other hand, the even more spectacular expansion of railway shares, which increased from only 1 per cent of business to 17 per cent.[41] All of Peter Brough's investments were in bank shares in 1833, for example, but by 1837 he had placed 11 per cent of the total in the shares of gas and water companies and a further 12 per cent in railway securities.[42] This rise to prominence of railways would not have been sustained, however, for the number of railway projects implemented fell away in the late 1830s, while numerous banks

Table 3
Value & Distribution of Business done by
John Robertson & Co., Stockbrokers, Edinburgh,
January 1833-April 1836

	Location						Sector				
Area	1833	1834	1835	1836	1833-6	Sector	1833	1834	1835	1836	1833-6
Local	95%	90%	89%	88%	91%	Rail	1%	6%	3%	17%	5%
Rest of						Ship	—	—	—	1	—
Scotland	4	9	11	6	8						
						Canal	2	—	5	—	2
Scotland	99	99	100	94	99	Bank	74	64	60	53	65
						Ins.	2	7	11	12	8
England	—	—	—	5	1	Water					
						& Gas	18	18	17	15	16
Europe	—	1	—	—	—						
						Ind. &					
						Comm.	2	4	4	2	3
India	1	—	—	—	—						
						Gov.	1	1	—	—	1
Foreign	1	1	—	—	1						
(£000's)						(£000's)					
Total	152	148	136	72	508	Total	152	148	136	72	508

Source: John Robertson & Co., Sale Book, 1833-6.

were successfully promoted, especially in Glasgow. In Peter Brough's portfolio, bank shares rose from a low of 76 per cent of the total in 1838 to 84 per cent in 1840, at the expense of both gas, water and railway securities.[43] In terms of security, nothing approached banks in the 1830s, with the Edinburgh stockbroker, Reid, writing in 1840 that:

> Railways are justly regarded at best but hazardous ventures, and we would advise capitalists to be on their guard when they embark on them.

In contrast, he considered banks as '. . . virtually the parents of everything in the form of joint-stock schemes in this country', and unreservedly recommended them.[44] For many, in the 1830s, such as Thomas Binnie, a Glasgow builder; the Bairds, ironmasters; Walter Fergus, a Fife landowner; or Peter Brough, bank shares dominated the investments they made in joint-stock enterprise.[45]

The other notable feature about the transactions handled by stockbrokers was that they were overwhelmingly in the shares of local companies. Each area had its own banks, railways, gas, insurance and other companies which attracted the interest of local investors. For instance, between 1833 and 1836, over 90 per cent of the transfers made by John Robertson were in joint-stock concerns operating in Edinburgh and its area, while a further 8 per cent were located in the rest of

Scotland, especially Glasgow, and the remainder were divided between England and abroad. The lists of stocks for sale and wanted published by stockbrokers in other parts of Scotland suggest strongly that the same was true for each region of Scotland.[46]

The continuing development and expansion of the Scottish share market in the 1830s was based on the securities of banking companies, with investors largely interested in their own local concerns. Railways played only a minor role in comparison, and certainly the spread of stockbrokers cannot be readily attributed to their influence.[47] These stockbrokers did more than facilitate transactions in shares on a local level, for their existence created a ready market for the securities of joint-stock concerns, and this was a market that had national coverage. In turn, this market made joint-stock enterprise much more attractive to investors, as the stocks and shares they issued could be easily sold or bought. Therefore, money placed in shares became more readily realisable, and so investors were encouraged to subscribe to the stock of new ventures as it would not be locked up indefinitely. As Watson himself remembered about the 1830s:

> When, however, a market for the purchase or sale of the shares of joint-stock companies was established, the stocks of the then existing companies came to change hands frequently. A new field was opened up for joint-stock enterprise.[48]

During the 1830s stocks and shares became a much more popular outlet for savings, especially for such middle and upper income groups as those in the professions, or shopkeepers, merchants, manufacturers, and others.[49] For somebody like Peter Brough, with a comfortable income and little inducement to spend it on furthering his retailing business, stocks and shares represented a remunerative, interesting and fairly secure means of investing his accumulating wealth. Thus, by 1838, his fortune amounted to £17,012, and 92 per cent of that was in the securities of joint-stock banks, railways and gas companies.[50] This was undoubtedly an extreme example, but it illustrates the growing importance of transferable securities as a means of wealth-holding in Scotland, and so the importance of stockbrokers and the market they were creating.

NOTES

1. Checkland, op. cit., pp. 326-7, 335, 337.

2. T. H. Marshall, *The History of Perth* (Perth 1849) p. 470; Reid, op. cit., p. 26.

3. *F.J.* 16 October 1846; MacMillan *Scotland*, op. cit., p. 345.

4. Cotterill, op. cit., p. 208.

5. Vamplew (1970), op. cit., p. 429; Lythe, op. cit., p. 50.

6. Robert Allan, *Monthly Circular,* September 1840; Reid, op. cit., pp. 31-3; W. Graham, *The One Pound Note in the History of Banking in Great Britain* (Edin. 1911) p. 203.

7. Lythe, op. cit., p. 58; Reid, op. cit., p. 18.

8. Reid, op. cit., pp. 21, 26, 49; Cotterill, op. cit., pp. 215, 230, 741; MacMillan, *Scotland*, op. cit., p. 345.

9. Vamplew, op. cit., p. 429; Lythe, op. cit., p. 56; *E.W.J.* 6 December 1837; *Tait's Edinburgh Magazine* (1837), p. 336; *E.R.* July 1836, p. 422; *G.H.* 1 February 1836.

10. *G.H.* 19 December 1834; Sale Book of John Robertson & Co., (Edin. 1832-6): List of 28 subscribers to the London & Southampton Railway, 1834; W. S. Davidson to W. Leslie, 22 March 1836.

11. C. Davidson to Col. Forbes, 8 March 1836; *General observations on the Principal Railways, written by a Liverpool Resident* (Lon. 1838) p. xi.

12. MacEwan, op. cit., p. 248.

13. *Memoirs,* op. cit., pp. 187-8; *Records of the Glasgow Stock Exchange Association, 1844-1926* (Glasgow 1927) p. 1.

14. Pigot & Co., *Commercial Directory of the Whole of Scotland* (Lon. 1837) p. 582; *D.P. & C.A.* 12 September 1834; *A.F.P.* 2 April 1884.

15. *E.D.* 1830-40.

16. *D.P. & C.A.* 21 February 1834.

17. *D.P. & C.A.* 17 January 1834, 24 January 1834, 31 January 1834, etc.; *A.H.* 1 September 1832, etc.; *G.H.* 6 January 1834, etc.; C. Davidson to Col. Forbes, 8 March 1836, 18 March 1836.

18. Mitchell, Grahame & Mitchell: Book of Newspaper Advertisements, Glasgow, 1828-1841.

19. Logan, op. cit., p. 163.

20. Keith, op. cit., pp. 14, 18; *Memoirs,* op. cit., pp. 162-3.

21. *The Baillie,* 23 October 1872; J. S. Jeans, *Western Worthies* (Glasgow 1872) p. 152; *The Lord Provosts of Glasgow* (Glasgow 1883) pp. 279, 295; *Local and Municipal Souvenir of Glasgow,* 1837-1897 (Glasgow 1897) p. 34; *Memoirs,* op. cit., pp. 187-8.

22. *E.D.* 1830-40.

23. *D.P. & C.A.* 14 March 1834; *D.D.* 1834, 1840.

24. *A.D.* 1830-40; *A.H.* 25 April 1868; *A.F.P.* 2 April 1884.

25. *A.H.* 29 December 1838.

26. *D.P. & C.A.* 1 April 1836.

27. *E.D.* 1830-40; *A.D.* 1838-40; Pigot, op. cit., pp. 99, 582.

28. Stock and Sharebrokers in Britain: Occupational Category in 1841 Census.

29. Sale Book, op. cit., 1832-6; Allan, op. cit., 10 January 1840.

30. *E.W.J.* 20 April 1836; Sale Book, op. cit.

31. Allan, op. cit., 29 February 1840: Newcastle Share List, 2 September 1842.

32. Allan, op. cit; James Watson, *Monthly Circular* (repr. in *G.H.*, e.g. 4 August 1834); *G.H.* 3 January 1834, etc.

33. *A.H.* 29 December 1838.

34. Sale Book, op. cit., 8 October 1834.

35. Sale Book, op. cit., 1832-6; cf. *A.J.* 24 June 1835; *A.H.* 20 January 1838.

36. C. Davidson to Col. Forbes, 8 March 1836; J. Mitchell, *Reminiscences of My Life in the Highlands* (1883, repr. 1971) I, p. 18.

37. Sale Book, op. cit., 1832-6. (Gave the names and addresses of all clients including those for whom James Watson was acting.)

38. Reid, op. cit., pp. 172-7.

39. Scottish Joint-Stock Companies listed by Alexander Grey, 1834. repr. in *G.H.* 4 April 1927; Allan, op. cit., 1835.

40. J. B. Sturrock, *Peter Brough: A Paisley Philanthropist* (Paisley 1890) p. 81.

41. Sale Book, op. cit., 1832-6.

42. Sturrock, op. cit., pp. 234-254.

43. Sturrock, op. cit., pp. 234-254.

44. Reid, op. cit., xxvi, pp. 36, 51-2; Cotterill, op. cit., p. 741.

45. Binnie, op. cit., p. 100; Corrins, op. cit., p. 277; Sturrock, loc. cit; D. I. A. Steel, The Linen Industry of Fife in the later 18th and 19th Centuries (Ph.D. St. Andrews 1975) p. 155.

46. Sale Book, op. cit., 1833-6; cf. *A.H.; D.P. & C.A.; G.H.*

47. For a contrary view cf. B. L. Anderson, 'Law, finance and economic growth in England: Some long-term influences' in B. M. Ratcliffe (ed.), *Great Britain and her World, 1750-1914* (Man. 1975).

48. Memoirs, op. cit., pp. 187-8.

49. Cotterill, op. cit., p. 194.

50. Sturrock, op. cit., pp. 57, 234-254.

PART III:

THE FORMATION OF THE STOCK EXCHANGES, 1840-1850

There is, perhaps, nothing that has a greater power in inducing people to save than the knowledge that there are plenty of available means by which savings can be profitably and safely invested.

T. Thomson, 'The Effect on Commerce of the Law of Limited Liability', *Journal of the Institute of Bankers,* vii, 1886, p. 500.

It was by establishing stock exchanges throughout the Kingdom that facilities were given for the formation of the large and important railway and other undertakings which have tended so much to develop the resources of the country, and at the same time form a channel for the investment of its surplus capital.

Sir James Watson, 19 October 1881, quoted in *Memoirs and Portraits of One Hundred Glasgow Men* (Glasgow 1886) pp. 187-8.

7

The 'Railway Mania', 1843-5: I

THE Scottish economy was passing through a deep recession in the early 1840s with much of the development and construction work connected with mining and manufacturing at a halt due to overcapacity. Industries as diverse as iron, textiles, and shipping were experiencing severe difficulties which resulted in much unemployment and idle equipment.[1] Aberdeen's spread of industrial and commercial activity usually allowed it to escape the worst of any recession, but even in that city the economic problems of the times were becoming apparent in the course of 1842:

> Aberdeen, as most of its merchants, shipowners, and shopkeepers can testify, has not failed to participate in the general distress of the country, but it has not suffered to the same extent as some other localities. We have had and have still our unemployed workmen, and many of our business-men, instead of realizing a profit, have not been able to defray their current expenses; but, on the whole, whether owing to the variety of trades in which our population are engaged, or a sort of good luck combined with enterprise and prudence, we have been able to get over the last two years without any serious inroads on our commercial stability, or much outward appearance of destitution.[2]

Bankruptcies among Scottish business-men rose steadily from a mere 59 in 1838-9, to a peak of 566 in 1841-2, while a number of the smaller banks were forced to close, such as the Leith Banking Co., the Renfrewshire Banking Co., and the Southern Bank of Scotland, which were all discontinued in 1842.[3]

Despite the recession, savings continued to grow in Scotland, especially in the industrial and urban areas, with deposits in joint-stock banks rising by a third between 1836 and 1845 to reach £33m. The expansion of deposits placed in the Scottish savings banks was even more spectacular, for they held only £74,000 in 1836, but over £1m by 1844. A total of 80,000 people had money in the savings banks and around 4,000 had deposits of £100 and over.[4] While only a small minority in Scotland were in a position to save significant sums of money, those who did had no wish to let it remain idle, but were keen to place their savings where they were secure, available, and brought a return.[5] In 1844, a Scottish bank accountant maintained that:

> Of the thirty millions of Scotch money lodged in our Scotch banks, nearly one half is money not employed in business, but deposited simply for the sake of the interest which it brings, and which, if it ceased to carry interest, would be withdrawn, and invested elsewhere. Nay, of the sum lodged under the head of Cash Deposit Accounts, and which is held to represent a portion of the Country's money floating in business, there are large balances which remain permanently at the credit of the depositors, and that, therefore, come as properly under the head of capital invested on interest as the sums lodged on Interest Receipts.[6]

Therefore, by the mid-1840s there were considerable savings in Scotland, and these were responsive to the differing attractions of the various forms of investment, depending upon the interest being paid.

Government stock and land continued to be unattractive in the 1840s, suffering from low yields and a lack of availability. Private Scottish investors made only limited purchases in the funds, preferring to obtain the interest paid by their banks, although Scottish banks and insurance companies themselves did have considerable holdings for their reserves.[7] By 1847 at least half of the land in Scotland was under entail, which seriously curtailed sales, while existing landowners were active in the market in order to augment and rationalise their own holdings.[8] Defaults by U.S. States and companies, along with lingering doubts concerning South American securities, made overseas investment an unpopular alternative to domestic investment. Another popular outlet for spare funds was the construction or purchase of houses for renting, but there was relatively little house-building in the 1840s, largely due to a lack of demand for new accommodation.[9] Again, as in the 1820s, this left the stocks and shares of joint-stock companies as one of the few investment outlets both capable of paying a reasonable return and of expanding to meet the needs of investors.[10] Joint-stock company securities were also attractive in their own right as they involved few problems with regard to uncertain and complex titles, lengthy and expensive conveyancing, and the other impediments that bedevilled the purchase or sale of land, houses or mortgages.[11] Stocks and shares were also flexible investments as the amount involved could be more easily altered to fit individual circumstances, compared with land or housing. However, over bank deposits, joint-stock securities had only the advantages of possible higher yield and capital gain, for on all other criteria of security, flexibility, liquidity, and accessibility, deposits were superior.

Thus, under these conditions any return to prosperity and confidence, accompanied by a substantial increase in savings, would put initial pressure upon bank deposits as an investment outlet, and then the stocks and shares of joint-stock companies, if the banks could not absorb all the available funds at a reasonable rate of interest. Economic recovery was evident by 1843-4 and was further stimulated by a series of excellent harvests from 1842 to 1844, which had the usual consequences of spreading an air of confidence and of releasing bullion, previously committed to trade, for use in internal finance.[12] By 1844 an abundance of capital over immediate requirements was reported from every corner of Scotland and even earlier in some parts. An observer in Edinburgh noted in February 1843 that 'Money at present seems too plentiful an article with capitalists.'[13]

However, in the early 1840s there was little sign of any impending speculation in shares, or of a rash of joint-stock company promotions, for available funds were easily absorbed by the banks. The rate of interest paid on deposits was increased from 3 per cent per annum to 3.5 per cent per annum in February 1841, and remained at that level until August 1842.[14] This high level of interest paid on deposits encouraged investors to leave their savings in the banks rather than purchase stocks and shares. Robert Allan, the Edinburgh stockbroker, blamed much of the lack of activity in the share market on the high interest rates paid by the banks, as in April 1842:

> The profitless rate of interest which our Banks still retain upon Deposit Money is one cause of this, but as it is evident they cannot much longer afford to allow 3.5 per cent on cash at call — while discounts in London are obtainable even at a less rate — this bar to an improvement in our prices must speedily be removed.[15]

Of course the recession and uncertainty also dampened down interest, but it was the opportunities available in bank deposits that diverted the attention of potential investors in the shares of joint-stock concerns.[16] There were occasional flurries of activity in the share market, such as in June 1841, but none were sustained for long.[17]

By late 1842 the surplus of funds for investment was beginning to make itself felt on the banks, with the rate of interest being progressively reduced as they found it difficult to place the money deposited with them remuneratively. In February 1843 the British Linen Bank reduced its rate of interest on deposits by 0.5 per cent per annum as '. . . the greatest difficulty occurs in placing it (money) to advantage'.[18] The rate of interest paid by Scottish banks fell from 3.5 per cent per annum in 1842, to only 2 per cent per annum in 1843.[19] With this substantial decline, investors began to seek out more high-yielding investments, turning to stocks and shares as early as September 1842, as Robert Allan observed:

> The reduction of the rate of interest on deposits has had its natural effect of causing more inquiry for stock, and consequently of raising prices.[20]

The continuation of this fall, not only on bank deposits but also on all forms of loans on heritable security arranged by the legal profession, resulted in, according to Allan in February 1843,

> . . . an impetus to transactions in shares of the first-class-securities, such as we have not seen for some years.[21]

However, this demand for shares in 1842-3 petered out for, once interest rates had settled down at their new levels, and the necessary upward adjustments had been made to security prices, the activity in stocks and shares quickly subsided. Investors were still uncertain as to the course of economic events and the trends in interest rates and share prices. Despite optimistic predictions in April, Allan was forced to admit, in May 1843, that:

> . . . throughout the country, . . . in the face of an increased trade, abundance of money at low rates, and a decided reduction in general expenditure, share property of almost every description commands little attention.[22]

As late as October 1843 there had been little in the way of a sustained recovery in the prices of, and demand for, joint-stock company shares, which somewhat surprised Allan:

> . . . on the whole, we have not that demand for good stocks, which the continued abundance of money, and the low rate of interest allowed by the Banks, would lead us to expect.

It was in the following month of November 1843 that brisk, sustained activity in shares began in Scotland.[23]

A second excellent harvest had been gathered by late 1843, and low or falling interest rates had become a permanent feature of the capital market. Consequently, the confidence of investors was sufficiently enhanced to permit the venturing of substantial sums in the purchase of joint-stock company shares.[24] When, in January 1844, he reflected upon the previous year, James Watson, the Glasgow stockbroker, noted the change that had occurred:

> . . . a great improvement has taken place in the shares of many of the joint-stock companies during that period. While this must be considered to have arisen chiefly from the great abundance of unemployed capital in the market, it is evident also that it has been in part produced by a growing conviction of the safety and eligibility of such investments.[25]

This improvement continued throughout 1844, with another good harvest, and reached its peak in 1845. According to Allan, the scale of share business was 'unprecedented' in January 1845, while in February he was of the opinion that 'the share market perhaps never exhibited a more animated appearance than it has done during the past short month'.[26] March was 'Another month of roaring business, . . .' and, even in May, activity in shares continued unabated, although it usually slackened at that time of year.[27] It was not until July 1845 that any real sign of a decline in buying and selling was to be found, and it was November before the speculative activity was finally spent,[28] and then rather abruptly, from the viewpoint of Robert Allan:

> The Railway mania of 1845 has terminated this month in as thorough a panic as the loudest prognosticator of evil ever contemplated; and perhaps a more suddenly heavy fall in the value of share property never before occurred.[29]

The increasing movement of capital into stocks and shares led to steadily rising prices. These, in turn, eventually encouraged further purchases, not as a permanent investment, but rather with the intention of reselling once prices had risen even further.[30] Caledonian Railway shares, with £5 paid, rose from £6 each on the last day of January 1845 to £9.75 on the last day of May, and, by the end of October, they stood at £12.25 each, having reached £16.25 in the course of that month. However, as early as the end of November the price had fallen to just over £7. Similar dramatic increases, and later decreases, were recorded for the shares of other Scottish joint-stock companies during 1845.[31] In the course of the speculation the return to be obtained, or the prospects of the company involved, mattered less than the potential profit to be made through buying and selling, and thus the speculation developed a momentum of its own. Nevertheless, the origins of the speculation lay in the operation of the economy and the availability of savings looking for outlets. Without that capital the speculation would soon have petered out.[32]

As early as August 1845 the *Times* had warned its readers that the speculation was only a temporary phenomenon, which any number of events could bring to a close:

> ... under the most favourable circumstances, speculations of such a character and to such an extent, cannot be for long successful ... it is impossible to rely upon the continuance of productive harvests or on the uninterrupted maintenance of friendly intercourse with all foreign countries; ... any rumour of war or apprehension of scarcity must at once dispel their visions of inordinate gain, and plunge them, and all connected with them, in irretrievable ruin.[33]

In addition to these external events, speculation generated its own collapse, for any attempt by numerous investors to realise their gains from higher share prices, without other investors being willing to purchase at these values, would lead to falling prices and a panic among overcommitted investors, and thus initiate a rush of selling, bringing the speculation to a close as confidence was lost.[34] Allan himself regarded the panic of November 1845 as an inevitable and natural consequence of the preceding speculative mania.[35]

As it was, the harvest of 1845 was very bad, calling forth extra commercial capital in order to purchase emergency supplies from abroad. Stocks and shares had been a temporary home for some of these funds, and so their holders attempted to realise their assets and obtain the cash necessary for trade, but this was impossible for all. Trading firms found that either their capital was tied up in unsaleable shares or severely reduced by crisis disposals of securities. At the same time many investors had borrowed on the strength of their portfolio of stocks and shares and used the funds obtained in this way to indulge in more speculative purchases, which in turn could be pledged for further sums, and so on. The Perth Banking Company, for example, had lent Robert Allan £10,000 by 1845 on the security of 178 Edinburgh and Glasgow Railway shares.[36] However, as share values declined, so did the security upon which the loans were based, leading the lender to call in his loans, especially as the demands from trade created more remunerative openings for the employment of capital. This tightening of credit forced speculators to unload the stocks and shares that they were holding in anticipation of a rise, so further depressing price levels. A strong reaction was inevitable, with such powerful influences as these operating in the market, and, as with the speculation itself, a panic carried its own momentum in which stocks and shares became unmarketable and the confidence of investors was destroyed. By the end of 1845 the speculative mania was over.[37]

Accompanying the speculation in stocks and shares was the promotion of numerous new joint-stock companies in Scotland. Few new concerns had been promoted in the early 1840s, when economic conditions held out little prospect of success. Not one new railway scheme was authorised from 1838 to 1843, and not one new bank appeared between 1840 and 1844.[38] One of the few to appear was the Scottish National Insurance Company, which was established in Edinburgh in 1841. This venture had the modest aim of raising an initial capital of £50,000, but found great difficulty in doing so, despite the strenuous efforts of the promoters. A total of only £20,000 was raised.[39] The joint-stock companies that appeared in the early 1840s tended to be small local concerns with a limited capital requirement, but serving an important need, such as gas or water supplies.[40] However, the very same conditions of confidence and an abundance of capital that led to the speculative mania in shares also nurtured a boom in joint-stock company promotions:

... the public of Glasgow are too speculative, and too well aware to what account capital can be turned in these times, to allow cash to accumulate in their account at their bankers, and be contented with interest at the rate of two per cent

was the considered opinion of the *Bankers' Magazine's* Scottish correspondent in March 1845.[41]

Over a year before, in January 1844, Allan had observed that 'The effect of this superabundance of money is already exhibited in a disposition to enter on a variety of new undertakings ...'[42] This disposition became more pronounced in the course of 1844 and 1845, with the number and paid-up capital of the Scottish joint-stock companies listed by Allan rising from 48 and £14.9m in 1840 to 94 and £20.1m in 1845.[43] In railways alone, the plans for 115 new Scottish companies had been deposited with the Board of Trade by December 1845.[44] Company promotion was not confined to the large cities, but was widespread in Scotland in 1844-5:

... every local newspaper contains an array of local projects in the form of Insurance, Gas, Water, Cemetery, Iron, Coal, Heritable Investment Companies, etc etc. and this list is daily on the increase,[45]

complained the *Glasgow Herald* in April 1845. Some medium-sized towns were centres of promotional activity, in which large numbers of the wealthy participated. Perth was one such town, with four railway projects alone, which had a capital requirement of over £3m. The most popular concern, the Scottish Central Railway, had its shares oversubscribed by the Perth public.[46] Inverness was another medium-sized town which became an important centre of company promotion, including two major railways with a capital requirement of £2m.[47]

Dundee was the only important centre that remained relatively aloof from the boom in company flotations. A total of only 11 joint-stock concerns were promoted in the city over the years 1843-5, and their capital requirement was as low as £1.5m.[48] This amount of capital was substantially less than the sums smaller towns such as Perth or Inverness hoped to raise for their schemes. Aberdeen was a city the same size as Dundee, and over the same period 15 new joint-stock companies with a capital requirement of £7.2m were seriously promoted in Aberdeen.[49]

Although Dundee and Aberdeen were cities with similar populations, their composition was entirely different. Dundee's population was growing rapidly, with a large number of workers attracted to the city by the prospect of employment in the textile mills. In contrast, the population of Aberdeen had grown only slowly and had a balanced social composition to reflect that fact. The difference between the two cities was highlighted by the Irish component, as the Irish were mainly in the low-wage, unskilled, industrial occupations. Nineteen per cent of Dundee's population of 79,000 in 1851 were Irish, compared to only two per cent of Aberdeen's 72,000. As a consequence incomes and savings were far greater in Aberdeen than Dundee.[50]

However, this does not fully explain Dundee's limited participation in company promotion compared with Perth or Inverness. What was largely absent from the new concerns which were appearing in Dundee was railway companies.

Whereas Aberdeen had a total of eight projects under consideration in 1844-5, with a proposed capital of £4.7m, Dundee had only two, with a combined capital of only £0.6m. By the mid-1840s a number of important Dundee-based railway companies were already in operation, while there was not one around Aberdeen. The railways established in the Dundee area had not proved themselves to be conspicuously successful, apart from the Arbroath and Forfar, and were regarded as 'bad speculations' locally.[51] This disillusionment with the existing railways was reflected in the unwillingness of Dundee investors to become involved in new railway schemes, despite their popularity elsewhere in Scotland, especially in the neighbouring town of Perth.[52] The Scottish Midland Junction Railway was one of the two lines designed to link Dundee's local railway system with the national network, but received scant support in the area, according to the *Dundee Advertiser* in November 1844:

> The scheme has been before the public for many months, without even an attempt to allocate the stock; and in this quarter it has met with almost no pecuniary support, being looked upon as chimerical, and will be allowed to fall to the ground, without the aid of capital from a distance.[53]

In fact, the assistance of English investors was regarded as the only way of raising the finance required to construct the line.[54] Investors in such other Scottish towns and cities as Aberdeen, Perth and Inverness possessed no railways of their own and were yet to be disillusioned about their merits, while those in Glasgow and Edinburgh, who were acquainted with railway enterprise, were reasonably pleased with the results as a considerable coal traffic buoyed up receipts of the lines with which they were involved. In the end, after the mania was over, both Aberdeen and Dundee were left with schemes requiring an estimated capital of £1m.

Although the period of speculation and company promotion in the mid-1840s is referred to as the 'Railway Mania', both by contemporaries and historians, railways were not the only new ventures projected at the time. There was the usual variety of banking, insurance, gas, industrial and other companies all seeking public favour, along with a few, more novel, enterprises. 'A mania for joint-stock speculations of all hues is beginning to develop itself . . .' was the view of the *Glasgow Herald* in April 1844.[55]

Joint-stock banks had been the major feature of company formation in both the 1820s and 1830s, but not one bank was set up successfully in the 1840s, despite conditions which encouraged their creation. Many smaller banks had either closed or amalgamated in the early 1840s, leaving scope for new concerns when prosperity returned. The number of banks in Scotland, for example, fell from 30 in 1840 to only 20 in 1844. New avenues for banking business also opened up in the 1840s, with the construction and running of railways requiring large amounts of temporary credit. The Bank of Scotland, for example, made a number of substantial loans to the North British and other railway companies in 1845.[56]

Banks were also regarded by investors as the soundest and most profitable forms of joint-stock enterprise, and the shares of existing concerns were very popular. In the course of 1844 demand for bank stock outran supply in both Edinburgh and

Glasgow, as investors sought to place their money in safe, marketable securities which had a good yield. James Watson in Glasgow reported in March 1844 that:

> A large business has been done in shares during the month, and in most instances higher prices have been obtained. The demand has been chiefly for the stock of the Banks; . . . The market has become bare of almost the whole of these stocks, from the large purchases made of them.[57]

Under circumstances such as these a rash of new banking ventures was to be expected, as promoters took advantage of the investor's desire to purchase bank stock, which could not be fulfilled from the amount existing in the market. In the prospectus of the Aberdeen Commercial Banking Company, issued in April 1844, the promoters were quite explicit in citing that situation as a major reason behind the formation of the concern:

> At present, the demand for Bank Stock, by parties who are unconnected with any of the local establishments, and transact their business with the Branches of distant Banks, is beyond the supply, except at a high premium; and it is believed that the number of influential persons so situated, and ready to participate in such an adventure at the present is sufficient to secure its success.[58]

Numerous substantial banks were formed in 1844-5 in Scotland, but not one of them became established in the way that banks had in previous decades. In Aberdeen two new banks were promoted in 1844, the Aberdeen Commercial Banking Co. and the Aberdeenshire Banking Co., with a combined capital requirement of £0.75m. A further three banks appeared in Edinburgh, the Dunedin Bank of Scotland, the North British Bank, and the Edinburgh, Leith and Glasgow Bank, despite that city's proliferation of banking companies, while five were promoted in Glasgow between 1843 and 1845, namely the Glasgow Joint-Stock Bank, the Glasgow Bank, the Bank of Glasgow, the Glasgow Banking Co., and a Glasgow-based North British Bank. Altogether, there were attempts to found at least ten joint-stock banking companies in Scotland in the mid-1840s, and their requests for capital totalled around £7m.[59] It was not the counter-attraction of railways that led to the failure of these new Scottish banks to become established. Many of them did attract substantial financial support: the Glasgow Bank's issue of shares was over-subscribed, and by July 1844, 2,000 investors had been attracted to the venture. For the Bank of Glasgow, the Dunedin Bank, and the two Aberdeen banks, the situation was similar, for they also attracted a considerable degree of public interest.[60]

What killed off these banks was the passage of Peel's Banking Acts of 1844 and 1845. These acts restricted the issue of notes to existing banks and, in Scotland, note issue was considered such a vital part of banking that neither the promoters nor the public were willing to press ahead with the establishment of non-note-issuing banks. It was felt that they could not compete with those established banks that had the right to issue their own notes.[61] Consequently, banking projects were either abandoned or merged with one or other of the existing banks. The City of Glasgow Bank, for example, made agreements with the promoters of the Aberdeen Commercial Bank and the Edinburgh-based North British Bank to establish branches in these cities and issue the shareholders of these banks with City of Glasgow shares. National, Western and Clydesdale banks also absorbed newly promoted banking companies.[62] Without the government's legislation many new banks would, almost certainly, have been established in Scotland but, as it was, none had more than a temporary faltering existence before they disappeared.

Eventually a substitute for banks was discovered in the form of investment or exchange companies, which lent money on the security of stocks and shares, particularly railway shares. This was a branch of business with which the traditional institutions were somewhat unwilling to become involved, but which was of growing importance in the mid-1840s as investment went increasingly into stocks and shares rather than land, houses or other property. Kinnear, one of the founders of the first exchange company, the Glasgow Commercial Exchange Company, described the thinking behind their appearance:

> In the year 1844, several gentlemen in Glasgow, who knew the demand for such accommodation, conceived the idea of forming a company for the express purpose of undertaking such business, which should adapt every department of its business so as to grant the required accommodation on safe and legitimate principles.[63]

The company commenced business in May 1845, accepting deposits from the public, upon which a higher rate of interest than that of the banks was paid, and money was lent upon the security of stocks and shares. This was nothing more than a specialised banking service, and as speculation grew, so did the business of these companies, for they lent to investors on the strength of their existing holdings in order that they could indulge in further speculation.[64]

The success of this company led to its imitation, with numerous other exchange or investment concerns being formed all over Scotland, although Glasgow remained the home of the movement, with a total of eight established in 1845.[65] In Edinburgh, the City of Edinburgh Exchange Association and the Edinburgh Commercial Company were promoted in response to the great, and increasing, business being done in railway and other stocks in the city.[66] Two more were founded in Aberdeen, the Northern Investment and Exchange Co. and the North British Exchange, Reversionary and Guarantee Co., while Dundee and Stirling had one each.[67] Many of those who promoted and financed the exchange companies were connected with local banking enterprise and had seen the potential openings created by the banks' conservatism. If more banks had been promoted, it is likely that the increased competition would have forced all banks to adopt a more liberal and adventurous lending policy, and so limit the scope for such new projects as the exchange companies.

Insurance continued to be a favourite form of joint-stock enterprise in the mid-1840s, with life and guarantee companies being the vogue, such as the Dundee-based East of Scotland Life Assurance, Reversionary Interest, and Annuity Company, the Bon-Accord Life and Fire Assurance Company, which was formed in Aberdeen, and the Glasgow-originated West of Scotland Guarantee Association. As the demand for all forms of insurance was growing, it was easy to justify the appearance of yet more companies.[68] Altogether, the number of insurance companies listed by Allan rose from 13 in 1843 to 20 in 1845.[69]

Another traditional area for joint-stock enterprise was the provision of urban services, particularly gas and water. By early 1844 a spate of new gas companies was already in formation and had been enthusiastically received by investors, especially Glasgow's new gas company:

> ... the most remarkable feature of the month has again been the Glasgow New Gas Company, whose shares, from £4.15 premium, have steadily advanced as high as £7.55, and are now selling — with £1 additional paid — at £6.15,

reported Allan in January 1844. The success of this concern stimulated the establishment of new gas companies throughout Scotland, especially in towns and cities already provided with gas, according to Allan:

> This extraordinary rise has tended materially to the formation of several new Gas Companies; Aberdeen, Paisley, and Dundee, have all at once found out the necessity of supporting rival Gas Lights, and the shares of the two former have been run up to 10s and 18s premium.[70]

Three companies were proposed for Edinburgh alone in 1844-5. Altogether, between 1843 and 1846, some 35 new gas companies were actually established in Scotland in such towns as Aberdeen, Ayr, Dundee, Dumfries, Falkirk, Glasgow, Greenock, Hamilton, Paisley, Perth and Stirling. Some of these companies had been unsuccessfully promoted in earlier years but now found finance easy to obtain.[71] By December 1843 the Aberdeen New Gas Company had received applications for £46,705 worth of stock from 9,341 local investors, and could afford to reject the subscriptions of 3,343 non-local people, as it was felt that they would contribute little to the success of the company.[72]

A few water companies were also promoted in 1844-5, such as three in Glasgow and one in Dundee. The Dundee Water Company was a perennial project, but 1844 was considered an opportune moment to bring it forward again '... on account of the price of iron and labour, and the reduced rate of interest'. Not all of these concerns received public support, with only one out of the three projected in Glasgow obtaining the finance it required.[73] A number of urban property companies also appeared in the mid-1840s, encouraged by 'The low price of materials and labour, and the difficulty of investing small sums satisfactorily, ...'[74] In Edinburgh a scheme to widen the North Bridge had been put forward in the past but had lapsed. During the boom it was revived as the Victoria Arcade and Exchange, which was to be a joint-stock venture, whose profits would be derived from the letting of the shops and offices to be erected along the side of the bridge. Cockburn considered the project 'A most abominable conception', which was an opinion shared by the Council, who refused to give the necessary approval although the finance appeared to be available.[75]

The great innovation in the provision of urban facilities by joint-stock enterprise in the mid-1840s was the rise of the cemetery company. Burial in the increasingly crowded cities was a problem of some duration, and the appearance of concerns offering a solution was generally welcomed, as for example by the *Scotsman* in March 1845:

> While the rage for speculation generally is to be deprecated, yet the great importance of having internments at a distance from the centre of the city is a most important object connected with the health and comfort of the inhabitants; and there is no doubt that it will meet with public support.

A small cemetery company, capitalised at £7,500, had been in existence in Edinburgh for some time, but in 1844-5 five new concerns were promoted with a combined authorised capital of £80,000.[76] Cemetery companies were not confined to Edinburgh, but mushroomed in most other congested cities and large towns, such as Glasgow, Paisley, Greenock and Dundee.[77]

Joint-stock enterprise did not completely overlook industrial and commercial possibilities in the 1840s, with a number of schemes being put forward, especially in Dundee, where a glass works, a fishing venture and a bakery company were promoted, and Glasgow, which had another glass works, an iron foundry, a coalmine, and a graving dock.[78] Most of these concerns were conversions of existing private firms into public companies. All three of the iron companies formed in Scotland in 1844-5 were created by the amalgamation of private malleable iron foundries into regional groupings, and their subsequent flotation as joint-stock companies.[79] Although these iron companies were successfully promoted, few of the other industrial or commercial concerns received public support. The Glasgow Graving Dock Company had to be abandoned in September 1844, because the promoters were unable to raise the necessary capital. Similarly, the Aberdeen White-Fishing Company, which proposed to catch fish off Aberdeen for sale in the industrial areas of Scotland and England, was not taken up by the public, despite favourable comment concerning the feasibility of the scheme.[80] Even those ventures that were established attracted minimal support, with the Ayrshire Malleable Iron Company having only 200 shareholders and failing in 1847.[81] Few industrial or commercial joint-stock ventures had been successful in the past, compared to concerns operating in the service sectors, and so investors were not encouraged to risk their savings in these enterprises, while the availability of other joint-stock companies meant that they did not have to try.[82]

NOTES

1. A. Birch, *An Economic History of the British Iron and Steel Industry* (Lon. 1967) p. 173; R. H. Campbell, 'Early Malleable Iron Production in Scotland' *B.H.* 4 (1961-2) p. 26; A. M. C. MacEwan, The Shotts Iron Company (M.Litt. Strathclyde 1972) p. 215; B. Lenman, *From Esk to Tweed* (Glasgow 1975) p. 111; *Journal of Henry Cockburn, 1831-54* (Edin. 1874) II, p. 2; *A.H.* 27 November 1841, 4 March 1843.

2. *A.H.* 24 December 1842.

3. *Sc.M.* 9 August 1845; Banks of Issue (Scotland): A Return, P.P. (38) 1845.

4. R. Cameron, 'Scotland, 1750-1845' in R. Cameron (ed.), *Banking in the Early Stages of Industrialization* (N.Y. 1967) pp. 66, 73; J. A. Wenley, 'On the History and Development of Banking in Scotland' *J.I.B.* 3 (1882) p. 138; G. R. Porter, 'Sketch of the Progress and Present Extent of Savings Banks in the United Kingdom' *J.R.S.S.* 9 (1846) pp. 3, 5-6; I. Levitt & C. Smout, *The State of the Scottish Working-Class in 1843* (Edin. 1979) pp. 9, 134.

5. E. T. Powell, *The Evolution of the Money Market, 1385-1915* (Lon. 1916) p. 273.

6. *Words of Warning to the People of Scotland on Sir Robert Peel's Scotch Currency Scheme* (Edin. 1844) p. 11.

7. *Words,* op. cit., p. 12; *Econ.* 19 April 1845.

8. J.R. McCulloch, *A Treatise on the Succession to Property* (Lon. 1848) pp. 55-6, 65; J. R. McCulloch, *A Descriptive and Statistical Account of the British Empire* (Lon. 1854) I, pp. 567-8; Cockburn, op. cit., I, p. 170; F. M. L. Thompson, 'The Land Market in the Nineteenth Century' *O.E.P.* 9 (1957) p. 293.

9. *B.M.* May 1844, July 1844, September 1844; A. K. Cairncross & B. Weber, 'Fluctuations in Building in Great Britain, 1785-1849', *Ec.H.R. 9 (1957) pp. 288, 295.*

10. C. W. Boase, *A Century of Banking in Dundee* (Edin. 1867) p. 550; Robert Allan, Monthly Circular (Edin. 1838-1844).

11. L. Levi, *History of British Commerce, 1763-1870* (Lon. 1872) p. 332; A. R. B. Haldane, *New Ways through the Glens* (Lon. 1962) p. 47.

12. W. W. Rostow, 'Bagshot and the Trade Cycle' in *The Economist, 1843-1943: A Centenary Volume* (Oxf. 1943) pp. 159-60; A. W. Kerr, *History of Banking in Scotland* (Lon. 1918) p. 218; Boase, op. cit., p. 440; *Econ.* 13 April 1844; *B.M.* May 1844; *I.L.N.* 4 November 1843.

13. Anon., *Edinburgh Journal* (1823-1847), 10 February 1843; *G.H.* 15 April 1844; *E.W.J.* 13 March 1844; *Sc.M.* 6 January 1844.

14. Boase, op. cit., p. 550.

15. Allan, op. cit., April 1842.

16. Allan, op. cit., February 1841.

17. Allan, op. cit., June 1841, August 1841.

18. Circular issued by the British Linen Bank, 10 February 1843, repr. in C. A. Malcolm, *The History of the British Linen Bank* (Edin. 1950) p. 120.

19. Boase, op, cit., p. 550; Anon., *Edinburgh Journal,* op. cit., 10 February 1843.

20. Allan, op. cit., September 1842.

21. Allan, op. cit., February 1843.

22. Allan, op. cit., May 1843, April 1843, March 1843.

23. Allan, op. cit., October 1843, November 1843.

24. T. Tooke, *A History of Prices* (Lon. 1848) IV, pp. 63-4; *I.L.N.* 3 February 1844, 24 February 1844, 6 April 1844.

25. *G.H.* 15 January 1844.

26. Allan, op. cit., January – February 1845.

27. Allan, op. cit., March – May 1845.

28. Allan, op. cit., June – December 1845; Anon., *Journal,* 4 November 1845.

29. Allan, op. cit., November 1845.

30. Allan, op. cit., March 1844; J. Morrison, *English Railway Legislation* (Lon. 1848) p. 5; *Times,* 30 August 1845, 14 October 1845; *Econ.,* 4 October 1845.

31. D. M. Evans, *The Commercial Crisis,* 1847-8 (Lon. 1848) pp. 4, 7, 12, 20, 26.

32. *D.P. & C.A.* 28 October 1845.

33. *Times,* 30 August 1845.

34. C. P. Kindleberger, *Manias, Panics and Crashes: A History of Financial Crises* (Lon. 1978) pp. 102-4, 113.

35. Allan, op. cit., November 1845.

36. Munn, op. cit., p. 222; J. Shand, Calcutta to W. Shand (his father), late of Glasgow, 3 July 1846 (The firm, Bruce, Shand, Stewart & Co., operated in Glasgow, Calcutta and London. Two of its partners, namely Wm. Shand (a brother of James) in London and J. C. Christie in Glasgow, had been speculating with their own and the firm's money during the 'Railway mania'.)

37. Allan, op. cit., March 1846; H. Scrivenor, *The Railways of the United Kingdom statistically considered* (Lon. 1849) p. 20; H. Pollins, *Britain's Railways: An Industrial History* (Newton Abbot 1971) p. 39; Kerr, op. cit., p. 214.

38. W. Vamplew, 'Sources of Scottish Railway Capital before 1860' *S.J.P.E.* 17 (1970) p. 436; R. C. O. Matthew, *A Study in Trade-Cycle History: Economic Fluctuations in Great Britain, 1833-1842* (Cam. 1854) p. 112; Banks, op. cit.

39. W. F. Gray, *A brief Chronicle of the Scottish Union and National Insurance Company,* 1824-1924 (Edin. 1924) pp. 153-4; Allan, op. cit., January 1841.

40. M. S. Cotterill, The Scottish Gas Industry up to 1914 (Ph.D. Strathclyde Univ. 1976) pp. 121-131; *A.H.* 31 December 1842.

41. *B.M.* March 1845.

42. Allan, op. cit., January 1844.

43. Allan, op. cit., 1840, 1845.

44. Vamplew. op. cit., p. 426.

45. *G.H.* 28 April 1845.

46. D. Peacock, *Perth: Its Annals and its Archives* (Perth 1849) pp. 567-8; J. Mitchell, *Reminiscences of my life in the Highlands* (1883-4, repr. 1971) II, pp. 152-3, 157.

47. Mitchell, op. cit., p. 159; Cockburn, op. cit., II, p. 129.

48. *D.P. & C.A.* 10 November 1843, 15 March 1844, 1 November 1844, 29 November 1844, 27 December 1844, 18 April 1845, 20 May 1845, 10 October 1845, 24 October 1845.

49. *A.H.* 16 December 1843, 18 May 1844 et seq.

50. C. Mackie, *Historical Description of the Town of Dundee* (Glasgow 1836) p. 219; H. Hamilton, *The Industrial Revolution in Scotland* (Oxf. 1932) p. 110; L. J. Saunders, *Scottish Democracy, 1815-1840* (Edin. 1950) pp. 118, 136, 141.

51. F. Wishaw, *The Railways of Great Britain and Ireland* (Lon. 1840) pp. 1-6, 78-82; O. S. Nock, *The Caledonian Railway* (Lon. 1961) pp. 21-3; *D.P. & C.A.* 12 April 1844, 1 November 1844.

52. A. J. Warden, *The Linen Trade, Ancient and Modern* (Lon. 1864) p. 618.

53. *D.P. & C.A.* 1 November 1844.

54. *D.P. & C.A.* 6 December 1844.

55. *G.H.* 5 April 1844.

56. Banks, op. cit.; C. A. Malcolm, *The Bank of Scotland* (Edin. 1948) p. 111; S. G. Checkland, *Scottish Banking: A History, 1695-1973* (Glasgow 1975) p. 421; M. Reed, *Investment in Railways in Britain, 1820-44* (Oxf. 1975) p. 230; *Memoirs and Portraits of One Hundred Glasgow Men* (Glasgow 1886) pp. 99-100.

57. *D.P. & C.A.* 29 March 1844; Allan, op. cit., June 1844, September 1844.

58. *Prospectus: Aberdeen Commercial Banking Company* (Aberdeen 1844).

59. A. Keith, *The North of Scotland Bank Ltd., 1836-1936* (Abdn. 1936) p. 43; J. M. Reid, *The History of the Clydesdale Bank, 1838-1938* (Glasgow 1938) pp. 49, 127; *B.M.* June 1844 – May 1845, October 1845; *Prospectus: Dunedin Bank of Scotland* (Edin. 1844); M. A. Whitehead, The Western Bank and the Crisis of 1857 (M.Litt. Strathclyde Univ. 1978) p. 17.

60. *B.M.* June 1844, July 1844, August 1844, December 1844; Keith, op. cit. p. 43.

61. J. Clapham, *The Bank of England: A History* (Cam. 1944) II, pp. 186-7; Munn, op. cit., p. 157; Whitehead, op. cit., p. 19; Allan, op. cit., March 1845; Reid, op. cit., p. 49; Keith, op. cit., p. 43; R. S. Rait, *The History of the Union Bank of Scotland* (Glasgow 1930) p. 270; W. F. Crick & J. E. Wadsworth, *A Hundred Years of Joint-Stock Banking* (Lon. 1936) p. 384.

62. *B.M.* July 1844, August 1844, September 1844, March 1845; Whitehead, op. cit., p. 17.

63. G. Kinnear, *A History of the Rise of Exchange Companies in Scotland* (Glas. 1848) p. 12.

64. Kinnear, op. cit., pp. 11, 12, 14.

65. Tooke, op. cit., IV, p. 365.

66. *Sc.M.* 9 April 1845.

67. Keith, op. cit., p. 37; *D.P. & C.A.* 10 October 1845; *G.H.* 5 May 1845.

68. Allan, op. cit., January 1845; *D.P. & C.A.* 27 December 1844; *F.J.* 16 October 1846; *B.M.* June 1845, November 1845.

69. Allan, op. cit., 1843 & 1845.

70. Allan, op. cit., January 1844.

71. M. S. Cotterill, The Scottish Gas Industry up to 1914 (Ph.D. Strathclyde Univ. 1976) pp. 121-131; 1137-1139; *D.P. & C.A.* 10 November 1843, 17 November 1843; *E.W.J.* 14 February 1844; R. M. Smith, *The History of Greenock* (Greenock 1921) p. 47.

72. *A.H.* 14 December 1843; Cotterill, op. cit., pp. 1, 135.

73. *D.P. & C.A.* 15 March 1844; J. Burnett, *History of the Water Supply to Glasgow* (Glasgow 1869) p.22.

74. *A.H.* 1 November 1843.

75. Cockburn, op. cit., pp. 117-8 (12 June 1845); *Sc.M.* 2 August 1845.

76. *Sc.M.* 15 March 1845, 26 March 1845. Cf. *S.R.G.* 17 May 1845.

77. *G.H.* 17 February 1845; Allan, op. cit., January 1845.

78. *D.P.* & *C.A.* 7 June 1844, 18 April 1845, 20 May 1845, 24 October 1845; *G.H.* 3 March 1845, 11 April 1845, 13 September 1845.

79. A. Slaven, *The Development of the West of Scotland, 1750-1960* (Lon. 1975) p. 122; Campbell, op. cit., pp. 26, 32.

80. *G.H.* 13 September 1844; *A.H.* 18 May 1844.

81. Allan, op. cit., December 1847; C. A. Whatley, The Process of Industrialisation in Ayrshire (Ph.D Strathclyde Univ. 1975) p. 220.

82. Cf. S. D. Chapman, 'Working Capital in the British Cotton Industry, 1770-1850' *E.B.H.C.P.* 1075; P. L. Cottrell, Investment Banking in England, 1856-1882 (Ph.D. Hull 1974) p. 71.

8

The 'Railway Mania', 1843-5: II

NOTWITHSTANDING the promotion of banks, insurance companies, urban utilities and industrial concerns, company formation in the mid-1840s was directed increasingly towards railways. The estimated capital requirement of the principal Scottish projects of 1844-5 totalled over £8.8m and, in addition to these, there were innumerable local railway schemes. Co-existing with such proposed major trunk lines as the North British, the Caledonian, and the Great North of Scotland, with capital requirements often well in excess of £1m, were ventures such as the Glasgow, Barrhead, and Neilston Direct or the Morayshire railway, whose capital needs were of the order of £50,000 or £150,000.[1] In 1840 Allan listed 8 railways with a paid-up capital of £1.9m but, by 1845, he recorded 46 railways capitalised at £5.7m, when they provided 49 per cent of the number and 28 per cent of the capital of the Scottish companies which interested Edinburgh investors. Railways had grown rapidly in importance in 1844-5, both in terms of absolute numbers and capital, and in comparison with other forms of joint-stock enterprise.[2] Many contemporaries saw the promotional mania of the mid-1840s as being confined to railways. According to the *Edinburgh Weekly Journal* in October 1844:

> It is to the gigantic extension of the railway system and its promising field for investment that men's minds are now turned. Every capitalist is inflamed with visions of unprecedented profits . . . All that they (promoters) have to do is to take care that the schemes promise to be profitable, and that the district holds out hope of sufficient traffic; they may safely leave to the public the mode of procuring the means. Nothing, in fact, can affect the security of railways as a profitable investment, except that some invention shall supersede them.[3]

This emphasis of certain contemporary opinion on railway promotions has led many to ascribe the mania itself to the attractions of railway enterprise and the benefits which it brought. Improvements in technology, which made the railway a far superior form of transport, the completion of existing lines and their successful operation, and the willingness of established companies to support new projects in order to boost their own traffic, were seen as the fundamental factors behind the promotional mania in 1844-5.[4] In Scotland, the opening of the Edinburgh and Glasgow Railway in 1842 has been seen as triggering the subsequent mania for railway schemes in the country.[5] However, even most contemporaries could see that it was not so much the intrinsic worth of railways which demanded that finance be made available for their construction, but rather that the comparative want of profitable employment for capital in other areas of the economy '. . . had the effect of diverting the public to railway property as the most eligible and favourite investment for their money; . . .'[6]

Few of the existing railways had fulfilled their investors' expectations, though they had been a great boon in Central Scotland and were of immense use to the producers and consumers of coal. Even the most recent line, the Edinburgh and Glasgow Railway, had taken years to complete, and cost £1.25m compared with the original estimate of £550,000.[7] A workable rail technology had long been available, while many of the most promising Scottish routes had been mapped out years before.[8] As in previous decades, many of the railways projected in 1844-5 had been promoted unsuccessfully in the past, such as the lines between Dundee and Perth, Glasgow and Carlisle, and Aberdeen and Dundee. A favourable report had been prepared on the Dundee to Perth railway in 1835, but it was ten years before the plan was implemented. Similarly, the proposal to construct a railway from Glasgow to Carlisle, linking Scotland and England by a west coast route, had been actively canvassed in the mid-1830s, but was eventually laid aside until March 1844, when it re-appeared as the Caledonian Railway.[9] Ballantyne, one of the Glasgow-based promoters, indicated quite clearly in September 1839 why the project was not being proceeded with, and what action the promoters intended to take:

> In consequence . . . of the revulsion in the money market which took place this spring, nothing further has been done in regard to the proposed railway. Indeed, we have the impression here that it must sleep until a reaction occurs in the public mind as to the value of such undertakings. At the same time it might be expedient that the parties interested should meet and understand one another, and that a general survey should be now made, in order that we might avail ourselves of any change.[10]

Consequently, there were many railway schemes already organised and ready for implementation but mothballed by their promoters until a favourable opportunity to raise the finance appeared. The years 1844-5 were such a time, and so all these projects were unleashed upon the public.

Although the majority of the trunk lines, and many of the secondary ones, promoted during the mania were the product of many years of deliberation and organisation, others were less carefully thought out. The enthusiasm for railways led to a number being floated without much consideration of either their utility or viability. However, even many of these lines were intrinsically sound projects despite their hasty formation. The successful promotion of a main trunk route could lead to the speedy appearance of subsidiary companies, whose lines would act as branches and feeders of the central route. Also, the formation of one trunk company often stimulated the promotion of other concerns, favouring alternative routes and serving the towns and villages that were to be bypassed by the original enterprise. Naturally, not all of these companies had been previously considered, for they were responses to recently changed circumstances.

Events in north-east Scotland illustrate what was taking place during the mania. The Great North of Scotland Railway was projected as the link between Aberdeen and Inverness via the inland agricultural centres of Inverurie, Keith, Huntly, Elgin, and Nairn. Following the promotion of this company, there came a rash of small local concerns intending to link up with the main line, such as the Alford Valley Railway, the Banffshire Railway, the Deeside Railway, the Morayshire Railway, and the Great North of Scotland Extension Railway. At the same time, other interests in Aberdeen proposed the Aberdeen, Banff, and Elgin railway, which would follow the coastal route to Elgin, and serve such important fishing and agricultural towns as Fraserburgh, Banff, Macduff and Buckie. In order to link up with this scheme, Inverness interests proposed the Inverness and Elgin railway, as they had no wish to see control of the whole Aberdeen to Inverness route fall into the hands of Aberdonians and leave them without any control over such a potentially important transport connection.[11]

Both the main routes had their respective merits, although the Great North of Scotland line was of more obvious benefit, as it connected landlocked centres, and both were organised by respectable Aberdeen legal firms, who had founded successful joint-stock companies in the past. The supporters of each route attempted to attract as much local support as possible, especially that of the country gentry through whose land the track was to be laid.[12] It was not to be expected that all companies promoted would be successful in obtaining support, as the two Aberdeen-based schemes were certainly regarded as alternatives backed by different sectional and regional interests. Either one or the other would be allowed to proceed, or a compromise would be reached. Two other Aberdeen concerns, the Aberdeen and East Coast Railway, and the Aberdeen, Dundee and Perth Railway amalgamated to form the Aberdeen Railway, which would construct a single line south from the city.[13]

There was an economic justification for almost all of the railway projects of the mid-1840s, in view of the improved transport they provided for the areas they passed through and the towns they connected.[14] Typical of the views of many contemporaries regarding the proposed railways was that expressed in the *Dundee Advertiser* in December 1844, concerning the Scottish Midland Junction Railway:

> I do not say that it will for many years pay a return on the capital invested, but it will enrich the district of Strathmore, and thus will lay the foundation of the future though it may be remote prosperity to the Railway itself.[15]

In this the author was quite correct for, interacting with the economy, such railways did eventually generate sufficient traffic to justify their construction. Railways, for example, stimulated increased use of gas through the provision of cheaper coal, which in turn benefited the railways by an increased carriage of coal.[16] What was obvious was that there was insufficient capital available at the time to finance all the proposed lines, and that many would not make an adequate return to shareholders for some years.[17]

Certainly a promotional mania took place in 1844-5, with some companies being floated solely to satisfy the avarice of promoters and the demands of investors and speculators. In June 1845 the Scottish correspondent of the *Bankers' Magazine* traced the progress of the mania in Glasgow:

> A few months more than two years ago, speculation raised its hydra-head in Glasgow, by the success of a new Gas Company, the shares of which rose immediately to 200 per cent premium. This scheme was followed, in about six months afterwards, by a bank, which, amalgamating with the National Bank of Scotland, was formed into the Glasgow branch of that very popular establishment. The result of this arrangement was, of course, a high premium, and then

followed an insatiable demand for something new. Scheme after scheme was broached, the shares subscribed for, premiums pocketed, and still the speculators did with success that which poor Oliver Twist, in the novel, failed to effect — they 'asked for more' — and got it. Even now the mania still rages on the banks of the classic Molendinar, and the denizens of St. Mungo are pocketing their premiums, and trying to laugh in their respective sleeves.[18]

It seems quite clear that the flotation of companies in Glasgow developed its own momentum during the mid-1840s, with the intrinsic worth of certain enterprises being completely subordinated to the possibilities of gain for those involved in the formation of the company, such as the promoters themselves, lawyers, brokers, technical experts, and so on. By restricting the issue of shares, and giving the impression of massive over-subscription, the promoters of a company could make it appear that the flotation had been a success and that the shares were in demand, thus enhancing the value of the shares in the market. At that stage, the promoters and their friends could gradually unload their own holdings and so obtain a premium over their face value, because others felt that the company was now firmly in public favour with its shares likely to rise even higher in price.[19] There were many cautious investors who were wary of subscribing to the issue made by a new and untried company until they saw how it turned out, as they had no wish to be committed to a concern that was only poorly supported and thus inadequately financed. They waited until the outcome of the flotation was clear and, if the future of the enterprise looked certain, they then purchased shares. Consequently, speculators hoping for further price rises and investors trying to discern a well-founded concern provided the fraudulent promoter with ample scope for his operations.[20] Of course, many companies during the mania did have their share issues legitimately oversubscribed. The Caledonian Extension Railway offered the public the opportunity to subscribe for 60,000 shares in April 1845 and received applications for 300,000. In Aberdeen, the Aberdeen, Great North of Scotland, the Deeside and Alford Valley railways were all oversubscribed six or seven fold.[21] It was legitimate oversubscriptions such as these, and the subsequent premium that the shares were traded at, that gave some the idea of manipulating company promotions for their own benefit.

Although these abuses originated in Glasgow and reached their peak there, with the Edinburgh lawyer R. E. Aytoun using events in Glasgow as the basis of his contemporary satire upon company promotion, they were not absent in the other Scottish cities, especially Edinburgh. However, in Edinburgh they took place later and were on a smaller scale.[22] According to the *Bankers' Magazine* in June 1845:

The disease did not spring up with any degree of virulence in the metropolis of Scotland till last July, when the Metropolitan Cemetery, the Second of the kind, was first announced to the lieges. . . . The premium which ensued on the Metropolitan Cemetery was the watch-word for 'the spread' of other cemeteries, and Edinburgh and Leith were speedily supplied with graveyards — more than sufficient for the internment of the entire inhabitants of both places . . . Loan Companies, ie. pawnbroking establishments, Life Assurances, Washing and Bleaching Greens, and other companies of a less sombre cast than churchyards, alternately occupied the public attention, till Railways took the field, and in their favour everything else has been ceded.[23]

Nevertheless, by far the greatest number of joint-stock companies promoted during the mania were sound concerns, reflecting the legitimate aspirations of the promoters, and meeting real needs in the economy.[24] The speculation in shares and excessive promotion of companies owed much more to the actions of the investor himself than to any small minority such as fraudulent promoters. Investors were far too willing to subscribe for shares for which they could not pay either immediately or eventually, when the capital was all called up. Their intention was to hold the shares only temporarily until they could be sold at a premium, and then repeat this again and again, with the scale of operations magnified by easy credit, especially from the new exchange companies:

> Everywhere in advance of the real capitalists, there is a large and indefatigable corps of sharpshooters, amongst whom are many of the largest applicants for shares, whose capital just suffices to meet the deposit upon the shares they apply for, and who do not seek an investment for capital which they do not possess, but who trust, by creating an artificial scarcity of shares, and thereby investing them with a fictitious value, to dispose of them at a premium to parties who, having capital to lose, are exceedingly apt to be less prompt in rushing upon investments than the speculators we allude to.[25]

An illustration of what was taking place comes from Aberdeen. There Oswald, George & Co., a local stockbroking firm, subscribed for 5,000 of the Aberdeen, Banff and Elgin Railway Company's shares and, once they were allotted the number applied for, they gradually sold them on the market for varying premiums, resulting in a profit of £1,000 for themselves.[26] Numerous other people did likewise in the expectation of also realising quick capital gains. The *Economist* estimated that only 2 per cent of the subscribers to the Scottish railways promoted in 1845 had any intention of fulfilling their commitments.[27] However, irrespective of the intentions of investors, their willingness to subscribe to each new issue, and later to purchase shares at a premium, encouraged more and more joint-stock companies to be formed, as there appeared to be an inexhaustible supply of capital to support such enterprises.

The very nature of railway shares encouraged speculation. A newly promoted railway issued shares upon which only 10 per cent was paid up and, if the government sanctioned the scheme, the rest was gradually called for over the space of a year or more. With each call the value of a share changed and, as completion of the line approached, so the speculative element in the shares declined. In response to each change the interest of particular groups of investors declined or grew with, for example, banks and insurance companies, usually only willing to invest in established dividend-paying lines.[28] The small deposit required, the changing nature of railway shares, and the prospect of resale at an enhanced price, encouraged speculation in railway shares, owing to the great uncertainty that hung over the future of the company at almost every stage of its formation and the construction of the line. As the Scottish correspondent of the *Bankers' Magazine* observed:

> Anything in the shape of a Railway seems to be acceptable — no matter whether the contemplated line be a good one or not. The only question asked is — 'will it go to a premium.'[29]

This, in turn, stimulated the promotion of far too many railway companies. By the end of November 1845, 94 railways had been promoted in Scotland over the previous year, with an estimated capital requirement of £36.5m, but only £180,764 had been paid to the Court of Exchequer in Scotland on account of deposits upon the shares of Scottish railway companies. The remainder was yet to be called.[30] One of the difficulties, in the later 1840s, was that too much capital had been committed to railway construction, so leaving insufficient available, temporarily at least, for other areas of the economy, such as everyday trade and business.[31] This situation was rendered even more acute by the bad harvest of 1845 which necessitated a demand for bullion, raised interest rates, and led to general deflation. This left many holders of shares committed to expenditures which they had no hope of meeting.[32] Many had not the funds to pay the calls on shares that they held, and had little inclination to do so once share values began to fall and interest rates to rise, thus offering secure alternative investments with acceptable yields.[33] The interest paid by Scottish banks, for example, was raised to 3 per cent in November 1845, and to 4 per cent in February 1847.[34]

From every area, and from every new company, came the same report of the great difficulty which was experienced in getting each successive call paid up.[35] Allan noted in June 1847 that calls '. . . will not be paid so long as money is current at 6 or 7 per cent . . .'[36] This meant a desperate situation for railways, for as long as the railway was uncompleted it was unable to generate traffic and earn revenue. Essentially an unfinished line was unproductive and the investment was wasted. Attempts to press ahead with the line meant forcing the payment of calls and so resulted in even more depressed share prices as investors attempted to dispose of their holdings at any cost, because of the uncalled commitment and liability, and eventually insolvencies among shareholders. Bankruptcies in Scotland more than doubled between 1845 and 1848, reaching a peak of 553 in that year.[37]

Railways whose works were already well under way by the end of 1845 could resort to borrowing since tangible assets existed as security. However, even in these cases it became increasingly difficult to obtain outside finance:

> . . . Railway companies have either found it impossible to raise money upon Debentures at all, or where they have succeeded, upon terms which in ordinary times would be considered exorbitant

was the view of Blaikie, one of the directors of the Aberdeen Railway.[38] Companies had to resort to a variety of devices in order to complete the construction, including loans from contractors, local institutions, and wealthy local shareholders.[39] The Aberdeen Railway was one that did persevere, though under great difficulties, including the reluctance of shareholders to pay their calls. By February 1849 the Company had managed to raise £1.5m, but of this only 56 per cent represented the original share capital, while 19 per cent was in the form of debentures, another 19 per cent came through the issue of preference shares, and the remaining 6 per cent from miscellaneous loans.[40]

Those companies that had not begun operations when the boom collapsed usually postponed work '. . . until the circumstances of the money market should become more favourable . . .', according to the committee of the Great North of Scotland Railway in December 1847.[41] There was almost unanimous agreement that the only remedy for the current difficulties was the abandonment of many of the new railway lines, even some of those upon which money had already been expended, so that either the shareholders could be partially repaid or, at least, released from their heavy obligations.[42] Of the Scottish railways that did receive parliamentary approval — and many did not — 15 were actually abandoned while others were either long delayed before commencing construction, or were completed only in part.[43]

Railway companies were not the only joint-stock concerns that faced enormous problems in becoming established after the ease of their promotion in the mid-1840s. Many other companies also were either abandoned or disappeared. Almost all of the investment or exchange companies had collapsed by 1850 for, as the shares upon whose security they had lent money became worthless, those borrowing the money defaulted on their loans, leaving the companies holding the shares. Consequently, the investment concerns could neither pay the interest on the deposits that they held nor repay these deposits, and thus they had no option but to wind up their business.[44] Most of the few industrial concerns formed in 1844-5 also failed, with all three iron companies bankrupt by the end of the decade.[45] Amalgamations were also commonplace as the newly formed companies tried to ensure survival either by merging with each other or coming to terms with the established concerns against which they had been going to compete. As early as April 1846 the Aberdeen New Gas Light Company and the Aberdeen Gas Light Company were discussing a merger, which finally took place in September of that year.[46]

Altogether, the number of Scottish joint-stock companies listed by Allan fell by over a fifth in the course of 1846 due to abandonment, bankruptcy or amalgamation.[47] General economic conditions in the late 1840s were not conducive to the success of either new or established companies, with a succession of bad harvests, incomes and demand depressed, and the confidence of investors temporarily destroyed by the collapse of the speculative mania and promotional boom. The economy as a whole was passing through a very difficult period and many old-established family firms collapsed, especially in the textile industry.[48] In the mid-1840s joint-stock enterprise in Scotland had taken a great step forward in certain areas of the economy, primarily finance, urban services, and mass transportation, especially the latter. Despite the later reverses, with the collapse of the boom, from then on these activities would be the sole preserve of joint-stock companies, with only minor exceptions.

However, these were the sectors of the economy in which the joint-stock form had been of growing importance in the previous decades. The 'Railway Mania' did not represent a new departure but a culmination of previous trends, for joint-stock ventures had not yet invaded, successfully, the primary and secondary economic activities. Scotland was rapidly becoming an industrial and commercial nation, but joint-stock companies had a negligible presence in both manufacturing and distribution, for these remained the preserve of the single entrepreneur or the partnership and informal means of direct finance. Joint-stock enterprise had come a long way in the first half of the nineteenth century, but remained confined to a certain limited sector of the economy which it did, however, increasingly dominate.

NOTES

1. *The Scottish Railway Shareholder's Manual* (Edin. 1849) p. 12; E. F. Carter, *An Historical Geography of the Railways of the British Isles* (Lon. 1959) pp. 93, 98; H. G. Lewin, *The Railway Mania and its Aftermath, 1848-1852* (Lon.1936) pp. 474-480.

2. Allan, op. cit., 1840-1845.

3. *E.W.J.* 25 October 1844.

4. M. C. Reed, *Investment in Railways in Britain, 1820-44* (Oxf. 1975) pp. 27, 29; A. G. Kenwood, 'Railway Investment in Britain, 1825-1875' *Ec.* 32 (1965) p. 316; A. C. O'Dell & P. S. Richards, *Railways and Geography* (Lon. 1971) pp. 102, 181.

5. *Memoirs*, op. cit., p. 176.

6. *Sc. M.* 6 January 1844, cf. *A.H.* 27 April 1844.

7. *Memoirs*, op. cit., p. 175.

8. C. Maclaren, *Railways Compared with Canals and Common Roads and their uses and advantages explained* (Lon. 1825) p. 30.

9. H. V. Mulligan, Early Railway Developments in Angus (M.A. St. Andrews 1952) p. 33; G. Graham, *The Caledonian Railway: Account of its origin and Completion* (Glasgow 1888) pp. 12, 51, 68, 70, 77; *E.W.J.* 10 April 1844.

10. A. Ballantyne to Hope Johnstone (M.P. for Dumfriesshire) September 1839, repr. in Graham, op. cit., pp. 15-16, cf. *A.H.* 24 March 1844 for the Aberdeen Railway.

11. *A.H.* 8 February 1845, 22 March 1845, 12 April 1845; J. Mitchell, *Reminiscences of my life in the Highlands* (1833-4, repr. 1971) II, pp. 158-9; A. Keith, *The North of Scotland Bank Ltd., 1836-1936* (Abdn. 1936) pp. 35-6.

12. Circular letters issued by Stronach & Grainger 18 April 1845 and by Adam & Anderson 8 April 1845.

13. *A.H.* 22 March 1844.

14. *Scottish Railway Shareholder's Manual* (Edin. 1849) p. 12.

15. *D.P. & C.A.* 6 December 1844.

16. Cotterill, op. cit., p. 262.

17. *Times*, 30 August 1845, 14 October 1845; *Econ.*, 4 October 1845; Anon., *Edinburgh Journal* (1823-47) 20 September 1845.

18. *B.M.*, op. cit., June 1845.

19. *G.H.* 5 April 1844, 10 February 1845, 14 February 1845, 17 February 1845; G. Kinnear, *A History of the Rise of Exchange Companies in Scotland* (Glas. 1848) p. 17.

20. *E.W.J.* 7 November 1844; *A.J.* 15 October 1845.

21. *E.W.J.* 23 April 1845; *A.J.* 15 October 1845; W. Watt, 'Fifty Years' Progress in Aberdeen' *T.A.P.S.* (1903) p. 105.

22. 'How we got up the Glenmutchin Railway and how we got out of it' *Blackwoods Magazine*, October 1845.

23. *B.M.* June 1845.

24. Mitchell, op. cit., II, p. 166; *S.R.G.* 27 September 1845.

25. *G.H.* 5 April 1844.

26. Letter to the Shareholders of the Aberdeen, Banff, and Elgin Railway by Stronach & Grainger (Abdn. 16 January 1846).

27. *Econ.* 28 March 1846; Watt, op. cit., p. 105; Keith, op. cit., p. 49; *A.H.* 12 July 1845, 24 January 1846; *B.M.* August 1845; *Sc.M.* 2 July 1845; Anon., ms. Edinburgh Resident, 12 March 1846.

28. E. V. Morgan, 'Railway Investment, Bank of England Policy and Investment Rates, 1844-8' E.H. 4(1940) p. 334; M. C. Reed, 'Railways and the Growth of the Capital Market' in M. C. Reed (ed.), *Railways in the Victorian Economy* (Newton Abbot 1959) p. 164; S. G. Checkland, *Scottish Banking: A History, 1695-1973* (Glasgow 1975) p. 421; T. Tooke, *A History of Prices* (Lon. 1848) IV, p. 65; *S.R.G.* 27 September 1845.

29. *B.M.* June 1845.

30. *S.R.G.* 29 November 1845; H. Tuck, *Railway Shareholder's Manual* (Lon. 1847) p. 297.

31. Clapham, op. cit., p. 199; *Times* 14 October 1845; *Econ.* 4 October 1845.

32. J. H. A. MacDonald, *Life Jottings of an old Edinburgh Citizen* (Edin. 1915) p. 21; *S.R.G.* 27 September 1845, 1 November 1845.

33. *Econ.* 20 November 1847, 21 October 1848; C. N. Ward-Perkins, 'The Commercial Crisis of 1847' *O.E.P.* (1950) p. 13; Mitchell, op. cit., II, pp. 166-7; Carter, op. cit., p. 201; J. Morrison, *English Railway Legislation* (Lon. 1848) p. 8; A. W. Kerr, *History of Banking in Scotland* (Lon. 1918) p. 214; H. Pollins, *Britain's Railways: An Industrial History* (Newton Abbot 1971) p. 39; Morgan, op. cit., pp. 334-5.

34. C. W. Boase, *A Century of Banking in Dundee* (Edin. 1867) p. 550.

35. Cf. railway company reports reprinted in *Scottish Shareholder's Manual*.

36. Allan, op. cit., June 1847.

37. Boase, op. cit., pp. 310-518.

38. Statement by Mr. Blaikie relative to the Aberdeen Railway (Abdn. 1848) p. 6; Mitchell, op. cit., II, p. 168.

39. H. Pollins, 'Railway Contractors and the Finance of Railway Development in Britain' *J.T.H.* 3 (1957-8).

40. *A.H.* 23 October 1847, 4 December 1847, 5 February 1848, 22 July 1848, 2 December 1848, 30 December 1848, 3 February 1849.

41. *A.H.* 4 December 1847; M. Barclay-Harvey, *A History of the Great North of Scotland Railway* (Lon. 1949) p. 9.

42. A. Moffat, *Scottish Railways: Their Present and Future Value considered as an Investment for Capital* (Edin. 1849).

43. Lewin, op. cit., pp. 474-9, 480.

44. Keith, op. cit., p. 37.

45. A. Slaven, *The Development of the West of Scotland, 1750-1960* (Lon. 1975) p. 122; R. H. Campbell, 'Early Malleable Iron Production in Scotland' *B.H.* 4 (1961-2) 32.

46. *A.H.* 18 April 1846, 5 September 1846, 12 September 1846.

47. Allan, op. cit., 1846.

48. C. Gulvin, *The Tweedmakers: A History of the Scottish Fancy Woollen Industry, 1600-1914* (Newton Abbot 1973) p. 94; Watt, op. cit., p. 107; Keith, op. cit., p. 55; *A.H.* 6 May 1848, 5 May 1840; A. M. C. MacEwan, The Shotts Iron Company (M.Litt. Strathclyde Univ. 1972) p. 251.

9

Glasgow, Edinburgh and Aberdeen, 1844-5

DURING the 'Railway Mania', the number and capital of Scottish joint-stock companies increased greatly, as did the investors interested in stocks and shares. As early as March 1845 the *Edinburgh Weekly Journal* noted that, in Scotland,

> At present there are in active operation . . . nearly 100 Railway, Banking, Insurance, Canal, Mining, Steam, Gas-Light, Water, and other great public undertakings, all more or less prosperous, based upon a capital of nearly £50m., and embracing a proprietary of many thousand individuals.[1]

By the end of 1845 Robert Allan's list of Scottish joint-stock enterprise totalled 94, which was almost twice the number that concerned him a year before, while in Glasgow, where promotions and interest reached their peak, 135 different Scottish joint-stock companies were attracting public attention.[2] In addition, there was a multitude of other concerns which were either too local or too ephemeral to reach the lists of Edinburgh and Glasgow brokers. Although many cautious investors avoided the more speculative joint-stock companies, especially the newly promoted railways, joint-stock enterprise attracted widespread interest in the mid-1840s and led to the involvement of most of Scotland's wealthy men.[3] Peter Brough, for example, knew numerous people in Paisley and its district who had invested in various of the joint-stock schemes.[4]

The mania did not lead merely to an increase in the scale of joint-stock enterprise and in the size of the investing public, but also to a massive expansion in the turnover of shares, for the attendant speculation meant the repeated purchase and sale of stocks and shares for the capital gain:[5]

> The prevailing rage for gambling in Railway scrip has only within the last two months seized upon the inhabitants of Scotland . . .

observed the *Bankers' Magazine* in June 1845, when it also reported that, as a consequence,

> . . . the offices of the sharebrokers in Edinburgh and Glasgow are now regularly besieged; from morn till noon, — from noon till dewy eve, aye, and even later than that, by parties who wish to sell, and parties who wish to buy — the former class being usually predominant.[6]

The variety, complexity, volume and rapidity of this speculative activity necessitated the use of specialists in order to match bargains.[7]

The few stockbrokers practising in Scotland in the early 1840s were inundated with business. As a result, those who had regarded the profession as rather disreputable and unlikely to pay even a moderate return, now saw it pay handsome

H

profits to those engaged in it.[8] Consequently, it was not long before stockbroking was invaded by people who knew something about stocks and shares and who felt that they could handle the business effectively and so reap the rewards for themselves. Alexander Dowell, for example, had been engaged in all forms of property transfer in Edinburgh since the late 1830s, but in 1845 he decided to become a stock and share broker, devoting his whole time and attention to the business.[9] He was one among many in Edinburgh. In 1844 there were 4 individuals, 3 partnerships, and 4 companies operating stockbroking businesses in Edinburgh, while by 1846 there were 15 individuals, 14 partnerships and 6 companies. The situation was similar in the rest of Scotland, with the number in Aberdeen trebling and those in Glasgow expanding almost sixfold.[10]

It was not only in the main cities that new stockbrokers appeared in the mid-1840s, for they set up business in virtually every significant town in Scotland at that time. William Pringle began as a stock and share broker in Leith in February 1845, W. T. Provand in Greenock in May, John M'Kinnell in Dumfries in July, James T. Wingate in Stirling in September, and John M. Douglas in Cupar in October.[11] Perth did not have one stockbroker in 1844, but by April 1845 three were practising in the town and a fourth had set up operations by October.[12] Even Inverness, in the far north, could boast two stockbrokers, one of whom, John Thomson, announced to the public in April 1845 why he felt it necessary to commence business:

> Having latterly devoted much time and attention to the subject of buying and selling Government, Bank, Railway and other stocks, it has been suggested to me by several valued and influential friends, that I might beneficially add to my present profession that of stockbroker. When it is considered that Railroads are, comparatively speaking, in their infancy — how extensive are the transactions in their stocks — how enormous the investments daily making therein, and how very large are the purchase and sales by parties in this town and neighbourhood, it will at once occur to those interested, that the services of a stockbroker are much required in the North. This is now more especially the case, as Railway communication will shortly be extended to our Northern capital, and it is confidently anticipated that it will soon be carried farther northwards.[13]

Everywhere stockbrokers appeared readily in response to the public's needs and the opportunities for gain.

The multiplication and geographic spread of stockbrokers was not the only significant effect that the 'Railway Mania' had upon the Scottish share market. Accompanying this quantitative growth was a major qualitative change in the structure of the market itself. In the large cities the rapid expansion of business, and the equally rapid growth in the number of brokers, made it difficult to settle share bargains between brokers, on behalf of clients, as it had been done in the past. Unless the stockbroker, engaged to effect a purchase or sale, had a suitable client already waiting for the exact number of shares in that company at the required price, which was increasingly unlikely, it was essential that other brokers were consulted so that their clients could be canvassed. It was by these means that the market operated.

However, the expansion of both transfers and brokers, allied to the increased complexity of the business and the necessity for swift action in the case of speculation, put the existing means of contact under pressure, as it was already rather slow and cumbersome. While it was perfectly feasible to visit the offices of 7 other stockbroking firms when business was slack, as in Edinburgh in 1840, it was not possible to do so when there were some 34 firms, and business was enormous, as in Edinburgh in 1845. Nor was it very advantageous to wait around at a public meeting place all day on the chance that another broker with matching business would turn up. Public meeting places themselves were hardly the most conducive spots for the conduct of an orderly business by a large group of people during the speculative enthusiasm of the 'Railway Mania' when the daily, if not hourly, fluctuations in share values were of interest to numerous members of the public who wished to participate in their own capacity.[14]

It was as a solution to these growing difficulties that the creation of the first stock exchanges in Scotland was proposed:

> ... considering the augmented number of stockbrokers and the increasing importance of the trade it is expedient in order to facilitate the transaction of business to form a Stock Exchange in Edinburgh.

This was the conclusion reached at a meeting of Edinburgh stockbrokers held in December 1844, and a stock exchange was duly formed by the brokers present.[15] Similar considerations had already led to the formation of a Stock Exchange in Glasgow in June 1844. The number of stockbroking firms in Glasgow grew very rapidly in 1844-5, while channels of contact and practices of business were less well established than in Edinburgh. At the same time 'The vast amount of business transacted in this city in stocks ...' necessitated some kind of formal organisation, which would render the arrangement of buying and selling more manageable.[16]

Although the number of brokers and the amount of business done in Aberdeen during the 'Railway Mania' remained small, when compared to Edinburgh and Glasgow, a stock exchange also came to be regarded as a necessity, and one was formed in October 1845, at the very end of the speculative boom. The *Aberdeen Journal* reported that:

> This Institution, so much required by the extension of business, and the necessity of having some central spot where everything relating to stocks and shares can be ascertained and settled on the spot, was opened on Thursday last, the Agricultural Hall in Market Street having been appropriated for the purpose.[17]

These stock exchanges were being formed by the stockbrokers themselves for their own convenience, and certainly the Aberdeen brokers had no doubt about the nature of the advantages that would ensue, according to the local press:

> ... the Brokers who have enrolled their names are satisfied that their transactions will be facilitated by their meetings in the Room twice-a-day — thereby saving much time in waiting on each other when orders were on hand; a necessary step until now, when bargains were on the tapis.[18]

Of the four major Scottish cities, only in Dundee was a stock exchange not formed during 1844-5. Dundee was the least affected by either the speculative mania or the promotional boom, and the business was not generated that required large numbers of stockbrokers or a stock exchange. In 1846 there were only three stockbroking firms in Dundee.[19] Elsewhere in Scotland the number of brokers and the volume of transactions never reached a level that necessitated a formal association.

Although stock exchanges were formed only in Glasgow, Edinburgh, and Aberdeen, more than three stock exchanges were established in Scotland during the 'Railway Mania'. In both Edinburgh and Glasgow, not one but three separate stock exchanges appeared in each city during 1845. The first exchanges formed were the creation of the old-established brokers, and they wanted to retain control of the business. Thus, many of the new entrants into the profession were excluded from membership of the recently founded stock exchanges in both Glasgow and Edinburgh.[20] Not only were the longer-established brokers trying to protect their own interests from newer members of the stockbroking fraternity, but they were also attempting to make share business a monopoly of stockbrokers. Solicitors, writers, advocates and other members of the legal profession were specifically excluded from the first stock exchanges formed. These very people had traditionally played a major role in arranging transfers and, as such, posed the greatest challenge to stockbrokers. When Daniel Paul was admitted as a member of the Glasgow Stock Exchange in September 1845, he had to make a declaration which included the statement that '. . . he had no connection with the Faculty of Procurators . . .', the legal body in Glasgow.[21] The entire Faculty of Procurators in Glasgow made a unified appeal for admission to the Stock Exchange at the end of September 1845, but their request was rejected almost immediately.[22]

In addition to those people who were excluded because they had only recently become brokers or because of their strong connections with a rival occupation, especially law, a number of long-established stockbrokers either did not become members of the early associations or left after a short time. This was because they were dissatisfied with the restrictions imposed upon the additional occupations that were permissible and upon the methods by which business had to be carried out, as, for example, Alexander Stevenson & Son, an Edinburgh firm which resigned due to both these grievances.[23] Consequently, there were many in both Glasgow and Edinburgh who were active dealers in shares, either as a full-time activity or as a component of some other business, but they were not members of the stock exchanges formed. In contrast, in Aberdeen, such people were too few to be of any significance.

As early as February 1845, a number of these people in Edinburgh attempted to form their own rival stock exchange, the Edinburgh and Leith Commercial and Stock Exchange Association. The basis of this stock exchange was very much wider than the one formed in December 1844, whose membership was confined to established stockbrokers, for this exchange was to be open to all who were interested in buying, selling and dealing in stocks and shares. Both brokers and their clients could join, and it was hoped to attract at least a membership of 300. However, the scheme was supported by only 6 Edinburgh stockbroking firms, and some of these began to drift away by April. Such a heterogeneous collection of individuals offered little scope for brokers needing some means to facilitate transactions, and this exchange never became properly established.[24] By September, another new stock exchange was in the course of formation, and many of the stockbroking firms that had supported the earlier venture participated in this one. These tended to be the more recent recruits to the profession. The City of Edinburgh Stock Exchange eventually appeared, in October 1845, with an initial membership of 7 stockbrokers. Transactions in all stocks and shares, especially those of banks and railways, would be handled on this stock exchange, while all bargains were to be settled weekly, with no exceptions, and no member could deal on his own account. Through these measures it was hoped to attract business from legitimate investors by restricting the possibility of speculation, as purchasers and sellers would be forced to pay for, or deliver, the stock agreed upon, rather than merely gamble on the changing prices — a practice indulged in by stockbroking firms themselves.[25]

However, by October business generally was already declining, especially speculation itself, and it was too late for certain brokers to distance themselves from the ill repute which the whole profession had fallen into through the abuses of a few. On 7 January 1846 the secretary, on behalf of the members of the City Stock Exchange, proposed an amalgamation between themselves and the Edinburgh Stock Exchange, but this was rejected on the 8th. It was not until 1854 that the two rival stock exchange associations finally merged to form one unified body. Over these eight years many of the new stockbroking firms had become large, established and respectable, and were equivalent to any of the older partnerships. The differences between the two sets of stockbrokers, which had been essentially the date of entry into the occupation, disappeared with time as the less committed individuals left. All those who remained were ready to accept the common set of rules that were necessary to regulate the business and to preserve it from outsiders. At the same time it was ludicrous to split the market in two, for the brokers themselves, whichever association they belonged to, did business with each other in order to match bargains and fix prices. The amalgamation in 1854 was merely formalising the *ad hoc* procedures adopted by individual brokers.[26]

The formation of rival stock exchanges in Glasgow began in April 1845 when the 'City of Glasgow Stock Exchange' was established. This exchange was designed deliberately to cater for those excluded from the Glasgow Stock Exchange, especially the numerous members of the Glasgow legal profession. By June, this exchange was in operation, but it attracted few lawyers. Its membership consisted almost entirely of new stockbrokers, many of whom had been rejected from membership of the Glasgow Stock Exchange as they were not considered to be sufficiently established.[27] An attempt was made to amalgamate the personnel of both stock exchanges in September 1845, when the 'Scottish Western Stock Exchange Association' was created. Many contemporaries regarded with surprise the fact that

> . . . the business of a share-agent has been hitherto confined to two companies, not co-operating, but looking on each other with jealousy and distrust, and each endeavouring to obtain a monopoly of employment.[28]

However, the interests of the established stockbrokers, with their existing clients and contacts, were too well entrenched for them readily to admit large numbers of new people to the profession, and so the proposed merger failed. After the application of the Faculty of Procurators to join the Glasgow Stock Exchange was rejected in September 1845, those lawyers to whom share business was still of some significance decided to form their own stock exchange. In October 1845 the General Stock Exchange was established with a membership consisting of 62 Glasgow lawyers.[29]

Eventually, in February 1847, the General Stock Exchange and the City of Glasgow Stock Exchange merged to form the Union Stock Exchange. The object was to form a more powerful opposition to the Glasgow Stock Exchange, which continued to resist any attempts at compromise or amalgamation. Gradually, as stockbroking business fell into depression and the established firms, who were members of the Glasgow Stock Exchange Association, dominated what remained, those who had only dabbled in stockbroking abandoned it to the specialists. This was particularly true of the lawyers and of those people who had become involved at the height of the speculation. As a result the membership of the Union Stock Exchange faded away, with those firms which remained in stockbroking transferring to the Glasgow Stock Exchange. By 1851 the Union Stock Exchange had ceased to exist and the era of rival exchanges had ended in Glasgow. There could be no official merger as the Glasgow Stock Exchange Association was adamant in its resolve to keep the legal profession out of the stock exchange for, once lawyers had direct access to the market there would be no need to use brokers as intermediaries, and so stockbrokers would lose an important part of their business.[30]

The whole concept of stock exchanges was challenged by the establishment of regular, well publicised auctions of shares, held either by brokers — who were not stock exchange members — or by auctioneers themselves. Auctions were a traditional means of arranging the disposal of shares and had been popular for a short time during the speculative mania of 1824-5. The abolition of the auction duties in April 1845, which reduced the expense of buying and selling by that means, combined with the great volume of share transactions during the 'Railway Mania', suggested to many that a weekly share auction would be a valuable alternative to the services offered by stockbrokers. The prices paid would be arrived at in open competition and neither buyer nor seller ought to feel that they had been cheated. Also, less popular shares could more easily find buyers if they were exposed to public sale.[31] Reid and Nicholson, an Edinburgh stockbroking firm, began to hold regular share auctions at the end of April, after having been refused permission to join the Edinburgh Stock Exchange earlier in the month. This auction was held each Saturday at 1 pm and encompassed '... every description of stock intrusted to them for this purpose . . .'[32] Another Edinburgh stockbroking firm, Alex. Stevenson & Sons, were also organising regular auctions by April 1845, and they referred to their auctions as a 'Stock Exchange', claiming that it was

> . . . a free and open market for the sale of the shares of Public Companies, where the prices can at once be fully and fairly ascertained, . . .[33]

It was not only in Edinburgh that these regular auctions of shares appeared. William Stuart & Son, and Hutchison and Dixon in Glasgow were both holding weekly share auctions in 1845, while George Stuart introduced a twice-weekly one in June of that year. In Aberdeen H. Macswein, an established auctioneer, had initiated a separate share auction by May 1845.[34] The problem with a weekly, or even twice weekly, auction of shares was that it did not respond swiftly enough to the rapid changes in the speculative market that existed during the 'Railway Mania' while, at the same time, it demanded personal attendance if an intermediary's fee was to be avoided. Consequently, auctions were both inconvenient for those busy people who were also investors and were also an imperfect market because of this limited attendance. Auctions also left the individual unaided in deciding what to purchase and at what prices. Altogether, it was much easier to consult and utilise a stockbroker who could give an informed view of the market and keep a close eye upon the constantly changing scene. Once the speculative interest of the public at large disappeared, so did the regular share auctions.

When the speculative and promotional mania collapsed at the end of 1845, the volume of share business declined dramatically, as the market for certain securities, especially the most speculative counters, disappeared and they became unsaleable.[35] However, business was sustained in 1846-7 as people desperately attempted to realise their stocks and shares at whatever price they would fetch, in order to avoid going bankrupt, while others bought at these levels with the intention of holding until recovery came. For instance, both Peter Brough and John M'Gavin, a Glasgow grain merchant, bought and sold extensively in 1846-8, with the object of acquiring the securities of sound companies at exceptionally low prices.[36] Also, turnover on the Aberdeen Stock Exchange, for example, fell from £21,265 in November 1845 to £14,521 in November 1846, and then completely collapsed, amounting to only £3,593 in November 1847 and £2,782 in November 1848.[37]

As a result there was soon insufficient business to support the vastly increased number of people who had been attracted to the stockbroking profession. John Miller, a Glasgow stockbroker and accountant, received an income of £259 in 1846 from the brokerage he charged clients for buying and selling shares. This rose to £277 in 1847 and then dropped precipitously to £92 in 1848 and only £60 in 1849. Miller survived only because he was also an accountant, and his growing income from arranging insurance and handling estates compensated for the decline in the profits from stockbroking. In 1846, of his total income of £405, 64 per cent came from stockbroking and 36 per cent from accountancy and allied activities, while, in contrast, by 1849 only 9 per cent came from broking and 91 per cent from accountancy, out of total receipts of £655. For Miller, the collapse of the mania brought financial compensations in that his services were required to handle the winding-up of bankrupt estates, some of which were presumably rendered insolvent owing to the fall in share prices and the inability to sell securities.[38] As Brough himself observed at the end of 1847, 'Thousands of persons who, twelve months ago, thought themselves rich are now totally ruined.'[39]

Unlike Miller, who tried to maintain the stockbroking side of his business, many others gave up and either returned to their previous occupations or sought new ones. Paxton, in Edinburgh, had been an auctioneer before becoming a stockbroker, and he returned to that employment when the boom was over. In contrast, Albert Cay, also in Edinburgh, had been a wine and tea merchant before setting up as a stockbroker and, when the business declined, he moved on to become an advertising and newspaper agent. Others who had set themselves up as brokers sought employment in other parts of the country, such as H. Oliphant and James Renton, who migrated to London in 1849. Altogether, stock exchanges suffered 'heavy losses' in their membership, 13 leaving Glasgow alone in 1848-9.[40]

In Glasgow, numbers were down from a peak of 107 firms in 1846 to only 63 in 1850, while in Edinburgh the summit was reached in 1847 with 39 firms, but in 1850 only 26 remained. Similar declines were recorded in both Aberdeen and Dundee.[41] In these cities the wealthier and less committed stockbrokers left the profession during the difficult years of the late 1840s.[42] Yet at least these cities retained stockbroking as an occupation: in the rest of Scotland it completely disappeared, even from such substantial towns as Greenock and Inverness.[43] The cities in which stock exchanges had been established did retain these institutions, but where more than one had appeared they gradually coalesced, in one way or another, so that a single exchange resulted. Those stock exchanges that resulted had also to restrict their operations by reducing overheads and dispensing with staff and facilities.

The 'Railway Mania' resulted in the spread of stockbrokers throughout Scotland, and the creation of at least 7 stock exchanges, of some form or another as well as engendering great public enthusiasm for joint-stock enterprise and transferable securities. Many have seen this as the very foundation of the capital market in Britain.[44] However, most of the creations of the mania did not last for many years after its collapse, with stockbroking in Scotland once again confined to the four large cities, where numbers fell greatly. Certainly, stock exchanges were firmly established in Glasgow, Edinburgh, and Aberdeen but, at that time, this was little more than the creation of a necessary, if minimal, formal organisation for an already operating share market, which was now under acute pressure from the volume of business it suddenly had to handle. These stock exchanges were the product of the stockbrokers themselves, and existed for their own convenience. They represented a more refined and organised tool in the share market and were not the creation of that market. It is from the personnel, not the institutions, that the beginning of the market can be dated. Without the stimulus of the 'Railway Mania', it is doubtful whether stock exchanges would have been established in the mid-1840s, for it was the speculative excesses which drove the volume of business to such levels that changes in the market were required at that time. These exchanges were the only permanent legacy of the mania, for the geographical extension of the market proved short-lived.

However, the stock exchanges formed in Scotland in 1844-5 did not act solely as central meeting places for stockbrokers to facilitate the transaction of business at regular times and in a mutually agreed fashion. They were also associations which regulated the conduct of their members, both in relation to each other, and with the public. On the Edinburgh, Glasgow, and Aberdeen Stock Exchanges most of the business of the committee consisted of resolving disputes between members over such issues as late delivery of shares, disagreement over agreed share transfer prices, or refusal to acknowledge that a bargain had been struck. These disputes declined in number as procedures became better known, accepted and modified in the late 1840s.[45] The stock exchanges also enforced uniform rates of commission on any business undertaken, and fined members who did not adhere to these rates.[46] They also co-ordinated the actions of their members in such areas as defaulting clients or in forcing companies to conform to their rules. Clients who refused to pay for shares that they had requested their broker to purchase could be boycotted by all brokers until settlement was made. A company whose affairs were suspect could have its quotation suspended until matters were cleared up. The Committee of the Aberdeen Stock Exchange considered the suspension of the Aberdeen, Banff and Elgin Railway in January 1846 a 'duty to the public', in the light of the considerable uncertainty hanging over the company's shares.[47]

The stock exchange associations acted as central agents for the communication of share market information as well as controlling the conduct of their members. In particular, the only accepted and reliable share price list became that of the Stock Exchange, not that of the individual broker:

> ... in order to insure perfect uniformity in the printed or published prices of stocks it is expedient that a share list be made up and published daily and such a list to be the only one to be circulated by the members,

ruled the Edinburgh Stock Exchange, for example, in March 1845.[48] With this list, the public could have absolute faith that changing prices did reflect genuine market conditions rather than being rigged by one or a few brokers for their own ends. It engendered far greater confidence on the part of the investor in the resale potential and value of transferable securities than could the prices of any individual stockbroker.

The stock exchange also acted as the main means of communication between groups of stockbrokers in each town or city in order to harmonise procedures and adopt uniform commission rates. Thus, for instance, it was through the agency of the stock exchanges in Edinburgh and Glasgow that the liability of stock-brokers for the default of their clients was harmonised in April 1845. The regular exchange of share lists between the separate stock exchange organisations was instrumental in creating a national market, as it publicised the share prices existing in each area, and in facilitating the movement of shares from one area to another in response to differing supply and demand acting through the price mechanism.[49] The actual functioning of this market, however, continued to rest with the stockbroker. Edinburgh and Glasgow Stock Exchanges exchanged share lists from the outset, and the Scottish stock exchanges were soon in receipt of lists from Bristol, Hull, Leeds, York and other English stock exchanges.[50]

The Scottish stock exchanges had, therefore, two main functions. Primarily, they embodied the existing share market in an institutional form, but the market continued to be in the hands of the stockbrokers, and the Exchange was utilised by them only as a more convenient way of transacting business. However, the stock exchanges also developed a secondary function, for they were also stockbrokers' associations, acting as final arbiters between stockbrokers, linking one group of stockbrokers with another, and relating the activities of stockbrokers to companies and the general public. It was this secondary role that was to grow in importance once the stock exchanges had been set up, giving an added dimension to the stock exchanges beyond their institutionalisation of an existing market.

NOTES

1. *E.W.J.* 26 March 1845.
2. Robert Allan, Monthly Circular (Edinburgh 1844 & 1845); Glasgow Stock Exchange List, 31 December 1845.
3. *S.R.G.* 5 April 1845, 27 September 1845.
4. J. B. Sturrock, *Peter Brough: A Paisley Philanthropist* (Paisley 1890) pp. 148-9.
5. J. T. Dawson, 'On the Accounts of the Bank of England' *J.R.S.S.* 10 (1847) p. 152.
6. *B.M.* June 1845.
7. Cf. the volume and variety of securities issued by the numerous Scottish railway companies. *Scottish Railway Shareholder's Manual* (Edin. 1849) pp. 49-92.
8. *A.H.* 15 November 1845.
9. *Sc.M.* 8 October 1845.
10. *E.D.* 1844 & 1846; *A.D.* 1844 & 1846; *G.D.* 1844 & 1846.
11. *Sc.M.* 8 February 1845; *E.W.J.* 30 July 1845; *D.P. & C.A.* 26 September 1845; *S.R.G.* 10 May 1845, 17 May 1845, 4 October 1845.
12. *D.P. & C.A.* 11 April 1845; *S.R.G.* 10 May 1845, 18 October 1845.
13. *S.R.G.* 19 April 1845, 17 May 1845.
14. Allan, op. cit., February 1845.
15. Edinburgh Stock Exchange Association: Minutes 16 December 1844.
16. *G.D.* 1844 & 1845; *G.H.* 24 June 1844; *E.W.J.* 26 June 1844.
17. *A.J.* 3 November 1845.
18. *A.J.* 3 November 1845; cf. *E.W.J.* 26 June 1844.
19. *D.D.* 1846.
20. Edin.: Minutes 16 December 1844, 2 June 1845, 4 January 1845, 6 January 1845, 11 January 1845, 14 January 1845; *Records of the Glasgow Stock Exchange Association, 1844-1898* (Glasgow 1898) p. 3; *Records of the Glasgow Stock Exchange Association, 1844-1926* (Glasgow 1927) p. 4; Appendix: List of Members.
21. Glasgow Stock Exchange Association: Minutes, 11 September 1845.
22. Glas.: Minutes 26 September 1845, 1 October 1845.
23. Edin.: Minutes 6 January 1845, 14 January 1845.
24. *Sc.M.* 26 February 1845, 23 April 1845; *S.R.G.* 5 April 1845; Edin.: Minutes 7 April 1845.
25. *Sc.M.* 27 September 1845, 4 October 1845.
26. Edin.: Minutes 7 January 1846, 27 September 1854.
27. *G.H.* 28 April 1845; *S.R.G.* 3 May 1845.
28. *G.H.* 26 September 1845; *S.R.G.* 27 September 1845.
29. Glas.: Minutes 1 October 1845; Glasgow (1844-98) op. cit., p. 20.
30. Glas.: Minutes 1 January 1851; *S.R.G.* 20 February 1847; Union Stock Exchange: Daily Share List 15 February 1847, 9 June 1849.
31. *S.R.G.* 26 April 1845.
32. Edin.: Minutes 11 April 1845, 18 April 1845; *S.R.G.* 26 April 1845.

33. *Sc.M.* 23 April 1845, 17 May 1845, 18 June 1845.

34. *G.H.* 9 June 1845, 16 June 1845, 15 September 1845; *The Banner* 23 May 1845.

35. Sturrock, op. cit., p. 146.

36. J. H. A. MacDonald, *Life Jottings of an Old Edinburgh Citizen* (Edin. 1915) p. 21; Sturrock, op. cit., pp. 117, 155, 157; *Memoirs,* op. cit., p. 191.

37. Aberdeen Stock Exchange: Record & Ledger, November 1845 – November 1848.

38. John Miller: Accounts, 1846-9.

39. Sturrock, op. cit., p. 149.

40. *E.D.* 1846-9; Edin.: Minutes, 27 January 1849, 2 July 1849; Glas.: Minutes, 3 July 1849.

41. *G.D.* 1846 & 1850; *E.D.* 1847 & 1850; *A.D.* 1847 & 1850; *D.D.* 1846 & 1850.

42. Glas.: Minutes, 3 July 1849.

43. *Slater's Commercial Directory of Scotland* (Lon. 1852).

44. M. C. Reed, 'Railways and the Growth of the Capital Market' in M. C. Reed (ed.), *Railways in the Victorian Economy* (Newton Abbot 1959) p. 162; M. C. Reed, *Investment in Railways in Britain, 1920-44:* (Oxf. 1975) p. 262; G. R. Hawke, *Railways and Economic Growth in England and Wales, 1840-1870* (Lon. 1970) p. 388; L. H. Jenks, *The Migration of British Capital to 1875* (N.Y. 1927) p. 132; P. L. Cottrell, Investment Banking in England, 1856-1882 (Ph.D. Hull 1974) pp. 46-7; B. L. Anderson, 'Law, finance and economic growth in England: some long term influences' in B. M. Ratcliffe (ed.) *Great Britain and her World, 1750-1914* (Man. 1975) p. 114.

45. Edin.: Minutes January 1845 — December 1849; Glas.: Minutes, September 1844 – December 1849; Abdn.: Minutes, November 1845 – December 1849.

46. Glas.: Minutes, 11 September 1845.

47. Abdn.: Minutes, 17 July 1845, 13 January 1846, 15 January 1846; 3 February 1846; To the Shareholders of the Aberdeen, Banff, and Elgin Railway: Stronach & Grainger, solicitors (30 January 1846, Abdn.).

48. Edin.: Minutes, 4 March 1845, 9 May 1845.

49. Edin.: Minutes, 7 March 1845, 8 April 1845; Glas.: Minutes, 2 April 1845.

50. Edin.: Minutes, 13 February 1845, 11 April 1845, 17 April 1845, 19 April 1845, 23 April 1845.

10

Stockbroking in the 1840s

THE stockbrokers who appeared in Scotland in the mid-1840s were the same in origin as those who were already established. They were drawn mainly from the allied activities of accountancy, and commission and insurance agency, with much smaller numbers having been auctioneers, merchants, or members of the legal profession.[1] Often, it was their existing clientele who encouraged them to become stockbrokers, either because of requests to handle share business, or because of the existing contacts they represented. The transition from one occupation to the other was relatively easy, as all were relatively new occupations with no restrictive apprenticeship periods or other major bars to entry:

> Mr Paxton, in returning his grateful thanks for the liberal patronage he has received since he carried on the business of Auctioneer for the sale of Heritable Property, begs to intimate that he has, in addition, commenced business as a stockbroker.[2]

This advertisement placed in the *Scotsman* in March 1845 was typical of the many that appeared during the mania, announcing entry into the stockbroking profession.

Of the Edinburgh stockbrokers who set up in business between 1844 and 1846, by far the largest group appear to have been practising as accountants in previous years. Many moved from one occupation to the other, depending upon prevailing business conditions, such as John Green, Samuel Clerk or J. Burns. Samuel Clerk, for example, was a stockbroker and accountant from 1839 to 1843, an accountant alone in 1844, and a stockbroker alone in 1845. The contribution of other occupational groups to the stockbroking profession in Edinburgh tended to be fairly evenly spread. Merchants had been purveyors of high quality foodstuffs, especially wine and tea. Those with a legal background were rarely solicitors or writers themselves but were their sons seeking a livelihood with good prospects and in an occupation where their fathers' connections could be of great assistance to them.[3] In Glasgow, the new entrants to stockbroking came even more predominantly from accountancy and very few had any legal connections.[4]

The origins of Aberdeen's new stockbrokers were much more varied; they were drawn from such trades as wine and spirit merchants, commission agents, shipbroking or the law. One person, W. N. Fish, had come to Aberdeen deliberately to undertake stockbroking.[5] Dundee's stockbrokers had equally diverse origins, having been either agents of one kind or another, or lawyers.[6] Neither Aberdeen nor Dundee had numerous accountants ready to enter stockbroking when business was booming, as did Edinburgh and Glasgow, and so there were more openings for others in these places. Outside the large cities it was usual for members of the legal profession to become stockbrokers, as there were few other suitable candidates and the business was of small enough size and relatively unsophisticated, so that it could be accommodated within a legal practice. John Douglas in Cupar, D. Prophet in Inverness, and John Kippen in Perth, for example, were all lawyers before becoming stockbrokers in 1845. Where accountants and commission agents did exist, they also often became stockbrokers, such as W. T. Provand in Greenock, who was an accountant.[7]

Although a number of those who became stockbrokers in 1844-5 abandoned their previous occupation, if they had had one, most tended to pursue both activities, with stockbroking being tacked onto an existing business or practice. A third of the stockbroking firms operating in Edinburgh in 1845 also acted as accountants, commission agents, insurance agents or auctioneers, and Edinburgh had the most committed stockbroking profession in Scotland. Only one Glasgow stockbroking firm did not have an additional occupation, for most practised as accountants and stockbrokers. It was not until 1846 that Aberdeen possessed a full-time stockbroker, while Dundee had none at all during the whole decade of the 1840s. Throughout the rest of Scotland every stockbroker had an additional occupation. In fact, it is quite clear that it was stockbroking that was the additional pursuit for the majority involved in the activity, and stockbroking was easily adopted or discarded by most agents, accountants or lawyers, depending upon its momentary attractions. When these faded after the collapse of the mania, stockbroking was quietly dropped as a specialist activity, though the firm might still dabble occasionally on behalf of a client. However, stockbroking was becoming a more specialised activity as the increase in business encouraged brokers to drop ancillary occupations and to concentrate upon buying and selling shares. Only 38 per cent of the Edinburgh stockbroking firms had no additional activity in 1840, but 68 per cent in 1845. Conversely, the collapse of the 'Railway Mania' had the same effect, for many of the firms who had outside pursuits decided to concentrate upon them and so left stockbroking, while the specialist stockbrokers merely attempted to survive. Between 1846 and 1850, while the number of Edinburgh stockbroking firms without an additional occupation fell by only one, those with such an activity were reduced from 15 to 9.[8]

The primary function of stockbrokers in Scotland altered little in the 1840s, for they continued to be 'agents in the transfer of shares,' to be utilised when stocks and shares were purchased or sold, or any such investment contemplated.[9] During the promotional boom of 1844-5 a secondary aspect of the stockbroker's business became of growing importance, namely involvement in obtaining subscriptions for share issues by new companies. Through his clients, the stockbroker was in contact with the very people who were also potential investors, for they had bought shares in the past. It was a simple matter for the broker to circulate his clients with the details of a new company, recommending purchase, and handling any subsequent business. To encourage stockbrokers to take such action on behalf of a new concern, these companies paid brokers a commission upon every share subscription obtained through their agency:

> The sharebrokers lent their willing aid, as they were paid a brokerage on the number of shares they could get subscribers for, besides another brokerage when the subscribers sold their shares again,

was the observation of Kinnear concerning the role of stockbrokers in the promotion of the exchange companies.[10] Thus, by 18 April 1845 the Edinburgh stockbrokers, for example, had collectively obtained subscriptions for 9,215 shares in the Edinburgh and Leith Water Company and received £23 7s. 6d. in commission by way of return.[11] A number of stockbrokers took an even more active role, for they acted as issuing houses for specific joint-stock companies, arranging the flotation of the entire enterprise in conjunction with the promoters and a legal firm. The Aberdeen stockbroking firm of Oswald, George & Co. handled the issue of shares by the Aberdeen, Banff and Elgin Railway, for example.[12] This latter role naturally declined into insignificance with the collapse of joint-stock company formation in the late 1840s.

In most respects the methods employed by stockbrokers in the transaction of their business, particularly the buying and selling of shares, did not change greatly in the 1840s. Personal contact between brokers and with clients remained the principal means of arranging such business. Those brokers who belonged to stock exchanges could not supplement personal contact with newspaper advertising, as this was banned by all the associations and replaced by a uniform share list of current stocks and their shares, which was issued to the local press. Advertisements offering shares 'For sale and purchase' gradually disappeared from the newspapers as a consequence. With the increased number of brokers in the cities it became important to maintain regular contact, and this was done not only through the organised stock exchange sessions, but also by informal meetings in each other's offices, which all continued to be clustered in the same district of each city. When the Edinburgh stockbroker, W. Kinnear, applied for membership of the Edinburgh Stock Exchange Association, he indicated that he already had

> . . . considerable transactions with many of the members of the Association, all of which were promptly and honourably implemented.[13]

Even after the formation of the stock exchanges there continued to be an active, but parallel, share market located in stockbrokers' offices and generally taking place outside stock exchange hours.[14] Contacts with clients continued to be easy, as they were generally residents of the town or city in which the stockbroker operated, or of the nearby vicinity. Virtually all the clients of Thomas Kennedy, a Glasgow stockbroker, came from Glasgow itself, for instance. For a substantial client such as Peter Brough the Glasgow stockbroker, James Watson regularly came out to Brough's office in Paisley to confer with him in 1845. By then, purchasing and selling stocks had become Brough's chief occupation, and there was a portfolio of shares worth almost £37,000 to manage.[15]

Transactions between different towns and cities were also upon a personal level, even where stock exchanges existed, for each stockbroker had his own contacts in other markets. These contacts were utilised when transactions could not be settled locally and another market offered the possibility of making a sale or a purchase.

For instance, John Robertson & Co., Edinburgh stockbrokers, were in constant communication with Buchanan, Aitken & Co., Glasgow stockbrokers, with regard to the supply and demand for specific shares and the prices at which deals could be made:

> We have yours of 25th and 26th inst. and now send contract for sale of 50 Stirling and Midland Junction — no more wanted. Nothing yet done in City Gas or Forth and Clyde — No Buyer of either but we have good hopes of selling the former . . . We may buy tomorrow 30 Dundee Water at or under £5. Have you any enquiry for Clydesdale Junction? We had a tolerable market today in extent of business.

Such was the missive from Buchanan, Aitken & Co. to John Robertson & Co. on 27 April 1848.[16] In Aberdeen, William George disposed of 20 shares in the Strathearn Junction Railway on behalf of W. J. D. Shephard, a Glasgow stockbroker, while Mr Burgess sold some North of Scotland Bank shares for an Edinburgh broker.[17] These links were not confined to Scotland, for similar contacts existed between Scottish stockbrokers and their colleagues in England, especially in London. The Edinburgh stockbroking firm of Lyon & Co. possessed '. . . intimate and family connection with some of the most influential members of the London, Liverpool and Manchester Stock Exchanges, . . .' in 1845.[18]

These connections also existed outside the main cities, as the stockbrokers who sprang up temporarily in the rest of Scotland in 1844-5 found it essential to develop communications with other brokers in order to remain in touch with market developments and to satisfy the requirements of their customers. John Thomson in Inverness claimed in April 1845 that:

> Every necessary information will be furnished, both as to British and Foreign stocks, and purchases or sales will be transacted, on the same terms, and at the same charges, as in London, Liverpool, Manchester, Dublin, Glasgow and Edinburgh. The latest quotations from these different cities (in each of which I have formed respectable connections) can always be supplied, and every attention and promptitude will be given to the execution of any orders entrusted to my care.[19]

The other Inverness stockbroker, D. Prophet, also possessed contacts in all the large cities in both Scotland and England by May 1845.[20] It was through this web of personal and business contact that both the regional and the national share market was maintained since, from the stockbroker himself, it extended to the local investing public, whether they were individuals, such as Peter Brough, or professional agents, such as members of the Scottish legal profession. Obviously, the disappearance of brokers outside the cities in Scotland reduced the scope of this market, but some compensation existed, for the lines of communication with those in the towns or countryside were lengthened as they looked to the brokers in the nearest city for access to the market.

The procedure employed by a stockbroker to transact business that could not be settled locally was fairly simple. If a Scottish stockbroker was approached by a client to buy or sell the stock of a company which was not popular locally, the broker did not put his client directly in touch with a broker in the most appropriate market, but contacted his corresponding broker in that market himself. This broker then bought or sold the requisite amount, informing the original broker of what had been done, and debiting or crediting him with the cost or receipts. The client was then billed for the cost of purchase or paid the money realised from a sale less, of course, the commission on the transaction, which was shared between the two brokers.[21] It was expected, however, that most buying and selling would be settled on the local market, rather than resort being made to the markets of other cities.[22] Only in cases where transactions were so infrequent and demand or supply so limited would purchases and sale be channelled through the correspondent system for settlement. There was, of course, a certain amount of arbitrage as stocks with more than a purely local appeal moved from one market to another in response to changing conditions of supply and demand.

Despite the expansion in the number of stockbrokers in Scotland during the 'Railway Mania', and the growing sophistication of their methods and institutions, they did not succeed in monopolising the share business in that decade. The legal profession, in particular, continued to play an important role in the cities and they held sway outside, once the collapse of the speculation had swept away the budding brokers from the smaller towns. The Committee of the Aberdeen Stock Exchange had noted in 1847 that 'In many smaller towns where there are no Stock Exchanges persons call themselves Brokers who are merely agents either Law or Mercantile.'[23] However, stockbrokers engrossed more and more of the buying and selling of shares, for only they possessed both the expertise required for an increasingly complex business and had immediate access to the market through contacts with other brokers and membership of a stock exchange. The stockbroker's willingness to share commission with those that passed business his way encouraged lawyers, bankers, accountants, and others to accept the subsidiary role of agents in the share market rather than attempt to undertake the full business themselves. It was easy for such people to pass a client's business on to a stockbroker and receive half the commission for almost no effort. Stockbrokers were willing to do this as it removed a major source of competition, increased their volume of business, and left them in control of the market.[24]

With a minimum charge of five shillings per transaction stockbrokers were not cheap, particularly if a small lot of low value shares had to be disposed of. Consequently, newspaper advertising continued to be resorted to in a few cases in order to arrange the sale or purchase of shares:

> Wanted to Purchase, 100 shares of Glasgow Gravitation Water Co., 50 shares Dundee Water Co. To save broker's commission, offers stating lowest price, addressed to No. 150, and left at the Herald Office, till the evening of Saturday, the 12th instant, will have immediate attention.[25]

This appeared in the *Glasgow Herald* in October 1845. However, advertisements themselves were not cheap and had to be paid for, whatever the outcome. At the same time it was far more convenient to use a stockbroker. As a result, such advertisements became increasingly rare and were called for only on particular occasions and circumstances. Newspaper advertising ceased to be a normal part of the share market as it had been in the past.

The relative composition of Scottish joint-stock enterprise changed considerably during the 'Railway Mania', with the importance of railways increasing at the expense of all other sectors. As late as 1843, almost 75 per cent of the capital was provided by banking, insurance and investment companies, as compared with a mere 14 per cent provided by railways, with gas, water, canals, industrial and other miscellaneous concerns taking up the rest. By 1846, the financial sector's capital contribution was down to 57 per cent, while that of railways had risen to 34 per cent.[26] It was not until the second half of 1844 that this composition began to change radically, with the growing emphasis upon railways rather than an expansion across the full range of joint-stock enterprise. Until then the business being transacted in the market reflected the range of companies available to the investor. Robert Allan referred to the 'good market for shares generally' in his July market report, for instance.[27] Financial concerns, especially banks, continued to dominate the share transactions handled by Scottish brokers up to the summer of 1844 and were then supplanted by railways in the realm of public enthusiasm.

Of course, the interests of Scottish investors were not wholly confined to the securities of Scottish companies, and these securities were not all held by Scottish investors. A large proportion of the shares issued by Scottish railways, especially the major trunk lines, were taken by English investors. Altogether, English shareholders were responsible for 38 per cent of the funds provided for Scottish railways by large investors in 1846. Certain lines, such as the Caledonian, the North British and the Inverness and Perth, had a majority of English shareholders. In 1849, 77 per cent of the capital of the North British Railway originated in England.[28] Allan reported in January 1845 that there was considerable English demand for North British shares, which was driving up the price, and that 'Vast quantities have consequently gone south . . .'[29] With such substantial English holdings of Scottish railway shares it was perfectly possible to have a purely English market in these securities, with both the seller and purchaser being resident in England, the deal being handled by an English stockbroker, and settled in an English market. There was no need for these holders of railway shares to utilise directly the services of a Scottish stockbroker. Consequently, not all the business generated by Scottish railway enterprise affected the Scottish share market, for it was done partly in London, Leeds, Liverpool, Manchester or some other major English centre.[30]

This growing English interest in Scottish railways was reciprocated by the Scottish investor, who made increasing purchases of English railway stock. As early as November 1841 Allan observed that

Considerable purchases have recently been made on Scotch account in some of the leading English lines, particularly South Western, Midland Counties, and York and North Midland.[31]

During the 1840s substantial Scottish holdings of the securities of English railways were being built up. The Liverpool and Manchester Railway had only 10

Scottish shareholders in 1838, but 29 by 1845, while the Grand Junction Railway had 4 in 1835 and 122 in 1845. Scots had invested only £2,000 in the Newcastle and Carlisle Railway in 1838, but £9,300 in 1844, while they held £94,000 of the stock of the Great North of England Railway in 1845 compared to a mere £4,700 in 1838. As English railway lines were completed and became dividend-paying concerns, they attracted Scottish investors seeking a secure and regular return on their capital. Scottish banking and insurance companies, for example, were interested in the securities of established English railway companies. The North Midland Railway had not one Scottish shareholder in 1836, but it had 69 in 1842, which was one year after it began to pay dividends.[32]

Other Scots were involved in the shares of newly promoted or unfinished English railways for the speculative element they offered. Charles Tennant, for example, the Glasgow chemical manufacturer, speculated in the shares of the Midland Railway in 1844-5, while Arthur Anderson, the Aberdeen lawyer, put his faith in 3,000 shares of the North Staffordshire Railway in 1845-6.[33] Many Scots such as Joseph Mitchell, the Inverness civil engineer, also possessed connections in England, which led them to become involved in various of the English railway schemes. He placed over £2,000 in the Midland Railway, because, as he explained himself,

> A relative of mine whom I frequently visited in Yorkshire recommended me to invest some of my professional savings in the stock of the Midland Railway. The line, he said, formed part of the great central route of communication between London and the North. It passed through a country rich in minerals, and connected great manufacturing towns. The works were of the most substantial character for they had the personal superintendence of the father of railways, Mr George Stephenson. I consequently purchased at various times some of the stock during the progress of the works.[34]

Peter Brough travelled extensively in England buying textiles for his drapery business and was able to gain first-hand knowledge of the English railway system which he put to use by purchasing extensive holdings in the York and North Midland Railway.[35]

However, apart from railways, which were of growing importance, there was very little Scottish involvement in other forms of English joint-stock enterprise. The Royal Bank of London, for example, was about the only English banking company in which Scottish investors were at all interested.[36] Again, with the exception of railways, most of the shares of Scottish joint-stock enterprise were taken by Scottish investors, usually from the locality in which the concern operated or was based. One third of the shares in the Kilmarnock Water Company, for instance, were taken by residents in Kilmarnock, with the remainder being held by investors from the neighbouring city of Glasgow.[37]

Consequently, in most cases Scottish investment in stocks and shares was directed exclusively to Scottish joint-stock enterprise and these companies relied upon the financial support of the Scottish public. Complicating this neat interdependence were railways, for, in that sector, not only was there considerable cross-investment between Scotland and England, but also turnover in railway shares was, proportionately, far greater during the mania than in any other joint-stock venture. In 1845, especially, railway shares absorbed most of the interest of the investor who was concerned with speculative gains rather than a long-term investment. As early as January 1845 Robert Allan had noted that 'Capitalists have shown a preference for railway investments, . . .' and, by March, he considered that little else was happening outside the market in railway shares. During May, June and July business was less dominated by railways, as transactions in banks in Edinburgh and exchange companies in Glasgow were considerable, but, by August, railways were again virtually monopolising attention. On the 18th of October 1845, for example, it was reported from the Edinburgh market that:

> . . . the amount of business done in railway shares has not been exceeded during any similar period.

Similar hectic activity in railway shares was also taking place in Glasgow and Aberdeen, with other joint-stock companies neglected.[38]

Although transactions in railway securities were far more numerous than the turnover in the shares of all other forms of joint-stock enterprise as a whole, the actual value of business done in railways was much less dominant. Interest in railway shares centred increasingly upon the issues of the recently promoted railway companies, where the speculative element was greatest. These shares, usually called 'scrip', had often little or nothing paid up upon them, and were traded frequently in large numbers at low values:[39]

> We have had . . . a most active market and principally in railway scrip shares, almost all of which have been largely dealt in, while the paid up stocks have been comparatively neglected,

was the report from the Glasgow market for the week ending 6 September 1845, and this was typical of what occurred during the mania.[40] In contrast, the more limited transactions in the stocks and shares of other companies had a much greater individual value. The vast volume of business in railway shares gave the sector an impression of overwhelming importance during the mania, but the actual relative value of these transactions was much less significant.

On the Aberdeen Stock Exchange the value of turnover in railway shares was only 28 per cent of total business in November – December 1845. However, the contribution would certainly have been much higher earlier in the year, before the collapse of the mania in October, and the decline in enthusiasm for railways. In addition, the Aberdeen area had no established and operating railway companies whose securities would provide an element of stability for the railway sector, rather than the largely speculative interest in either incomplete or unauthorised lines. However, Aberdeen did possess a number of important coastal steamship companies and their combination would approximate to the situation in Glasgow, Edinburgh or Dundee. The whole transport sector on the Aberdeen Stock Exchange comprised 47 per cent of the total value of turnover in the last two months of 1845.[41]

Therefore, the nature of the business being handled by Scottish stockbrokers during the mania was fairly diversified until 1844, with the securities of financial concerns still being of prime importance. In the course of 1844 this composition began to alter in favour of railways, but it was not until 1845 that they became dominant, providing half of all transactions, by value, even by the end of that year, by which time they were facing increasing disfavour.[42] Railway securities had come to play a much greater role in the portfolios of securities held by Scottish investors, though there was enormous variation between different individuals.[43]

The transactions carried out by the Scottish brokers were also overwhelmingly in the shares of Scottish companies, despite the interest shown in English railways. Certainly, the shares of railway lines such as the Shrewsbury, Oswestry and Chester Junction, the London and Windsor, or various Irish ventures, were traded by Scottish brokers, but this was a small part of their total activity.[44] In fact, not only were the concerns mainly Scottish, but investors all possessed their own local preferences. Each city or town continued to have its own set of locally owned and operated banks, insurance companies, urban facilities, and railways, and it was transactions in these that tended to dominate the business of the stockbroker and the investments of his clients. Only 14 per cent of the value of turnover on the Aberdeen Stock Exchange at the end of 1845 consisted of transactions in the securities of enterprises that were not based in the North-East of Scotland, and dealings in English railways provided most of that. The same was true for Thomas Kennedy in Glasgow, as the buying and selling of stocks and shares which he carried out for his customers was largely in the issues of Glasgow-based companies.[45]

During the mania there was little involvement in overseas investment, with no new Scottish companies being formed to invest or operate outside the country. The Scottish Australian Company, for example, failed to raise any additional funds in Scotland between 1843 and 1847, not through any difficulty in employing additional capital in Australia, but as a consequence of an unwillingness among Scottish investors to lend them the money. The North British Australasian Loan and Investment Company also faced the same difficulties.[46] This Scottish aversion to overseas involvement, during the mania, was not confined to Australia but applied generally, such as to the opportunities in railway construction on the Continent. Allan noted, in April 1843, that while '. . . considerable disposition to speculate in French railways had been exhibited in England, . . .' in Scotland '. . . there is no inclination to advance on foreign securities of the kind.'[47] It was not until after the collapse of the mania that there was some revival of Scottish interest in foreign investments. Kennedy, for example, was handling purchases and sales of Indian railway stock by 1846, while activity in the Aberdeen-based investment concerns had also picked up by the end of 1845. Altogether the rather fragmentary evidence suggests that the value of share turnover in Scotland in 1845 was composed of roughly 75 per cent local, 8 per cent in other Scottish companies, 15 per cent English and 2 per cent overseas.[48] Again, individual cases could differ markedly, with John M'Gavin, a Glasgow grain merchant, being largely interested in the securities of such Scottish railway companies as the Caledonian, North British, and Forth and Clyde Junction, while 80 per cent of Peter Brough's portfolio of investments in 1845 was composed of English railway stock.[49]

In the dramatic decline of business that followed the collapse of the speculative mania, with turnover on the Aberdeen Stock Exchange down by 764 per cent between November 1845 and November 1848, the nature and composition of the transactions handled by brokers changed substantially.[50] It was activity in the securities of the unproven joint-stock enterprises that suffered most in the general decline, for the shares of established and successful concerns continued to be traded in, though at a reduced level:

> Whilst in almost every department of speculation — railways, mining, or commercial — an almost unprecedented lethargy prevails — the necessary reaction of the over-activity and recklessness of a former period — banking and life assurance maintain the even tenor of their way, and the accumulating capital of the country instinctively selects these secure channels of investment and profit,

observed one contemporary in September 1849.[51] Even in the most difficult times there was always a market for securities of proven worth, and the difficulties that some had got themselves into as a result of the speculations forced the gradual disposal of these, and their acquisition by investors more advantageously placed.[52] In contrast, 'A certain class of Railway shares has hardly been saleable, . . .' said the *Scottish Railway Gazette* in December 1849.[53]

Consequently, in a city such as Aberdeen, with no established railways, the contribution of railway shares to this greatly reduced level of business fell dramatically from 24 per cent in 1846 to only 5 per cent in 1848. Over the same period, the proportion of business done in bank shares rose from 26 per cent to 50 per cent. It was transactions in bank, insurance, gas and established railway companies that engaged Scottish stockbrokers in the later 1840s and sustained those who remained in the profession. Investors who held shares in the more recent railway ventures, and could survive without realising the capital tied up in them, waited until a revival in railway fortunes and the money market would allow them to sell off their holdings. These people withdrew from the market temporarily. Retrenchment by investors and their preference for the familiar and the secure also enhanced the local component of share business, and involvement in distant investments including English railways declined, while English investors also tried to unload their holdings of Scottish railway securities.

The proportion of business done on the Aberdeen Stock Exchange in the shares of companies actually operating in the North-East of Scotland rose from 73 per cent in 1846 to 83 per cent in 1848, while that of other Scottish companies fell from 5 per cent to 1 per cent, and that of English companies from 9 per cent to 1 per cent.[54] Evidence from both Edinburgh and Glasgow tells a similar tale, with investors concentrating on the known, both in field of operation and the location of activity.[55] Only Indian railways, which had a government-backed minimum return, appeared to be an exception to this trend.

During the 'Railway Mania' there was a considerable change in the composition of stockbroking business in Scotland, with the investor's horizon being broadened both geographically and by a wider range of enterprise in which to participate.

However, the collapse of the mania witnessed a considerable retrenchment by the investor, as he again came to concentrate upon the securities of local companies operating in such long-established fields as banking, insurance, gas and water.

NOTES

1. *E.D.* 1840-6; *G.D.* 1840-6; *A.D.* 1840-6; *D.D.* 1840-6.

2. *Sc.M.* 2 March 1845.

3. *E.D.* 1840-6; A. W. Kerr, *History of Banking in Scotland* (Lon. 1918) p. 224.

4. *G.D.* 1840-6; S. G. Checkland, *Scottish Banking: A History 1695-1973* (Glas. 1975) pp. 380-1.

5. *A.D.* 1840-6; Aberdeen Stock Exchange Association: Minutes, 15 April 1848.

6. *D.D.* 1840-6.

7. *S.R.G.* 27 September 1845, 3 May 1845, 18 October 1845.

8. *E.D.* 1840-1850; *G.D.* 1840-50; *A.D.* 1840-50; *D.D.* 1840-50.

9. *D.P. & C.A.* 22 August 1845.

10. G. Kinnear, *A History of the Rise of Exchange Companies in Scotland* (Glas. 1848) p. 16. Cf. Rules of the Edinburgh Stock Exchange Association 15 May 1846, Rule 6.

11. Edin.: Minutes, 18 April 1845.

12. Edin.: Minutes, 1 February 1845; *G.H.* 17 February 1845; To the Shareholders of the Aberdeen, Banff, and Elgin Railway: Stronach & Grainger, solicitors (30 January 1846, Abdn.)

13. Edin.: Minutes, 7 April 1846; Glas.: Minutes, 11 September 1845, 6 June 1845; *S.R.G.* 6 September 1845, 13 September 1845, 25 October 1845.

14. Thomas Kennedy: Stock Books, 1845-7.

15. J. B. Sturrock, *Peter Brough: A Paisley Philanthropist* (Paisley 1890) pp. 116-7, 234-254.

16. Buchanan, Aitken & Co. to John Robertson & Co., 27 April 1848.

17. Abdn.: Minutes, 8 December 1845, 10 November 1846; Glas.: Minutes, 19 October 1847.

18. *Sc.M.* 8 October 1845; Glas.: Minutes, 4 June 1848; Abdn.: Minutes, 6 August 1846.

19. *S.R.G.* 19 April 1845.

20. *S.R.G.* 17 May 1845.

21. Case for the Joint Opinion of Mr Bramwell and Mr Willes re transactions in shares of Joint Stock Companies by Members of Aberdeen Stock Exchange (17 November 1854).

22. Glas.: Minutes, 23 November 1846; *The Edinburgh Stock Exchange, 1844-1944* (Edin. 1944) p. 16.

23. Aberdeen Stock Exchange Association: Draft Rules (Abdn. 1847) Rule 11.

24. Edin.: Minutes, 23 September 1845; Abdn.: Draft Rules.

25. *G.H.* 11 October 1845.

26. Robert Allan, *Monthly Circular, 1843-6.*

27. Allan, op. cit., April & July 1844.

28. W. Vamplew, 'Sources of Scottish Railway Capital before 1860' *S.J.P.E.* 17 (1970) pp. 431-2; B. Lenman, *An Economic History of Modern Scotland, 1660-1976 (Lon. 1977) p. 168; Scottish Railway Shareholder's Manual* (Edin. 1849) p. 1; J. Mitchell, *Reminiscences of my life in the Highlands* (1883-4 repr. 1971) II pp. 159-60.

29. Allan, op. cit., January 1845.

30. *D.P. & C.A.* 31 January 1845.

31. Allan, op. cit., November 1841.

32. M. C. Reed, *Investment in Railways in Britain, 1820-44* (Oxford 1975) pp. 120, 128, 164-5, 179, 186; P. L. Cottrell, Investment Banking in England, 1856-1882 (Ph.D. Hull 1974) pp. 83-4; Sturrock, op. cit., p. 117.

33. N. Crathorne, *Tennants' Stalk: The Story of the Tennants of the Glen* (Lon. 1973) p. 120; A. Anderson to H. J. Rawden, 18 January 1863.

34. Mitchell, op. cit., II, pp. 229-30.

35. Sturrock, op. cit., p. 153.

36. *B.M.* June 1845.

37. M. S. Cotterill, The Scottish Gas Industry up to 1914 (Ph.D. Strathclyde 1976) pp. 1, 391; *S.R.G.* 10 May 1845.

38. Allan, op. cit., January – May 1845; Market Reports from Edinburgh and Glasgow in *S.R.G.* 5 April 1845 – 20 December 1845; Glasgow Stock Exchange: Daily Share List, 16 September 1845 – 31 December 1845; Aberdeen Stock Exchange: Record & Ledger, October – December 1845.

39. Reed, op. cit., p. 93 ('scrip' was derived from the word sub*scrip*tion).

40. *S.R.G.* 6 September 1845; cf. *S.R.G.* 12 April 1845.

41. Abdn.: Record, November – December 1845.

42. Kennedy, op. cit.

43. Sturrock, op. cit., pp. 234-254; J. R. Kellett, 'The Private Investments of Glasgow's Lord Provosts' *A.M.* November 1969, p. 602.

44. *B.M.* June 1845.

45. Kennedy, loc. cit.; Abdn.: Record, loc. cit.

46. D. S. MacMillan, *The Debtor's War* (Melbourne 1960) p. 41; J. Anderson, *To the Shareholders of the North British Australasian Loan and Investment Company* (Ellon 1848) pp. 4, 7; A. G. Kenwood, 'Railway Investment in Britain, 1825-1875' *Ec.* 32 (1962) p. 320.

47. Allan, op. cit., April 1843.

48. Kennedy, loc. cit.; Abdn.: Record, loc. cit.; *A.H.* 4 October 1845.

49. Sturrock, op. cit., pp. 234-254; *Memoirs and Portraits of One Hundred Glasgow Men* (Glas. 1886) p. 191.

50. Abdn.: Record, November 1845 – November 1848; Glas.: List, 1846-9; Allan, op. cit., 1846-9; *S.R.G.* 1846-9 (Market Reports), e.g. 10 April 1847.

51. *A.H.* 22 September 1849.

52. A. Moffat, *Scottish Railways* (Edin. 1849) p. 3; J. Morrison, *English Railway Legislation* (Lon. 1848) pp. 8, 38; T. Tooke, *An History of Prices* (Lon. 1848) IV, p. 360.

53. *S.R.G.* 29 December 1849.

54. Abdn.: Record, 1846-8.

55. Allan, op. cit., April 1848.

PART IV:
THE PROFESSION AND ITS INSTITUTIONS, 1850-1900

Nothing short of a study of these local share lists will convince the observer how great has been the contribution of these local exchanges to the most remote and minute irrigation of national prosperity and the ubiquitous fostering of productive enterprise.

E. T. Powell, *The Evolution of the Money Market, 1385-1915* (London 1916) p. 538.

11

Income, Wealth and Investment

BUILDING upon the foundations laid before 1850, the Scottish economy continued to develop strongly in the second half of the nineteenth century along the lines already established. Undoubtedly, the most dynamic element was the engineering and allied industries, based upon the coal and iron ore of Central Scotland, especially the Glasgow region. In 1851 the heavy industries employed only 5 per cent of the total Scottish labour force, while by 1901 their share was 15 per cent. Altogether, in 1907, heavy industry accounted for 50 per cent of the manufacturing labour force and produced 55 per cent of industrial output in Scotland. Prime amongst these industries was shipbuilding, with the Clyde becoming one of the leading shipbuilding areas of the world. Scottish shipyards launched 70,000 tons of shipping in 1862, but 520,000 tons in 1902. A complex of other manufacturing industries complemented shipbuilding by being both ready to supply its every requirement and maintain an independent existence for themselves. Steel production in Scotland, for example, rose from 84,500 tons in 1880 to 963,345 tons in 1900, by which time it was providing one third of the British output, and the Scottish steel industry was heavily dependent upon the Scottish shipyards for outlets. Glasgow also became the largest railway locomotive engineering centre in Europe, while other branches of engineering, such as textile equipment, sugar refining machinery, railway appliances, and machine tools, flourished either in Glasgow itself or in numerous other subsidiary centres such as Kilmarnock or Aberdeen.[1]

For these industries the world, rather than the British market, became of major importance at an early stage, with a growing proportion of output being exported. However, this external demand was not confined to a small number of specialist activities, but gradually affected all sectors of the Scottish economy. Industrialisation in the world meant a need for coal, iron and, later, steel, which Scotland was well placed to provide. Scottish coal output, for example, grew from 7.5m tons in 1854 to 39m tons in 1908, and a rising percentage was destined to supply foreign industry or transport with power. In 1854 a mere 5 per cent was exported, but by 1896 this had reached 21 per cent. Within Britain itself the demand for Scottish coal continued to expand, especially from the London gas works.[2] The existence of a large expatriate population with rising incomes also meant a lucrative market for the everyday items of Scottish manufacturing industry. Beer and whisky production, for example, gradually became export-orientated. In 1850 the Scottish beer industry produced 0.5m barrels, of which only 4 per cent was sent abroad, but in 1900 output reached 2.1m barrels and 6 per cent was exported. Similarly, Scotch whisky was being shipped overseas in growing quantities to satisfy the tastes of British emigrants who had settled in such places as Australia or South Africa.[3] Even service activities such as insurance or shipping catered for increasingly wide markets. Edinburgh-based insurance companies came to conduct business throughout the world, while Glasgow-owned shipping lines carried not only British cargo from, or to, British ports but any cargo between any ports. In 1906, for example, there were 230 shipping companies in Glasgow operating 1,021 ships, half of them overseas.[4]

Within Scotland itself the prosperity of these manufacturing and commercial sectors meant a growing demand for food, raw materials, and all the other requirements of an increasing population in receipt of rising incomes, which lived in an expanding urban, industrial economy. Market forces, for example, pervaded the whole of Scottish agriculture, whether it was in Ayrshire, meeting Glasgow's needs, or in North-East Scotland, where the demands of London were of paramount importance. Fishing was transformed from a coastal activity with a limited hinterland market into a major industry utilising rail and steamship connections to serve urban markets, not only within Britain, but also in Continental Europe. By 1886, for example, almost 70 per cent of the Scottish herring catch was exported.[5]

As early as 1858 the transformation in the Scottish economy was evident in an area such as St. Rollox in Glasgow:

> The whole district for miles is now teeming with manufacturing life; potteries, glass-works, saw mills, wood-yards, flax and cotton-mills, iron foundries and machine-shops, coal depots, earthenware manufactories, railway stations, and a busy hard working and commercial population occupy almost every inch of the ground.[6]

This pattern was repeated again and again in the second half of the nineteenth century, and its consequences pervaded the whole of the Scottish economy, bringing employment and prosperity to most people. However, certain sectors did not gain by exposure to the market forces of the world economy. A disadvantaged region such as the Highlands, with poor agriculture, no coal, and limited access to markets, saw its population gradually drift away to better opportunities elsewhere. Agriculture, as a whole, faced difficult conditions in the later nineteenth century as foreign competition undermined its once monopolistic position in the domestic market. The Scottish grain distillers, for example, had almost entirely switched to using imported maize instead of domestically produced barley and oats by the 1880s. In many minerals, domestic production was supplemented and then replaced by foreign sources, such as in iron ore, with 200,000 tons being imported as early as 1880. Within industry itself certain branches were unable to meet competition, not so much from abroad as from England. The textile industries employed 18 per cent of the Scottish labour force in 1851 but only 10 per cent in 1901, and this decline was not only a relative but also an absolute one. Only certain small sections of the industry such as jute textiles, fancy woollens or cotton thread managed to compete successfully with producers in Lancashire and Yorkshire.[7] Even the heavy industries began to experience problems by the early twentieth century. A review of the Scottish steel industry in 1913-14 concluded that:

> The competition to be met in the world's markets is becoming more severe, coming, as it does, from quarters which are more favourably placed with regard to costs of raw materials and labour.[8]

However, while problems existed in the late Victorian and Edwardian Scottish economy, they were not to manifest themselves until the changed circumstances following the First World War. Until that time the economy remained a buoyant one, slowly altering to meet new developments and opportunities in technology and markets.[9]

This economy produced growing income and wealth for its population, especially in the prosperous regions of Central and Eastern Scotland. Income in Scotland is estimated to have doubled between 1854-5 and 1885, and nearly doubled again by 1910, when it was running at £82m per annum.[10] This represented not only a substantial increase in per capita incomes, but also a rising proportion of total British income being received in Scotland.[11] Savings increased proportionately, or even more so, as the middle income groups were those who gained most from the development of the Scottish economy, and they could afford not to spend all they earned.[12] Kerr reflected in 1898 that in Scotland 'Capital has been steadily increasing at a greater ratio than the population, . . .'[13] As early as 1874-5, there were some 125,000 people in Scotland with deposits of £100 or over in the Scottish banks.[14] An example of the growth of Scottish wealth was the expansion of savings held by these Scottish banks, since deposits grew from £35m in 1850 to over £107m by 1900. This was over a period when there was increasing competition for this money from a variety of other institutions, and bank deposits fell substantially as a proportion of total investment.[15] All in all, one anonymous writer in 1886 could justifiably claim that Scotland was '. . . one of the richest countries in the world'.[16]

The growth of the Scottish economy required vast inputs of capital in order to finance its further expansion. Railways, heavy industry, agriculture and construction were all sectors which were capable of absorbing almost limitless supplies of savings. As Paish observed in 1908:

> . . . there is a vast amount of new capital every year embarked in the erection of houses, in the building of ships, in the construction and equipment of factories, in the decoration and stocking of shops, . . .[17]

By 1910, according to Crammond, the capital invested in Scottish railways reached £132m, while a further £309m was tied up in housing. In contrast, the Scottish brewing industry employed a capital of £0.6m in 1850, but £6m by 1900.[18] All sectors of the Scottish economy witnessed both a deepening and a spread in the use of capital.[19] A report on the agriculture of Forfar and Kincardine in 1881 noted that

> . . . a very large sum of money has been expended in these counties since 1850 in the draining and fencing of arable land.[20]

The finance for most of these developments was largely obtained from the rising profits and income being generated within each industry itself, or even from within individual firms or families. Activities as diverse as fishing; coalmining; the whole range of manufacturing including iron and steel; textiles, paper, brewing, and distilling; or commercial operations such as the timber trade or shipping, were all heavily dependent for their capital upon funds provided by the entrepreneurs themselves, their friends and acquaintances, and supplemented by trade credit and bank loans. The bulk of finance required continued to be mainly in the form of working capital, which facilitated the use of these personal or temporary sources.[21] Only around half the capital in coalmining in the 1870s was fixed, despite the heavy demands made by deeper pits, and the need for expensive drainage and haulage equipment. In brewing two-thirds of the capital was for trading purposes as late as 1900.[22]

Even before the joint-stock era, there were opportunities for outside investors to participate directly in these industrial or commercial ventures. The distillers and whisky blenders, for example, were required to carry large stocks of spirits from time to time over the year, and they looked for outside assistance in order to finance this burden. According to evidence given in 1891 to the Select Committee on British and Foreign Spirits,

> It is an investment which is very much thought of and carried out to a very large extent in Scotland by gentlemen outside the trade altogether; there is a very large amount of money invested by the public; men who have money saved, instead of investing in railways and other things, invest it in whiskey; it is a very good and safe investment indeed.

Through a web of contact those in the whisky trade could mobilise sufficient funds to finance the carrying over of the large stocks that they held, and investors were more than willing to provide the necessary capital as the return was from 10 to 15 per cent per annum.[23] A similar situation existed in the iron industry where supply and demand were not always in accord, not only over the year, but from year to year. Consequently, large but fluctuating stocks of pig iron could be built-up, and the holding of these had to be financed until an upturn in demand absorbed them. This was done through the market in pig iron warrants and attracted a wide variety of investors, especially in the Glasgow region.[24]

The participation of outside investors was not confined to the provision of temporary funds to finance stocks, but also took a more direct form in certain activities. In the fishing industry it was common for those with some connection with the industry, such as fish salesmen and outfitters, to provide a portion of the capital necessary to begin operations, and to receive a return on their investment.[25] Merchants who had made money by selling textiles, coal or iron, often invested in the manufacture or mining of the product they sold.[26] Other merchants or industrialists who had accumulated large profits from one branch of industry often switched to finance another area which was felt to have greater potential. The Fife linoleum industry drew both capital and enterprise from the ailing linen textile industry in the region, while there was a similar movement in Glasgow away from textiles and into heavy industry and shipbuilding.[27] For example James Scott, owner of a Glasgow cotton spinning enterprise, invested a considerable sum of money from 1871 onwards in developing the Scottish shale oil industry.[28]

Of all the activities which drew upon finance through an informal or personal web, shipping remained one of the most dependent. This had traditionally been financed by a system of 64ths, whereby up to 64 people agreed to provide the capital necessary to construct and operate each individual ship. Even after this method was abandoned — and it lasted a considerable time — the same means were used to provide the capital for much of Scotland's shipping. Commonly a shipbroker canvassed a small circle of friends, relatives, acquaintances, and business contacts with each new proposal. Shipbuilders were always ready to subscribe a part of the capital, or extend credit, as it held the possibility of securing an order, and suppliers of ships stores were similarly placed. Ship's captains could also be tapped for funds with the promise of a good berth. A new firm of shipbrokers found it difficult to raise all the capital needed and had to rely heavily upon the partners' own savings and those of the immediate family. The Donaldson Brothers, for instance, set up as shipbrokers in Glasgow in the 1850s and obtained all their initial funding from close relatives and through the sale of some property they owned. However, once the success of a few ships and their voyages had been proved and publicised, finance became much less of a problem. There were profits to be reinvested, both by the shipbrokers themselves and by those clients who had participated from the beginning, while it was also easy to widen the circle of financial support as the brokers had the reputation for success which would provide something of a guarantee to potential investors.[29]

Despite the growing capital requirements of the Scottish economy, not all those directly involved reinvested the profits and savings generated. Many in agriculture put money aside in the eventuality of a series of difficult years, as had happened in the past. Of those who had made fortunes in the textile industry, some invested the proceeds and retired to live on the interest, while others sought alternative outlets for the income being generated, as the industry itself had limited prospects in Scotland. Even such successful activities as iron and coal, chemicals, whisky blending or jute textiles were at times generating profits greater than the entrepreneurs involved could completely employ comfortably within the industry. One jute firm, Cox Brothers of Dundee, was earning profits for its partners averaging £36,000 per annum between 1877 and 1893, and these sums were in excess of both the partners' personal requirements and the needs of the company.[30]

At the same time there existed a growing income that was not committed to any specific productive sector. In 1885, around half the estimated annual income being received by the people of Scotland could be so classified, and by 1910 the proportion was as high as three-quarters.[31] There existed a large number of Scottish landowners who received a growing income from their property, not only because of its farming capability, but also because of its new-found proximity to an expanding town or because of the mineral wealth that lay beneath the soil. Robert Ramsay, for instance, was a Midlothian landowner who, by the 1870s, enjoyed earnings of £2,300 per annum from renting out the farms he controlled and an additional income of over £11,000 per annum in royalties for the coal-mining being carried out on his property.[32]

During the second half of the nineteenth century there continued to be recurring periods when there appeared to be no suitable openings for the abundant savings available for investment. The early and late 1850s, the mid 1860s and 1870s, the early and late 1880s, and the mid 1890s were all such times.[33] Typical of the situation that developed on these occasions was that in the mid-1870s when, according to the *Aberdeen Free Press:*

> The value of money has now reached a point at which it has never before stood, and practically no employment can be found for the great mass in bankers' hands . . . The look-out is gloomy for those having the disposal of large sums . . . It is difficult to forsee what the ultimate result of this plethora of unemployed money will be, but in former times, when somewhat similar circumstances have ruled, although in a less marked degree, it has generally led to indulgence in heavy speculation, either in stocks or produce of some description.[34]

These speculations and ensuing crashes became progressively milder after mid-century but still occurred regularly, disrupting the general workings of the capital market and giving the impression, at least, that not only was capital available in abundance for any feasible investment, but that investors were actively seeking any suitable outlet for the funds that they had at their disposal.[35]

During the second half of the nineteenth century the channels of investment available to the general public in Scotland widened considerably.[36] These ranged from participation in such trade investments as whisky stocks or tramp steamers, to the opportunities in a wide variety of joint-stock enterprises. However, traditional outlets for savings continued to be important, although of changing popularity. The purchase of a landed estate had always been considered a safe haven for those with substantial amounts to invest, but land was in limited supply and what did become available was often purchased in large blocks by the very wealthy, or by those intending to farm it themselves.[37] Large numbers of estates, for example, were bought by the Glasgow entrepreneurs who had made fortunes in coal, iron, engineering or shipping. In the 1850s alone the six Baird brothers spent collectively £1,115,000 of their profits from coal mining and iron manufacture on acquiring landed estates throughout Scotland, such as Knoydart in Inverness-shire, Strichen and Auchmedden in Aberdeenshire, Stichill in Berwick and Roxburgh, and Auchendrane and Muirkirk in Ayrshire. Arthur Pollock, a timber merchant and shipowner, and James Weir, a marine engineer, were among the many others who followed the Bairds' example.[38]

However, the depression in agriculture from the 1870s onwards undermined the value and security of rural land as an investment, leading to a precipitous contraction in land sales and then a prolonged depression for the rest of the century. The great fall in the value of farm produce seriously affected the ability of the tenant farmer to pay the rent at which he had contracted to take the farm. Some farmers went bankrupt, while others abandoned agriculture. Rents had to be reduced or farms remained unlet. The yield on land as an investment was already low, and the fall in rents pushed that return even lower. At the same time there was no longer the guarantee that land would increase or even retain its value as it had done in the past, or that a regular income would be generated, for foreign competition had destroyed the domestic industry's control over its home market.[39] By the late nineteenth century only the very rich could afford both the large initial outlay involved in land purchase and accept the low returns and insecurity involved.

For the small investor, deposits in Scottish banks had long been popular because of the interest paid, the ease of withdrawal, and the almost total security. Increasingly, however, the attractions of bank deposits had been declining as their ability to pay a competitive rate of interest fell.[40] The Scottish banks were finding it more and more difficult to obtain openings for the money deposited with them in secure and remunerative loans to Scottish industry or commerce. At the same time their investments in government stock were becoming both more difficult and less profitable, as the size of the National Debt contracted and the interest paid was reduced, both by conversion and by pressure of demand. There was always a substantial demand for government securities from insurance companies or industrial and commercial firms, as they used them as a reserve fund against a sudden financial crisis or as a home for temporarily idle cash. Scottish gas companies, for example, held their reserves in the form of government stock. In addition, savings banks had to invest all their deposits in government stock. As long as government stock paid any positive interest it would be purchased and held by institutions and individuals who had either no alternative investment or regarded it as marginally superior to the holding of cash, for which there was no return.[41] As an investment though, government stock was of little direct value and was held by the Scottish banks 'rather for protection than for profit', according to the North of Scotland Bank, as early as 1866.[42]

Consequently, the character of deposits in Scottish banks gradually changed after 1850 so that they were no longer the repository of savings seeking a secure and remunerative long-term investment, but the temporary home of funds awaiting a more attractive opening or of the fluctuating balances being created by everyday commercial business:

> The investment deposit which used to lie year after year undisturbed, except for interest calculation, is a thing of the past,

wrote Kerr in 1898.[43]

Only the Scottish branches of foreign banks could pay sufficient interest to attract substantial long-term deposits. These appeared in Scotland as early as the 1860s, and by the 1880s Indian and Colonial banks had established a network of branches and agencies throughout Scotland.[44] Their success was soon evident, with the *Scottish Banking and Insurance Magazine* commenting in February 1879 that,

> Even under the disadvantages of the want of local connection they have proved formidable rivals of the home companies. This is much conduced to by the higher rates of interest which they — especially the Canadian companies — offer for deposits.[45]

By October 1883 one estimate placed the total deposited with these institutions at £10m, and this amount grew substantially in the course of the decade.[46] However, these foreign banks could never hope to tap Scottish savings to the same extent as the indigenous banking system, even with higher interest rates, for they did not possess the necessary branch network, nor did they enjoy the complete confidence of the Scottish investing public. The Australian banking crisis of 1893, for example, when numerous depositors lost money, confirmed to many the risks involved in placing their savings in unfamiliar institutions.[47]

Housing was a major and expanding area of capital expenditure in the Scottish economy, amounting to an estimated 23 per cent of the total in 1885, and 29 per cent in 1910.[48] As population grew and migrated to the towns and cities there was an ever increasing need for urban accommodation.[49] Annual capital formation in dwellings approached £5m per annum by 1900, while other forms of building work, such as commercial and industrial property, averaged £6m per annum. Between 1872/3 and 1906/7, 90,316 houses and 7,108 shops were built in Glasgow at a cost of £19.9m, and about a third of that construction was necessary, not for the additional population pouring into Glasgow but to replace property that was no longer satisfactory and had to be demolished. In the 1890s alone over 11,000 houses were pulled down in Glasgow.[50]

The general standard of housing in Scotland also steadily improved in the second half of the nineteenth century, with the number of people to a room and the rooms per house all rising, while services such as hot water supply, electric lighting and an internal bathroom became commoner. One-roomed houses, for example, comprised 34 per cent of the total housing stock in 1861, but only 18 per cent in 1901 and 13 per cent in 1911. Even the quality of building improved as houses became more substantial and streets wider.[51] The cost of building a tenement rose as much as 60 per cent between 1862 and 1902, and continued to rise thereafter, as more work, time, and materials were needed to construct and furbish the higher quality of accommodation.[52] There was continual scope for further improvement in the quantity and quality of the housing stock available to the Scottish population, as it was never completely adequate for their needs throughout the 1850-1914 period, especially in industrial towns and cities such as Clydebank, Coatbridge, Govan, Dundee, Kilmarnock, Glasgow, Greenock, and Falkirk. Fraser estimated in 1907-8 that there were 400,000 living in overcrowded conditions in Glasgow alone, while the Scottish Land Enquiry Committee thought that housing conditions in Scotland as a whole were 'little short of scandalous' in 1914.[53]

A significant measure of house purchase and construction took place on behalf of the owner-occupier who utilised some of his accumulated savings to buy himself a house or to have one built, especially in the growing suburban areas. As Mitchell observed in 1882,

> In Dalkeith, as in most other thriving towns, the shop-keepers, tradesmen, and professional men have in many cases ceased to reside at their places of business, and have provided themselves with dwellings in the suburbs . . .[54]

People such as Arthur Bell, a Perth whisky blender, or Peter Brough, a Paisley draper, bought or had built for themselves substantial houses once their businesses were established and they had the money to spare. Previously they had resided for many years in rented accommodation.[55] Altogether, there was a considerable growth in owner-occupation by the middle classes, with many houses built and paid for outright by the occupant or his relatives, or else a

K

mortgage was raised through the agency of the family solicitor. Thomas Binnie, for example, was a Glasgow builder and he advanced money to those of his workers who wanted to buy their own houses.[56] For these people a house was not so much an investment that had to bear a direct financial return as a reflection of their desire for greater comfort and status.

However, most housing was constructed not for owner-occupation but for letting at a rent that would produce an acceptable return for the investment made, and was thus an integral part of the capital market:

> Parties erecting detached houses for their own occupation do not consider the question of interest for their outlay, but those who speculate for letting purposes necessarily do; . . .

reported the *Aberdeen Free Press* in May 1876, and this was true for the whole period.[57] The construction or purchase of housing for let was financed through a diverse but intimate web of personal and institutional contact in which the local lawyer was normally of paramount importance.[58] The real upsurges in property construction came in the area of building houses for let, and this fluctuated considerably as it was dependent upon such internal variables as the costs of building materials, the wages of building workers, and the amount of unlet housing on the market, and also upon such external factors as the rate of interest, the existence of alternative investments, and the state of economic prosperity and confidence. Of all these factors a low rate of interest, combined with limited outlets for savings in secure investments, was the one that did most to promote a building boom, such as in 1872-6 or 1893-1903.[59]

The speculative builders, who were responsible for the construction of most of the rented property during these boom periods, had only limited capital of their own and relied heavily on borrowed funds for the finance they required to embark on the construction of extensive tenements and other property. It was only a few builders, such as Thomas Binnie in Glasgow, or James Steel in Edinburgh, who had the capital available to purchase land and construct property on it for their own account and then to retain some of the property for themselves for the income it produced.[60] Traditionally, the case was that '. . . builders finance their operations very largely by short period loans', according to the Scottish Land Enquiry Committee. It was general practice for a builder to erect a block of tenement houses with loans obtained from institutions such as banks or insurance companies, or from wealthy individuals, and secured by a mortgage or bond over the property. Additional working capital, apart from that possessed by the builder himself, could be obtained by selling the right to the feu-duty or annual ground rent, while extensive trade credit was also available, extending to four months in the case of timber suppliers.[61] In the Polmadie district of Glasgow by far the majority of tenements built between 1874 and 1903 were owned initially by builders, but they quickly sold them to others so that their own capital was released, short-term loans were repaid, and profits were realised. The ultimate purchasers were either small tradespeople from Glasgow itself, such as publicans, grocers, bakers, and butchers, or professional house factors who managed property on behalf of a network of investing clients.[62] Andrew Melrose, an

Edinburgh tea merchant, and James Scott, a Glasgow textile manufacturer, both diverted some of the profits of their trades into property in their respective cities.[63]

The loans obtained by these builders were not wholly local in origin, for the greatest need for housing, and thus finance, was in the Glasgow region, but it was in the rural areas of Scotland or in cities such as Edinburgh or Aberdeen that those people with savings, who were most willing to invest in property, existed. In Glasgow too many alternative openings existed for those with trade connections. The City of Aberdeen Land Association, for example, found in the mid 1870s that it was receiving a far greater volume of deposits from the Aberdeen public and legal fraternity than it could possibly use, because it paid a rate of interest a half per cent higher than the banks. Demand from local builders or owner-occupiers was insufficient to absorb more than a small proportion of the funds at their disposal. By October 1877, £255,484 was deposited with the Association, which had only been formed in March 1875.[64] However, the Association did receive numerous proposals from Glasgow builders seeking loans to finance the construction of tenements. After a searching enquiry, involving a deputation visiting Glasgow, they came to the conclusion that, if caution were exercised, there was '. . . no reason to desist from seeking securities in Glasgow'.

Not only were there abundant openings for capital in Glasgow property but the Glasgow borrowers paid 5-6.5 per cent on the sums they borrowed, compared with the 4.25-5 per cent of the Aberdeen borrowers, and the security was considered to be the same. The Aberdonians attributed this willingness of the Glaswegians to pay more money to the greater demand in Glasgow. By December 1876 over £90,000 had been lent out in the Glasgow region, and this was 80 per cent of the total deposits placed with the Association. Altogether, some £158,000 was channelled into loans on Glasgow property before it was decided to abandon the deposit side of the business.[65] A similar situation existed in Edinburgh, with much money from that city also being used to finance housing construction in Glasgow. The Edinburgh-based Property Investment Company of Scotland, for example, lent a total of £102,500 to nine different Glasgow clients, mainly builders, over the period June 1875 to October 1877.[66]

However, urban property, wherever located in Scotland, did not present either a continuously growing outlet for capital or one that guaranteed a reasonable return without considerable insecurity. The building cycle was not a smooth one and it was prone to over-construction, as it was determined at least as much as by the interests of investors as by those requiring rented accommodation:[67]

> The briskness of the building trade in the towns is by many attributed to the fact that there is a great difficulty in investing money at a fair rate of interest, . . .

reported the *Aberdeen Free Press* in 1894, for instance.[68] Consequently, there were times when house property was considered to be 'a drug in the market', as in the years 1881-3.[69]

At these times it became difficult to dispose of property. These occasions happened periodically, as in the late 1870s when the City of Glasgow Bank stopped payment, confidence disappeared, and credit became tight. In such a situation Glasgow builders could not obtain the funds necessary to continue operations, and two-thirds of them were bankrupted. This brought down some of the creditors who had been financing these builders, as they were left with a mass of empty and often unfinished property which they could not easily sell, but they were themselves committed to repay deposits and loans. The Western Heritable Property Company, which had been formed in 1877, was, by 1882, '. . . hopelessly insolvent, and can no longer carry on its business'.[70] The North British Property Investment Company, which was formed in Edinburgh in 1872, had a typical tale of woe to tell that applied to all large investors in property for let, whether private or institutional:

> . . . owing to overbuilding of the class of property on which the company had given advances, followed by a protracted period of depression and glut in the property market, many of the company's borrowers became insolvent — and the company sustained considerable losses.

This company never did recover.[71]

Not only were property sales and prices depressed at these times, but it also became difficult to obtain a remunerative income from property. As a result of over-building there was often a temporary shortage of suitable tenants, and so the property remained unlet, producing no income, or rents were lowered, producing a reduced income and the problems of poor tenants who found it difficult to pay the rent regularly. In Glasgow the proportion of housing unlet rose from a mere 2.5 per cent in 1873 to a peak of 11.2 per cent in 1880, and then fell gradually, reaching 2.3 per cent in 1902.[72] At the same time it was expensive to buy and sell property, as the legal costs could be quite considerable, especially on the smaller property.[73]

For many small investors direct investment in property was not an attractive home for their savings due to the substantial initial investment, the heavy transfer costs, and the hazards that the renting of property involved, while the rate of return was low, declining steadily from 4 per cent per annum in the 1860s to only 3.25 per cent per annum in the 1890s.[74] In 1891 potential house purchasers were warned that they should

> . . . bear in mind that in calculating the interest you will receive on the money spent in buying it, you must deduct from the gross rent you expect to receive, not only the cost of repairs, the land-tax, the insurance against fire, but the money which would fail you if the House remained unlet for a time. If you employ a person to collect the rent, a certain amount of commission will be required by him, and will be the cause of a further deduction.[75]

Mortgages and feu-duties were regarded as safer and more desirable investments, but their availability was, of course, a direct function of house building itself, and if that was limited, so were the investment opportunities in that direction.[76] Consequently, property investment was not always available as an outlet for savings, while its yield and security were not always such as to make it immediately desirable to all, especially the small investor. As other avenues for investment continued to open up in the 1850-1914 period, property lost some of the monopoly it had once had of the funds of the cautious investor.[77]

There were a growing number and variety of joint-stock companies waiting to attract the investor's attention, and stocks and shares became more and more attractive to the investor.[78] By mid-century a fairly sophisticated market in second-hand securities was in existence, giving the investor confidence that he could realise an investment in the shares of a joint-stock company both quickly and at low cost. At the same time, stocks and shares could be, increasingly, combined in an almost infinite variety of quantity, rate and return, and degree of risk to suit the requirements of almost any investor. Property could certainly not match that, for only deposits in banks had a similar flexibility and liquidity. Consequently, stocks and shares came to occupy a far more important proportion of Scottish wealth-holding in the second half of the nineteenth century than they had ever done before, with innumerable people holding most — or a significant part — of their assets in the form of transferable securities. Even the Bairds, with their massive land purchases, placed a greater proportion of their accumulating wealth in stocks and shares. Throughout Scotland investors increasingly turned to the stocks and shares of joint-stock enterprise as a convenient and remunerative home for any significant amount of savings they accumulated.[79]

Table 4
Estimated Capital and Annual Income in Scotland, 1885 and 1910

Sector	Distribution of Capital		Distribution of Income	
	1885	1910	1885	1910
Total	£792m	£1,062m	£44m	£82m
Land	26%	14%	17%	7%
Housing	23	29	28	25
Farming & Fishing	8	*	18	2
Mining & Quarrying	1	1	2	3
Railways & Canals	14	13	10	7
Gas & Water	2	2	1	1
Public Companies	10	29	10	27
Trade & Professions	7	*	9	6
Misc. Profits & Incomes	1	*	2	11
British Funds	4	*	3	3
Foreign Investment	1	12	1	13

* The capital element of these sectors is distributed amongst the others.

Source:
1885: R. Giffen, *The Growth of Capital* (London 1889) p. 164.
1910: E. Crammond, 'The Economic Position of Scotland and her Financial Relations with England and Ireland' *J.R.S.S.* 75 (1913) pp. 168-9.

NOTES

1. T. J. Byres, The Scottish Economy during the 'Great Depression', 1873-1896 (B.Litt. Glasgow 1963) pp. 11-20, 367, 421-3; J. Butt, *Industrial Archaeology of Scotland* (Newton Abbot 1967) p. 23; J. Mackinnon, *The Social and Industrial History of Scotland* (Lon. 1921) p. 103; J. Napier, *Life of Robert Napier* (Edin. 1904) pp. 241-2; *Souvenir Handbook of Glasgow* (Glasgow 1904) pp. 10-11; A. McLean (ed.), *Local Industries of Glasgow and the West of Scotland* (Glasgow 1901) pp. 35-91; C. A. Whatley, The Process of Industrialisation in Ayrshire, c. 1707-1871 (Ph.D. Strathclyde 1975) p. 26; B. Lenman *An Economic History of Modern Scotland, 1660-1976* (Lon. 1977) pp. 173, 181; I. F. Gibson, 'The Establishment of the Scottish Steel Industry' *S.J.P.E. 5 (1958) pp. 36-7; I. F. Gibson, The Economic*

History of the Scottish Iron and Steel Industry (Ph.D. London 1955) p. 232; M. L. Simpson, 'Steel Works: A Twenty-One Years' Review' J.W.S.I. & S.I. 21 (1913-14) p. 56.

2. J. A. Hassan, The Development of the Coal Industry in Mid and West Lothian, 1815-1873 (Ph.D. Strathclyde 1976) pp. 97, 102, 120; Byres, op. cit., pp. 29, 427-433, 438-441; Butt, op. cit., pp. 24, 90; Whatley, op. cit., pp. 61-3; Lenman, op. cit., p. 173.

3. I. Donnachie, *A History of the Brewing Industry in Scotland* (Edin. 1979) pp. 147, 153; R. B. Weir, The Distilling Industry in Scotland in the Nineteenth and early Twentieth Centuries (Ph.D. Edin. 1974) pp. 480, 500.

4. P. D. Holcombe, Scottish Investment in Canada, 1870-1914 (M.Litt. Strathclyde 1975) p. 149; J. Shields, *Clyde Built* (Glasgow 1949) p. 19.

5. E. H. Whetham, 'Prices and Production in Scottish Farming, 1850-70' *S.J.P.E.* 9 (1962) p. 238; J. H. Smith, 'The Cattle Trade of Aberdeenshire in the Nineteenth Century' *A.H.R.* 3 (1955); M. Gray, *The Fishing Industries of Scotland, 1790-1914* (Abdn. 1978) pp. 59, 63, 89, 170-2; Whatley, op. cit., p. 34.

6. *Commercial Enterprise and Social Progress, or Gleanings in London, Sheffield, Glasgow, and Dublin* (Lon. 1858) p. 119.

7. Gray, op. cit., pp. 182-3; Gibson (1955), op. cit., pp. 249, 311; Weir, op. cit., p. 295; Byres, op. cit., pp. 12, 34-6, 51-7, 131-5, 610-628; McLean, op. cit., pp. 11, 17, 144.

8. Simpson, op. cit., p. 55.

9. Byres, op. cit., p. 922; Simpson, op. cit., p. 53; R. D. Corrins, William Baird & Co.: Coal & Iron Masters, 1830-1914 (Ph.D. Strathclyde 1974) p. 53; Hassan, op. cit., p. 176; D. Pollock, *Modern Shipbuilding and the Men engaged in it* (Lon. 1884) pp. 159-161.

10. Lenman, op. cit., p. 192; R. Giffen, *The Growth of Capital* (Lon. 1889) p. 164; E. Crammond, 'The Economic Position of Scotland and her Financial Relations with England and Ireland' *J.R.S.S.* 75 (1913) pp. 168-9.

11. M. G. Mulhall, *Fifty Years of National Progress, 1837-1887* (Lon. 1887) p. 113.

12. L. Soltow, 'Long-run changes in British Income Inequality' *Ec.H.R.21* (1968) p. 29; *Econ.* 19 July 1856; M. G. Mulhall, *Industries and Wealth of Nations* (Lon. 1896) pp. 100-2.

13. A. W. Kerr, *Scottish Banking during the period of Published Accounts, 1865-1896* (Lon. 1898) p. 6; A. W. Kerr, *History of Banking* (Lon. 1918) p. 273.

14. J. A. Wenley, 'On the History and Development of Banking in Scotland' *J.I.B.* 3 (1882) p. 146.

15. S. G. Checkland, *Scottish Banking: A History, 1695-1973* (Glasgow 1975) pp. 426, 744; R. H. I. Palgrave, *Notes on Banking* (Lon. 1873) pp. 15, 17; Wenley, op. cit., p. 140; Byres, op. cit., p. 257.

16. *Memoirs and Portraits of One Hundred Glasgow Men* (Glasgow 1886) XI.

17. G. Paish, 'Our New Investments in 1908' *Statist* 2 January 1909.

18. Crammond, loc. cit; Donnachie, op. cit., p. 147.

19. Corrins, op. cit., p. 53; Hassan, op. cit., p. 176.

20. J. MacDonald, 'On the Agriculture of the Counties of Forfar and Kincardine' *T.H. & A.S.* (1881) p. 132.

21. Gray, op. cit., pp. 95, 100, 178; D. I. A. Steel, The Linen Industry of Fife in the later Eighteenth and Nineteenth Centuries (Ph.D. St. Andrews 1975) pp. 239, 360; Hassan, op. cit., pp. 178-9; Donnachie, op. cit., p. 160; Weir, op. cit., pp. 426, 532-3; R. Perren, *John Fleming & Co., 1877-1977* (Abdn. 1978) pp. 5, 14, 18; A. M. Dunnett, *The Donaldson Line: A Century of Shipping, 1854-1954* (Glasgow 1960) pp. 5-7, 13-17; Gibson (1955) op. cit., p. 461; G. Gulvin, *The Tweedmakers: A History of the Scottish Fancy Woollen Industry, 1600-1914* (Newton Abbot 1973) p. 128; L. Weatherill, *One Hundred Years of Papermaking: An Illustrated History of the Guardbridge Paper Company Ltd., 1873-1973* (Guardbridge, Fife 1974) pp. 66-7; Gibson (1958), op. cit., p. 26.

22. Hassan, op. cit., p. 177; Donnachie, op. cit., pp. 147, 162.

23. Weir, op. cit., pp. 472-3 (Evidence of James Greenlees).

24. Gibson, op. cit., pp. 363-369.

25. Gray, op. cit., p. 178.

26. Steel, op. cit., p. 239; Hassan, op. cit., pp. 178-9.

27. Steel, op. cit., p. 382; Byres, op. cit., p. 51.

28. *Memoirs*, op. cit., p. 279.

29. Dunnett, op. cit., pp. 5-7, 13-17; J. L. Carvel, *Stephen of Linthouse* (Glasgow 1950) p. 75; Pollock, op. cit., p. 30; J. Smith, *Rise and Progress of the City Line* (Glasgow 1908) p. 202; G. R. Taylor, *Thomas Dunlop & Sons: Shipowners, 1851-1951* (Glasgow 1951) p. 33; J. Stephen to T. Dunlop, 21 December 1887; J. Neil to T. Dunlop, 26 December 1884.

30. J. Keith, *Fifty Years of Farming* (Lon. 1954) p. 21; Byres, op. cit., p. 92; Gulvin, op. cit., p. 129; B. Lenman & K. Donaldson, 'Partners' Incomes, Investment and Diversification in the Scottish Linen Area, 1850-1921' *B.H.* 13 (1971) p. 11; R.H. Campbell, *Carron Company* (Edin. 1961) p. 263; Weir, op. cit., p. 426, 434, 463-5.

31. Giffen, loc. cit.; Crammond, loc. cit.

32. Hassan, op. cit., pp. 141-3.

33. J. Clapham, The Bank of England: A History (Cam. 1944) II pp. 222-3; P. L. Cottrell, Investment Banking in England, 1856-1882 (Ph.D. Hull 1974) pp. 122, 577, 579; *A.H.* 14 August 1875; *A.F.P.* 24 May 1876, 2 October 1876, 7 February 1881, 15 February 1881, 27 December 1889 et seq.

34. *A.F.P.* 1 May 1876.

35. C. P. Kindleberger, *Manias, Panics and Crashes: A History of Financial Crises* (Lon. 1978) p. 217; G. Clare, *A Money Market Primer and Key to the Exchanges* (Lon. 1900) p. 136.

36. Wenley, op. cit., p. 149; W. Bartlett & H. Chapman, *A Handy-Book for Investors* (Lon. 1869) pp. 1-5.

37. *A.H.* 27 July 1861; *A.F.P.* 21 July 1879; F. M. L. Thompson, 'The Land Market in the Nineteenth Century' *O.E.P.* 9 (1957) p. 303.

38. Corrins, op. cit., pp. 282-3; *Memoirs*, op. cit., pp. 16-20, 263-4; W. J. Reader, *The Weir Group: A Centenary History* (Lon. 1971) p. 25.

39. Lenman, op. cit., p. 197; Smith, op. cit., p. 118; Keith, op. cit., p. 21; J. Cruickshank, 'Changes in the Agricultural Industry of Aberdeenshire in the Last Fifty Years' *T.A.P.S.* (1935) p. 1; *A.F.P.* 23 September 1880.

40. Holcombe, op. cit., p. 41; Kerr (1898), op. cit., p. 165; J. Nicol, *Vital Social, and Economic Statistics of the City of Glasgow, 1885-1891* (Glasgow 1891) p. 369; G. A. Jamieson, 'On some of the Causes and Effects of the Fall in the Rate of Interest' *A.M.* 1 (1897) pp. 22-3; Byres, op. cit., p. 231; P. L. Payne, 'The Savings Bank of Glasgow, 1836-1914' in P. L. Payne (ed.) *Studies in Scottish Business History* (London 1967) p. 168.

41. Jamieson, op. cit., pp. 8, 22-3; *A.F.P.* 8 January 1877, 19 December 1895; Mulhall, op. cit., pp. 71, 75; Holcombe, op. cit., p. 147; M. S. Cotterill, The Scottish Gas Industry up to 1914 (Ph.D. Strathclyde 1976) pp. 835, 841, 843.

42. North of Scotland Bank: Annual Report (Abdn. 1866).

43. Kerr (1898), op. cit., p. 16; Byres, op. cit., pp. 256-7.

44. J. S. Fleming, 'On the Theory and Practice of Banking in Scotland' *J.I.B.* 4 (1883) p. 149; *S.B. & I.M.* December 1885; *A.H.* 29 March 1862; *A.F.P.* 13 October 1890; J. D. Bailey, 'Australian Borrowing in Scotland in the Nineteenth Century' *Ec.H.R.* 12 (1959-60).

45. *S.B. & I.M.* 1 February 1879.

46. *S.F.* October 1883; *S.B. & I.M.* December 1885; *A.F.P.* 13 October 1890.

47. *A.H.* 29 March 1862; *A.F.P.* 28 December 1894; Holcombe, op. cit., p. 127; S. B. Saul, 'House Building in England, 1890-1914' *Ec.H.R.* 15 (1962-3) p. 133.

48. Giffen, loc. cit.; Crammond, loc. cit.

49. R. G. Rodger, Scottish Urban Housebuilding, 1870-1914 (Ph.D. Edin. 1975) pp.131-4, 496; R. G. Rodger, 'Speculative Builders and the Structure of the Scottish Building Industry, 1860-1914' *B.H.* 21 (1979) p. 229; Byres, op.cit., p. 537.

50. Rodger (1975) op. cit., pp. 477-8; W. Fraser, 'Fluctuations of the Building Trade, and Glasgow's House Accommodation' *P.R.P.S.G.* 39 (1907-8) pp. 22, 30-1; H. W. Bull, Working-Class Housing in Glasgow, 1862-1902 (M.Litt. Strathclyde 1973) p. 13.

51. R. N. Millman, *The Making of the Scottish Landscape* (Lon. 1975) p. 194; H. W. Bull, op. cit., p. 9; Fraser, op. cit., p. 23; I. H. Adams, *The Making of Urban Scotland* (Lon. 1978) p. 157.

52. Bull, op. cit., p. 11; J. McKee, Glasgow Working Class Housing between the Wars, 1919-1939 (M.Litt. Strathclyde 1977) p. 2.

53. Lenman, op. cit., p. 202; Bull, op. cit., pp. 39, 81; Fraser, op. cit., p. 39; *Socttish Land: The Report of the Scottish Land Enquiry Committee* (Lon. 1914) xxxiii, p. 283; Adams, op. cit., p. 93.

54. A. Mitchell, *Political and Social Movements in Dalkeith, 1831-1882* (Dalkeith 1882) p. 227.

55. Weir, op. cit., p. 492; J. B. Sturrock, *Peter Brough: A Paisley Philanthropist* (Paisley 1890) p. 171.

56. Adams, op. cit., pp. 188, 193-4; Rodger (1975), op. cit., pp. 430-1, 435; Rodger (1979), op. cit., pp. 233, 235; Mitchell, op. cit., pp. 23, 100; E. J. Cleary, *The Building Society Movement* (Lon. 1965) p. 46; T. Binnie, *Memoir of Thomas Binnie, Builder in Glasgow, 1792-1867* (Glasgow 1882) p. 91.

57. *A.F.P.* 26 May 1876; Saul, op. cit., pp. 129, 132-3, 134; *The Land: The Report of the Land Enquiry Committee* (Lon. 1914) II, pp. 82-5.

58. Rodger (1975), op. cit., p. 438; Rodger (1979), op. cit., p. 235; Holcombe, op. cit., p. 42.

59. Bull, op. cit., pp. 10, 67; Fraser, op. cit., p. 39; *Scottish Land*, op. cit., pp. 382, 388-9; Rodger (1975), op. cit., pp. 173, 361, 389, 445-6; Rodger (1979), op. cit., pp. 229, 241.

60. Rodger (1975), op. cit., pp. 417-8; Rodger (1979), op. cit., p. 236; Binnie, op. cit., p. 104; Memoirs, op. cit., p. 34.

61. M. A. Whitehead, The Western Bank and the Crisis of 1857 (M.Litt. Strathclyde 1978) p. 29; Adams, op. cit., pp. 166-7; Bull, op. cit., p. 60; Fraser, op. cit., p. 37; Perren, op. cit., pp. 12, 15; *Scottish Land*, op. cit., p. 388; Rodger (1975), op. cit., pp. 432, 437-8, 441; Rodger (1979), op. cit., pp. 226, 234-6; Holcombe, op. cit., p. 164.

62. McKee, op. cit., pp. 72-7.

63. H. & L. H. Mui, *William Melrose in China, 1845-1855* (Edin. 1973) lxxii; *Memoirs*, op. cit., p. 279.

64. City of Aberdeen Land Association: Minutes of Directors' Meeting 4 July 1876, 2 October 1877; Annual Reports 1876-1881.

65. City of Aberdeen Land Association: Report to the Directors by the Treasurers relative to the Deposit Branch of their Business, December 1876; Report by the Committee of Directors relative to Loans on house property in Glasgow, 1877; Report by A. Anderson on Glasgow Loans, 10 June 1880; Edmonds & Macqueen to A. Anderson, 11 June 1880; Anderson to Edmonds & Macqueen, 16 June 1880; Memo by A. Anderson 16 July 1880; Annual Report, 1881.

66. Property Investment Company of Scotland: Ledger, 1875-7.

67. Saul, op. cit., p. 133; E. W. Cooney, 'Long Waves in building in the British Economy of the Nineteenth Century' *Ec.H.R.* 13 (1960-1) p. 267.

68. *A.F.P.* 28 December 1894.

69. *A.F.P.* 28 January 1882; *S.B. & I.M.* May 1881, January 1883.

70. Whitehead, op. cit., p. 23; Memoirs, op. cit., pp. 41-2; Rodger (1975), op. cit., pp. 401, 439; Rodger (1979), op. cit., pp. 226, 236; Western Heritable Property Company Ltd.: Petition by City of Aberdeen Land Association, 10 July 1882.

71. North British Property Investment Co.: Petition to Lords of Council & Session 12 April 1905; cf. *Memoirs*, op. cit., p. 42.

72. Fraser, op. cit., pp. 24-7; Byres, op. cit., pp. 481, 490; J. Mann, 'Better Houses for the Poor — Will they pay?' *P.R.P.S.G.* 30 (1898-9) pp. 84-5; Adams, op. cit., p. 168; McKee, op. cit., p. 2.

73. *Scottish Land*, op. cit., pp. 344-5; Rodger (1975), op. cit., p. 206.

74. Jamieson, op. cit., pp. 22-3; Fraser, op. cit., p. 36; *A Guide to the Unprotected in every-day matters relating to Property and Income* (Lon. 1891) pp. 105-6; *S.P.G.* 4 March 1892, 18 March 1892.

75. *Guide*, op. cit., p. 97.

76. *S.R.G.* 2 February 1850; *E.P.R.* 24 May 1879; *Guide*, op. cit., p. 90.

77. *Scottish Land*, op. cit., pp. 388-9.

78. R. L. Nash, *A Short Inquiry into the Profitable Nature of our Investments* (Lon. 1881) p. 6; W. Bagehot, *Lombard Street* (Lon. 1896) pp. 138-9.

79. Corrins, op. cit., pp. 85-6, 275-280; Appendix A., Steel, op. cit., pp. 381-2; Weir, op. cit., p. 492; Mui, op. cit., p. lxxiv; Sturrock, op. cit., 234-254.

12

The Pervasion of Joint-Stock, 1850-1900

IN the second half of the nineteenth century the number and capital of Scottish joint-stock companies expanded steadily and they came to occupy an important position in ever more varied areas of the economy. This pervasion of joint-stock enterprise was clear to contemporaries in the 1870s and 1880s, such as this writer in *Blackwood's Magazine* in 1885:

> Every succeeding year exhibits an increase in the proportion of the national wealth that has passed out of personal control into the control of joint-stock companies . . . the great industries of the country are passing rapidly out of private hands into the maelstrom of joint-stock management . . . One by one the merchant princes of a generation ago are either retiring from the field, or are converting themselves into companies.[1]

By 1900 there were estimated to be 2,593 Scottish joint-stock companies in operation, with a paid-up share capital of £121.0m, compared with 728 companies with £36.4m as recently as 1884.[2] However, most of these joint-stock companies were small concerns with a minimal number of closely connected shareholders, and were no different from the family firms or partnerships of the past. They made no appeal to the capital market and were financed by the traditional informal means, aided by bank and trade credit, while their shares were only nominally transferable. Although their form was that of a joint-stock company, they remained essentially private firms, and as such continued to dominate the Scottish economy. Even in Aberdeen, which by 1904 was 'honeycombed with limited liability companies', the proportion of industrial capital owned and directed by private enterprise was far greater than that possessed by joint-stock companies.[3]

Nevertheless, the number and importance of public joint-stock companies continued to expand in Scotland. In 1840 there were 106 such concerns, but by 1900 the figure had risen to 520. The growth of total paid-up capital (shares, debentures, etc.) was even more rapid, with an increase from £18.6m in 1840 to £120.9m in 1880, and then to £408.1m in 1900. There was thus an increase of 390 per cent in numbers and 2,094 per cent in paid-up capital in the Scottish joint-stock enterprise, known in the market, over the period 1840-1900. The composition of this enterprise also changed considerably in the second half of the century. Banking and insurance were eclipsed by railways in terms of paid-up capital, while areas such as manufacturing industry, mining, property and retail distribution all reached positions of importance, if only temporarily.[4]

It was undoubtedly railways which dominated Scottish joint-stock enterprise in the second half of the nineteenth century, with the capital they raised growing from a total of £26.6m in 1850 to £166.1m in 1900, while the length of the network expanded by 3,326 miles.[5] However, it was to be many years before railways were generally regarded as safe and remunerative investments after the over-indulgence of the 'Railway Mania' and the vast capitalisation and low or non-existent profits that followed it.[6] 'At present, no scheme, however wise, proper and necessary, will receive the slightest support,' reported the *Aberdeen Herald* in 1850, and this was true throughout Scotland, despite an availability of capital and a growing confidence amongst investors.[7] Established railway companies found it almost impossible to raise fresh capital, while attempts to revive postponed projects were to no avail.[8] It was only gradually, in the 1850's, that railways came back into public favour, and, really, they had to await the period of easy money ushered in by the Californian and Australian gold discoveries before investors again purchased railway securities in large numbers.[9] It was with a cry of relief that Robert Allan announced in November 1852 that:

> Railways have got the wind into them at last! Quotations, in almost every instance, exhibited marked and satisfactory improvements on those of the preceding month.[10]

Not only did existing railway companies find increasing favour among investors, but new schemes were put forward and taken up by the public.

The mania had left a legacy of numerous railway projects of either local importance, or links in the national network, that had been abandoned before any work had commenced. These proposed lines had not been forgotten by their promoters, but merely withheld until the prospects of raising the required capital improved, as they had by the 1850s. Such was certainly the case with the railway lines between Perth and Inverness, Aberdeen and Inverness, or Dumfries and Castle Douglas.[11] However, railways never recovered the enthusiasm of the 'Railway Mania', being regarded, at best, as reasonably secure investments capable of producing a low but acceptable return. 'The days are gone when large profits were expected from investments in railroads; . . .' wrote one writer in 1854.[12] This remained true in the 1860s, with any rise in interest rates, or the appearance of alternative investments, quickly reducing the railway companies' ability to raise the required finance.[13]

More than ever the newly projected railways had to rely upon the financial support of those who could expect to benefit from the actual construction of the line, or from the improved transportation provided. Railway contractors, locomotive builders and iron manufacturers, for example, assisted in providing or obtaining the capital necessary to build many lines in the 1850s and 1860s, as it was a means of keeping themselves in business when orders were scarce. Similarly, local support became more important than ever, as it was only those who foresaw advantage from the line who would accept the low returns and a real element of risk. Landowners were asked to contribute to railway development because it

> . . . would add greatly to the value of their estates, even if they received little or no return from the tolls or profits,

according to Notman, trying to canvas support for the Deeside Railway in 1850.

The Duke of Sutherland, for example, spent £226,300 on building railway lines through his estates during the second half of the century.[14]

In the 1850s, 697 miles of new railway line were built in Scotland, mostly by new companies, or those that had existed in name only since the collapse of the mania. However, by the mid 1860s, after a series of amalgamations and acquisitions, five large Scottish railway companies emerged, and between them they controlled 98 per cent of the country's railway system. The Great North of Scotland Railway, for example, took over 11 local railway concerns, having already provided, in aggregate, 40 per cent of their capital. All had been no more than branches or extensions of its Aberdeen – Inverness trunk line.[15] Although separate railway companies continued to be formed, most were closely linked to one or other of the existing combines and were heavily dependent upon them for finance. Both the Glasgow Central Railway, and the Lanarkshire and Dumbartonshire Railway were part of the Caledonian Railway Company's network. Similarly, both the Forth Bridge Railway Company and the West Highland Railway were integral parts of the North British Railway's network, and were heavily backed by that concern.[16]

After the late 1860s there was little independent promotion of new railways in Scotland, and the extension of mileage was largely the work of established companies. Consequently, new railway construction became much more a product of company policy than an attractive investment in its own right. The West Highland Railway, for example, was considered to have very poor prospects when it was promoted in 1889, but the North British Railway considered it a worthwhile venture as it benefited the company's existing network.[17] Nevertheless, interest rates and the availability of capital remained the major determining factors in the capital expenditure planning of established railways and the promotion of new concerns. The Forth Bridge scheme was put forward first in 1865, and then in 1873, but on both occasions it failed to obtain sufficient finance. Similarly, during the 1880s, there was a rash of suburban railway schemes, such as the Dundee Suburban Railway and the Edinburgh, Stockbridge and Leith Railway, but almost all remained dreams, as investors were not willing to provide the necessary funds. In the 1890s the reverse was true for, with interest rates low and alternative investments temporarily unattractive, there was a minor boom in the promotion of railway companies to serve remote rural areas, such as in the Highlands, or to improve urban services, such as in Glasgow.[18]

The growth of the Scottish economy gradually justified the initial heavy over-capitalisation of the railway system, while management slowly learned how to organise the giant enterprises under their control, so as to produce regular and reasonably satisfactory returns. At the same time, the re-organisation in the 1860s, and the subsequent extension of the respective networks, created five major companies whose prosperity was widely based upon the considerable and varied traffic generated both in the economy as a whole and, more especially, in the particular regions and routes that they served. Consequently, railway stocks and shares became desirable investments owing to the security that they offered and the regular dividends which they paid.[19] The changed attitude of investors was quite clear by the mid 1870s, as in this comment in the *Aberdeen Herald* of September 1875:

> Railway Stock in Scotland is looking up. The Great North besides paying all dividends on the guaranteed and preference stocks, is paying a dividend at the rate of 3 per cent on the ordinary stock . . . The ordinary shareholders of the North British who, like the ordinary shareholders of the Great North, had long been accustomed to go without a dividend are now getting 4 per cent, and the Caledonian, which was paying but 2 per cent a year ago, is this year paying 6.25 per cent.[20]

The securities of Scottish railways were increasingly popular with investors who wanted a safe and liquid outlet for their funds. A company such as the Glasgow-based Tharsis Sulphur and Copper Company, for instance, possessed considerable surplus and reserve funds, which they mostly placed in the securities of the Caledonian Railway.[21]

The increasing size and density of population within the cities and towns of Scotland presented opportunities for some form of mass transit system and, in the 1870s, there was a rash of joint-stock tramway company promotions, with concerns formed in Glasgow in 1872, Edinburgh in 1874, and Dundee and Aberdeen in 1877. Companies were also formed in smaller towns like Greenock and Stirling. These tramways were not entirely novel creations, as a number were based upon privately owned onmibus companies which were already in operation. Some of the omnibus companies themselves were converted into joint-stock concerns. In Glasgow the volume of traffic was such that an underground railway, the Glasgow District subway, was promoted in 1887, although construction was not begun until 1891, and it remained uncompleted until 1898. Initially, many investors had grave misgivings about these tramway ventures and held back from providing the necessary capital but, as the tram became an essential feature of urban life, this reluctance on the part of the investor disappeared. By 1900, for example, the expenditure by passengers on transport in Glasgow had reached £33,000 per week, and of this 36 per cent was going to the tramways as opposed to 42 per cent on the railways and subway.[22] Therefore, a new dimension was added to rail transportation in the shape of tramway companies, and here again the joint-stock form was dominant.

Shipping had long been a field in which the joint-stock enterprise had played an important role, due to the risks involved and the capital required. However, the joint-stock company had been largely confined to coastal shipping operations providing a regular service on specific routes, and few new concerns in this line were promoted in the second half of the century. One exception was the Aberdeen and Glasgow Steam Shipping Company, which was established in 1881 with a paid-up capital of only £18,000 and had as its aim the breaking of the Caledonian Railway's monopoly of the transportation of goods between those two cities.[23] Generally, the established coastal navigation companies provided all the service that was required, expanding their own capital to meet the needs of new routes or ships. The London and Edinburgh Shipping Company, for example, had been established as early as 1809, and its paid-up capital rose from £70,000 in 1870 to £139,730 in 1900.[24]

Aside from the regular coastal lines, most other shipping ventures were traditionally financed by an informed web marshalled by a shipbroker or by families and partnerships. Even concerns such as the European and Columbian Steam Navigation Co. of 1850, with a capital of £400,000, the Albion Shipping Co. of 1864, with a capital of £138,000, or the British and Burmese Steam Navigation Co. of 1874, with a capital of £135,400, were still private operations whose capital was provided by a few friends and associates.[25] It was common practice for those involved in shipping finance to take a stake in specific vessels, leaving the employment of the ship and the voyages it undertook to a firm skilled in maritime management. These ships might be placed throughout the world, carrying any goods available, or utilised on a set route with a specific cargo. Whatever the case, there was a great element of risk involved in the participation in the finance of a single ship or a single route. Participation in maritime finance was largely confined to those investors with a knowledge of, connection with, or interest in shipping, and though there were substantial numbers in these categories, the investing public at large were little involved, and the shares in individual vessels were not easily marketable.

It became increasingly clear that finance would be more readily obtained if the individual ships were combined into a single fleet, with the income and capital of each investor resting upon their total performance rather than upon one ship and upon one voyage. Dividends would, thus, be more secure and less liable to fluctuation, and so more attractive to investors in general, rather than just to those with some involvement in shipping.[26] Nevertheless, it was not until the early 1880s that such a changeover began to take place, with a rash of conversions at that time. In Dundee, five new shipowning companies appeared in 1881-2. These included the Dundee Loch Line Steam Shipping Co., where shares to the value of £90,000 were issued to the existing owners of the vessels and £30,000 was obtained from the public.[27]

During the 1890s the arrangements of other shipbroking firms were formalised in the form of a joint-stock company, with public support being attracted. Established private shipping concerns were also converted into joint-stock enterprises. The single ship venture did not disappear, but also acquired a joint-stock shape. Companies were promoted to own and operate only one vessel. Two such companies were the Glasgow Steamship Co. of 1881, with a paid-up capital of £24,000, and the 'Klyde' Steamship Co. of 1882, with a paid-up capital of £25,000. For those willing to accept considerable risk for a commensurate but fortuitous chance of gain, single ship ventures remained attractive.[28]

The timing of these conversions and promotions owed far more to the willingness of the investing public to absorb the issues of shipping companies than to conditions within the shipping industry. An attempt was made to convert the Allan Line Steamship Company into a joint-stock concern in 1872 but was unsuccessful. In the mid 1890s the transition was easily made, despite the company's being capitalised at £1m and the shipping industry being generally depressed.[29] Similarly, the firm of Donaldson Brothers, Shipbrokers, did not re-organise the ships it handled into an integrated shipping company, the Donaldson

Line, until 1913.[30] The firm had continued to operate until then on the basis of each ship having a unique set of owners and profits being paid out at the end of each voyage. It may have been useful to adopt a more rational and comprehensive system of shipownership and management, but it was not a necessity, and numerous shipping companies and shipbrokers continued to operate without the benefit of re-organisation.[31]

The continuing growth of Scotland's urban population required the provision of such additional facilities as gas and water, which had traditionally been provided by joint-stock enterprise. Gas companies, for example, were formed in ever smaller towns, while those already established in the larger and more rapidly growing urban areas had to re-invest profits and raise extra capital in order to finance the improvement, expansion, and extension of their service. Between 1853 and 1903 the capital of the Glasgow and Aberdeen gas industries each rose by around 600 per cent. The industry's total capital was a mere £0.9m in 1853, but £5.3m in 1900.[32] However, new services were increasingly required by an urban population that was not only becoming more numerous, but also possessed more money and leisure than before, while the possibilities available to them were growing in variety.

Hotels, hydropathics, public halls, music halls, theatres, public baths, and steam laundries proliferated in and around Scottish towns and cities in the second half of the nineteenth century, and many were in the form of joint-stock companies. Peter Chalmers, for example, promoted and managed six companies each owning a single hotel located in one of Scotland's holiday centres, such as the Dreadnought Hotel in Callander, the Grand in St. Andrews, or the Royal in Portree.[33] There was even a rage for joint-stock steam laundries in the late 1870s and early 1880s, with all major Scottish cities coming to possess at least one.[34] Dundee was not to be omitted from this trend, according to the *Dundee Advertiser* in 1880:

> A few months ago a number of influential gentlemen in Dundee, becoming aware that steam laundries were established institutions all over England, and were being gradually introduced into Scotland, initiated a movement whereby the community of Dundee could participate in the advantages of such an institution. A limited liability company thereafter formed on the lines of companies already in existence . . .[35]

Developments in technology also manifested themselves in the larger cities, with joint-stock concerns being formed to exploit electricity generation and supply, such as the Clyde Valley Electric Power Co. and the Lothians Electric Power Co., or the provision of a telephone exchange and a local network. J. G. B. Lorrain founded the Scottish Telephonic Exchange Company in 1879 and, subsequently, aided in the establishment of other local concerns, including the Dundee and District Telephone Company.[36]

In Scottish cities joint-stock enterprise also invaded the field of property construction and ownership, attracted during the periods when the value of land and houses was rapidly increasing and large profits were being made by individuals buying, selling and letting property. The Scottish Equitable Property

Company claimed, in 1875, that the rental of house property in Edinburgh had been doubled during the previous ten years, while land values had risen even more, and similar claims were made for Aberdeen at that time.[37] However, the prosperity of these joint-stock property concerns was heavily dependent upon the state of the property market, and many collapsed in the depressed period of the late 1870s and early 1880s. The formation of new property companies ceased until the recovery, during the mid 1890s, of interest in property. Even then, these property ventures never recovered the enthusiasm among investors which they had possessed when they were first formed in the 1870s.[38]

The investors who financed these enlarged urban facilities were only partly motivated by the promised rate of return, as they expected to benefit in other ways, either individually or communally. According to the annual report of the Airdrie Public Hall Company in 1870:

> The Hall was got up more with a view to meet a great public want in the town than to yield a revenue to the shareholders . . .[39]

The same sentiment prevailed in many other concerns providing urban services. So, for instance, '. . . drama and not dividends was to be the care of the company', reported the *Dundee Year Book* in 1885, concerning the Dundee Theatre and Opera House.[40] In the case of public baths, the shareholders expected to benefit through improved public health, although they would be unlikely to use the facilities themselves. The shareholders of the Aberdeen Baths Company claimed in 1886 that '. . . we do not seek a profit in investing our money in this scheme . . .'[41] Some of the property companies also had as a prime consideration the provision of satisfactory accommodation for the working classes, rather than the realisation of good returns on secure investments.[42]

However, this mixture of philanthropic ends with the objects of the investor became less and less necessary as the municipalities themselves increasingly provided the services required by a town or city's population. They had traditionally provided functions such as police or sewage disposal, but from the 1850s onwards municipal authorities both acquired existing joint-stock companies in the fields of gas and water supply or transportation and extended their involvement into housing, although their commitment in that area was very limited. Glasgow corporation acquired the water companies in 1855, the gas companies in 1869, electricity generation in 1891, the tramway company in 1894, and the telephone system in 1900; Dundee took over gas in 1868, and water in 1869; Aberdeen purchased gas in 1871, and tramways in 1892; while Edinburgh waited until 1888 to take control of gas. Numerous other local authorities bought out the joint-stock concerns operating in these areas.[43] Altogether, in gas, in 1900, the paid-up capital of the municipal undertakings totalled £4.4m, compared with the mere £0.9m still controlled by joint-stock enterprise.[44] The local authorities spent heavily upon these new responsibilities, with Glasgow spending £4.5m on water works alone between 1855 and 1913.[45.] As a result, at least one-fifth of the total amount of municipal securities in existence by 1900 did not represent a novel creation but merely the substitution of the debentures, and annuities, of the local authority for the stocks and shares of joint-stock enterprise.[46] The remainder reflected the increased spending of councils upon education, sewage, harbour improvements, or urban renewal. Through the Glasgow Improvement Trust and the Clyde Navigation Trust, Glasgow Corporation spent large sums on the demolition of slum dwellings in central Glasgow and the building of a better class of property, and also upon dredging and maintaining an ocean-going channel from Glasgow to the sea. Over £5.7m alone was raised by the Navigation Trust between 1858 and 1900, for instance.[47] The growing position of the municipal authorities represented both a substitution of their control for that of local joint-stock concerns, and an extension of public influence into areas where either the private individual had been supreme, or where no service had been previously provided. While joint-stock enterprise had to accept a diminished, though more varied, role in the realm of urban services, the role of the capital market was enhanced, as the municipal authorities relied heavily upon publicly raised funds to finance their actions. Low interest rates and cheap capital could facilitate a programme of acquisition and expenditure, while high interest rates and capital shortage forced local government to bide their time and either halt, or delay, planned programmes.[48]

Banking and insurance had once been popular areas for new joint-stock enterprise, but there were only limited additions to the field after 1850, with the established concerns being dominant. Both in insurance and banking, size was an indication of security, and so the existing companies attracted the support of both policy holders and depositors, while new concerns found it difficult to become established. At the same time legislation had made it impossible for new banking companies to appear in the traditional areas of business. In fact, the number of banks declined. Both the Western Bank of Scotland and the City of Glasgow Bank collapsed, in 1857 and 1878 respectively, while others, especially those located in Dundee and Perth, were taken over by either Edinburgh or Glasgow banks in the 1850s and 1860s. The exchange banks hardly survived the collapse of the mania, and their function of lending on the security of shares was undertaken by the banks themselves. Altogether, the number of Scottish banks fell to only 10 in 1896, and their paid-up capital was a mere £9.3m, although their control of the business was greater than ever. The long-established Scottish banks met little opposition in their own field and needed little in the way of extra capital to finance their extended operations, as that grew gradually out of the business they conducted.[49]

It was only in the peripheral areas of banking and finance that any new and substantial joint-stock companies were formed. A number of loan companies appeared in the main Scottish towns and cities. These were essentially pawnbroking establishments lending on the security of small items. Their capital requirements were low, and that was easily obtained as they were popular with investors, since they paid high and regular dividends. In 1887 the Northern Loan Company of Aberdeen could have raised twice the capital of £15,000 for which they had asked.[50] During the 1860s and 1870s investment companies which lent on the security of land and property were popular, such as the Edinburgh-based Heritable Securities Investment Association, which had attracted £275,000 in shares, debentures and deposits by 1869.[51] However, the collapse of the property boom in the late 1870s meant not only a temporary end to the promotion of these companies, through the unfavourable circumstances, but also avoidance of them by investors for years afterwards, due to the great difficulties in which many of the concerns had found themselves when their borrowers defaulted and the property proved unsaleable.[52] In domestic finance nothing appeared to rival the banks, although the property investment companies made an attempt which ended in failure in the late 1870s.[53]

The same type of situation prevailed in insurance, for it was those companies established before 1850 that tended to dominate the traditional fire, life and marine areas of the industry. Existing companies expanded through mergers and by the appointment of agents and branches in new areas. The Northern Insurance Company of Aberdeen, for example, absorbed six other insurance companies between 1847 and 1866, including such substantial enterprises as the Western Fire and Life of Glasgow, and the Forfarshire and Perthshire of Dundee. At the same time the company not only enlarged its network of operations in Scotland but also extended them into England and abroad.[54]

In the relatively novel fields of insurance, new companies were formed and grew. The traditional fields were dominated by established concerns, although a few fire, life and marine concerns did appear, such as the Scottish Fire Insurance Co. in Edinburgh in 1864.[55] Numerous new insurance companies were promoted in the early 1880s, for example, to operate in the fields of accident, boiler and plate glass insurance. These were areas in which insurance was increasingly required, with the growing installation of high pressure boilers or plate glass windows, but they were not adequately covered by the policies issued by the existing companies. Government legislation, for instance, made accident insurance something of a necessity and thus opened up a completely new market for insurance, of which those forming new insurance companies were quick to take advantage. In Scotland, the Scottish Employers' Liability Assurance Company was the first in this recently opened field. According to the *Aberdeen Free Press* in 1890:

> The passing of the Employers' liability Act in 1881, having materially increased the liability of masters to their servants in the matter of compensation for injuries, suggested the idea that a company should be floated in Aberdeen whereby such risks might be insured. To this end a company was formed in August 1881, ... The success which has attended the Company's operations has induced similar companies to be floated, ...[56]

Changes in the market provided opportunities for new concerns such as the General Accident of Perth, but in most areas the established companies consolidated their positions in the second half of the century, leaving little scope for new entrants.

Few industrial and commercial concerns had taken the joint-stock form before 1850. Government legislation passed in 1856 and 1862 certainly facilitated the formation of joint-stock trading and manufacturing ventures in Scotland in the second half of the century, but there is no evidence of a causal link. It was not until the 1870s that the new laws were seriously resorted to, and even by the mid 1880s

L

the use to which they were put was limited.[57] The *Economist*, in 1855, had been of the opinion that '. . . the law as it at present exists appears scarcely to be an impediment to their formation', and expressed doubt in 1856, '. . . if encouragement be really given by this act to the formation of companies'.[58] Instead of drawing up partnership agreements, a growing number of entrepreneurs utilised the joint-stock legislation to form small private companies with little more than the minimum number of seven shareholders. Most accepted the limited liability that registration offered as a bonus rather than a major factor. Many companies had only partly paid shares, leaving their shareholders still liable for large sums in the case of bankruptcy. It was not until the City of Glasgow Bank collapse, in 1878, that the dangers of unlimited liability were made clear to the investing public at large, and even after that insurance companies with a substantial uncalled liability remained popular with investors. Out of a portfolio of investments totalling £273,962 in 1884, the Glasgow merchant, William Stirling, had a further liability amounting to £41,603 (15 per cent), largely incurred through his holdings in insurance, finance, trading and manufacturing companies.[59] The government had made it easy to form joint-stock companies and offered an inducement to register, with the limited liability provision, but it took other factors to stimulate the promotion of new concerns or the conversion of existing enterprises.

The scale of industry's capital requirements continued to grow in the second half of the century with the needs of technology and the market. In 1850 each brewery had a capital of £2,700, while in 1900 this figure had risen to £50,000. Capital expenditure of this kind necessitated, in most cases, the support of a greater number of people than ever before as individuals alone were not always available both to provide all the capital and accept all the risks involved. In the mid-nineteenth century, for example, there was a growing size of partnership operating in coal mining, which was becoming increasingly capital intensive, while heavy industry gradually outgrew the private means of finance available to it. All sectors of the Scottish economy witnessed the same development, with an increasing need for a high initial capital before operations could even begin, so as to generate further profits for re-investment.[60]

Nevertheless, few new industrial and commercial companies attempted to raise their initial capital directly from the general public, via an issue of shares. Most of the finance required was provided by those involved in originating and promoting the scheme, together with their immediate contacts. Many of the joint-stock coal companies relied upon the support of small groups of business associates, and numerous other joint-stock enterprises, in a variety of fields, did likewise, such as in brewing, distilling, paper making, shale oil, or even steel manufacture. The Steel Company of Scotland, for example, was formed in 1871 with a capital of £105,000 which was obtained from only 28 people.[61] In the case of the Bon Accord Distillery Company in 1876, for example:

> The preliminary arrangements were made very quietly . . . before any shares were offered in a semi-private way to a limited circle of gentlemen, no less than £18,000 of the capital (£30,000) had been subscribed by the originators of the scheme,

reported the *Aberdeen Free Press*. Similarly, the North British Distillery Co. of Edinburgh had obtained its entire capital of £75,000 in 1885 before the public were fully aware that such a concern was being promoted.[62]

However, there were three developments which gradually opened up industrial and commercial enterprise to the participation of the general investing public. Many of the joint-stock companies that had been formed, almost privately, came to seek additional capital. This they did by issuing shares or debentures, not only to existing holders but more widely. At the same time many of the original investors either sold all, or part of, their substantial holdings, to reduce their exposure to risk, or their securities were subdivided amongst relatives, or otherwise disposed of, on their deaths. By this process once 'private' joint-stock companies became 'public'. The North British Rubber Company was formed in 1856, with a paid-up capital of £50,000, provided by only 10 investors, most of whom were American. In 1880, the company's paid-up capital had risen to £195,000 and its shareholders to 98, the majority of whom were Scottish. Even more dramatic was the transformation of the Scottish Wagon Co., which had a paid-up capital of £14,160 provided by 14 people on its establishment in 1861, but a capital of £252,000 held by 773 people in 1900.[63] Similar transformations existed in other joint-stock companies, with many disappearing from the scene, while some became substantial concerns with a public following.

A few new joint-stock companies were formed which appealed directly to the public from the very beginning. By the late nineteenth century, for example, a growing number of joint-stock companies were started to purchase, and own, fishing trawlers and, by 1914, such concerns provided almost half the Aberdeen fleet. This was a fairly novel departure in Scottish fishing. Similarly, both Glasgow and Aberdeen attempted to establish a jute industry to rival that of Dundee. The vehicle used in both cases was a joint-stock company, with the Glasgow Jute Co. being formed in 1865, and the Aberdeen Jute Co. in 1873. Neither was a success. The Glasgow Company obtained £244,185 from 170 shareholders by 1870, but was wound up in 1877. The Aberdeen Company hoped to raise £200,000 but, despite strenuous efforts by the promoters, not even a third of that was obtained. By 1880, £64,253 had been paid up by 859 shareholders. As with the Glasgow concern, the Aberdeen venture met the entrenched opposition of the Dundee manufacturers in a difficult industry, and never became successfully established in the city. The capital was progressively written down and the shareholders gradually deserted the venture, so that the paid-up capital was a mere £21,249 in 1900, held by 589 shareholders.[64] Unfortunately the majority of the completely new joint-stock companies that did appeal for public support from their inception were not successes, having either to be wound up after the capital was exhausted or limping along paying small or non-existent dividends to those who had been impressed by the grandiose visions of profits. This was as true in an established field such as jute textiles as in a new departure such as the manufacture of electrical equipment. The shares of the British Electric Light and Power Company of Scotland were 15 times over-subscribed by the public in 1882, but the company was in liquidation within a few years.[65]

Indubitably, the major component of industrial and commercial joint-stock enterprise was the conversion of established private firms into public joint-stock companies. Previously these firms had often been continued by other members of the entrepreneur's family, such as sons and sons-in-law, although this was not always feasible as the appropriate offspring might not exist, while others might wish to realise their inheritance. However, the capital involved in the enterprises steadily increased and made it more and more difficult to find other individuals with the finance necessary to purchase the business as a going concern. Many of the conversions had a capital in excess of £100,000. Thus, in consequence, it was necessary to re-organise the company in such a way that it became saleable and its owners could liquidate all, or part, of their holdings. The growth in the size of the firm itself increasingly required the more flexible organisation of a joint-stock company rather than a partnership. Prosser claimed, in 1898, that:

> Indeed the variety of circumstances in which advantage may be derived from incorporation is infinite, while any disadvantages resulting, provided the business is one suitable for incorporation, and the arrangements are carried out with due regard to the possibilities and requirements of the future, are insignificant.[66]

Examples do exist of private purchasers buying the assets of existing firms and continuing to develop the business. In this way the Smiths of Glasgow sold their extensive shipping and trading company to the Ellerman family of Liverpool in 1899 rather than float it off as a company, while the Sheffield steel making firm, John Brown & Co., used re-invested profits to purchase the Clydebank Engineering and Shipbuilding Co. in 1899 as an outlet for their steel forgings.[67] Again, many of the conversions did not involve any appeal to the public for funds, but were merely a re-ordering of the methods in business in the light of changing family, partnership, technology or market circumstances. The Distillers Company, for instance, was formed in 1877 as an amalgamation of six Lowland grain distillers in order to control the whisky trade more effectively in the face of severe competition. No public subscription was envisaged at the time and the capital of £0.9m was issued wholly to the partners of the amalgamating firms. Similarly, John Fleming & Co., a firm of Aberdeen timber merchants, was converted into a joint-stock company in 1890 at a time when it acquired its major rival in Aberdeen. All the capital continued to be held, however by the existing partners and their associates.[68] Thus, for reasons purely internal to the firm itself, and the conditions in which it operated, there was a growing tide of conversions in the second half of the nineteenth century in such areas of industrial and commercial enterprise as textiles, quarrying, shipbuilding, iron and steel, engineering, brewing, paper manufacture, and retail and wholesale distribution.[69]

However, for those firms that hoped to raise capital from the investing public — and they were growing in number — the determining factor in conversion was not the needs of the owners or general market conditions, but the ability to persuade the investor to subscribe for the stocks and shares issued. A few companies were of sufficient standing to attract interest whatever the conditions, but most had to await favourable circumstances in the capital market.[70] The opportunity to re-

register as a joint-stock company had existed since 1856, and the advantages from so doing had both been growing steadily and becoming more evident. But it was the willingness of the investor to absorb large amounts of securities issued by joint-stock industrial and commercial firms that determined their conversion into 'public' as opposed to 'private' joint-stock companies.

Increasingly, the private firm or private joint-stock company became aware of the possibilities of raising capital by a public issue which was both cheaper and more flexible than raising it from partners, banks, or by other means. These flotations and issues tended to be concentrated in periods when public confidence was high, interest rates were low, and alternative investments limited. The first wholesale conversions came in the mid 1860s (1863-5) and then in the early 1870s (1871-4), followed by the early (1881-3) and late (1887-8) 1880s, and finally from the early 1890s onwards. At times such as these it was possible to float almost any enterprise, including ones with the most dubious prospects.[71] According to the *Scottish Financier* in October 1883:

> The prospectus of the West Lothian Oil Company Limited, has just been issued. In ordinary times this would be put into the waste basket, but now when the oil mania is in full swing, there is little doubt that the shares will be over-applied for, and that the vendors will make a good thing out of it, . . .

The same periodical had as cynical a view, in November 1883, of the Glasgow Cotton Spinning Company, which was also being promoted:

> A period of continuous depression in the Lancashire cotton spinning trade would seem, at the first blush, to be unfavourable to the inauguration of such an enterprise as this, . . .[72]

The greatest boom in industrial and commercial flotations in the nineteenth century was in the 1890s, and most of these consisted of conversions of existing companies, with the vendors themselves, and their immediate associates, not only absorbing much of the capital raised, but also retaining all, or most, of the ordinary shares issued. It was debentures or preference shares that were normally offered to the investing public, not participation in the ordinary share capital and the control that that brought.[73] There seem to have been no unique features internal to industry which explain such a mass conversion as took place in the 1890s. In distilling, for example, many family firms became joint-stock concerns, and some raised substantial sums on the capital market to finance acquisitions and expansion, such as Distillers Company and John Dewar & Sons. Others, such as John Walker & Sons or James Buchanan & Co., seemed to have been able not only to survive but also to grow without any issue of shares to the public, as personal, bank, and trade credit provided all the funds they required. Consequently, conversion and flotation in the 1890s can hardly be attributed to circumstances internal to the industry, although they probably played a role.[74] The very numbers and variety of conversions in the 1890s suggest, as with the building and railway investment in that decade, that investors were turning in large numbers to other investment areas, as they had substantial sums to invest but had become disillusioned with existing outlets, especially those abroad.

As a result of these developments, joint-stock enterprise, reliant upon the capital market, came to pervade almost all areas of the Scottish economy, with most of the largest enterprises being public joint-stock companies. By 1900 there were some 200 industrial, commercial and allied concerns, with a paid-up capital of £43m, which relied partly or wholly on public support for their finance, while areas such as railways, banking and insurance were completely dominated by joint-stock enterprise. Nevertheless, there remained large areas of the Scottish economy in which the public joint-stock form had made either no impact at all, or one which was limited and particular, and these included almost all of distribution, agriculture, commerce, professional and personal service, and road haulage. Even in those branches of manufacturing industry, trade or fishing where public joint-stock companies were numerous, partnerships and private joint-stock companies continued to play a very important role. Joint-stock had pervaded the Scottish economy by 1900 but did not dominate it. This was certainly true of those concerns that were dependent upon public support.[75]

The most prominent feature of Scottish joint-stock company promotion in the second half of the century was the growing number of concerns, in an increasing variety of fields, that were formed to operate outside Scotland. Details are vague, but it has been suggested that total Scottish overseas investment, excluding that in the rest of Britain, rose from £60m in 1870 to £150m in 1885, £300m in 1900, and £500m in 1914.[76] Much of this investment was in the form of Scottish purchases of securities issued in England, Wales, and Ireland or abroad, and as early as 1853 Scots held stock in U.S. banks and insurance companies. Increasingly, numerous Scottish individuals and institutions held, for example, substantial amounts of English and United States railway securities. These investments ranged from the millions of pounds worth of North American or Australian railway stock, or land mortgage bonds, purchased by Scottish banks and insurance companies, such as the City of Glasgow Bank's £1.1m in the U.S. rail-road stock in 1878, or the £6m placed overseas by the Scottish Widows' Funds Life Assurance Society by 1900, to the much smaller foreign holdings of individuals, such as Peter Brough's £105,000 in English railways in 1880 or Arthur Bell's c.£15,000 in U.S. railroads by 1900.[77] Increasingly, in the late nineteenth century, institutional or individual investors seeking a secure outlet with a reasonable return turned to foreign securities. In the 1880s, for example, more than half of the value of total trustee funds available in Scotland for investment was estimated to have gone overseas, principally into government or railroad stocks.[78] Money also went abroad by other means such as the deposits in the Scottish branches of colonial banks and financial institutions, or by direct investment. The Baird family, for example, purchased a number of Spanish iron ore mines from 1871 onwards in order to supply their Scottish iron and steel making operations. A. J. Balfour was reputed to have invested the proceeds of the sale of his Scottish estates in land around Winnipeg, while Lord Aberdeen purchased a large fruit farm in British Columbia in 1890.[79]

With this tide of foreign investment it was only to be expected that joint-stock enterprise would seek to provide a means by which funds of all sizes, not just those of wealthy individuals or institutions, could be marshalled together and directed into profitable foreign openings by a skilled management. Hence appeared the investment, trust and mortgage companies, largely from the 1870s onwards. Such enterprises had been originally formed in Scotland in the 1830s, with the succession of Aberdeen-based U.S. and Australian companies, but interest among investors had lapsed as domestic outlets, especially railways, absorbed most available funds. Gradually, in the 1850s and 1860s, interest revived with, for example, the small New Zealand Scotch Trust established in Edinburgh in 1865. However, although demand for funds existed abroad at that time, especially since North American and Australian economic prosperity had been stimulated by gold discoveries, it was not until the 1870s that Scotland possessed large amounts of savings which could be attracted abroad. By then the declining requirements of infrastructure and heavy industry not only released finance for other sectors of the economy or for abroad but were also generating large profits and incomes which sought new avenues.[80]

Those who had been employed by institutions or wealthy investors to handle their growing portfolio of overseas securities, such as William Menzies in Edinburgh or Robert Fleming in Dundee, easily turned their experience to wider use. They formed companies that would simply raise capital in Scotland and invest it abroad, especially in the United States.[81] In addition to the share capital obtained, these companies raised substantial sums by issuing terminable debentures and accepting deposits from the public, secured by the uncalled portion of the share capital. This was also invested abroad, so that the company benefited from the differential between higher foreign than domestic interest rates. The North of Scotland Canadian Mortgage Company, for example, had £133,000 outstanding through debentures and deposits in 1876, and that had grown to £600,000 by 1902.[82] These companies confined their operations either to the loan of funds on the security of real estate, principally farm land, or to the purchase of railway or municipal securities. However, they gradually became more adventurous as their knowledge of investment, and the country in which they were investing, improved, while at times, the funds they had available to invest outran their preferred outlets, forcing them to accept alternative securities. The North British Canadian Investment Company, for example, had been formed to lend on farm mortgage in Ontario, but extended its field of operations into the prairie provinces and also began to lend to businesses and purchase municipal securities.[83] J. W. Barclay, Chairman of the North of Scotland Canadian Mortgage Co., summed up the philosophy of his company in February 1876, and this was typical of the simple aims of this type of enterprise:

> Practically the business of the Company was that of bankers. They received money here, where it was plentiful, and consequently yielded only a low rate of interest, and they lent it out in Canada, where capital was very scarce, and consequently the rate of interest very high, even on land, which, with the exception of consols, was considered the best security in any country.[84]

The first of these new investment companies appeared almost simultaneously in Dundee and Edinburgh with Robert Fleming's Scottish American Investment Trust being formed in Dundee in February 1873, and William Menzies' Scottish

American Investment Company being established in Edinburgh in March 1874. They were soon followed by a host of others promoted in these or other Scottish cities, or even in London, but catering for Scottish investors. The North British Canadian Investment Co. was formed in Glasgow in 1876, the North of Scotland Canadian Mortgage Co. in Aberdeen in 1875, and the Colorado Mortgage and Investment Co. in London in 1877.[85] By 1900 the paid-up capital of the Scottish overseas trust, mortgage, and investment companies totalled about £12.4m, and this was almost equivalent to the combined capital of the Scottish banks and insurance companies. Most of these companies were successful ventures and they became the major new component of joint-stock financial enterprise in Scotland in the second half of the century. They were especially numerous in Edinburgh, where the established Scottish banks, insurance companies and other institutions usually had large amounts of spare funds to invest and were always ready to lend to these investment companies, as withdrawals could be made at short notice. This was true to a lesser extent in the other Scottish cities. The investment companies absorbed a large volume of the capital which either sought safe outlets, such as mortgages or government securities, or which was only temporarily available as it had to be kept ready at short notice in order to meet the needs of trade, borrowers, or maturing insurance policies.[86]

Investment, trust and mortgage companies were certainly the largest and most successful of Scottish joint-stock enterprises formed to operate outside Scotland, but they were complemented by a growing number of other ventures, often of the most speculative kind. Few railways, utilities, or services were formed by Scots to operate in the rest of Britain or abroad. The most notable exception was the Oregonian Railway Company founded in Dundee in 1880 to build a railroad in the United States. At its peak, in 1888, this company had a paid-up capital of £426,560, including a loan of £49,000 from the British Linen Bank. The operation of the company was a failure and the assets were sold to an American company at a considerable loss to the shareholders, estimated at £300,000 in March 1889.[87] Most of Scotland's direct involvement with rail-road construction overseas was as part of other operations. The Glasgow-based Tharsis Sulphur and Copper Company, for example, spent £231,000 on building a railway in Spain from the mine to the coast so that the ore could be shipped out.[88] Similarly, most utilities such as docks or gas companies were off-shoots of other enterprises. The Scottish Wharf Company was founded in 1868 to construct and operate a wharf in London for the Edinburgh shipping trade and was eventually amalgamated with the London and Edinburgh Shipping Company in 1899.[89]

A number of Scottish-based companies were established to run a purely local shipping service in some of the world's remoter rivers and lakes, such as the Irrawaddy Flotilla and Burmese Steam Navigation Company in 1865, the African Lakes Corporation in 1878, and the La Platense Flotilla Company in 1886. However, Scottish shipping operations outside home waters were almost entirely carried out by the numerous companies and combines that operated 'tramp' vessels wherever there was a profitable cargo to be found.[90] More common were the land and property companies that were established to take advantage of the rising value exhibited by both farm and urban land in the recently settled parts of the world. The Dundee Land Investment Company was formed in 1878 and aimed to purchase extensive tracts of land in the sparsely populated parts of North America, to wait until farmers and others began moving into the area, and then sell off the land in small lots at a considerable profit. The Scottish Manitoba and North-West Real Estate Company, formed in Edinburgh in 1881, had the same object. It purchased both farm land and house property in the Canadian prairie provinces. However, most Scottish involvement with overseas real estate was confined to loans on its security rather than purchasing, holding and disposing of the land itself, for this could be as risky a business abroad as was property development in Scotland. The Scottish Manitoba and North-West Real Estate Company had lost over a third of its capital by 1893 due to a severe depreciation in the value of its holdings.[91]

The most numerous of all Scottish companies operating overseas were those that sought to exploit, directly, the mineral, agricultural, or forest resources of the world. Mining enterprises were formed in Scotland to operate in such areas as Australia, India, South Africa, Canada, the United States, or within other parts of the British Isles, especially Ireland. Unfortunately, the majority of all these mining companies turned out to be failures. The prospects held out by the promoters, which attracted considerable investment, often proved to be entirely inaccurate. By the time that that was discovered, however, the entire subscribed capital had usually been exhausted in the unsuccessful attempt to discover and develop the supposed mineral wealth. Companies as diverse as the Glasgow Port Washington Iron & Coal Co., formed in Glasgow in 1872 to mine coal and iron in Ohio, and which possessed a paid-up capital of £235,000; the Peruvian Nitrate Co., promoted in Leith in 1873 to mine nitrates in Peru and with £71,400 paid up; or the Achill Plumbago & Talc Co., founded in Glasgow in 1882, to mine lead and talc in Ireland, and with only £9,400 paid up, all failed either through the mineral deposits, or the market not turning out as expected. Far more uncommon were the successful Scottish mining ventures such as the Tharsis Sulphur and Copper Company, established in Glasgow in 1866 to mine copper pyrites in Spain, or a number of the Indian gold mining companies, which appeared in 1879-80. Charles Tennant, for example, was reported to have made around £2m from his investments in Scottish-based Indian gold mining companies, principally Mysore Gold Mining Co. and Gold Fields of Mysore, which both paid at least 100 per cent per annum in dividends between 1896/7 and 1905. It was occasional successes like these that under-lay the continued promotion of overseas mining companies, despite their exceedingly high mortality rate.[92]

Equally risky were those companies formed to undertake different types of farming operations throughout the world, which ranged from tea plantations in India to cattle ranching in the United States:

> . . ., tea shares as a class are investments of a decidedly speculative character, a small fluctuation in the price of tea making a vast difference in the amount available for distribution in dividends

claimed one Indian investment expert in 1911, and the same could be said of beef, wool, or any other agricultural product.[93] Increasingly, in the second half of the nineteenth century, the Scottish trading agencies operating in India promoted both large and small tea plantation companies in Scotland. Finlay, Muir & Co., a Glasgow-based Indian agency house, floated the North and South Sylhet Tea Companies in 1882 and the Consolidated Tea and Lands Co. in 1896. The North Sylhet Tea Co. had £280,000 paid up by 1890.[94]

Much more spectacular was the involvement with American cattle ranching in the early 1880s. Scottish investors had financed earlier substantial stock raising ventures such as the Glasgow-based Canterbury and Otago Association and New Zealand and Australian Land Co. in 1865/6. These together had a paid-up share capital of £1.3m in 1870, and grazed cattle and sheep on extensive land holdings in Australasia.[95] The U.S. cattle ranching mania, however, largely bypassed Glasgow, partly because of the lack of success, up to that time, of its existing involvements, especially the New Zealand and Australian Land Company and, more especially, because of the aftermath of the City of Glasgow bank collapse in 1878, which shattered confidence and ruined many Glasgow investors. The U.S. cattle ranching mania was built up by reports of the fabulous profits made in the business. After visiting the United States, James MacDonald, a Scottish farmer, reported in 1878 that the estimated return in Texas on stock-raising was 25 per cent per annum, and this was confirmed by many others as a conservative estimate.

Thus, beginning with the Prairie Cattle Company, formed in Edinburgh in 1880, a host of other cattle ranching companies were formed, such as the Matador Land and Cattle Company and the Swan Land and Cattle Company. Altogether, some £5m of Scottish money was invested in such enterprises in the course of the 1880s. However, like the mining ventures, most of these company formations turned out disastrously.[96] By 1890 the depreciation on the value of the Prairie Cattle Company's assets totalled £294,000, or 70 per cent of the paid-up share capital. In that year the Company ascribed its difficulties to

> ... over-estimates in the numbers of cattle in the herds acquired by the Company; to the titles of part of the lands having been cancelled by the United States Government; to losses of cattle incurred by the severity of recent seasons; and to the general depreciation in cattle and in grazing lands ...[97]

In contrast to mining or agriculture, very few manufacturing concerns were formed in Scotland to operate outside the country. Most were extensions of existing Scottish firms. The Tharsis Copper Co., for example, acquired a number of English metal refining plants to process the copper it was mining, while J. & P. Coats of Paisley came to own factories throughout Britain and the world which produced cotton thread.[98] India was one of the few places to attract independent Scottish manufacturing companies, especially jute textile mills such as the Samnuggur, Titaghur and Victoria of Dundee, or the India and Champdany of Glasgow. Most of these jute operations were founded in 1873.[99]

Overseas ventures such as copper or gold mining, tea or rubber plantations, sheep or cattle grazing, all had their moment of glory before the conditions that had created the craze disappeared. What remained were the stronger, or luckier, companies, paying good or reasonable dividends, while much of the capital raised had disappeared with the liquidation of the weaker concerns. What is clear is that the Scottish investor was as adventurous abroad as he was at home. While domestically the investor came to chance more on industrial, commercial, and oil, coal and iron ore mining concerns, he was doing likewise overseas, with the proliferation of oil, copper, and gold mining companies, cattle ranches, tea plantations, and a few industrial ventures. In fact, there was considerable coincidence between promotional booms in risky home and foreign ventures, such as the early 1870s with their domestic industrial and mining companies and overseas jute textile mills and mining ventures, and the early 1880s with their domestic electrical concerns and U.S. cattle ranches.

As a result of these substantial developments in all forms of joint-stock enterprise, both at home and abroad, the importance of stocks and shares in the economy grew enormously during the second half of the nineteenth century. This was both absolutely and as a share of total wealth. *Blackwood's Edinburgh Magazine* claimed in 1885, that:

> Out of the £8,720m of national capital in the U.K. very nearly one-half exists in the form of securities, which are daily passing from hand to hand, and are subject to all the fluctuations of a sensitive market.[100]

This greatly expanded joint-stock presence attracted the support of an equally enlarged investing public. By 1887, £101.8m worth of Scottish railway securities was in existence in the form of stocks and shares. This was held by 12,930 individual holders of debenture stock, 27,981 holders of ordinary shares, and a further 33,861 holders of preference and guaranteed shares. If one allows for duplication between different classes of securities and separate companies, this would suggest that there were around 50,000 separate investors with an average holding of £2,036. As early as 1876 the Caledonian Railway was reported to have approximately 15,000 shareholders, the North British 10,000 and the Glasgow and South Western 5,000.[101] Other branches of joint-stock enterprise also witnessed an increase in both the individual and collective number of investors, with J. & P. Coats having some 17,000 shareholders by 1907.[102] There were also a substantial turnover in securities with, in banks, an average of 8 per cent of the stock being bought and sold every year.[103] With such an amount of joint-stock capital, such a numerous body of investors, such a variety of enterprise, and such a regular and sizeable turnover of stock, it was essential to have a sophisticated market organisation and the skilled professionals that required.

It was necessary to have both the market organisation and the profession in Scotland, for the enterprises and their shareholders were, in most cases, peculiar to Scotland. The formation of large national companies such as the United Alkali Company in 1890, or the Calico Printers' Association in 1899, and the expansion of Scottish-based enterprise outside the country, as with J. & P. Coats, had led to the submerging of Scottish companies and Scottish shareholders in a British environment. In addition, Scottish holdings of securities issued by English or foreign concerns and governments, and non-Scottish investments in Scottish enterprise, also encouraged the creation of one central market with offshoots throughout Britain, rather than the existence of separate, but inter-connected, markets.[104] Up to 1900, the vigour of Scottish joint-stock company formation and the limited moves towards large British-based concerns meant that there remained a need for a separate Scottish stock exchange. However, neither Scottish joint-stock enterprise nor the Scottish investor confined operations to Scotland alone but gradually adopted a world perspective. At the same time, the Scottish economy and its finance were being slowly drawn into a British scale of operations.

Table 5
Scottish Joint-Stock Companies, 1900

Area of Operation	Number	Paid-up Capital
Total	520	£408.1m
Transport	11%	73%
Railways	6%	72%
Tramways	2%	—
Shipping	4%	1%
Financial	19%	7%
Banking	2%	2%
Insurance	6%	1%
Investment	11%	4%
Mining	12%	3%
Agriculture	5%	2%
Commercial & Industrial	37%	11%
Commercial	6%	1%
Food & Drink	13%	3%
Metal & Engineering	6%	2%
Textiles	4%	3%
Paper & Printing	3%	1%
Building Materials	2%	—
Chemicals	3%	1%
Urban Facilities	18%	5%
Gas & Water	1%	—
Services	9%	1%
Property	2%	—
Municipal Securities	3%	5%

Source: *The Stock Exchange Official Intelligence* (London 1900)

NOTES

1. *B.E.M.* 137 (1885) pp. 274-5; L. Levi, 'Joint Stock Companies', *J.R.S.S.* 33 (1870) p. 2.

2. T. J. Byres, The Scottish Economy during the 'Great Depression,' 1873-1896 (B.Litt. Glasgow 1963) p. 265.

3. Byres, op. cit., pp. 259, 270; W. Watt, 'Fifty Years Progress in Aberdeen' *T.A.P.S.* 4 (1900-1910) p. 120.

4. J. Reid, *Manual of the Scottish Stocks and British Funds* (Edin. 1842) pp. 172-7; *The Stock Exchange Official Intelligence* (Lon. 1900); T. Skinner (ed.), *The Stock Exchange Year-Book* (Lon. 1881).

5. G. R. Hawke & M. C. Reed, 'Railway Capital in the United Kingdom in the Nineteenth Century', *Ec.H.R.* 22 (1969) pp. 270-3; W. Vamplew, Railways and the Transformation of the Scottish Economy (Ph.D. Edin. 1969) p. 26. N.B. Not all of the paid-up capital in the market had been raised from the public, as some stock had been issued under par, as bonuses, or to capitalise re-investment.

6. P. L. Cottrell, Investment Banking in England, 1856-1882 (Ph.D. Hull 1974) p. 510.

7. *A.H.* 6 July 1850; *S.R.G.* 6 April 1850; Robert Allan, Circular, August 1851.

8. J. R. T. Hughes, *Fluctuations in Trade, Industry and Finance* (Oxford 1960) pp. 184, 192, 194; *S.R.G.* 14 December 1850; *A.H.* 20 December 1851; Allan, op. cit., November 1851.

9. J. Clapham, *The Bank of England: A History* (Cam. 1944) II, p. 223; T. Doubleday, *A Financial, Monetary and Statistical History of England from the Revolution of 1688* (Lon. 1859) p. 439; Allan, op. cit., December 1852.

10. Allan, op. cit., November 1852.

11. W. M'Ilwraith, *The Glasgow and South Western Railway* (Glasgow 1880) p. 85; *A.F.P.* 28 October 1853; Allan, op. cit., November 1852.

12. J. Thompson, *On the Existing State of our Herring Fishery* (Abdn. 1854) p. 46.

13. Cottrell, op. cit., pp. 444, 449.

14. Cottrell, op. cit., pp. 463, 491-2; R. R. Notman, *The Deeside Railway: A Letter to the Landed Proprietors of Deeside* (Abdn. 1850) p. 1; 'Railway Morals and Railway Policy' *Edinburgh Review* 100 (1854) p. 457; C. J. A. Robertson, 'The Cheap Railway Movement in Scotland: The St. Andrews Railway Company' *T.H.* 7 (1974) pp. 15-16; R. N. Millman, *The Making of the Scottish Landscape* (Lon. 1975) p. 183.

15. Vamplew, op. cit., pp. 26, 33-34; *Report by the Committee of Investigation to the Shareholders of Great North of Scotland Railway* (Abdn. 1865).

16. A. Mclean (ed.), *Local Industries of Glasgow and the West of Scotland* (Glasgow 1901) p. 124; W. M. Acworth, *The Railways of Scotland* (Lon. 1890) p. 51; J. Thomas, *The West Highland Railway* (Lon. 1965) p. 41.

17. Vamplew, op. cit., pp. 103, 147; Thomas, op. cit., p. 42.

18. Vamplew, op. cit., pp. 135, 137; Acworth, op. cit., p. 51; I. H. Adams, *The Making of Urban Scotland* (Lon. 1978) p. 118; Thomas, op. cit., p. 79; Mclean, op. cit., p. 124; *A.F.P.* 27 August 1890.

19. Cottrell, op. cit., p. 510.

20. *A.H.* 18 September 1875.

21. J. Scott & M. Hughes, *The Anatomy of Scottish Capital* (Lon. 1980) p. 33.

22. J. Butt, *Industrial Archaeology of Scotland* (Newton Abbot 1967) pp. 184, 187; J. P. McKay, *Tramways and Trolleys* (Princeton 1976) p. 173; *Memoirs and Portraits of One Hundred Glasgow Men* (Glasgow 1886) p. 227; Mclean, op. cit., pp. 126, 131, 263; *A.H.* 30 September 1871; *A.F.P.* 20 August 1876.

23. Aberdeen & Glasgow Steam Shipping Co. S.C.R.O. BT2/1,026; *A.F.P.* 11 April 1881.

24. London & Edinburgh Shipping Co.: S.C.R.O. BT2/155.

25. D. Laird, *Paddy Henderson* (Glasgow 1961) pp. 35. 47-8, 99; Albion Shipping Co. S.C.R.O. BT2/181.

26. L. Mackinnon, *Recollections of an Old Lawyer* (Abdn. 1935) pp. 85, 88; *A.F.P.* 9 June 1883.

27. *D.Y.B.* (1882) p. 25; *D.Y.B.* (1891) p. 58; Dundee Loch Line Steam Shipping Co. S.C.R.O. BT2/1,040; Dundee Gem Line Steam Shipping Co. S.C.R.O. BT2/1,097; Albany Shipping Co. S.C.R.O. BT2/1,127.

28. J. Mackenzie, 'Shipowning by Shares and by Single Ship Limited Companies' *A.M.* 2 (1898) pp. 103-7; Glasgow Steamship Co. S.C.R.O. BT2/1,030; The 'Klyde' Steamship Co. S.C.R.O. BT2/1,162.

29. Cottrell, op. cit., p. 672; Gem Line, op. cit., Petition 21 June 1895; Albany Line, op. cit., Petition 10 December 1895.

30. A. M. Dunnett, *The Donaldson Line* (Glasgow 1960) p. 55.

31. J. Shields, *Clyde Built* (Glasgow 1949) p. 19.

32. M.S. Cotterill, The Scottish Gas Industry up to 1914 (Ph.D. Strathclyde 1976) pp. 121-131, 152, 1415-1421, 1567.

33. H. H. Bassett (ed.), *Men of Note in Finance and Commerce* (Lon. 1900-01), 'Major Peter Chalmers'.

34. *A.F.P.* 27 March 1894.

35. *D.P.* & *C.A.* 12 July 1880.

36. H. H. Bassett, *Business Men at Home and Abroad 1912-13* (Lon. 1912) 'J. G. B. Lorrain'; *D. Y.B.* (1884) p. 71; Scott & Hughes, op. cit., p. 58; Cotterill, op. cit., p. 1304.

37. *S.B.* & *I.M.* 2 April 1879; *The Real Property Trust: Prospectus* (Edin. 1876); *Land Feuing Company: Prospectus* (Glasgow 1874); *The Scottish Equitable Property Improvement and Investment Company: Prospectus* (Edin. 1875); Circular from Sir A. Anderson, 3 February 1875.

38. *S.B.* & *I.M.* December 1880, May 1881; *E.P.R.* 24 May 1879; *A.F.P.* 16 June 1896.

39. Airdrie Public Halls Co. S.C.R.O. BT2/234.

40. *D. Y.B.* (1885) p. 51.

41. *A.F.P.* 17 July 1886.

42. *A.F.P.* 18 July 1878.

43. Mclean, op. cit., pp. 215, 218, 263; Cotterill, op. cit., pp. 1035, 1048, 1037; A. M. Munro, *Aberdeen Today, 1886-1907* (Abdn. 1907) pp. 28, 33; A. Mackie, *An Industrial History of Edinburgh* (Glasgow 1963) p. 67; *D.Y.B.* (1887) p. 80; I. H. Adams, *The Making of Urban Scotland* (Lon. 1978) pp. 162, 166-7.

44. Cotterill, op. cit., p. 1567.

45. H. W. Bull, Working-Class Housing in Glasgow, 1862-1902 (M.Litt. Strathclyde 1973) p. 24.

46. *S.E.O.I.* (1900) 'Corporation Stocks'.

47. Bull, op. cit., pp. 49, 56, 84; *S.E.O.I.* (1900) 'Clyde Navigation Trust'.

48. Cotterill, op. cit., p. 1048; Bull, op. cit., p. 67.

49. S. G. Checkland, *Scottish Banking* (Glasgow 1975) pp. 344, 465, 510; A. W. Kerr, *Scottish Banking during the period of Published Accounts, 1865-1896* (Lon. 1898) pp. 23, 301, 31, 122; W. M. Mitchell, *Our Scotch Banks* (Edin. 1879) p. 75; M. A. Whitehead, The Western Bank and the Crisis of 1857 (M.Litt. Strathclyde 1978) pp. 8, 104, 165; A. T. Innes (ed.), *Report of the Petition of Wm. Muir and others* (Edin. 1878) pp. 5-8; R. H. Campbell, 'Edinburgh Bankers and the Western Bank of Scotland', *S.J.P.E.* 2 (1955) p. 133; G. MacGregor, *The History of Glasgow* (Glasgow 1881) pp. 446, 493; *S.R.G.* 26 May 1849.

50. *Northern Loan Company: Report* (Abdn. 1887).

51. Cottrell, op. cit., p. 563; Heritable Securities Investment Association, S.C.R.O. BT2/124.

52. *S.B.* & *I.M.* May 1881; North British Property Investment Company, S.C.R.O. BT2/395; The Aberdeen Heritable Securities Investment Company: Articles of Association, 1872.

53. *Phillips' Investors' Manual* (Lon. 1887) p. 169.

54. The Northern & Allied Co.'s Staff Magazine, 16 (1936) pp. 225-294; W. F. Gray, *A Brief Chronicle of the Scottish Union and National Insurance Company, 1824-1924* (Edin. 1924) pp. 175, 182.

55. Scottish Fire Insurance Company, S.C.R.O. BT2/175.

56. *A.F.P.* 7 March 1890; *S.F.* August 1883.

57. J. B. Jeffreys, Trends in Business Organisation in Great Britain since 1856 (Ph.D. London 1938) p. 118; T. Napier, 'The History of Joint Stock and Limited Liability Companies' in *A Century of Law Reform* (Lon. 1901) pp. 388, 394; F. Gore-Browne & W. Jordan, *A Handy Book on the Formation, Management and Winding up of Joint Stock Companies* (Lon. 1902) p. 5; J. Mann, 'Glimpses of Early Accountancy in Glasgow', *A.M.* 58 (1954) p. 298.

58. *Econ.* 27 January 1855, 28 June 1856.

59. Byres, op. cit., pp. 650-1; Scottish Fire Insurance Company S.C.R.O. BT2/175; W. J. Anderson to W. Stirling, 4 December 1884.

60. Byres, op. cit., p. 650; I. Donnachie, *A History of the Brewing Industry in Scotland* (Edin. 1979) p. 162; J. A. Hassan, The Development of the Coal Industry in Mid and West Lothian, 1815-1973 (Ph.D. Strathclyde 1976) p. 161.

61. Hassan, op. cit., p. 187; Donnachie, op. cit., p. 172; R. B. Weir, The Distilling Industry in Scotland in the Nineteenth and early Twentieth Centuries (Ph.D. Edin. 1974) pp. 332, 375, 510, 515; I. F. Gibson, The Economic History of the Scottish Iron and Steel Industry (Ph.D. London 1955) p. 448; L. Weatherill, *One Hundred Years of Papermaking* (Guardbridge 1974) pp. 1, 66-7; *Glasgow Morning Journal* 3 March 1866; *A.F.P.* 19 January 1889.

62. *A.F.P.* 21 June 1876; Weir, op. cit., pp. 336, 373-5.

63. North British Rubber Company, S.C.R.O. BT2/18; Scottish Wagon Company, S.C.R.O. BT2/81.

64. M. Gray, *The Fishing Industries of Scotland, 1790-1914* (Abdn. 1978) p. 179; Glasgow Jute Company, S.C.R.O. BT2/202; Byres, op. cit., p. 65; Aberdeen Jute Company, S.C.R.O. BT2/483; *A.F.P.* 25 January 1873, 8 February 1873, 22 February 1873, 14 March 1874.

65. *A.F.P.* 29 April 1882, 3 May 1882; H. O. O'Hagan, *Leaves from my Life* (Lon. 1929) I, p. 118; Phillips, op. cit., p. 199; J. Butt, 'The Scottish Oil Mania of 1864-6' *S.J.P.E.* 12 (1865); J. Nicol, *Vital, Social and Economic Statistics of the City of Glasgow, 1885-1891* (Glasgow 1891) p. 369.

66. J. Prosser, 'The Incorporation of Trading Companies' *A.M.* 2 (1898); Jeffreys, op. cit., p. 109; *S.E.O.I.* (1900) 'Breweries & Distilleries', 'Commercial & Industrial', 'Iron, Coal & Steel'.

67. J. Smith, *Rise and Progress of the City Line* (Glasgow 1908) p. 202; A. Grant, *Steel and Ships: The History of John Brown's* (Lon. 1950) p. 37; Shields, op. cit., p. 96.

68. Weir, op. cit., pp. 290, 297, 320, 332; R. Perren, *John Fleming & Co. Ltd., 1877-1977* (Abdn. 1978) p. 22.

69. W. Diack, *Rise and Progress of the Granite Industry in Aberdeen* (Abdn. 1950) pp. 31, 92; J. L. Carvell, *The Coltness Iron Company* (Edin. 1948) p. 53; *Then and Now, 1751-1899: The Culter Mills Paper Co. Ltd.* (Abdn. 1899) p. 20; M. Blair, *The Paisley Thread Industry* (Paisley 1907) p. 63; C. Gulvin, *The Tweedmakers* (Newton Abbot 1973) p. 158; D. I. A. Steel, The Linen Industry of Fife in the later Eighteenth and Nineteenth Centuries (Ph.D. St. Andrews 1975) p. 383; J. L. Carvel, *Stephen of Linthouse: A Record of Two Hundred Years of Shipbuilding* (Glasgow 1950) p. 92; Donnachie, op. cit., p. 173; S. G. E. Lythe & J. Butt, *An Economic History of Scotland, 1100-1939* (Glasgow 1975) p. 229; *D.Y.B.* (1892) p. 55, (1893) p. 6, (1897) p. 48; Grant, op. cit., p. 43.

70. *Econ.* 23 June 1900; *A.F.P.* 30 June 1888; L. Hannah, 'Mergers in British Manufacturing Industry, 1880-1918' *O.E.P.* 26 (1974) pp. 7-8.

71. Byres, op. cit., pp. 650-654; Gulvin, op. cit., p. 158; Hassan, op. cit., pp. 176, 185, 187, 188.

72. *S.F.* October & November 1883.

73. Donnachie, op. cit., pp. 167, 172, 176-7; Weir, op. cit., p. 513.

74. Weir, op. cit., pp. 531-3, 510-16, 555-56, 568; R. B. Weir, *The History of the Malt Distillers' Association of Scotland* (York 1974) pp. 12, 20, 61.

75. *S.E.O.I.* (1900); Byres, op. cit., pp. 655-6.

76. B. Lenman, *An Economic History of Modern Scotland, 1660-1976* (Lon. 1977) p. 193; Lythe & Butt, op. cit., p. 236.

77. Steel, op. cit., pp. 381-2; R. D. Corrins, William Baird & Company: Coal & Iron Masters, 1830-1914 (Ph.D. Strathclyde 1974) pp. 86, 275, 277, 280; Weir (Ph.D.), op. cit., pp. 434, 492; Cottrell, op. cit., p. 694; J. B. Sturrock, *Peter Brough: A Paisley Philanthropist* (Paisley 1890) pp. 234-254; B. Lenman & K. Donaldson, 'Partners' Incomes, Investment and Diversification in the Scottish Linen area, 1850-1921' *B.H.* 13 (1971) pp. 12, 15; R. E. Tyson, 'Scottish Investment in American Railways: the case of the City of Glasgow Bank, 1856-1881' in P. L. Payne (ed.), pp. 389, 390, 400; P. D. Holcombe, Scottish Investment in Canada, 1870-1914 (M.Litt. Strathclyde 1975) pp. 115, 151, 152, 166; C. A. Malcolm, *The Bank of Scotland, 1695-1945* (Edin. 1948) p. 130; North of Scotland Bank: Annual Reports, 1874-8; W. J. Anderson to W. Stirling, 4 December 1884; *U.S. Senate: Report to the Secretary of the Treasury* (Washington 1854) pp. 20, 33.

78. Holcombe, op. cit., p. 188.

79. A. R. Hall, *The London Capital Market and Australia, 1870-1914* (Canberra 1963) pp. 116, 119; Corrins, op. cit., pp. 189, 192; Holcombe, op. cit., p. 71; Byres, op. cit., p. 289; J. M. Gibbon, *The Scot in Canada* (Abdn. 1907) p. 22; *British Columbia: Its Position, Resources and Climate* (1893) p. 9.

80. *S.B. & I.M.* February 1879; H. Burton & D. C. Corner, *Investment and Unit Trusts in Britain and America* (Lon. 1968) p. 320; New Zealand Scotch Trust, S.C.R.O. BT2/212.

81. R. B. Weir, *A History of the Scottish American Investment Company, 1873-1973* (Edin. 1973) p. 3; W. T. Jackson, *The Enterprising Scot: Investors in the American West after 1873* (Edin. 1968) p. 22.

82. *A.F.P.* 23 March 1876; Holcombe, op. cit., pp. 264-8, 293-6, 304-5, 373; F. W. Field, *Capital Investments in Canada* (Toronto 1911) pp. 17-18.

83. *S.B. & I.M.* February 1879; Holcombe, op. cit., pp. 270, 278, 285.

84. *A.F.P.* 4 February 1876, 23 March 1876.

85. Weir, (1973), op. cit., p. 5; Jackson, op. cit., pp. 13-43; Burton & Corner, op. cit., pp. 17, 320; Holcombe, op. cit., pp. 362, 301-2; G. Glasgow, *The Scottish Investment Trust Companies* (Lon. 1932) pp. 38, 45, 52, 54, 60, 62, 68; J. C. Gilbert, *A History of Investment Trusts in Dundee, 1873-1938* (Lon. 1939) pp. 5, 8; C. H. Walker, 'Unincorporated Investment Trusts in the Nineteenth Century' *Ec.H.* 4 (1940) p. 345; W. H. Marwick, 'Scottish Overseas Investment in the Nineteenth Century', *S.B.M.* 27 (1935-6) p. 3; W. G. Kerr, 'Scotland and the Texas Mortgage Business' *Ec.H.R.* 16 (1963-4) p. 91; W. G. Kerr, *Scottish Capital on the American Credit Frontier* (Austin 1976) p. 171; 'Scottish Capital Abroad' *B.E.M.* 136 (1884) pp. 476-7; C. H. Marshall, 'Dundee as a Centre of Investment', *British Association Handbook,* 1912, pp. 354-5.

86. *S.E.O.I.* (1900); Holcombe, op. cit., pp. 309, 311, 316; Byres, op. cit., p. 304; *Scottish Land: The Report of the Scottish Land Enquiry Committee* (Lon. 1914) pp. 388-9.

87. Oregonian Railway Company, S.C.R.O. BT2/963; *A.F.P.* 7 March 1889; Lenman & Donaldson, op. cit., p. 11.

88. S. G. Checkland, *The Mines of Tharsis* (Lon. 1967) pp. 105-6.

89. Scottish Wharf Co., S.C.R.O. BT2/281.

90. D. Laird, *Paddy Henderson* (Glasgow 1961) pp. 114-157, 158-169; Irrawaddy Flotilla & Burmese Steam Navigation Company, S.C.R.O. BT2/188; Marwick, op. cit., p. 115.

91. *A.F.P.* 1 August 1878; Jackson, op. cit., 30-31, 211; Gilbert, op. cit., pp. 35, 56; Scottish Manitoba North-West Real Estate Company, S.C.R.O. BT2/1008.

92. C. C. Spence, *British Investments and the American Mining Frontier, 1860-1901* (New York 1958) p. 34; Kerr (1976), op. cit., p. 60; Jackson, op. cit., p. 141; K. Robinson, *The Mining Market* (Lon. 1907) p. 177; Checkland, op. cit., pp. 105-6, 123; P. M. Edwards, 'Scottish Investment in the American West', Scottish Colloquium Proceedings, p. 415, Guelph, 1972; Marwick, op. cit., p. 112; N. Crathorne, *Tennants' Stalk* (Lon. 1973) pp. 138-141; Glasgow Port Washington Iron Coal Co., S.C.R.O. BT2/399; Peruvian Nitrate Co., S.C.R.O. BT2/480; Achill Plumbago & Talc Co., S.C.R.O. BT2/1180; H. Bassett (ed.) *Men of Note in Finance and Commerce* (Lon. 1900-1), 'Sir Charles Tennant'.

93. G. H. Le Maistre, *The Investor's India Year Book* (Calcutta 1911).

94. Marwick, op. cit., p. 115; *James Finlay & Co. Ltd., 1750-1950* (Glasgow 1951) p. 105; North Sylhet Tea Company, S.C.R.O. BT2/1157.

95. Canterbury & Otago Association, S.C.R.O. BT2/197; New Zealand and Australian Land Company, S.C.R.O. BT2/229.

96. Kerr (1976), op. cit., p. 27; Jackson, op. cit., pp. 76-80; Edwards, op. cit., pp. 72-3; 'Outlying Professions' *B.E.M.* 136 (1884) p. 585; W. M. Pearce, *The Matador Land and Cattle Company* (Norman 1964); H. R. Mothershead, *The Swan Land and Cattle Company* (Norman 1971); Marwick, op. cit., p. 111; H. O. Brayer, 'The Influence of British Capital on the Western Range-Cattle Industry' *J.E.C.H.* 9 (1949) pp. 90-93; J. F. Rippy, 'British Investments in Texas Lands and Livestock', *S.W.H.Q.* 58 (1955) pp. 332-4; R. V. Clements, 'British Investment in the Trans-Mississippi West, 1870-1914', *P.H.R.* 29 (1960) p. 39; J. MacDonald, *Food from the Far West* (Edin. 1878); W. A. Baillie-Grohman, *Camps in the Rockies* (Lon. 1882) pp. 426-43; J. S. Tait, *The Cattle Fields of the Far West* (Edin. 1884) pp. 13, 30.

97. Prairie Cattle Company, S.C.R.O. BT2/1003.

98. H. W. Macrosty, *The Trust Movement in British Industry* (Lon. 1907) p.128; Checkland, op. cit., p. 111.

99. Marshall, op. cit., pp. 349; 355-56; James Finlay, op. cit., p.91; Byres, op. cit., p.74; India Jute Company, S.C.R.O. BT2/232; Champdany Jute Company, S.C.R.O. BT2/496.

100. *B.E.M.* 137 (1885) p.276.

101. *Econ.* 22 January 1887; *Financial Register and Stock Exchange Manual,* 1876.

102. Hassan, op. cit., p.185; Holcombe, op. cit., pp. 374-380; M. Blair, *The Paisley Thread Industry* (Paisley 1907) p.63.

103. M. A. Whitehead, The Western Bank and the Crisis of 1857 (M.Litt. Strathclyde 1978) p. 173; Clydesdale Banking Company, S.C.R.O. BT2/123.

104. M. S. Cotterill, The Scottish Gas Industry up to 1914 (Ph.D. Strathclyde 1976) pp. 1, 391; Byres, op. cit., pp. 90, 100.

13

The Expansion of the Market

IN the 1850s no stockbrokers operated outside Glasgow, Edinburgh, Aberdeen and Dundee, and the numbers in these locations had declined considerably from the peaks of 1845/6. There was only a third of the number of firms operating in Glasgow in 1853 that there had been in 1846, for example. During the second half of the nineteenth century stockbroking not only recovered the losses incurred in the late 1840s, to become a larger and more widespread profession, but also grew in status and skill so that its position within the economy and society was greatly enhanced. Growth in the numbers of stockbrokers continued to be concentrated in the periods of speculation, when transfers were active, but there was now both a large volume of regular business to support an expanding number of firms, and an internal momentum of growth stemming from the profession itself. Stockbroking firms in Edinburgh, for instance, rose from 18 in 1862 to 23 in 1866, in the course of the mid 1860s speculation, but had only fallen back to 20 in 1872 before beginning to pick up again.[1]

Fluctuations in income continued to occur, bankrupting some stockbrokers, such as William Gordon in Aberdeen in 1868, but most survived the lean periods to reap the benefits when business was active. John Miller, a Glasgow stockbroker, saw his brokerage income rise from a mere £98 in 1862 to £5,474 in 1867 before falling away again. Increasingly, the growing number of larger and older-established stockbroking firms were generating sufficient income to be able to cope with such wide variations. Miller's brokerage income increased from an average of £170 per annum in the 1850s to £1,950 in the 1860s and £4,407 in the 1870s, before dropping to £3,889 in the 1880s and £2,482 in the 1890s. At the same time the money left in the firm by Miller and his associates was also generating substantial income, as it was either being lent at interest to clients in order to finance buying and selling operations, or being used by the firm itself for such purposes.[2] When Peter White, another Glasgow stockbroker, died in 1881, he was possessed of a fortune estimated at over £200,000.[3]

Over time, stockbroking firms became part of the fabric of economic life, each with their own circle of clients and a basis of fairly steady business on their behalf. In 1898 it was said of Andrew Ogilvie, a Dundee stockbroker, that 'His clients were many, and year by year the business which he directed increased in proportions', while another Dundee firm, W. & R. Ritchie, had 'built up a large and prosperous business' by 1900.[4] The Glasgow stockbroker, B. B. MacGeorge, was envied in 1904 by his fellow brokers, as 'his clients include many of the merchant princes of Glasgow, which means, in business parlance, that much of the best money in the city passes through his hands.'[5] No longer were stockbroking firms recent creations without the connections and assets necessary to withstand the vagaries of business. Stockbrokers themselves had become respected members of the community. William Auld, a Glasgow stockbroker, was regarded as 'a high-principled, upright and honourable gentleman' in 1886.[6]

By the end of the nineteenth century each of the major Scottish cities had its own sizeable and established group of stockbrokers. Foremost was Glasgow with 58 individual brokers, 48 partnerships and a further 15 stockbroking companies, compared with Edinburgh's 25 individuals, 20 partnerships and 2 companies. In comparison, the other major cities had a much smaller profession in 1900, with Aberdeen having 8 individuals, 4 partnerships and 2 companies, while Dundee had 9 individuals and 3 partnerships.[7] Stockbroking gradually expanded from these large city locations, for, as early as the 1860s, the occupation was appearing, or re-appearing, in some of the smaller towns, especially those that were important regional centres. Both Perth and Inverness had stockbrokers in the 1860s, and Arbroath, Dumfries, Greenock and Stirling came to possess their own by the late 1870s. During the 1880s and 1890s even more minor towns or centres came to have at least one resident stockbroker, such as Rothesay and Blairgowrie by 1882, and Elgin, Hawick and Paisley by 1899. By 1900 there was a total of 40 towns and cities in Scotland with a practising stockbroker, compared to only 4 in 1850. However, the profession remained located in the four major cities, although their domination was declining. In number of firms alone — which over-emphasises the importance of the small country firms — 97 per cent of Scottish stockbrokers worked in the cities in 1873/4, and 69 per cent in 1900/1. All the major stockbroking firms operated in one of the main cities, especially Edinburgh or Glasgow. Nevertheless, the 60 individual stockbrokers, 23 partnerships and 1 company established in the rest of Scotland by 1900 ensured that in each Scottish town of significance there existed a known professional available for transacting business.[8]

Stockbroking was also becoming a much more specialised profession, with brokers concentrating upon share transfers and attendant activities at the expense of the various additional occupations they had formerly undertaken. In the 1850s, 86 per cent of John Miller's income had come from the commissions he received from his accountancy business, and only 14 per cent from the brokerage derived from buying and selling shares on behalf of clients. In the course of the 1860s the emphasis changed: though the revenue from commission fees continued to rise, those from brokerage rose much faster. Consequently, in that decade he derived only 42 per cent of his income from commissions and 58 per cent from brokerage. During the 1870s he began to concentrate more and more of his time on stocks and shares, to the detriment of his accountancy business, so that the income from commissions fell absolutely while that from brokerage continued to rise strongly. In the 1870s, 75 per cent of the revenue came from share transfers and only 25 per cent from arranging life insurance, handling estates, and so on. This trend continued for the rest of the century, with the firm becoming much more a stockbroking than an accountancy operation. By the 1890s, 93 per cent of the income came from brokerage as opposed to 7 per cent from commissions.[9]

In Glasgow, stockbroking had traditionally been combined with accountancy, and this continued to be the case. Even by 1900 there still existed 38 firms that practised in both, despite attempts by some members of the Glasgow Stock Exchange to make stockbroking a full-time occupation. However, as the reference to John Miller has shown, stockbroking was no longer the poor relation of accountancy, but rose to equal or greater importance in most of the firms. At the same time a growing number existed whose full-time business was stockbroking. By 1900 there were 78 Glasgow stockbroking firms with no major ancillary activities, and only a further 2 that combined it with something other than accountancy.[10] In Edinburgh, most stockbrokers had been full-time, and this became more pronounced in the second half of the century. The other major Scottish cities followed the trend towards the separation of stockbroking from other activities. Dundee had four stockbroking firms in 1860, and all combined it with some other occupation, mainly accountancy or an agency. Robert Miller, for example, was also an insurance and mercantile agent and a wine merchant. By 1870, one full-time stockbroker, Andrew Ogilvie, was operating in the city and the additional pursuits had been reduced to either accountancy or the subsidiary insurance agency. This pattern became more pronounced, with 10 of Dundee's 16 stockbroking firms in 1900 being full-time, while the other 6 combined stockbroking with accountancy.[11]

Aberdeen's brokers had long combined the occupation with some form of agency business or the law. In 1860 James Black & Co. were also insurance and forwarding agents and produce brokers, while Joseph Willet was a commission agent and timber merchant. In the course of the next 40 years the combination of law and stockbroking disappeared, while the agency business declined in popularity and was largely reduced to the subsidiary level of insurance agent. Accountancy took over as the commonest additional pursuit, while many firms came to concentrate solely on stockbroking. By 1900 Aberdeen had 5 full-time stockbroking firms, another 5 combined stockbroking with some minor agency business, and 6 were also accountants.[12] Outside these cities there were very few full-time stockbrokers. Two exceptions were Hugh Thomson in Inverness, a town with a vast rural hinterland, and J. Grant Maclean in Stirling, who created business for himself as an expert on insurance shares.[13] Most stockbrokers in the smaller towns combined the profession with some other substantial occupation, particularly accountancy, the agency of a bank, or, to a lesser extent, legal practice. In 1900, 58 of Scotland's stockbrokers, working outside the four main cities, were also bank agents and a further 8 were solicitors.[14] Outside the cities stockbroking remained a subsidiary activity.

During the second half of the century the Scottish stockbroking profession was becoming much more specialist, with those involved either confining themselves solely to broking or combining it with a limited number of compatible ancillary occupations, especially accountancy. Even within firms the same specialisation was appearing. In the Glasgow stockbroking and accountancy firm of MacEwan and Auld, Andrew MacEwan devoted himself increasingly to the accountancy side of the business, while his partner, William Auld, managed the stockbroking side.[15] As stockbroking became a more important and wide-ranging profession, it required far greater expertise from those involved, rather than merely buying and selling on the direct orders of a client. Knowledge of the growing variety of securities involved was now necessary, as was the ability to time the deal and the market to obtain the best price. Such information and ability could only be obtained from a constant familiarity with the everyday business of stockbroking and the acquisition of expertise through specialisation. The gifted amateur or the part-timer had less and less of a place in the profession.

While many new stockbrokers entering the profession continued to come from those occupations providing contact with the wealthy, such as the retail trade or agency services, a growing number came from activities with close contacts with finance and investment, such as accountancy and banking. Both D. E. Outram, an Edinburgh broker, and G. G. Whyte, an Aberdeen broker, had been bank employees before entering stockbroking.[16] Even more numerous were those coming into the business who were sons of established stockbrokers or who had been clerks in stockbroking offices. As early as 1868, it was reported as common practice on the Glasgow Stock Exchange

> . . . for some time past to admit as members suitable parties, on commencing business on their own account, who have served five years as clerk with a Member . . .[17]

F. A. Grant became a stockbroker on his own account in Dundee in 1899 after being a clerk in the local firm of M'Intyre & Sievewright. In Aberdeen, R. B. Horne had been William Adamson's Chief Clerk before he became his partner in 1858. In May 1885 Adamson & Horne's chief clerk, David Smith, set up in business for himself. G. G. Whyte started his own stockbroking business in Aberdeen in 1880 after having served his apprenticeship in the city. John Carrick, whose father was an architect, joined the Glasgow stockbroking firm of John Dykes in 1882 after sojourns in both London and Calcutta. After experience with that firm, and in the United States, he set up on his own account as an accountant and stockbroker, becoming a member of the Stock Exchange in 1888.

The many sons who joined their fathers in the business included Andrew MacEwan and Robert Aitken in Glasgow and J. R. Mudie in Dundee. R. B. Horne was joined by his son in 1885, and his son-in-law in 1887.[18] It was increasingly those with either an inherited financial stake in stockbroking or an expertise gained through long apprenticeship who came to predominate in the profession. The Glasgow stockbroker Robert Campbell Mackenzie had both. Not only had his father been a stockbroker, but he himself had been apprenticed to the partnership of Auld & Guild before joining his father's firm of Aitken, Mackenzie & Clapperton.[19]

As the stockbroking profession grew in size and age it was increasingly able to generate the personnel required from within its own ranks, either in the shape of those employees who had risen to positions of responsibility, such as head clerk, or from the families of the partners themselves. No longer was the business open to all comers who felt that they had both the contacts and the knowledge to conduct it. Entry from outside was still possible, however. Two Aberdeen stockbrokers, namely Charles Williamson and D. L. Lunan, who began in 1894, were set up in business by their parents, respectively a soap and candle manufacturer and a chartered accountant. James Tytler, also an Aberdeen stockbroker, had begun in 1866 with the aid of friends and possessed no capital of his own.[20] These outsiders could also be very successful. F. F. Begg, whose father was an Edinburgh doctor, migrated to New Zealand, where he obtained employment as a clerk in the Union Bank of Australia. When he returned to Scotland, he became a partner in a leading firm of Edinburgh stockbrokers. He moved to the London Stock Exchange in 1887.[21]

According to a London stockbroker, Montague Newton, in 1878:

> ... men go into the Stock Exchange now as a sort of refuge for the destitute ... There is no inquiry made when a man applies for admission to the Stock Exchange as to his capacity for that work.[22]

Even in 1878 this was untrue of Scotland, and it became progressively more difficult for people from outside to be accepted into the profession, though it remained possible. Through the stock exchange associations, and the refusal, or admittance, to membership, the established stockbrokers in Scotland's main cities could make it difficult for any new stockbrokers to set up in business successfully. These associations took their responsibilities regarding new entrants to the profession very seriously. On the Edinburgh Stock Exchange in 1873 it was felt that:

> ... considering the amount of business now done in our Exchange ... (and) the responsibilities incurred by members in the transaction of it ... it was of importance that great care should be taken as to the admission of members.[23]

This caution was embodied in the constitution of the Edinburgh Stock Exchange Association.[24]

Entry into the associations, and thus the stock exchanges, was not prohibited, but it became more controlled and more difficult as the existing membership sought both to restrict numbers, and so preserve the available business for themselves, and to ensure that the growing integrity of the profession was maintained and furthered. Undesirable or unnecessary members could simply be refused admission, while the less committed were discouraged by the need to pay higher and higher entrance fees and to provide greater and greater financial security. By 1887, entry into the Scottish Stock Exchanges was by election, with two-thirds of the committee, or membership, having to be in favour. Once admitted, Glasgow demanded an entrance fee of £400, and Edinburgh £210, plus a contribution to the capital fund, while both Aberdeen and Dundee requested smaller sums. In addition, successful candidates had to provide a minimum security of £3,000 in the case of Glasgow, £1,500 in Edinburgh, and £500 in Aberdeen.

However, concessions were normally made for the sons of partners, or clerks of some standing, who were often admitted at half-price, while security could be provided by their father or employer.[25] Candidates in these categories appear to have had much less trouble in gaining admittance, although even they were carefully scrutinised. The Dundee Stock Exchange refused J. O. Brickman admission in 1895, although he had been a broker's clerk, because he possessed a capital of only £400. He was also involved in rather speculative company promotions, especially distilleries, and this may have influenced their decision. Nevertheless, Brickman was finally admitted in 1899 when his assets totalled £1,360.[26] Similarly, the Aberdeen Stock Exchange refused R. C. Allan membership in 1884 because the amount of business he handled was considered to be insufficient.[27] Increasingly, new members had to prove themselves, or needed acceptable connections, before the exchange associations consented to their admission, and this became increasingly costly to achieve. Edinburgh's entrance fee, for example, reached £315 by 1899, and the association had dispensed with exceptions.[28]

Admittance to membership of the local stock exchange was an important control over the numbers in the stockbroking profession. The stock exchange was the central market for share dealing in the major cities, and a bar to entry placed the stockbroker concerned at a disadvantage compared to those who were members. When R. C. Allan was refused membership of the Aberdeen Stock Exchange, he quite candidly admitted that decision was 'attended with considerable hardship', as he had found and would find it difficult to conduct his business without access to the contacts and information of the stock exchange.[29] Stockbrokers did operate without being stock exchange members, but they were very few in number in the large cities. It was only in the smaller towns, where there were no stock exchanges, that they flourished. Nevertheless, the numbers of the stockbroking profession in Scotland did grow substantially in the second half of the century. A total of 271 firms were in operation by 1900, compared to only 62 in 1873.[30] Membership of the stock exchanges also rose, with those belonging to the Glasgow Stock Exchange increasing from 40 in 1850 to 188 in 1900.[31]

Entry into the Scottish stockbroking profession became increasingly difficult after 1850, while the sources of new recruits narrowed to either stockbroking itself or to closely allied financial pursuits such as banking or accountancy. However, the profession continued to grow in numbers, location, expertise and status, while a knowledge of stockbroking was also of growing use for other aspects of business. Some stockbrokers left the profession to enter a variety of other areas of business, and many were very successful in their chosen fields. Henry Forrester, for example, gave up a career in stockbroking in 1875 to manage a Glasgow dye works. Nathaniel Spens retired from stockbroking in 1890, aged 40, and became a management consultant.[32] By 1900, stockbrokers had lost both their air of novelty and hint of disrepute to become one of Scotland's best regarded professions.

Accompanying the growth and spread of the stockbroking profession in Scotland was the formation of two further stock exchanges, namely Dundee in 1879 and Greenock in 1888. Traditionally their appearance has been seen as the gradual completion of the stock exchange network in Scotland in response to the growing importance of stocks and shares within the investment choices of the Scottish population.[33] Certainly both Dundee and Greenock appear to fit this pattern. Dundee was, alternatively, the third or fourth largest Scottish city, while Greenock was, usually, the fifth largest. Thus, in terms of population their formation can be easily justified. Both cities were also increasing in income, wealth and prosperity prior to the establishment of their stock exchanges.

Dundee was a major textile town, being the foremost jute manufacturing centre in the world. Despite periodic slumps, this industry was a prosperous one, producing higher profits and higher wages which, in turn, stimulated the whole economy of the region. As a result of this growth the annual income of Dundee was estimated at £1.5m by the early 1880s.[34] However, Dundee's wealth and income remained concentrated in the hands of the immensely rich. Fleming, a timber merchant in both Dundee and Aberdeen, reflected upon this fact in his autobiography:

> Dundee, . . ., has multitudes of workers living in tenements, great numbers of very wealthy merchant princes, with great mansions in the west end or at Broughty Ferry, and not nearly such a large number of the fairly well-to-do . . . fortunes of £100,000 to £1,000,000 are quite common in Dundee . . .[35]

Nevertheless, there was a growing number of people in Dundee with moderate incomes and the ability to save and invest, who would require the services of a local stockbroker rather than a specialist working solely on their behalf, as some of the very wealthy had:

> There is considerable wealth in the town, and it is far more widely diffused than it was a quarter of a century ago,

concluded the *Dundee Year Book* in 1878. As early as 1864 there were over 1,000 middle-class subscribers to a housing scheme in the city.[36]

Greenock also underwent a phase of rapid economic growth based upon its position as a major port on the Clyde estuary, through which the exports and imports of Glasgow and West Central Scotland could flow. There was a succession of substantial harbour developments in the nineteenth century, involving the construction of more commodious facilities in order to cope with both the expanding volume of traffic and the increasing size of ships.[37] At the same time the town was becoming a major sugar refining centre due to its access to the abundant coal reserves of Ayrshire and Lanarkshire, and the cane sugar of the Caribbean and Mauritius.[38]

Reflecting the growing affluence and population of both towns was the increase in the number of stockbrokers. By 1878 there were 9 stockbroking firms in Dundee compared with 7 in 1867 and 2 in 1851, while Greenock had 5 firms in 1888, only one in 1866, and none in the 1850s, although there had been at least one during the 'Railway Mania'. [39] However, many in both places utilised outside stockbrokers. The wealthy Dundonians often transacted business directly with stockbrokers in other British cities, or even in the U.S.A., as they had sufficient funds and the expertise to justify the trouble involved in establishing contacts with distant brokers.[40] In Greenock, it was proximity to the better services offered by the Glasgow stockbroking firms that reduced the business available to the unspecialised local brokers, for whom accountancy, property management, or some other pursuit, was their primary business.[41] This use of Glasgow brokers by Greenock investors became much easier in the 1880s, with the establishment of a telephone link between the two towns in 1882, and the growth of a dense telephone network in Central Scotland. However, there remained many in both Dundee and Greenock who found it far more convenient to use a local agent to conduct their buying and selling of shares, and to consult over matters of investment.

The need for, and the use of, local stockbrokers did not necessarily mean that a local stock exchange would eventually be formed. Many informal share markets existed in Scotland by the late nineteenth century, but only Dundee and Greenock formed stock exchanges. The stockbrokers in Fife, for example, were even producing their own 'Fife Share List' by the 1870s, although this consisted mostly of small gas companies operating in the locality.[42] In Perth there were movements afoot to form a small local stock exchange in 1898, but this came to nothing.[43] Other substantial towns, such as Paisley and Arbroath, or regional centres such as Inverness, Perth and Stirling, despite having an active stockbroking and investing fraternity, never established stock exchanges. In 1900, for example, Perth had 8 stockbroking firms, while Arbroath and Paisley had 5 each, compared to Greenock's 9 and Dundee's 16.[44]

From before the 'Railway Mania' there had been an active market in shares in Dundee leading to the production of a regular 'Dundee Stock List', reprinted in the *Dundee Press*. This listed the local joint-stock enterprises whose securities were traded, and the current prices determined by the Dundee market.[45] Local banks, railways, utilities and insurance companies, whose stocks and shares were largely held in Dundee and its vicinity, had their transactions settled and prices set by the collective action of the Dundee stockbrokers, with only indirect reference to outside market conditions. The small number of brokers made it unnecessary to formalise these contacts into a stock exchange. However, as the number of brokers in Dundee rose, reaching 9 firms by 1878, and as the business they handled increased, their need to settle transactions between themselves did not increase proportionately, and may even have declined, for Dundee lost control over much of its own joint-stock enterprise.[46] All Dundee's insurance companies and banks were taken over by other Scottish or English concerns in the 1850s and 1860s, while most of the railways became part of either the Edinburgh-based North British, or the Glasgow-based Caledonian railway networks.[47]

Consequently, by 1870, all that remained of locally owned and managed joint-stock enterprise in Dundee was one small railway, a coastal shipping company, gas and water works, a cemetery, a building company, and three speculative whaling ventures.[48] Dundee investors continued to have large holdings in banks, railways and insurance. In 1882, it was estimated that Dundee holdings of the stock of various Scottish and English insurance companies, such as the Northern, Queen, and Royal, totalled £100,000.[49] In each case, however, these holdings were now only a minor component of a company's issued stocks and shares, rather than the majority holding in a small local concern, as had been the case before amalgamation. The *Dundee Year Book* reflected, in 1882, on what had happened to the nature of local railway shareholdings as a result of amalgamation:

> At the time of transfer all these lines were chiefly held by local shareholders, but since the stocks have become guaranteed preferences it is probable that considerable amounts have gone into the general investment market, while a fair proportion is still held here.[50]

Holders of Dundee Bank stock, Forfarshire and Perthshire Insurance Company shares, or Dundee and Arbroath Railway stock, tended to be largely local so that any buying or selling would normally be confined to investors living in Dundee or its area, and thus necessitate regular consultation between local brokers and the creation of some form of local settling facilities where bargains could be matched and prices arranged. In contrast, the majority of holders of Royal Bank stock, Northern Insurance Company shares, or Caledonian Railway stock, would tend to be from either Edinburgh, Aberdeen, or Glasgow, the home offices of these concerns, or from Scotland as a whole. The main market for transfers in these stocks would tend to be where the majority of their shareholders resided, not in Dundee, from where only a minority came, since a Dundonian investor's holdings in the Royal Bank, Northern Insurance, or Caledonian Railway, were no different from any other investor's but his local securities were. Consequently, it became necessary for Dundee stockbrokers to direct many of their clients' buying and selling orders to other markets as they could not be settled by the local brokers alone. The Dundee stockbrokers, Henderson and Parker, advertised in 1871,

> Stocks and shares, bought and sold on the London, Liverpool, Glasgow and Edinburgh Exchanges.

They even went so far as to open an office in Glasgow in 1874 in order to facilitate business.[51]

Joint-stock enterprise in Greenock had always been much more limited than in Dundee, and so the pressure for local settling facilities was much less. What few companies there were mainly met a similar fate to Dundee's, being largely absorbed by such large Glasgow-based concerns as the Caledonian Railway, Glasgow and South Western Railway, or Clydesdale Bank. In addition, unlike Dundee, when the Greenock municipal authorities acquired the gas and water companies, they did not issue transferable stocks, debentures or annuities in exchange. Instead, they created a debt upon which they paid interest and redeemed gradually. Thus, while Greenock investors were owed around £0.75m by the town in 1888, that debt was not in a form that required the services of any stockbrokers, let alone local ones. All that existed in the way of joint-stock enterprise in Greenock by the 1880s were four small concerns, namely the Greenock Heritable Co., the Greenock Stevedore Co., the Greenock Steamship Co., and the West End Baths.[52] As a result, there existed even less need for a local stock exchange in Greenock in 1880 than in Dundee in 1870.

The market for the securities that interested the investors of each town lay, increasingly, elsewhere, especially Glasgow or Edinburgh. With the growing investment of savings in stocks and shares, there was a growing need for stockbrokers, but the long-term trend in both places was not conducive to the establishment of a local stock exchange. These brokers were perfectly capable of channelling this business to the appropriate market, through their stockbroking contacts, and although the sharing of commission may have irked, it was the position faced by every broker who was asked by a client to buy and sell securities whose market lay elsewhere.[53] The need for some form of local settling facilities was much greater in Dundee than in Greenock, but even there the brokers were perfectly capable of dealing with any local business on an *ad hoc* basis as it arose.[54] In both towns the stockbrokers were a fairly small and close-knit group which made contact easy, while the transactions to be handled between them were not burdensome.[55] Nevertheless, stock exchanges were formed in both Dundee and Greenock, suggesting a reversal of the observed trend.

In most areas of joint-stock enterprise, there was little sign of a revival in Dundee during the 1870s. The Northern Marine Insurance Company had been formed in 1868, but it had a paid-up capital of only £25,000, provided by just over 50 shareholders. Nothing further appeared in either insurance or banking. A few short and inexpensive railway lines were constructed, such as the St. Andrews, and only infrequently traded. The Dundee and District Tramway Company was established in 1877, but its paid-up capital amounted to only £10,000, coming from about 100 investors. Joint-stock shipping companies showed little expansion until the early 1880s, after the formation of the Stock Exchange, when there was the conversion of the fleets of a number of ship-owning firms into public companies. A few new urban facilities were provided in the shape of public halls, but their total capital was under £16,000. There was no significant conversion of Dundee's industrial stock companies during the 1870s, although a few large coal mining concerns in Fife did become public in 1872. The Fife Coal Co. and the Lochore & Capledrae Cannel Coal Co. had between them a paid-up capital of almost £200,000 in 1880, and this was held by 337 investors. However, these were Edinburgh-based concerns and drew their financial support from that quarter.[56]

There is the impression of innovation in municipal finance during the 1870s, with the corporation issuing annuities to the value of £212,710 in 1868-9. This did not, however, represent any net addition to local securities in circulation, but was the conversion of the existing stock of the gas and water joint-stock companies into municipal annuities. It was not until the 1880s that the city itself began to raise substantial amounts of new capital for municipal improvement. A total of £903,780 was raised between 1884 and 1889, for example, by the issue of transferable debentures. However, this municipal stock had a different market from that available to the local joint-stock companies. The corporation issued fixed interest securities guaranteed by their ability to raise money from the rates. This made these issues very attractive to personal and institutional investors from outside the region, for income was not dependent upon the sales of gas or supply of water by small local concerns, but upon the earning power of the whole town through its corporate body. Consequently, Dundee corporation stock was more widely held than ever were the issues of the companies it acquired.[57]

The one real area of expansion in joint-stock enterprise in Dundee during the 1870s was in the field of investment, trust and mortgage companies channelling funds overseas. In Dundee, Robert Fleming formed the Scottish American Investment Trust in 1873 to invest in U.S. railroad bonds. In three issues, £1.1m was raised by January 1875. Also in 1873, William Reid, a Dundonian resident in the United States, formed the Oregon and Washington Trust Investment Company to invest in land mortgages in the north-west of the United States. By 1877 this company had obtained £177,557 from the Dundee public. In 1876 the Dundee Mortgage and Trust Investment Company was established by Reid and his associates to invest in both railway bonds and land mortgages throughout North America. By 1878 a total of £289,821 had been raised. Finally, the same group organised the Dundee Land Investment Company in 1878 to purchase land in the American West for resale once prices had risen. In 1881 the capital of that company totalled £115,280.[58]

Consequently, by the late 1870s around £1.7m had been invested in the shares and debentures of the investment, trust and mortgage companies of Dundee. Most of this capital was raised in Dundee itself, often from small shareholders. The first issue of the Scottish American Investment Trust attracted 385 investors, of whom more than half invested less than £400 each. Similarly, 230 investors subscribed to the Dundee Mortgage & Trust Investment Co. in 1876. Almost all of the shareholders came from Dundee or the surrounding area.[59] At the same time the success of these numerous Dundee ventures led Dundee investors to subscribe to the issues of investment companies begun elsewhere in Scotland, in the expectation of a similar performance. By the early 1880s it was estimated that Dundee investors had placed up to £1m in non-local investment companies.[60] In the Edinburgh-based Scottish American Mortgage Co., for example, 34 per cent of the shareholders were from Dundee, and they provided 39 per cent of the capital.[61] The Dundee companies themselves also became more permanent enterprises. The Scottish American Investment Trust expected to terminate after 10 years, but in March 1879 it was re-organised on the basis of indefinite duration. At the same time the Oregon and Washington Trust Investment Co. was merged with the Dundee Mortgage and Trust Investment Co. to provide a stronger grouping under the control of William Mackenzie, who had been secretary to both companies.[62]

As a result of these investment company developments in the 1870s, Dundee investors not only invested some £3m abroad, but they also placed it through a small number of companies whose shareholders came largely or substantially from Dundee and its vicinity. These local investors were also numerous. This stimulated both a growing demand for the services of stockbrokers and a need for a better local market, as much more buying and selling was now taking place between investors resident in Dundee and its area. It was to meet this need that the Dundee Stock Exchange Association was formed in March 1879 by nine stockbrokers practising in Dundee.[63] As the *Dundee Advertiser* reported in April 1879:

Although during the last ten or fifteen years there has been a great increase in the number and amount of transactions in stocks and shares, both general and local, in Dundee, the stockbrokers have had no regular place or times of meeting. As the number of brokers has grown with the amount of business the want of a local Stock Exchange has been increasingly felt, and it was accordingly resolved recently to form an Exchange ... Two meetings will be held daily. Hitherto brokers have been subjected to considerable inconvenience in communicating with each other, having to go from office to office. Now at two periods every day they will come together, and transactions which were previously carried through elsewhere will be completed in Dundee.[64]

It was not the general investment needs of the Dundee investor that created the Dundee Stock Exchange in 1879, but the fact that his investments became concentrated on a small number of companies, which Dundee investors dominated, making the market for their shares a local rather than a general one. Enterprising promoters such as Fleming, Reid and Mackenzie were those who were actively responsible for the formation of a Dundee exchange, not the growing wealth of the community, for that could have continued to find its way into non-local enterprises. The new stock exchange was dependent for business upon the buying and selling of these investment company securities. In the period May to December 1879, 63 per cent of the transactions were in the stocks, shares, and debentures of investment, trust and mortgage companies, with 40 per cent being in the Dundee-based concerns alone. Consequently, without this revival of local joint-stock enterprise, centring almost solely upon overseas investment, it is unlikely that a formal market would have been established in Dundee in 1879. Later developments, such as the conversion of local companies into public joint-stock concerns, might have had the same effect, for Dundee was a large and wealthy city with a rapidly expanding investing public, but the actual creation of the exchange was a product of the boom in overseas investment and the form it took in Dundee.

In Greenock, there was no revival at all in local joint-stock enterprise during the 1870s or 1880s in either traditional or novel branches. The single event that led to the formation of the Greenock Stock Exchange in 1888 was the difficulties encountered by the town's over-ambitious harbour building programme. By 1878 the council had decided on a bid to make Greenock the premier port of the West of Scotland, surpassing Glasgow itself. The construction of a large wet dock, a graving dock, and an entirely new harbour — the Great Harbour — was set in motion. However, the work of the Clyde Navigation Trust ensured that increasingly large ocean-going ships could still reach Glasgow, removing much of the necessity for an intermediate trans-shipment point at Greenock. At the same time, the hoped-for coal export trade failed to materialise, while the major bulk import, raw sugar, declined in the face of competition from European sugar-beet producers.[65]

In order to finance harbour construction, the Greenock Harbour Trust resorted to heavy borrowing, and by May 1887 a debt of £1.5m had been accumulated. This was in the form of non-transferable short-term bonds upon which interest was paid annually. When these bonds matured they had to be repaid, but, as they were considered to be safe investments, they were either regularly renewed or replacement finance was easily obtained. With the new expenditure, the size of the debt was almost doubled, but the income out of which the interest was paid fell with the decline in traffic.[66] The inevitable result was reached in May 1887 when the Greenock Harbour Trust had to announce that they could not pay the interest due to the bond holders, let alone redeem maturing bonds.[67] A panic ensued amongst those who had lent money to the Trust, ensuring that no further funds could be raised without the greatest difficulty in order to maintain interest payments until construction was complete and trade and revenue revived.[68]

The only solution was to reform the Trust's borrowing into a long-term debt upon which interest would be paid, when possible, with the prospect of eventual redemption. The Trust's assets could hardly be sold to pay off its debts, as they consisted of harbours, piers, and docks, so a parliamentary bill was lodged in December 1887 with the object of consolidating the whole debt into ordinary and preference debenture stock, and this bill received the Royal Assent in July 1888.[69] Under this legislation the holders of bonds regarded as having priority, amounting to £430,673, had the option of exchanging them for Debenture Stock 'A', paying 3.5 per cent per annum, or otherwise waiting until their bonds could be paid off in full. Creditors holding bonds to the value of £359,950 (84%) accepted the offer of conversion. The other bond holders, to whom £1,103,838 was owed, were given no option but to exchange their holdings for Debenture Stock 'B', paying 4 per cent per annum. Stock 'A' had first call upon the Trust's revenue, while Stock 'B' could only share what remained, although its claim was cumulative.[70]

As a consequence of this conversion, the Greenock Harbour Trust's essentially short-term but renewable debt became a long-term transferable debt in the form of debenture stock. However, many holders of the bonds had no wish to hold debenture stock indefinitely and wished to realise the investment in which they were trapped. The natural market for their stock would have been the Glasgow Stock Exchange, for the largest proportion of the Trust's debt was held in the West of Scotland. Of the borrowings extant in May 1887, 45 per cent originated from Glasgow and the West of Scotland, 32 per cent from Edinburgh and the rest of Scotland, and 23 per cent from England.[71] Naturally there was an extreme unwillingness on the Glasgow Stock Exchange to become involved with the debenture stock of the Greenock Harbour Trust. Not only were there legitimate fears concerning the solvency of the whole venture, in the light of the Trust's continuing difficulties, but there was also an understandable unwillingness to aid an institution whose very purpose was to undermine the prosperity of Glasgow.[72]

Greenock Harbour Trust Debenture Stock remained unquoted on the Glasgow Stock Exchange throughout 1888, leaving the stock without a recognised and convenient market for its holders.[73] In order to remedy this difficulty the stockbrokers in Greenock decided to form their own stock exchange. By its establishment they expected to monopolise the substantial turnover in Harbour Trust Stock and so enhance their own business. The Greenock Stock Exchange was opened on the 24th of September 1888 'with the object of conducting business in Harbour Trust Stocks and other Investments', according to the local stockbroking firm of Hardie and Allan.[74] What limited transactions there were,

were largely confined to Harbour Trust debentures. Despite the creation of the stock exchange, Glasgow continued to provide the market for almost all the securities in which Greenock investors were interested. This included the stock of the Harbour Trust as early as 1890.[75] Glasgow stockbrokers regarded their Greenock rival as an unwelcome and unnecessary intrusion, and refused to recognise its existence, while not all of Greenock's own stockbrokers bothered to join.[76]

Consequently, the establishment of the Greenock Stock Exchange was due to a peculiar set of circumstances for, without the difficulties of the Harbour Trust, there would have been very little need to form a local stock exchange. The town was too near Glasgow and lacked the established, locally owned joint-stock enterprise ever to justify a local market without some unique occurrence, such as the conversion of a floating debt of £1.5m into transferable securities. In Dundee, there was always the possibility that a stock exchange would be formed, for the city had the size and the position to justify it, but that could not be said of Greenock. Specific, but different, developments were necessary in both cases before stock exchanges were formed. Without these events it is unlikely that Greenock would ever have had a stock exchange but possible that one would have been formed in Dundee.

After 1850 the stockbroking profession in Scotland grew in size, stature and skill, while two further institutions were added to the three already in existence. However, these new stock exchanges were very different from those established in 1844/5. The Greenock Stock Exchange was a very small market both in the volume of business and the range of securities in which it dealt. It was very much a marginal addition to the facilities available as, even in Greenock, investors had to have daily direct, or indirect, recourse to other markets, especially Glasgow. In fact, the Glasgow Stock Exchange remained the central market for that area of Scotland, and the Greenock Exchange was largely irrelevant. The Dundee Stock Exchange was much more important, but even it was not on the same level as the older institutions. Although there was considerable business on the Dundee Exchange, it centred mainly on the investment companies and the other varieties of overseas enterprise originated in the city. Dundee investors' interest in such major areas as banking, insurance and railroads continued to be directed to non-local institutions, and thus to non-local markets. The overseas ventures were complemented by a growth of joint-stock companies operating domestically, but the Dundee market never possessed either the volume or variety of business of the longer-established Scottish stock exchanges. Nevertheless, Dundee filled an important gap in the Scottish stock exchange network, while Greenock was largely superfluous, for its function was little different from that of the independent stockbrokers who operated throughout Scotland by the late nineteenth century.

NOTES

1. *Slater's Commercial Directory of Scotland* (Lon. 1852); *G.D.* 1846, 1853; *E.D.* 1862-1872.
2. *A.H.* 12 April 1868; John Miller, Private Ledger, 1850-1900; *Econ.* 22 Dec. 1900.
3. R. Brown, *A History of Accounting and Accountants* (Edin. 1905) pp. 225-6.

4. *D.Y.B.* (1898) p. 82; (1900) p. 71.

5. *The Bailie,* 9 March 1904.

6. *Memoirs and Portraits of 100 Glasgow Men* (Glasgow 1886) p. 188.

7. *G.D.* 1900; *E.D.* 1900; *A.D.* 1900; *D.D.* 1900.

8. *The British and Foreign Stock Exchange and Joint Stock Companies' Directory* (Lon. 1863); *The Stockbrokers' Directory of Great Britain and Ireland* (Lon. 1873/4); *United Kingdom Stock and Sharebrokers' Directory* (Lon. 1900/1); *Slater's,* op. cit., 1878 & 1882; *Stubbs' Directory* (Lon. 1892, 1896); *Royal National Directory of Scotland* (Lon. 1899).

9. Miller, Ledger, op. cit.

10. *G.D.* 1850-1900; Glasgow Stock Exchange Association: Minutes, 24 December 1895.

11. *E.D.* 1850-1900; *D.D.* 1850-1900.

12. *A.D.* 1850-1900.

13. *I.D.* 1894-5; *S.C. of F. & I.* February 1899; J. Grant Maclean, *Prices of Insurance Companies' Shares* (Stirling 1890).

14. *United Kingdom Stock & Sharebrokers' Directory,* op. cit.

15. *Memoirs,* op. cit., p. 188.

16. *The Bailie,* 4 February 1885; H. H. Bassett, *Business Men at Home and Abroad, 1912-13* (Lon. 1912), 'G. G. Whyte'.

17. Glasgow, Minutes, 13 December 1868.

18. *The Bailie,* 17 February 1897, 28 June 1899; *Memoirs,* op. cit., p. 188; Bassett (1912), op. cit., 'G. G. Whyte'; *D.D.* 1887, 1899; Horne & Mackinnon, 1845-1945 (Abdn. 1946).

19. *The Bailie,* 10 June 1908.

20. *A.D.* 1866, 1894; *A.F.P.* 3 May 1889.

21. Bassett (1900-1), op. cit., 'F. F. Begg'; Bassett (1912), op. cit., 'F. F. Begg'; *The Bailie,* 3 July 1895.

22. Report from the Commissioners on the London Stock Exchange, *B.P.P.* C2157-1 (1878) Q4268 p. 166.

23. Edinburgh Stock Exchange Association: Minutes, 4 June 1873.

24. *Constitution, Rules and Bye-laws of the Edinburgh Stock Exchange Association* (Edin. 1883) p. 11.

25. *Phillips' Investors' Manual* (Lon. 1887) pp. 341-4.

26. Dundee Stock Exchange Association: Minutes 23 October 1895, 17 August 1899; *D.D.* 1896; R. B. Weir, *The History of the Malt Distillers' Association of Scotland* (York 1974) p. 22.

27. Aberdeen Stock Exchange Association: Minutes 28 November 1884.

28. *Rules of the Edinburgh Stock Exchange* (Edin. 1899) p. 11.

29. R. C. Allan to Sec., Abdn. St. Ex. 28 November 1884.

30. *Stockbrokers' Directory,* op. cit.; *U.K. Directory,* op. cit.

31. *Records of the Glasgow Stock Exchange Association, 1844-1926* (Glasgow 1927) pp. 11, 16; W. A. Thomas, *The Provincial Stock Exchanges* (Lon. 1973) p. 287.

32. *Memoirs,* op. cit., p. 222; Bassett (1900-1), op. cit., p. 203.

33. M. Edelstein, 'Rigidity and Bias in the British Capital Market, 1870-1914' in D. N. McCloskey (ed.), *Essays on a Mature Economy: Britain after 1840* (Lon. 1971) p. 89; Thomas, op. cit., pp. 286-7.

34. B. Lenman, et al, *Dundee and its Textile Industry* (Dundee 1969) pp. 23-33, 67; B. Lenman & A. Donaldson, 'Partners' Incomes, Investment and Diversification in the Scottish Linen Area, 1850-1921' *B.H.* 13 (1971) p. 3.

35. J. Fleming, *Looking Backwards for Seventy Years, 1921-1851* (Abdn. 1922) pp. 53, 40.

36. *D.Y.B.* (1878) 6; Lenman (1969), op. cit., p. 91; Lenman & Donaldson, op. cit., p. 11.

37. J. Bird, *The Major Seaports of the United Kingdom* (Lon. 1963) p. 89; I. A. G. Kinniburgh, 'Greenock: Growth and Change in the Harbours of the Town', *S.G.M.* 78 (1960) pp. 92, 95; G. Williamson, *Old Greenock* (Paisley 1886) pp. 199-202.

38. T. J. Byres, The Scottish Economy during the 'Great Depression', 1873-1896 (B.Litt. Glasgow 1963) p. 96.

39. *D.D.* 1851, 1867, 1878; *Gr.D.* 1865-88; *S.R.G.* 18 October 1845.

40. W. & T. Jackson, *The Enterprising Scot* (Edin. 1968) p. 22.

41. *G.T.* 25 September 1888; *Gr.D.* 1865-88; *S.B.* & *I.M.* November 1882; B. T. Robson, *Urban Growth* (Lon. 1973) pp. 166, 169, 171.

42. *D.P.* & *C.A.* 28 July 1879.

43. Moir, Wood & Rorie, Accountants and Stockbrokers, Perth to Sec, Abdn. St. Ex. 16 December 1898.

44. *U.K. Directory,* op. cit.

45. *D.P.* & *C.A.,* e.g. 1850, 1860, 1870.

46. *D.D.* 1878.

47. S. G. Checkland, *Scottish Banking: A History, 1695-1973* (Glasgow 1975) p. 465; W. Vamplew, Railways and the Transformation of the Scottish Economy (Ph.D. Edin. 1969) pp. 33-4; *A.F.P.* 4 March 1889.

48. Dundee Stock List D.P. & C.A. 1870.

49. *D.Y.B.* (1882) p. 26.

50. *D.Y.B.* (1882) p. 24.

51. *D.D.* 1871, 1874.

52. *G.T.* 25 September 1888; *Centenary of the Shaws Water Company's Works* (Greenock 1927) p. 20.

53. *G.T.* 25 September 1888.

54. *D.P.* & *C.A.* 29 April 1879.

55. *Gr.D.* 1888; *D.D.* 1878.

56. *D.Y.B.* (1882) pp. 25-6; Northern Marine Insurance Co., S.C.R.O. BT.229, Dundee & District Tramway Co., S.C.R.O. BT2/778; C. J. A. Robertson, 'The Cheap Railway Movement in Scotland: the St. Andrews Railway Company' *T.H.* 7 (1974) pp. 15-16; Lochore & Capledrae Cannel Coal Co. S.C.R.O. BT2/432; Fife Coal Co. S.C.R.O. BT2/449.

57. *S.E.O.I.* (1900) pp. 96-7; M. S. Cotterill, The Scottish Gas Industry up to 1914 (Ph.D. Strathclyde 1976) p. 828.

58. J. C. Gilbert, *A History of Investment Trusts in Dundee, 1873-1938* (Lon. 1939) pp. 14, 19, 20, 35, 36, 39, 40, 49, 56, 58; Jackson, op. cit., pp. 22, 24, 27, 30-1.

59. Jackson, op. cit., p. 23; W. G. Kerr, *Scottish Capital on the American Credit Frontier* (Austin 1976) p. 171.

60. *D.Y.B.* (1882) p. 27.

61. Kerr, op. cit., pp. 103-5.

62. Gilbert, op. cit., pp. 23-4, 44; Jackson, op. cit., p. 33.

63. Dundee, Minutes, op. cit., 28 March 1879, 31 March 1879.

64. *D.P.* & *C.A.* 29 April 1879.

65. Bird, op. cit., p. 89; Kinniburgh, op. cit., p. 95; Byres, op. cit., p. 114; A. Maclean (ed.), *Local Industries of Glasgow and the West of Scotland* (Glasgow 1901) pp. 186, 287.

66. 'Greenock Harbour Bonds' *A.M.* 3 (1899) pp. 264-6; *S.E.O.I.* (1890) pp. 90-1.

67. *N.B.E.* March 1889; *G.T.* 5 September 1888.

68. R. M. Smith, *The History of Greenock* (Greenock 1921) p. 170.

69. *N.B.E.* March 1889; Smith, op. cit., p. 173.

70. *S.E.O.I.* (1890) pp. 90-1, (1891) pp. 98-99.

71. Smith, op. cit., p. 172.

72. Smith, op. cit., p. 173; Bird, op. cit., p. 89.

73. Glasgow Daily Share List, 3 January 1888 – 31 December 1888.

74. Circular issued by Hardie & Allan, 21 September 1888; *G.T.* 25 September 1888, 1889, 1895, 1900.

75. *S.E.O.I.* (1890) p. 91; Glasgow Daily Share List, 2 January 1900 – 31 Dec. 1900; Glasgow: Minutes, op. cit., 10 July 1894; *Constitution and Rules of The Greenock Stock Exchange Association* (Greenock 1888) Rules 2, 3, & 37.

76. Glasgow: Minutes, 23 September 1900, 13 November 1900; Edin. Committee Minutes, 3 January 1901; Abdn.: Minutes, 3 December 1900; *Gr.D.* 1900; Thomas, op. cit., p. 287.

14

Stockbroking: Functions and Operations

IN the second half of the nineteenth century Scottish stockbrokers came to occupy a central role in the process of investment.[1] Their main function continued to be that of buying and selling shares on behalf of clients, and they became almost the only channel through which such business was carried out. Transfers between individuals continued to exist, as did newspaper advertisements and auctions, but they were only very irregular occurrences prompted by special circumstances, rather than an integral part of the market.[2] Advertisements were resorted to in the case of the shares of tiny local companies with a limited appeal, for their securities were rarely transferred and had no ready market or known price.[3] In the case of auctions, it was usually bankruptcy, or sometimes death, that necessitated their use in order to dispose of large amounts of stock in a small company. Such was the case with an auction in Keith, in April 1889, to dispose of 1,550 shares in the local distillery.[4]

Stockbrokers also gradually ousted all other intermediaries from share dealing. Accountants, solicitors and bank agents continued to handle a certain amount of transfers, but they possessed neither the contacts nor the knowledge which were becoming of increasing importance in the buying and selling of securities. Thus, investors turned in growing numbers to the stockbrokers for the arrangement of all business connected with stocks and shares.[5]

Through their exclusive membership of the stock exchanges the stockbrokers in the large cities could monopolise share dealing since only they had access to the central market for shares. Other professional groups had, as a consequence, no alternative but to relinquish the role they had once played. Outside the cities with stock exchanges, the stockbroker was much more susceptible to competition from lawyers, accountants and others, as they too could channel business to the most appropriate market. However, throughout Scotland members of these other professions resorted to stockbrokers themselves in order to have the transactions of their clients expertly performed, usually receiving a part of the commission charged by the broker:

> . . . Some members of the Association have been in the practice of dividing commission with or allowing a remuneration to writers and other parties in Glasgow employing them on behalf of Trustees or otherwise . . .,

reported the Glasgow Stock Exchange in 1861. This was common practice in the whole of Scotland and continued until at least the end of the century, despite the stock exchange associations' attempts to stop such payments. Their purpose was

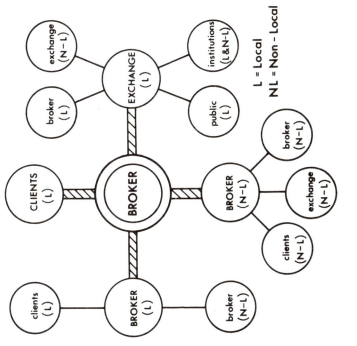

L = Local
NL = Non - Local

Inter-connections in the Share Market

to drive out completely all competitors by forcing investors to deal directly with the stockbrokers if they wanted to buy and sell stocks and shares.[6]

The only group that continued to deal in securities independently, in the face of the hostility of stockbrokers and their associations, were the Scottish banks. They continued to arrange transfers in their own shares for any customer, and refused to alter this procedure despite repeated requests to do so. The stockbrokers felt understandably aggrieved, for the banks used the prices set in the stock exchanges for the transfers they arranged, but the brokers obtained nothing by way of commission for this service. In January 1899 the Glasgow and Edinburgh Stock Exchanges jointly petitioned the banks, asking them to stop the practice, and their appeal contains the whole justification for their monopoly of the buying and selling of stocks and shares:

> The Committees of the Glasgow and Edinburgh Stock Exchanges, having under consideration the practice of many of the Scotch Banks of acting as Agents in the buying and selling of their own stocks, beg respectfully to represent the unfairness of this proceeding to the Brokers of their Exchanges, in as much as advantage is taken, without acknowledgement, of the facilities provided by markets established by them, without which the prices of Bank Stocks could not be satisfactorily ascertained. The Brokers consider that, being among the best customers of the Banks, they are entitled to some consideration in this matter, and they therefore, ask that applications for purchase or sale should be referred to Brokers connected with the Stock Exchanges.[7]

It was the action taken by the stockbrokers that set the prices which ruled in the market, and this market was supported by the facilities created and financed by the stockbroking firms who were members of the stock exchanges. Those individuals and institutions who were not stock exchange members contributed nothing in terms of money or business towards the maintenance of this market, but could only operate by virtue of the prices set in this market. Unless non-members directed the buying and selling to members, and shared commissions, or the member stockbrokers handled the whole business themselves, the members obtained no remuneration at all from those transfers handled by outsiders. These transactions bypassed the market, but were dependent upon it. The aim of the stock exchanges was to force all business through the hands of those stockbrokers who belonged to stock exchanges, where that was possible, so that all who used the market contributed to its upkeep. Naturally this would leave the stock exchanges and their members in a very strong position. The banks remained exceptions as they refused to alter their practice, despite the implied threat of the 1899 petition.[8] However, they were minor exceptions, for they confined their dealings to their own shares and passed on business in other securities to stockbrokers.[9] As a result the stockbrokers gradually dominated all purchases and sales of stocks and shares in Scotland, partly through their ability to force others out of the business, but mainly because of the better service they provided.

Although buying and selling shares was the primary function of stockbrokers, they became far more than the simple tools of their clients. Apart from general orders, the stockbroker was left to exercise a great deal of discretion as to how and when, and at what price, the deal was finally made. The client had to rely upon the stockbroker's expertise in achieving the best price possible. W. N. Neilson, a Glasgow engine manufacturer, held substantial stock in both the Caledonian and North British Railways, and was actively engaged in buying and selling their stock, both for capital gain and to realise part of his own investments. J. & G. Moffat, stockbrokers in Glasgow, acted for him, not only carrying out his orders but also giving advice, which was usually taken. On 6 February 1889, for instance, their opinion was that, 'we incline to think it would be better to clear out altogether', and by the fourteenth of that month some £36,000 of stock in the two railways had been sold.[10]

The Glasgow stockbroking firm of Kerr, Anderson, Muir & Main transacted business on behalf of Alfred Nobel, especially in Nobel Explosives and Nobel Dynamite Trust.[11] This was not a simple matter of making sales and purchases, but required the whole of the firm's expertise in gauging the market, as this letter to Nobel in February 1889 clearly illustrates:

> The market for these shares (Nobel Dynamite Trust) has for some time past been a very restricted one and it has been hardly possible to either buy or sell a few hundred shares in a day without putting the price up or down. The speculative account in these has been reduced to the very smallest dimensions and until it is increased and the dealings become more active we fear it would be extremely difficult if not quite impossible, to operate on a large scale without causing some disturbance. Your wire asks how long it would take to place 13,000 shares. We really could not indicate any time for the placing of such a lot as this at from 9½ to 10; but with say 2,000 or 3,000 on a market such as we have had lately it would probably take a couple of accounts. In this estimate we are taking it that no other large seller comes on. It might be necessary and advisable if you wish to undertake any large operation to create a more active market and we fancy this could be done with little cost.[12]

Stockbrokers were not just passive intermediaries in the market, doing as they were told by their clients. They used their accumulated experience and market knowledge, not only to carry out deals but also to advise investors as to what was the best course of action, especially with regard to the timing of purchases or sales. In December 1886, for example, Kerr, Anderson advised Nobel to hold onto his Clydesdale Bank shares as they expected the price to rise.[13]

In cases where clients were actively involved in the buying and selling of securities for speculation, and required additional finance for that purpose, the stockbrokers were even more valuable. Speculators relied heavily upon the expertise of their broker to get in and out of the market so as both to avoid losses and make gains. Stockbrokers also possessed contacts that allowed speculations to be financed by borrowings, with the securities being bought to act as collateral. Banks were always willing to lend on the security of first-class stocks, such as the stock of British and major U.S. railways. Some large stockbroking firms also possessed funds of their own which could be lent. The normal arrangement, in 1887, was for the client to pay 20 per cent of the market price of the securities being purchased for resale. The remaining 80 per cent was borrowed on the security of the stocks purchased, allowing the lender a 20 per cent margin against a fall in price and a possible default. A rate of interest of 4 per cent per annum was charged for the loan, plus 1 per cent per annum payable to the stockbroking firm for arranging the finance.[14]

The use of borrowed funds was not confined to those who could not afford to pay for stock outright, but was commonplace amongst wealthy investors, whose very assets made it easy to obtain credit. John Muir, for example, was the Lord Provost of Glasgow and a senior partner in the Glasgow firm of James Finlay & Co., East India merchants. In 1890/91 he made substantial purchases of Broxburn Oil Co. shares through Kerr, Anderson. In May 1890 Kerr wrote:

> In regard to financing these, I presume, in view of the low rate of interest at present you would like me to arrange a loan for as long a period as possible, which would be three months. The rate, unless there is a change will be 3½.

As a result, £4,700 was borrowed from the British Linen Bank on the security of the Broxburn shares, and the loan was extended at regular intervals, although the rate of interest was raised to 5½ per cent in October 1890.[15]

Similarly W. A. Coats, of the wealthy Paisley family of thread manufacturers, was actively involved in the mid-1890s in buying shares in J. & P. Coats, and in selling part of his very substantial holding of debentures in the firm, as he aimed both to make capital gains and to increase the rate of return obtained. These share purchases relied heavily on a loan of £50,000 obtained from the Royal Bank in Glasgow. However, in 1898 credit was becoming tight owing to a greater demand for money for trade purposes and the possibilities of war, and the Royal Bank was asking for repayment:

> The loan of course at present stands in the banks' books as made to us and as we have of course other considerable loans for other clients the manager may want us to reduce a little, while he might be quite willing to let the loan remain should you so desire it if made to you direct. I have put this to him also, but from what Michie (of the Royal Bank) said when I called for him it might be wise for you to be prepared to meet the amount on the 28th. Supposing the Royal won't renew on any terms I might be able to obtain a loan for you from one of the other banks if you wished it.
>
> But it might not, in the present state of market, be very easy to realize at present without putting the shares down for there is very little doing in them and markets generally are very nervous and business all round reduced to a minimum owing to the state of politics.[16]

The bank did not renew and, under these circumstances, the only alternative was for the client to provide the finance from his own resources or to sell the securities, and accept the low prices resulting.

It is quite obvious that the buying and selling of securities was not always a simple matter. A keen insight into current market conditions was required in order to judge the timing of a sale or purchase. In addition, an accurate estimation of the repercussions of any action taken was necessary, if the interests of the client were to be observed. Finally, clients often required far more than the purchase of a certain number of designated securities at a specified price. These frequently necessitated the arrangement of finance, until the stock was sold again or the funds were raised to complete the purchase. Consequently, what appears to be at first sight a very simple task was actually a sophisticated operation in which timing and market knowledge were of crucial importance. At the same time it involved the mobilisation of short-term funds, through banking contacts, to finance the purchase and holding of long-term securities. Short-term funds could be borrowed at low rates of interest, while long-term investments paid a much higher rate of return. If the former could be used to finance the holding of the latter, the investor could reap a return in the form of the difference between the two interest rates, although accepting the risk entailed in having, possibly, to repay short-term borrowings and liquidate the stocks and shares at low prices.

Knowledge of the market, and the securities traded in it, made stockbroking an ideal profession to advise investors on their investments. This had been a function of solicitors, primarily, although accountants, bankers, and others had also performed it. However, as stocks and shares grew in importance as investments and multiplied in numbers and variety, it was increasingly only the stockbroker who possessed the information and skill necessary to match an investor's objectives with the appropriate securities. The legal profession continued to dominate other investment outlets, particularly property, but stocks and shares became more and more the preserve of the stockbroker, who was seen to be the person to consult in such matters.[17]

Investors sought the aid of their stockbroker in re-arranging their existing portfolio of investments on a more rational basis. The Glasgow merchant, William Stirling, for instance, entrusted his whole portfolio of securities to William Anderson of Kerr, Anderson for his scrutiny and advice in 1884:

> As desired by you I have gone carefully over all your investments and now beg to hand you herewith a detailed statement of all your securities with notes appended to each,

wrote Anderson to Stirling after a number of personal consultations. This had involved considerable research by Anderson, as some of the companies were not well known and he had to 'make inquiries in the best informed quarters' in order to estimate their worth. His recommendation to Stirling was to leave the bulk of the portfolio of £274,000 untouched and to make only gradual and marginal changes.[18] Despite the fact that stockbrokers' only income was derived from clients buying and selling shares, the advice that they gave was not always to buy and/or sell, but to hold, if that was the most appropriate course of action. For the established stockbrokers with a strong and wealthy clientele, it was the interests of the client which were foremost, since it was with them that the long-term survival of the firm rested. Investors with funds to invest also readily consulted the stockbroker about the best prospects available, in order to combine both income and security. Muir & Scott, for example, were a firm of Edinburgh stockbrokers who readily dispensed such advice in the 1890s.[19]

Even the small investors who were gradually coming to purchase stocks and shares sought the assistance of stockbrokers, not only to carry out transactions but also to tell them what to invest in. According to George Anderson, an Aberdeenshire farm servant, writing in 1900:

It was a Mr Napier that told me to go to Mr Anderson (An Aberdeen Stockbroker) if I had any money to spare, that was when I left home, my Father and Mother died suddenly, and I had to leave a farm where I was brought up. So Mr Napier went with me to Mr Anderson and he asked me how much money I had and I told them I had just £40 but I would not give them more than £30. So he said to give him £35 and I would soon get it doubled and I gave him £32.

Unfortunately John Anderson, the broker, defrauded George Anderson and other clients of the savings they entrusted to him, thus demonstrating that, although the stockbroking profession had become honourable and respected as a whole, individual rogues remained.[20]

Stockbrokers did not have to be approached by investors seeking advice and aid; they frequently offered it without obligation in the hope that it might lead to business. The impression in Edinburgh, in 1897, was that investors were inundated with information and suggestions from stockbrokers.[21] The profession kept their clients well informed about general investment trends, with many of the larger firms, such as Bell, Begg & Cowan in Edinburgh, issuing a 'Monthly List of Scotch Stocks' which gave full details of a large number of joint-stock companies which were felt to be of interest to the Scottish investor.[22] Most firms also made specific offers and recommendations to their clients. William McKinnon, an Aberdeen stockbroker, regularly circulated his clients with a list that indicated the shares in demand, and those that were available for purchase, in order to encourage them to buy or sell.[23] Hardie and Allan, in Greenock, informed interested clients about stocks and shares that came into their hands but lacked a ready market, such as the West Auckland Brewery Co. in 1888:

We have a small number of the shares of this Company for disposal, and we shall be glad to receive an offer from you if you are disposed to increase your holding.[24]

Similarly, J. & G. Moffat wrote to W. N. Neilson, after they had sold his Caledonian and North British holdings, and enclosed a list of recommended stocks in six different Scottish and English railways '. . . in case you may think of re-investing in that class of property . . .'[25] As stock exchange investment became more complex, with the rapid expansion in numbers and the variety of securities in the market, the investor, though becoming better informed himself, was also forced to rely heavily upon the expertise of the stockbroker. At the same time the broker sought to improve the position of his clients through information and suggestions, for they then became more satisfied with the services he provided, and were encouraged to alter their portfolio in the light of changing conditions as related to them by the broker.

The contacts and trust established by brokers, in order to buy and sell stocks and shares, were also ideal for the raising of fresh capital by companies. The stockbroking profession was in direct communication with the existing shareholders in joint-stock enterprise, and they were the most likely subscribers to further issues by established companies, or the flotation of entirely new concerns. It became normal practice for joint-stock companies, municipal authorities and others trying to raise capital to pay commission to stockbrokers for any subscriptions to new issues obtained through the offices of that broker.[26]

Innumerable Scottish stockbrokers were involved in raising capital for joint-stock enterprise. The initiative normally came from the companies themselves. They approached the brokers and asked for their assistance in obtaining the required finance. The Scottish Ontario and Manitoba Land Company, for example, was promoted in 1879, and it invited the Edinburgh stockbroking firm of Bell, Begg and Cowan to '. . . give their support to this company on condition of their being paid brokerage on shares introduced by them'.[27] By April 1882 the company had a paid-up capital of £90,000, indicating that their appeal for funds had met with reasonable success.[28] Similarly, with the flotation of the North of Scotland Canadian Mortgage Co. in Aberdeen in 1875, local stockbrokers were given a commission of 6d per share for every one subscribed through them. In 1891 the company approached Lawrie & Ker, stockbrokers in Edinburgh, in order to sell their stock to institutional investors in that city, and by 1893 they had issued £90,000 worth of 4 per cent debenture stock, which was quoted on the Aberdeen and Edinburgh stock exchanges.[29]

In many cases the stockbrokers were purely passive agents, passing on to their clients the prospectuses and subscription forms sent to them by companies or authorities. The Equitable Mining Association of London, for example, wrote in 1888 to W. Gordon, an Aberdeen stockbroker, inquiring

> . . . whether it would be agreeable to you to act as local Broker to the Equitable Mining Association now in course of formation and of whose sketch Prospectus I beg to hand you a copy here in . . . The commission proposed to be allowed on subscriptions for shares is 2.5 per cent on the amount. I shall feel pleasure in sending you a supply of prospectuses for distribution amongst your clients.[30]

Scottish companies were far less solicitous, expecting the automatic support of their local stockbrokers, at the very least. The Aberdeen Comb Works Co., for example, was promoted in 1899, and the stockbrokers in Aberdeen were automatically circulated with prospectuses to send out to their clients.[31]

However, the stockbrokers did not have to circulate their clients with the offers sent to them, let alone recommend them. Stockbroking firms had reputations to uphold and had little desire to put their clients into a venture that was likely to turn out badly and discredit them. Kerr, Anderson turned down the opportunity to help promote the Centennial Gold Mining Co. in 1885, for:

> Our opinion of this Company is not favourable after reading the prospectus and the name of the Chairman — who has been connected with a good many unsuccessful ventures — is sufficient to deter us from recommending any one to take an interest in it though we have no particular information in regard to its prospects.[32]

Conversely, if a stockbroking firm was impressed by a proposal it could actively promote it among its own clientele, especially those who were likely to support it, and encourage other stockbroking firms, especially those with whom it was associated, to bring it to the attention of their own clients with a favourable report.[33]

Many others, apart from stockbrokers, were involved in the raising of capital for new companies, especially solicitors, bankers, accountants, and the personal contacts of the promoters themselves.[34] However, stockbrokers increasingly became central to the whole process, as it was they who not only were in touch with most of the potential investors but also held the greatest sway in the realm of stocks and shares. In 1875 the City of Aberdeen Land Association was forced to accept the Aberdeen stockbrokers' very high demand for a commission of 2/6d per share on all subscriptions obtained by them, as they needed their co-operation in order to get the shares taken up.[35] Stockbrokers such as F. W. O. Brickman in Dundee, John Carrick in Glasgow, or Faithfull Begg in Edinburgh were all actively involved in the financing and promotion of new ventures and did not confine their operations to the trading in issued securities.[36] J. W. Bowhill, for example, who was a partner in the Edinburgh stockbroking firm of Bell, Begg & Cowan, was a director of the British Assets Trust, the Scottish American Investment Trust, Edinburgh American Land Mortgage Co., Electrical Securities Trust, and South African and General Investment and Trust Co. in 1912.[37] Stockbrokers were also involved in the underwriting of issues by new or established companies, which became a commoner practice. Kerr, Anderson, for instance, helped underwrite the issue of £1,026,000 4 per cent convertible preference stock in 1904 for the North British Railway. It was a simple matter for stockbroking firms to marshall selected clients into a group so that the success of an issue was guaranteed. If the issue was not taken up by the investing public, they and their clients absorbed the amount agreed upon. If the issue was a success, they had obtained a commission, for themselves and their clients, without having to use any of their own money, merely promising that it would be available.[38]

Along with solicitors, stockbrokers were involved in the direct channelling of money overseas, for they accepted money on deposit or by way of debenture for overseas concerns. They also arranged investments in mortgages upon rural or urban property in the British colonies and the U.S.A.[39] In January 1883 Bell, Begg & Cowan circulated their clients to let them know that:

> We are now prepared to receive money in sums of £500 and upwards, for investment on security of First Mortgages of Improved Farms and Town properties in New Zealand or the North-Western States of America . . . At present a return of six to seven per cent, after allowing for all deductions, can be obtained, . . . The Loans run from three to five years, according to agreement. Should the borrower desire to pay off the advance when due, our agents employ the money in a new security; but more frequently an extension of the original period is arranged. On the other hand, should the money be required by the lender during the currency of any loan, a transfer of the security can be effected at small cost . . . We have confidence in suggesting these Loans as a medium for the investment of money not required on very short notice. We are quite satisfied that our corresponders may be thoroughly relied upon . . .[40]

Stockbrokers used their domination of the secondary market to enhance their position in the raising of capital, at the expense of other groups. A stock exchange quotation for a company's securities was solely in the hands of the stock exchange associations, not the companies themselves. It was in the power of the stock exchanges to refuse, or grant, a quotation, but a company could not demand it.

The stock exchanges were entirely controlled by stockbrokers, and they became more and more unwilling to allow new securities to be quoted unless the services of stockbrokers had been utilised in their issue:

> ... quotations were more favourably received when the name of a broker appeared upon the prospectus,

was the considered opinion of the Edinburgh Stock Exchange in 1883.[41] If a joint-stock company wanted their stocks and shares to have a recognised public market, they were increasingly obliged to involve the stockbroking profession in the financing operations. By this device stockbrokers were helped to become central characters in the capital market. However, it was their contacts and expertise that were mainly responsible for their climb to that position.

Consequently, although stockbrokers continued to be regarded as buyers or sellers of securities on the instructions of clients, the role they fulfilled was becoming far greater than that.[42] They controlled the market in issued securities, and their knowledge and expertise was vital, not only for the timing of investment, but also to advise what to invest in. Investors came to rely more and more on the judgement of their broker, while the brokers themselves took much more initiative by suggesting alterations in investments and by bringing additional possibilities to the attention of their clients. However, this was only one part of the functions fulfilled by stockbrokers, for they also grew in importance within the primary market. By approaching the stockbroking profession and persuading them to circulate offers and prospectuses, in the hope of a recommendation to purchase, joint-stock companies and other bodies obtained access to the very people likely to subscribe, namely existing investors. Local, regional, national and international enterprises and authorities all relied upon this means to raise at least part of the finance that they required, and stockbrokers increasingly supplanted other professions in this role. The functions of a stockbroker became much more complex and varied after 1850 than they had been before, and his activities straddled the whole of the capital market.

In order to carry out these multifarious tasks, stockbrokers established an ever-widening web of contact that stretched from local clients to international links. For each broker, clients tended to live in the locality. All the regular clients of the Aberdeen stockbroker, John Anderson, in 1897-8, came from Aberdeen itself, or the surrounding towns and villages, while nearly all the clients of Miller & Quaile, a firm of Glasgow stockbrokers, came from Glasgow and its vicinity between 1895 and 1900.[43] Stockbrokers did have a few clients not living locally, but these had usually been acquired through people moving out of the area, but retaining contacts. One of the clients of William Hogarth, an Aberdeen stockbroker, was Colonel Birch who had originally resided in Aberdeen but had since left the district.[44] There was little need for investors to look further than their local stockbrokers, for every stockbroker had his stockbroking contacts in other centres — correspondents — through whom the buying and selling orders that could not be transacted locally could be transmitted to the most appropriate market. It was claimed, in 1887, that:

> ... at the present time Investors have practically the same advantages in dealing with Provincial Brokers as they would have by going direct to the London Stock Exchange.[45]

David Halley, a Dundee stockbroker, contacted William Hogarth in Aberdeen in 1890 in order to arrange the sale of four Northern Insurance Company shares, an Aberdeen concern, on behalf of Halley's stockbroking contact on the Liverpool Stock Exchange.[46] Normally arrangements were less complicated than this, being usually direct and bilateral, as in this typical example from Glasgow in 1861:

> ... Mr McEwan (a broker) of Liverpool had instructed Messrs. MacEwan & Auld (Glasgow brokers) to sell Canada shares at the opening of this Exchange (Glasgow) on Saturday last; and to telegraph the result; and Mr Auld had accordingly executed the order, advising by telegraph, about 12 o'clock, immediately at close of the Exchange.[47]

Certainly, as early as the 1870's, there was extensive telegraphic communication between individual stockbrokers in different locations.[48] In the 1890s Miller & Quaile, for example, were in constant contact by telegraph with L. Powell, Sons & Co. on the London Stock Exchange, confirming by post the business that they had asked to be done.[49]

As the telephone network improved in the 1880s it was increasingly used by stockbrokers to communicate with each other, such as between Kerr, Anderson in Glasgow and Bell, Begg and Cowan in Edinburgh in 1884.[50] The Glasgow firm of MacNair, Allan, Young & Rowan went so far as establish a private telephone line between themselves and their London correspondent and, by 1914, they were '. . . linked up by private wire with all the important stock markets in the Kingdom'.[51] By letter, telegraph and telephone stockbrokers throughout Britain were in direct communication with each other. The development of the services available made communication both easier and more immediate.

Through discreet inquiries between the partners of established stockbroking firms, each new broker being dealt with at a distance could be classified according to position and standing. Without a satisfactory reference it would have been difficult for a stockbroker to build up professional contacts outside his own locality and thus get his non-local business transacted. In response to an inquiry from the Liverpool stockbroking firm of J. & J. Irwin in 1888, Kerr, Anderson informed them that:

> ... we think Messrs J. R. Ferguson & Smith are quite safe for any engagements they may make and are possessed of moderate capital.
> The Junior has just been admitted a member but the Senior in his previous partnership did a quite safe business.[52]

As stockbroking firms did a growing business on behalf of distant stockbrokers, buying and selling on their orders with no pre-payment of money or pre-delivery of securities, it was essential that these other firms could be trusted. References from other local firms with whom contact was already established was the only way that this could be achieved without detailed investigation.

This correspondent system was not confined to members of the stock exchanges, but encompassed stockbrokers in all the smaller towns. These country brokers channelled most of their buying and selling orders to a specific member of the most appropriate neighbouring stock exchange and received a share of the commission in return. In 1886 Kerr, Anderson bought stock in the Grand Trust Railway of Canada to the value of £20,000 for R. Davidson, an Inverness stockbroker, on behalf of one of his clients.[53] J. Grant Maclean in Stirling claimed, in 1888, to have contacts '. . . on all the Stock Exchanges' who would buy and sell on his behalf, but he operated an extensive and specialised business in insurance company shares, listing over 130 in 1890.[54] Links even extended outside the United Kingdom, for many of the larger Scottish stockbroking firms had direct contacts with overseas stockbrokers. By the 1890s Bell, Begg & Cowan had regular dealings with various New York stockbrokers, including Vermilye & Co. and Maitland, Phelps & Co. Bell, Begg & Cowan circulated their American contacts with the nature of securities in demand, or for sale, and received back relevant offers. Again, communication was by telegraph, with confirmation and more detailed instructions being conducted by letter.[55]

The scale and sophistication of a Scottish stockbroker's operations grew substantially in the half century after 1850, with improvements in communications and a widening of contacts. However, the principles remained exactly the same. Each stockbroker had his own circle of clients, whether personal or institutional, for whom he conducted business or handled new issues, or whom he circulated with investment information. The stockbroker was also in regular contact with his local colleagues, often through the stock exchange sessions, and with non-local stockbrokers, especially those who were his established correspondents. These non-local links grew as contact became easier with improvements in telegraphic and then telephonic networks. At the same time it became more and more important to communicate with stockbrokers outside the local market in order to find out what influences were at work and to match buying and selling orders in the growing amount of securities which were common to more than one market. Through these external links the stockbroker was put in indirect contact with the investing public as a whole, as these distant stockbrokers each had their own clients and their local stockbroking colleagues. These links had existed before 1850, but they increased greatly in scale, speed and importance in the second half of the century.

NOTES

1. W. R. Lawson, *The Scottish Investors' Manual* (Edin. 1884) p. 16; *D. Y. B.* (1893

2. *D.P. & C.A.* 23 November 1860, 29 July 1879; *G. T.* 17 August 1888; *A.F.P.* 7 May 1881, 12 April 1889, 15 May 1889, 3 April 1890, 25 May 1893, 4 October 1895; J. B. Jeffreys, Trends in Business Organisation in Great Britain since 1856 (Ph.D. London 1938) p. 118

3. *A.F.P.* 4 September 1893.

4. *A.F.P.* 5 April 1889, 27 August 1895.

5. W. Bartlett & H. Chapman, *A Handy-Book for Investors* (Lon. 1869) p. 1; *D.Y.B.* (1894) p. 50.

6. Glasgow Stock Exchange Association: Minutes, 12 October 1852, 9 October 1861, 11 April 1862, 16 April 1863, 13 December 1898, 27 December 1898, 10 January 1899, 24 April 1899; Edinburgh Stock Exchange Association: Minutes, 30 November 1876, 19 June 1885, 21 October 1891, 20 December 1893, 9 May 1894, 29 May 1900; Aberdeen Stock Exchange Association: Minutes, 14 December 1858.

7. Edin.: Minutes, 4 April 1888, 22 December 1898; Glas.: Minutes, 13 December 1898, 27 December 1898, 10 January 1899.

8. Glas.: Minutes, 24 April 1899.

9. *A.F.P.* 21 December 1895.

10. J. & G. Moffat to W. N. Neilson, 6 December 1888, 31 January 1889, 6 February 1889, 9 February 1889, 11 February 1889, 14 February 1889.

11. Kerr, Anderson, Muir & Main to Alfred Nobel, 5 June 1884, 16 June 1884, 20 June 1884 etc.

12. Kerr to Nobel, 14 February 1889.

13. Kerr to Nobel, 29 December 1886.

14. J. & C. Moffat to W. N. Neilson, 11 February 1889; Kerr to Fraser, Stodard & Co., 1 November 1884; Kerr to M. A. Phillip, 29 November 1887.

15. Kerr to J. Muir, 30 April 1890, 2 May 1890, 7 May 1890, 6 August 1890, 8 May 1890, 13 October 1890, 16 October 1890, 14 May 1891.

16. Wm. Anderson to W. A. Coats, 5 December 1894, 10 December 1894, 5 April 1898, 7 April 1898.

17. R. G. Rodger, Scottish Urban Housebuilding, 1870-1914 (Ph.D. Edin. 1975) pp. 435, 438; Jeffreys, op. cit., pp. 329-32; *S.F.* November 1883; Report from the Commissioners on the London Stock Exchange, *B.P.P.* c.2157-1 (1878) pp. 168, 4281; *A Guide to the Unprotected in every-day matters relating to Property and Income* (Lon. 1891) p. 2; Lawson, op. cit., p. 16; *D.Y.B.* (1893) p. 51; *D.Y.B.* (1894) p. 50.

18. W. J. Anderson to W. Stirling, 4 December 1884.

19. P. D. Holcombe, Scottish Investment in Canada, 1870-1914 (M.Litt. Strathclyde 1975) pp. 38-40 (including quotations from the correspondence of Muir & Scott).

20. G. Anderson to M. Mackinnon, Sec., Abdn. St. Ex., 23 June 1900; L. Mackinnon, Report on John Anderson's debts for the Aberdeen Stock Exchange Association, 1900.

21. Edin.: Com. Minutes, 22 February 1897.

22. Bell, Begg & Cowan, *Monthly List of Scotch Stocks* (Edin. 1882-1897).

23. W. Mackinnon to G. Cooper, 10 March 1894; Abdn.: Minutes, 9 November 1900.

24. Hardie & Allan, Circular Book, 25 July 1888.

25. J. & G. Moffat to W. N. Neilson, 12 February 1889.

26. F. Gore-Browne & W. Jordan, *A Handy Book on the Formation, Management and Winding Up of Joint-Stock Companies* (Lon. 1902) p. 128; Report, op. cit., 184Q4702.

27. Scottish Ontario & Manitoba Land Co. to Bell, Begg, & Cowan, 19 December 1879, quoted in Holcombe, op. cit., p. 292.

28. Holcombe, op. cit., pp. 293-6.

29. Holcombe, op. cit., pp. 301-3, 313.

30. Equitable Mining Association of London to W. Gordon, 29 August 1881.

31. D. R. Stewart & Co., agents for the Aberdeen Comb Works Co., to Sec., Abdn. St. Ex., 19 April 1899.

32. Kerr to M'Intyre & Sievewright, Dundee stockbrokers, 22 December 1885.

33. Kerr to Bell, Begg and Cowan, 28 July 1884; W. J. Anderson to Wm. Hector 15 June 1898.

34. Edin.: Com. Minutes, 22 February 1897; Edmond & Ledingham, solicitors, Abdn. to Sec., Abdn. St. Ex., 10 May 1890, 14 October 1890; P. L. Cottrell, Investment Banking in England, 1856-1882 (Ph.D. Hull 1974) pp. 420-424; *The Bailie*, 15 August 1900.

35. City of Aberdeen Land Association: Memorandum of Meeting, 9 February 1875.

36. R. B. Weir, *The History of the Malt Distillers' Association of Scotland* (York 1974) p. 22; *The Bailie,* 17 February 1897, 3 July 1895.

37. H. H. Bassett, *Business Men at Home and Abroad,* 1912-13 (Lon. 1912), 'J. W. Bowhill'.

38. Kerr to L. Messel & Co., 20 September 1904; J. Fitzpatrick & V. S. Fowke, *The Secretary's Manual on the Law & Practice of Joint Stock Companies* (Lon. 1902) pp. 59-61.

39. *A.F.P.* 5 October 1895.

40. Bell, Begg and Cowan, Circular, January 1883.

41. Edin.: Comm. Minutes, 14 September 1883.

42. R. H. I. Palgrave (ed.), *Dictionary of Political Economy* (Lon. 1894-1901) I, (1894), p. 181.

43. Mackinnon, *Report,* op. cit.; Miller & Quaile to L. Powell, Sons & Co., 14 January 1895 – 12 June 1900.

44. *A.F.P.* 20 January 1891.

45. *Phillips' Investors' Manual* (Lon. 1887) p. 339.

46. D. A. Halley to Sec., Abdn. St. Ex., 3 July 1890.

47. Glas.: Minutes, 28 January 1861.

48. *The Stockbrokers' Directory of Great Britain and Ireland* (Lon. 1873-4) p. 3.

49. Miller & Quaile to L. Powell, Sons & Co., 14 January 1895 – 12 June 1900.

50. Kerr to Bell, Begg and Cowan, 28 July 1884.

51. *The Bailie,* 29 July 1914.

52. Kerr to J. & J. Irwin, Liverpool, 24 September 1888; Kerr to H. Cook & Sons, Manchester, 10 July 1886.

53. Glas.: Minutes, 12 October 1852, 11 April 1862, 9 October 1894; Edin.: Minutes, 9 May 1894.

54. Kerr to R. Davidson, 9 August 1886; *N.B.E.* 1 September 1888; J. Grant Maclean, *Prices of Insurance Companies' Shares* (Stirling 1890).

55. Maitland Phelps & Co. to Bell, Begg & Cowan, 17 June 1896; Vermilye & Co. to Bell, Begg & Cowan, 15 June 1896.

15
Stock Exchanges: Functions and Operations

IN the same way as the significance of stockbrokers in the economy increased after 1850, the importance of stock exchanges not only grew in parallel but also grew within stockbroking itself. The functions of stockbrokers and stock exchanges were never synonymous, but the stock exchanges came to play a far greater role within both the capital market and the profession than ever before. However, their prime function remained the provision of a local market for stocks and shares.[1] Most Scottish stock exchanges continued to retain a long list of local joint-stock companies whose shares were held locally, and in which interest was largely confined to one area. Concerns as diverse as the Glasgow and South-Western Railway, the City of Glasgow Bank, the Scottish American Investment Co., and the Matador Land and Cattle Co. drew most of their shareholders from one particular area of Scotland rather than the country as a whole, let alone Britain.[2]

The *Stock Exchange Year-Book* for 1875 noted that the shares of numerous Scottish companies were either held in particular localities or in Scotland as a whole, and were traded in Scottish markets:

The company is not quoted in the London List, and the shares are chiefly dealt in in Scotland,

was their observation regarding the Edinburgh-based Standard Life Assurance Co. For the Tharsis Sulphur & Copper Co., a Glasgow concern, they indicated that 'The shares are not quoted in the London List, but they are freely dealt in at Glasgow'.[3] This was true of innumerable other Scottish companies, even many of those quoted on the London Stock Exchange, and this situation prevailed until at least the end of the century. In 1900 there existed 196 public joint-stock companies with a paid-up capital of £203m, whose headquarters were in and around Glasgow and whose main market for their shares was the Glasgow Stock Exchange. In Edinburgh there were 182 companies with £159m paid up, while Aberdeen had 76 with £33m, and Dundee 34 with £6m.[4]

Even in a field such as overseas investment each city had its own concerns. Whereas Dundee investors channelled their funds through such concerns as the Scottish American Investment Trust and the Alliance Trust Co., Aberdeen investors concentrated upon the Texas Land and Mortgage Co. and the Colorado Land and Mortgage Co. The North British Canadian Investment Co., formed in 1876, and the North of Scotland Canadian Mortgage Co., founded in 1875, were two concerns with basically the same objectives, but the former was based in Glasgow and the latter in Aberdeen. Consequently they each drew most of their shareholders, but not all, from their respective home areas and their securities were largely traded on their local stock exchanges.[5] The vitality of local joint-stock enterprise in Scotland was maintained throughout the period with both new ventures, such as concerns operating overseas, and the growing conversion of established industrial and commercial concerns into public companies.

The local stock exchanges provided a market for the securities issued by local enterprise and there were three main types of 'local' company. There were those companies that were local because they operated in the one locality and had their head office there, as in the case of railways, gas companies, banks, or industrial and commercial concerns. A large proportion of their shares were often owned in the area in which they operated. These enterprises were completely local through the coincidence of control, operation, and ownership. Of secondary importance were those that were local because their headquarters was in the area, although they also operated elsewhere. Typical of these were companies operating overseas, whether they were tea plantations, cattle ranches, textile mills, copper mines or financial organisations. Their shares were actively traded on the Scottish stock exchanges, not in the countries within which they operated. However, even within Scotland a number of companies operated in one part of the country but were owned and had their head offices elsewhere. Substantial Edinburgh-based companies operated in the Fife coal measures, while Glasgow interests were present in the West Lothian coalfield, and it was in Edinburgh or Glasgow that the market for their shares lay.[6] These companies were local in terms of control and ownership, but not operation.

Finally, there were those ventures that were local because of the personnel involved, with their head office and field of operation elsewhere. The association of Sir Robert Burnett, J. Badenoch-Nicholson, or J. W. Barclay, M.P. with a new enterprise, although its head office was in London, was sufficient to attract a large number of investors from North-East Scotland. Concerns such as the Espuela Land and Cattle Co., the British and New Zealand Mortgage and Agency Co., or the Texas Land and Mortgage Co. had far more numerous shareholders from Aberdeen and area than from elsewhere, and the market for their shares was on the Aberdeen Stock Exchange. This was true of other London-based companies.[7] These companies were local solely because they were largely owned by investors from one locality. As Lowenfeld observed, in 1909, the market for a company's shares was where the majority of the shareholders resided.[8] Thus the 'long lists of local stocks which are dealt in at all hours of the day', according to *Blackwood's Edinburgh Magazine* in 1885, represented far more than enterprise confined to one limited locality, for they were also the collective investment decisions of the region's wealthy, channelled into specific joint-stock enterprises.[9]

Consequently, in these 'local' companies the best, and often the only, market for their stocks and shares lay in the local stock exchange. Most, or all, of the potential buyers and sellers lived in the catchment area of the local stockbrokers and the local stock exchange and there was little need to look outside the region to settle transactions. For instance, 100 shares in the British and New Zealand Mortgage and Agency Co., which belonged to George Thomson, an Aberdeenshire merchant, were sold via the Aberdeen Stock Exchange to James Main, an

Aberdeen cork manufacturer, in 1887.[10] Nowhere outside the locality could a larger or more active market be found in 'local' securities than on the local stock exchange:

> . . . investors in the districts where Joint Stock businesses are carried on find it more convenient to buy and sell shares through the local exchanges, where there is often a freer market, and where closer prices are frequently obtained than upon the London market,

observed the *Dundee Year Book* in 1898.[11] It was openly acknowledged, in the late nineteenth and early twentieth centuries, that the best market for a wide range of securities, including those of major banks, railways, insurance companies and industrial and commercial concerns, lay with the stock exchange in which these companies operated or had their head office.[12]

When stockbrokers had to buy or sell on behalf of clients they normally tried their local stock exchange first, if there was any possibility of the transaction being carried out there, in order to put business in the way of fellow members so that they could all benefit. The stock exchange rules certainly assumed they would utilise the local market as much as possible.[13] If the sale or purchase could not be effected locally, then another market was broached by the stockbroker through the web of correspondents. In October 1889 Kerr, Anderson had 200 shares in the Marine Insurance Co. to sell for a client at £34.25, but could not find a buyer in Glasgow. They then sent the order to Harvey, Brand & Co., a firm of London stockbrokers, who also experienced difficulty, but, after a week of trying, they managed to dispose of the shares at the required price.[14] London was always a market of last resort. However, dealings in the securities of specific companies tended to drift to the most active market, not generally but in those securities, and each of the Scottish stock exchanges had its own specialities. For example, the Aberdeen Stock Exchange was the recognised market for shares in the North of Scotland Bank, Dundee for the Alliance Trust, Edinburgh for Arizona Copper Co., and Glasgow for Nobel Explosives Co.[15] Business in the stocks and shares of companies such as these came partly from outside the locality through the correspondent system, as it was attracted by the volume of trading, the keen prices, and the ease of buying or selling.

However, this local basis to the Scottish stock exchanges was being undermined through the purchase by Scottish investors of non-local securities, such as government stock or U.S. railroad bonds. These were common to all markets and business tended to move to the larger stock exchanges where the market was more active. The security imparted by the conversion of the shares of local utilities into municipal stock also transformed these securities into that class generally held rather than largely unique to one market. However, even in these securities some trading took place on the smaller stock exchanges, such as Dundee and Aberdeen, while Glasgow and Edinburgh were themselves two of the largest exchanges in Britain and could thus offer attractive markets.[16]

Of even greater significance in the reduction of the position of the local market was the growth in the size of corporate enterprise. Many railways, banks, insurance companies and even industrial concerns expanded either through natural growth or the purchase of other companies so that their original local origins were obscured by a regional, national or even international scale of operations. The process, which was evident from the 1850s onwards, was two-way. Many Scottish enterprises were acquired by English companies or moved their head office to London, while certain Scottish companies expanded outside the confines of Scotland itself, as well as within that country.[17] Changes such as these had important repercussions on the share market. The Queen Insurance Company, an English concern, gradually moved into Scotland, opening a branch in Aberdeen in 1863. Through familiarity with the insurance policies issued by the company Scottish investors began to recognise its prospects and to acquire its shares. From March 1872 onwards its shares were traded on the Aberdeen Stock Exchange.[18] Conversely, the Tharsis Sulphur & Copper Company, a Glasgow company, acquired five metal extraction concerns in England and Scotland in 1868, and became the major British copper processing company by 1872. As a result of these purchases the company acquired a substantial number of shareholders outside Glasgow. In response to demands from these shareholders, the company resolved in 1876 to obtain quotations upon stock exchanges other than Glasgow in order to facilitate transfers.[19] The Distillers Company, a combine of Lowland grain distillers, did likewise, writing to Aberdeen Stock Exchange in 1883 to request a quotation as '... our company have a very large trade in Aberdeen and district'.[20]

Proximate stock exchanges, such as Edinburgh and Glasgow, had always had a number of securities in common, but increasingly the number of overlaps grew, as did the stock exchanges they covered.[21] Nevertheless, although the divisions between markets were being steadily eroded after 1850, there did still remain a substantial and distinctive regional grouping to joint-stock enterprise, and this justified the continued importance of local share markets.[22] Even in the stock of such major joint-stock companies as the Caledonian and North British Railways, whose shareholders were to be found throughout Scotland and England, the main markets for their securities lay in Scotland, especially Edinburgh and Glasgow. When J. & G. Moffat were selling W. N. Neilson's holding of £36,260 in these two companies, only the 'odd' lot of £260 was sent for disposal to London. The rest (99%) found purchasers via the Glasgow Stock Exchange.[23] How typical this was is impossible to say, yet it illustrates the ability of the Scottish stock exchanges to provide a ready market for 'local' securities, of whatever type, even in competition with the London Stock Exchange.

However, investors were not merely interested in buying or selling securities in the light of their finances and portfolio needs. Much stock exchange business was speculative, with investors attempting to realise quick gains as prices rose and fell. Many also tried to utilise short-term borrowed money so as to take advantage of the higher rate of return available on long-term investments. Successful speculation in shares depended upon a large turnover and rapidly changing prices, which allowed both a speedy transaction to be made and facilitated the buying and selling of large amounts without greatly disturbing the market. A speculator could hardly realise gains if his sales immediately depressed prices. He had to be able to sell all his holdings at, or near, the prevailing market price, without his first disposals bringing a precipitate decline. The converse was true with purchases. Ease of purchase and sale with little consequent alteration to price was also essential for those whose holdings rested upon borrowed funds, for there was always the possibility of forced liquidation should the loans be called in and no replacement finance be available.

These situations arose under two main circumstances. Large issues, such as those of governments or railways, could fluctuate slightly in price, so allowing substantial capital gains to be made through large holdings, but price changes were small. These were most suitable for those speculating with borrowed funds, for losses were minimised, as alterations in price were normally within narrow confines, and they also facilitated crisis sales, as the volume of stock in the market and the number of potential investors were large. Thus the action of any individual could go largely unnoticed. Volatile stocks also produced speculative opportunities for, though their capitalisation was small compared with railways or governments, turnover was large and price fluctuations rapid and wide. Mining companies were prime speculative counters as their fortunes were so dependent upon unknown geological conditions. Even some industrial or commercial concerns could become objects of speculation in cases where they were pioneering a new branch of business whose prospects were unknown, such as explosives production, retail outlets, or bicycle manufacture. These were ideal for those speculators who wanted to be in and out of the market quickly.

All the Scottish stock exchanges attracted speculation, even a small market such as Aberdeen. In the 1880s Hugh Mollison, an Aberdeenshire farmer, and James Nottie, an Aberdeen merchant, '. . . were in the habit of making joint adventures and speculating on the rise and fall of the market', with the Aberdeen broker, A. S. Sutherland, acting for them and the business being transacted on the Aberdeen Stock Exchange.[24] However, none of the 'local' stocks in Aberdeen possessed either the capital or volatility to attract large-scale speculation, and the general turnover of the market was too small to support much activity in that area. The same was true of Greenock and Dundee. Speculative business on these markets was limited and confined to a few stocks at specific times, such as the overseas investment companies in Aberdeen in the early 1850s, the cattle ranching mania in Dundee in the early 1880s, or Harbour Trust bonds in Greenock in the late 1880s. Turnover quadrupled on the Aberdeen Stock Exchange in 1853, compared with 1852, as a result of speculation in the Aberdeen-based Australian investment companies, while almost half of the transactions on the Dundee Stock Exchange, in 1885, were in U.S. cattle ranching companies, owing to the obsessive interest amongst investors.

Speculative business on the Edinburgh Stock Exchange was more regular, with odd flurries of intense activity promoted by such passing interests as copper and gold mining, oil developments or cattle ranches. Speculation in Edinburgh was very moderate, however, when compared with Glasgow. The Glasgow Stock Exchange was the second largest in Britain and so had the turnover to support speculation. Glasgow was also the centre for a number of joint-stock companies which attracted immense speculative interest.[25] Prime amongst these were mining ventures, either originating in Glasgow or attracted to Glasgow by the involvement of Glasgow investors. In 1886 '. . . an enormous business has been done . . .' in the shares of the Spanish mining companies of Tharsis, Rio Tinto, and Mason & Barry, according to Kerr, Anderson.[26] Glasgow was also the home of a number of new industrial concerns whose prospects were sufficiently unpredictable to attract speculators. One of the foremost of these, in the 1880s, was Nobel's Explosives Co., which '. . . for some time ranked as one of the footballs of the market', according to the *Scottish Banking and Insurance Magazine*, in October 1884. Liptons Ltd. took over this mantle in the 1890s, being the subject of a large amount of speculative dealing.[27] As early as 1856 it was estimated that one-third of all transactions on the Glasgow Stock Exchange were speculative, and the proportion had risen to around three-quarters by 1914.[28]

Nevertheless, even Glasgow had to give pride of place in speculative business to London. Glasgow stockbrokers, such as Foulds in the 1850s and Miller & Quaile in the 1890s, passed on much of the buying and selling of their clients' speculative stocks to their London correspondents.[29] This was even truer of the rest of Scotland, with either brokers or investors themselves bypassing the local market to carry out their transactions in London.[30] Consequently, while the larger Scottish stock exchanges of Edinburgh and, especially, Glasgow retained an important element of speculative dealing, the other stock exchanges provided only limited and intermittent outlets for this aspect of investment. Much of their business in this direction had to be transmitted to other stock exchanges through the correspondent system, in particular Glasgow or London. Even Edinburgh and Glasgow could not provide a complete market for speculation, and they in turn passed on some of their clients' business to London, the largest stock exchange in the world.[31]

Thus, the Scottish stock exchanges continued to fulfil the function for which they had been created, namely the provision of a market for the securities of local companies. However, the nature of the service they provided had changed significantly. 'Local' no longer merely encompassed the few joint-stock enterprises operating in the catchment area of the stock exchange, but represented much of the collective interests of the region's investors, and could extend into a wide variety of fields in many countries. 'Local' did not mean parochial. At the same time the scope of joint-stock enterprise and the needs and interests of investors were changing. Moreover, joint-stock enterprise was, increasingly, extending its area of operation beyond the confines of any one stock exchange and so was attracting a more general investing public. Nevertheless, 'local' companies remained of major importance, especially with the conversion of local firms into joint-stock concerns. Investors themselves were broadening their involvement in transferable securities by buying those of foreign enterprises and governments, as well as becoming involved in the issues of Scottish or British companies other than those with which their locality had special connections. In addition, their speculative requirements could not be regularly met by anything but the largest markets, and although Scotland possessed two of these in the Edinburgh and Glasgow stock exchanges, much of the business did flow to London.

The Scottish stock exchanges continued to have a vital role to play, but it was not as simple or as clear-cut as it had been. No longer could the local market provide an outlet for almost all of the locality's investment needs. All stock exchanges steadily lost some business to other markets, especially to the larger ones. In compensation, they also attracted trade in the securities for which they were the best, or most active, market. Kerr, Anderson were selling shares in the Nobel Dynamite Trust for Arthur Nobel in 1889 and warned him to confine his operations to the Glasgow market, for

> . . . should you send an order here and another to London or elsewhere, the latter through one channel or another, would be certain to find its way to this market and so compete with us.[32]

This was true of many stocks and shares, as each of the Scottish stock exchanges had its numerous specialities for which it was the recognised market. The stock exchanges were the markets for 'local' securities and specialised in particular types of business such as speculation in mining shares. As a result they attracted buying and selling orders, through the correspondent system, in these companies and in these areas of activity. Although most of that would be from local people, the coincidence between activity on the local stock exchange and the interests of local investors was gradually fading. The nature of business on the Dundee Stock Exchange, for example, gave a distorted view of the objectives of Dundee investors, as so much of their purchases and sales of railways, banks, insurance companies and other joint-stock concerns was passed on to other Scottish stock exchanges.

These changes meant a growing interdependence between stock exchanges and a need for improved communication so that the requirements of all investors could be brought to bear in the market place. This was achieved, firstly by the telegraph, and then by the telephone. Although the links were at the level of the stockbroker rather than the stock exchange, this need to communicate enhanced the position of the stock exchange up to 1900, for it was in the stock exchange that central facilities such as telegraph offices and telephone exchanges were provided for the use of stockbrokers who needed to contact their correspondents. The increasing installation of private telephones after 1900, linking broker with broker in a national network, arrested the growing importance of the stock exchange as a means of communication between stockbrokers.

Edinburgh, Glasgow and London were linked by telegraph in 1846/7, and Aberdeen was reached in 1854. The irregularity of early telegraphic communication, and its limited capacity, restricted the system's use for the transmission of stock exchange information, despite its immediate suitability for that purpose.[33] Nevertheless, the effect of the link was soon recognised, especially upon the Edinburgh and Glasgow markets, as described in the *Scottish Railway Gazette:*

... in so far as regards the purchase and sale of stock, and in all other respects where communication is mainly concerned, Mr Bain's electric telegraph has made Edinburgh and Glasgow one city.[34]

Once initial difficulties in the use and maintenance of telegraphic equipment had been overcome in the course of the 1850s, the telegraph became an essential tool of the stockbroker in maintaining contact with his correspondents and, thus, other markets. Such was the importance of these links that they influenced behaviour on each stock exchange. In May 1847 the Glasgow Stock Exchange rejected a move to alter the times of its meetings, as this

... would deprive the members of the use of the Edinburgh forenoon quotations, and also prevent them executing Edinburgh orders sent through between meetings.[35]

The use of the telegraph increased greatly, and there was a gradual recognition on the Scottish stock exchanges that it was not only useful to know what was taking place in other markets, such as their closing prices, but also that it was a necessary part of business to know such pieces of information so that buying, selling and prices could be altered accordingly.[36] Towards the end of the 1860s the Scottish stock exchanges were being kept open on local holidays, as the English stock exchanges were still operating and it would be inconvenient if they closed. The Scottish stock exchanges increasingly conformed to both the opening times of each other and to their more numerous English counterparts.[37] Both the Glasgow and Edinburgh Stock Exchanges were connected to the London Stock Exchange by direct telegraphic wires by 1880, but the Aberdeen and Dundee stock exchanges were not. The delay in communication that resulted placed them under 'considerable disadvantages', for they were less able to respond to and take advantage of the rapidly changing prices and conditions of supply and demand.[38] Similarly, the interruption to telegraphic communication between Aberdeen and the other stock exchanges in February 1901 had caused the Aberdeen stockbrokers 'heavy loss, not only to themselves but also to their clients, whose instructions they were unable to fulfil'.[39] The capacity of the Aberdeen Stock Exchange's telegraphic links with other exchanges was only an eighth, at most, of that of Glasgow by the late 1890s, and the volume of business transacted using the telegraph was even smaller.[40]

For all the exchanges and their members telegraphic communication became an indispensable means through which business was conducted and information received. However, from 1880 onwards the telephone supplemented, and then gradually replaced, the telegraph as a means of communication.[41] The first telephone was installed in the Glasgow Stock Exchange in 1880, but only for a trial period of three months. Such was the use to which it was put that its position was made permanent, while additional telephones were required in 1882.[42] Demand was so great that it was decided, in 1897, to ballot members each morning for the privilege of making the first calls. The inefficiency of the telephone system restricted its value in the early years and the Glasgow Stock Exchange went so far as to recommend its nationalisation in 1898, in the expectation that government control would lead to an improvement.[43] Although the telephone was still very much experimental, by 1900 it was rapidly usurping the position of the telegraph and adding a completely new dimension as stockbrokers obtained their own instruments. Immediate personal communication between brokers, not only in the same town but nationally, was now becoming possible, allowing the central facilities of the stock exchange to be completely bypassed on occasion. Stockbrokers needed to use the local stock exchange to transact only 'local' business, for other buying and selling operations could be transmitted to the appropriate market by telephone from the office itself.

Thus, developments in communication initially built up the position of the stock exchange, for it was there that contact could be made, not only with local but also with distant brokers, via the telegraph and telephone. As the telephone service improved, the need to resort to the stock exchange diminished, as office to office contact was now available both within a town and between towns. Physical contact became less and less necessary. This increasing ease of communication also encouraged inter-market specialisation and dependence, for it now required little effort to direct business to the most appropriate exchange rather than attempt to find buyers and sellers locally. Technological change was reinforcing the changes in investment patterns which undermined the original function of the local stock exchanges, although 'local' joint-stock enterprise ensured that these stock exchanges continued to have an important role to play. The membership of the Glasgow Stock Exchange rose almost five-fold between 1850 and 1900, while the value of business done on the Aberdeen Stock Exchange increased six-fold over the same period.[44]

The method used to transact business on the Scottish stock exchanges remained largely the same as at their inception in the mid-1840s:

> The names of the various stocks in the official List are called over by the Secretary, and, thereupon, buyers and sellers quickly come to an understanding about price, and transact their business direct, in the presence of the whole market, without the intervention of dealers . . .

This was how the system operated in Glasgow in 1898, and exactly the same procedure was used on the other Scottish stock exchanges at that time.[45] This mechanism was sufficiently flexible to cope with any normal changes in the volume and nature of business. The stocks called could be easily re-arranged in response to changing preferences, with any new ones being added to the list or merely called on request. An increase, or decline, in the volume of turnover could be accommodated by the alteration of the frequency and length of meetings.[46] This happened on the Aberdeen Stock Exchange in March 1877:

> Hitherto the members of 'change have only met once a day, at half-past twelve o'clock, but 'business' has now increased to such an extent that it is found necessary to hold two meetings — one at eleven, and the other at half-past one. This will not only facilitate the despatch of business in local stocks, but will be more convenient in transactions with the southern markets.[47]

Even the coming of the telegraph and telephone could be accommodated by this method of dealing. It became a custom that a stock could be called out of turn, or again, on receipt of information from another exchange regarding fluctuations in its price, or buying and selling orders.[48]

Only one occurrence forced any real alteration in this method of business and that was the boom in gold mining shares during the mid-1890s. Even the collapse of the Western Bank of Scotland in 1857 or, especially, the City of Glasgow Bank in 1878, had not produced any fundamental alterations in dealing methods, despite the panic produced among holders of bank stock. Between 1878 and 1880, for example, at least 34 per cent of the stock of Clydesdale Bank was disposed of by frightened holders.[49] However, such was the pressure of business during the 1890s gold mania, with not only an enormous turnover but also very rapidly changing prices, that existing procedures were subjected to very severe strain. Most stock exchanges coped with the problems until the excited speculation died down, but the volume of business was so great in Glasgow in 1895 that a remedy had to be sought. According to one observer, writing in 1898,

> The noise and confusion became unendurable, and, in May of that year, the Reading Room adjoining the Exchange Room was turned into a mining market, to which dealings in the shares of nearly all mining and land companies were transferred and in which they are still carried on.

In this additional market, the calling over of securities was abandoned. There was no set organisation to facilitate transactions, for those interested in the securities relegated to this 'mining' market had merely to go round each other until they completed the sales or purchases which they wanted to make. The resulting prices were then marked and brought to the attention of all present, animating another round of buying and selling as stockbrokers consulted their clients or correspondents in other markets, and then acted accordingly. The traditional system of transacting business was not abandoned in Glasgow, but the market was split in two. Stocks and shares with a steady turnover at slowly changing prices continued to be dealt in, utilising the call-over method. These comprised the bulk of the listed securities. Shares with a volatile price and in which there was a great deal of trading activity were relegated to a separate part of the exchange where those interested could congregate. Although the majority of securities were those of mining and allied companies, it was not purely a mining market, for any stock with the appropriate characteristics could be banished from the main floor, such as Lipton's Ltd.

As only a limited range of securities were traded in this market, and only those brokers interested in them were present, it was quite possible for a buyer to deal direct with a vendor without the aid of either an intermediary to call out stocks in turn or specialists, such as jobbers, who would make a market by being always willing to both buy and sell at a price. By 1898 this dual system was felt to be working well:

> It seems to suit the nature of the business and the separation has quite relieved the pressure and confusion in the Stock Exchange proper. In both departments business now proceeds smoothly, to the general satisfaction of the members, and no further change is likely to be called for until the business again assumes unmanageable proportions.[50]

Through the 'call-over' system, regular business in a specified list of securities with a low volume of turnover and moderately varying prices could be catered for. In most of the Scottish stock exchanges this was almost all that was required, except for speculative flurries which could usually be coped with by longer and more frequent sessions and after-hours trading. In the Glasgow 'mining' market, stocks which generated an extensive turnover at rapidly changing prices could also be catered for. The rough separation of the two ensured the survival of the market as a whole, for the regular market was not swamped or the speculative market constrained. The creation of this 'mining' market gave the Glasgow Stock Exchange an important flexibility in speculative dealings and helped to make it both the most important in Scotland, and second only to London within Britain.

The Scottish stock exchanges were not only markets but also associations of stockbrokers, and this role became of major importance in the half century after 1850 as the profession grew in size and responsibility. Although there was a marked diminution of disputes between members by the early 1860s, the settling of these remained an important part of all stock exchange committees' work. Moreover, while the need to supervise dealings between brokers declined, with all coming to understand and accept the rules and rates of commission, the associations found themselves having to police the relationship between stockbroker and client.[51] Increasingly the public came to regard the stock exchange associations as guardians of the profession, responsible for the behaviour of their members.[52] In order to improve and preserve the reputation of the profession as a whole, especially as trust was such an important element in their business life, the stock exchanges were forced to take action against errant stockbrokers and to vet potential members. Transgressors were expelled and suspect applicants rejected.[53]

The stock exchanges also came to represent the collective interests of their members in contacts with other institutions. They dealt with the government, for example, over the level of stamp duty on transfers.[54] Yet, of far greater importance was their control over the quotation of a company's securities, as it was the trade in these that provided much of the business of their members. It was, to begin with, fairly easy for a company to obtain a quotation, with the stockbrokers themselves taking the initiative, such as in this request from two Aberdeen brokers in 1862:

> As there have been two or three transactions in the 'Beariz Tin Streaming Company Limited' and as a quantity of the shares are locally held, we beg to request that this company be entered in our weekly share list.[55]

On the Glasgow Stock Exchange occasional efforts were made to generate new business by quoting companies that were popular elsewhere. Five South American nitrate companies obtained a listing in 1893 on the recommendation of a broker who '. . . could not give an undertaking that there would be dealings in the shares, if quoted', but 'he thought there probably would be, and that business was passing this market in consequence of them not being quoted'.[56]

However, this entrepreneurial zeal was unusual, for stock exchanges tended to quote only those securities which promised to, or already did, provide a substantial business for their members. The major grounds for refusing a quotation, and almost the only grounds in the early years, were that it would not generate sufficient turnover to be worth calling at each session, thus wasting the time of the members. In 1894 the Edinburgh Stock Exchange, for example,

> . . . agreed to quote the Montana Mining Company in the event of business becoming active in the shares, but to postpone in the meantime.[57]

This was the basic philosophy behind quotation on all the Scottish stock exchanges, for there was a limitation to the number of companies which could be called at each session, so that only those which provided a reasonable level of business for the members were admitted to the listing. Of course this varied between exchanges, for what was too low a turnover of shares in a major stock exchange such as Glasgow could be perfectly acceptable in a minor one such as Aberdeen.[58]

Joint-stock companies came to realise more and more that a quotation for their stocks and shares was useful in that it facilitated transactions, thus pleasing the shareholders and investors and also making it easier to raise additional capital. Consequently, a quotation was desirable for most public joint-stock companies.[59] This allowed the stock exchanges to force companies to alter practices that restricted the market in their shares or interfered with the stockbroker's handling of transfers. There was always the threat of refusal to quote or removal of quotation. As early as 1872 the Glasgow Stock Exchange was inclined to refuse a quotation for companies that had not placed two-thirds of their capital in the hands of the public. An issue restricted to that extent created a limited market in the shares, which was bad for business.[60] The Glasgow Stock Exchange, in the 1870s, was also refusing to quote companies which retained a right to veto share transfers. This added an element of uncertainty to transactions for the broker involved, as he did not know whether the transfer he had arranged would be acceptable to the company. Most companies withdrew the offending clauses in order to retain their quotation.[61]

All the stock exchanges began to demand a growing amount of information from companies before they decided to quote them. This information related solely to the size and composition of the paid-up capital, the number of shareholders, and any restrictions on the transfer of shares. What concerned the stockbrokers was the business which companies' securities would generate, not the financial stability or economic performance of the companies themselves. The stock exchanges, in the nineteenth century, did not see themselves as having a role to play in the protection of the investing public from its own folly.[62] Once quoted on one stock exchange, a company could be automatically quoted on another without further investigation.[63]

Although a quotation was very useful, it was not essential for a company to have one, and business was regularly done in the shares of non-quoted companies on all the Scottish stock exchanges, at the request of members with buying or selling orders. The transactions which resulted were inserted in the margins of the official list, with the name of the company and the current price being given. The British Oil & Guano Company was promised, in 1898, that the Aberdeen Stock Exchange

> . . . would publish the business done and after a time, if sufficient numbers of transactions took place, they would no doubt find a place in the List.[64]

Therefore, refusal to quote was only a limited weapon. It was in the interests of the stockbrokers themselves to have a company's securities quoted, as it facilitated buying and selling and encouraged activity in response to the publicly changing prices. However, as the public capital market grew in importance, fewer and fewer companies could afford to ignore the threat of non-quotation.

The stock exchanges also developed a role as disseminators of information relating to the business of their members. It was they who received the price lists of other stock exchanges and, to a lesser extent, communications from companies. Prospectuses, for example, were often sent to the stock exchanges for distribution to their members, rather than being sent to every individual broker, as with the London Financial Association in July 1863:

> I beg to hand you a notice of Preference Stock which this association has for sale — may I solicit the favour of placing it in the usual way on the Notice Board of your Stock Exchange, in order to bring it before your members.[65]

It was easier to communicate with one permanent institution than its numerous and changing membership. However, the exchanges were not just passive intermediaries in issues, as they also came to co-ordinate the actions of their member brokers in this field.[66]

In performing these functions the stock exchanges realised that many could not be carried out satisfactorily without the joint action of all the stock exchanges. An isolated action could merely result in that particular stock exchange being bypassed for another. On the Edinburgh Stock Exchange, in 1876, it was felt that

> . . . much of the business of Edinburgh is being diverted to London and other markets, through the restrictions placed upon members by the Rules prohibiting their dividing commission with Law Agents . . .[67]

Similarly, on the Glasgow Stock Exchange in 1880 there was a reluctance to take independent action over the transfer regulations of foreign railways, as it would drive business to other markets.[68]

From their inception the stock exchanges had to consult each other over a variety of matters, take joint action, and gradually assimilate their individual practices.[69] One of the many instances of collective action was that over forged transfers. The stock exchanges combined to force companies to accept responsibility for any losses which resulted from forged share certificates. Previously stockbrokers had been sued by clients who had purchased these non-existent shares.[70] Eventually, an association of stock exchanges was formed, in 1890, whose object was both formally to co-ordinate the position of stock exchanges upon matters of mutual interest, and to draw up a uniform set of rules and regulations in order to reduce misunderstandings and disputes between the brokers of separate stock exchanges.[71] Both Edinburgh and Glasgow stock exchanges joined the association, but Aberdeen, Dundee and Greenock did not. Although they were sympathetic to its ends, they did not feel it was worth while for them to become members, considering the changes they would have to make. Even the two Scottish stock exchanges that joined were most unwilling to alter their rules and regulations so as to conform to a common practice. The advantages that would accrue to their inter-market business were far outweighed by the disruption that would be caused to their domestic transactions.[72] Despite the growing necessity for concerted action, and the increased business between different stock exchange members, the Scottish stock exchanges were not yet ready to alter their internal regulations to fit a common pattern. The relationships between member brokers were still of greater importance than any collective contact with other stock exchanges.

As a result of the changing status of stockbrokers and the growing importance of the business they conducted, the stock exchange associations became involved in acting for the corporate benefit of their members. They arbitrated between members, policed the profession, and handled its affairs with other corporate bodies such as the government or joint-stock companies. Nevertheless, the stockbroker remained an independent entity, being a member of the stock exchange by choice and not an employee of it, as were the officials of banks or insurance companies. In addition, the activity on the stock exchange was only one part, though a major one, of the stockbroker's business. It was the stockbroker who was central to the market, not the stock exchange. The institution was still subservient to the individual at the end of the nineteenth century.

NOTES

1. *Phillips' Investors' Manual* (Lon. 1887) p. 339.

2. A. T. Innes (ed.), *Report of the Petition of Wm. Muir* (Edin. 1878) p. 8; *A.F.P.* 3 October 1878; W. T. Jackson, *The Enterprising Scot* (Edin. 1968) p. 13; W. G. Kerr, *Scottish Capital on the American Credit Frontier* (Austin 1976) p. 20.

3. T. Skinner (ed.), *The Stock Exchange Year-Book and Diary for 1875* (Lon. 1874) pp. 140, 169.

4. *S.E.O.I.* (1900), Personal extrapolation.

5. Jackson, op. cit., pp. 22, 68; Kerr, op. cit., pp. 50, 69; P. D. Holcombe, Scottish Investment in Canada, 1870-1914 (M.Litt. Strathclyde 1975) pp. 262-268, 293-96, 301-2, 312, 374-380; T. J. Byres, The Scottish Economy during the 'Great Depression' (B.Litt. Glasgow 1963) p. 215

6. J. A. Hassan, The Development of the Coal Industry in Mid and West Lothian, 1815-1873 (Ph.D. Strathclyde 1976) p. 187.

7. Kerr, op. cit., pp. 50, 64-5, 69; *A.F.P.* 3 November 1881, 24 June 1887, 26 June 1889; Holcombe, op. cit., pp. 221-9.

8. H. Lowenfeld, *All about Investment* (Lon. 1909) p. 234.

9. *B.E.M.* 137 (1885) pp. 775-6.

10. *A.F.P.* 24 June 1887.

11. *D.Y.B.* (1898) p. 45.

12. G. D. Ingall & G. Withers, *The Stock Exchange* (Lon. 1904) pp. 70, 89; *B.E.M.* 137 (1885) pp. 275-6; Report from the Commissioners on the London Stock Exchange, *B.P.P.* c2157-1 (1878) pp. 108, 321; R. H. I. Palgrave (ed.), *Dictionary of Political Economy* (Lon. 1894-1901) I, p. 770; *Encyclopaedia Britannica* (1887) pp. 556-7; E. T. Powell, *The Evolution of the Money Market 1385-1915* (Lon. 1916) p. 538; J. B. Jeffreys, Trends in Business Organisation in Great Britain since 1856 (Ph.D. London 1938) p. 340.

13. Glasgow Stock Exchange Association: Minutes, 23 November 1846, 14 February 1888; *Constitution, Rules, and Bye-laws of the Edinburgh Stock Exchange Association* (Edin. 1883) p. 11.

14. Kerr to Harvey, Brand & Co., 28 October 1889, 5 November 1889, 8 November 1889.

15. Abdn.: Minutes, 20 July 1899.

16. *Econ.*, 19 April 1884; J. Scott & M. Hughes, *The Anatomy of Scottish Capital* (Lon. 1980).

17. D. S. MacMillan, 'The Transfer of Company Control from Scotland to London in the Nineteenth Century: the case of the Scottish Australian Company, 1853' *B.H.* 12 (1970).

18. *Queen Insurance Co.: Annual Report* (Lon. 1863); Aberdeen Stock Exchange: Record of Transactions, March 1874.

19. S. G. Checkland, *The Mines of Tharsis* (Lon. 1967) pp. 111, 154; Sec., Tharsis Sulphur & Copper Co., to Sec., Abdn. St. Ex., 3 June 1876, 7 June 1876.

20. Sec., The Distillers' Company Ltd. to Sec., Abdn. St. Ex., 6 April 1883.

21. Glasgow: Minutes, 2 March 1875.

22. J. Scott & M. Hughes, *The Anatomy of Scottish Capital* (Lon. 1980) p. 46.

23. J. & G. Moffat to W. N. Neilson, 14 February 1889; Ingall & Withers, op. cit., p. 70.

24. *A.F.P.* 27 March 1888, 25 October 1883, 6 April 1888.

25. Cf. Ch. 16.

26. Kerr to A. Nobel, 28 November 1887.

27. *S.B. & I.M.*, 4 October 1884; Glasgow: Minutes, 5 April 1898.

28. Glasgow: Minutes, 22 February 1856; *Econ.*, 31 October 1914; Report on London Stock Exchange, op. cit., p. 326 Q8172.

29. Glasgow: Minutes, 12 February 1856; Miller & Quaile to L. Powell & Sons, 14 January 1895 – 12 June 1900.

30. *A.F.P.* 22 March 1877, 20 November 1878, 8 March 1892; *Econ.*, 19 April 1884.

31. Cf. Ch. 19.

32. Kerr to Nobel, 14 February 1889.

33. Edin.: Minutes, 6 January 1851, 7 January 1851, 14 January 1851, 16 October 1851; Glasgow: Minutes, 5 May 1847; Abdn.: Minutes, 10 March 1854.

34. *S.R.G.* 17 January 1846, 25 September 1847.

35. Glasgow: Minutes, 5 May 1847.

36. Glasgow: Minutes, 9 October 1879, 15 October 1879.

37. Glasgow: Minutes, 24 August 1869, 16 February 1875; Abdn.: Minutes, 31 October 1884, 9 July 1885, 28 October 1887.

38. Glasgow: Minutes, 7 October 1880; Edin.: Comm. Minutes, 12 February 1890; Abdn.: Minutes, 22 December 1897; G.P.O., London, to Sec., Abdn. St. Ex., 21 December 1899.

39. Abdn.: Minutes, 19 February 1901.

40. G.P.O., op. cit.

41. B. T. Robson, *Urban Growth* (Lon. 1973) pp. 166-171; *D.Y.B.* (1880) pp. 9-10; A. Mackie, *An Industrial History of Edinburgh* (Glasgow 1963) p. 75.

42. Glasgow: Minutes, 15 March 1880, 2 November 1880, 28 February 1882, 11 April 1893, 9 May 1893, 3 February 1897, 1 March 1898.

43. Glasgow: Minutes, 31 January 1899.

44. *Records of the Glasgow Stock Exchange Association, 1844-1926* (Glasgow 1927) p. 11; Abdn. St. Ex., Record of Transactions, 1850-1900.

45. *Records of the Glasgow Stock Exchange Association, 1844-1898* (Glasgow 1898) p. 8; Edin.: Minutes, 8 March 1888.

46. Glasgow: Minutes, 31 December 1874, 29 December 1885, 26 April 1895.

47. *A.F.P.* 9 March 1877.

48. *Records* (1898), op. cit., p. 8.

49. Innes, op. cit., p. 8; Clydesdale Banking Co. S.C.R.O. B.T.2/123; M. A. Whitehead, The Western Bank and the Crisis of 1857 (M.Litt. Strathclyde 1978) p. 165.

50. Records (1898), loc. cit; Glasgow: Minutes, 26 April 1895, 5 April 1898.

51. Glasgow: Minutes, 1 July 1851, 15 June 1852, 16 June 1856, 2 July 1861, 12 February 1862; Edin.: Minutes, 21 November 1862, 4 January 1864; Abdn.: Minutes, 1 November 1862.

52. *Econ.,* 23 November 1895; Fraser & Duguid, advocates, Abdn., to Sec., Abdn. St. Ex., 19 November 1898.

53. Glasgow: Minutes, 13 September 1865; Abdn.: Minutes, 29 January 1891, 9 March 1891, 21 April 1891, 5 June 1891, 12 October 1898.

54. Edin.: Minutes, 27 April 1893; Glasgow: Minutes, 5 April 1888; Dundee: Minutes, 15 April 1893.

55. W. Duncan & J. Ferguson to Sec., Abdn. St. Ex., 12 November 1862.

56. Glasgow: Minutes, 28 February 1893.

57. Edin.: Comm. Minutes, 19 January 1894.

58. Glasgow: Minutes, 10 January 1866, 21 February 1890, et seq.; Abdn.: Minutes, 20 October 1876, 8 May 1882, 29 April 1887 et seq.; Edin.: Comm. Minutes, 1 June 1880, 22 September 1880, 17 October 1881, et seq.

59. F. Gore-Browne & W. Jordan, *A Handy Book on the Formation, Management and Winding-up of Joint-Stock Companies* (Lon. 1902) p. 453; Correspondence of Abdn. St. Ex. with Aberdeen Market Co., 4 December 1870; Culter Paper Mills Co., 8 January 1874; Yorke Peninsula Mining Co., 12 December 1881; Great Western Steam Laundry Co., 30 March 1885; Wm. Longmore & Co., 3 February 1890.

60. Glasgow: Minutes, 23 February 1872.

61. Glasgow: Minutes, 15 December 1880.

62. Memorandum of Requirements for Official Quotation, Abdn. St. Ex., 21 Sept. 1901; Edin.: Comm. Minutes, 18 November 1897; Abdn.: Minutes, 3 April 1886, 28 April 1886, 24 June 1886, 22 January 1890; Sec., Texas Land & Mortgage Co. to Sec., Abdn. St. Ex., 14 January 1896; Sec., Glasgow St. Ex. to Sec., Abdn. St. Ex., 17 July 1901.

63. Edin.: Constitution, op. cit., p. 37; Edin.: Minutes, 2 December 1891; Sec., Guardian Fire & Life Assurance Office to Sec., Abdn. St. Ex., 8 May 1890.

64. Abdn.: Minutes, 4 May 1898; Glasgow: Minutes, 15 November 1892, 23 October 1894.

65. London Financial Association to Sec., Abdn. St. Ex., 16 July 1863, cf. Madras Irrigation & Canal Co., 13 August 1872; Aberdeen Jute Co., 21 Feb. 1873; North of Scotland Orkney & Shetland Steam Navigation Co., 19 July 1875; Birmingham Corp., 18 April 1877; Northern Investment Co. of N.Z., 25 June 1880; Great Western Steam Laundry Co., 21 March 1885; Hermand Oil Co., 23 July 1885; Sheffield Corp., 8 June 1889; London Chatham & Dover Railway, 9 June 1897; Ocean Trawling Co., 17 May 1899; Ben Reid & Co., 3 May 1900; Edin.: Comm. Minutes, 6 July 1882, 6 February 1897.

66. Edmunds & Ledingham, advocates, Abdn. to Sec., Abdn. St. Ex., 6 October 1898; City of Aberdeen Land Association to Sec., Abdn. St. Ex., 14 & 16 November 1874.

67. Edin.: Minutes, 30 November 1874.

68. Glasgow: Minutes, 7 January 1880.

69. Glasgow: Minutes, 5 September 1849, et seq.; Abdn.: Minutes, 25 January 1853 et seq.; Dundee: Minutes, 11 September 1890 et seq.

70. Edin.: Comm. Minutes, 23 January 1894.

71. Sec., Council of Associated Stock Exchanges, Liverpool to Sec., Abdn. St. Ex., 7 & 13 June 1890; Memorandum prepared by Liverpool Stock Exchange, 17 March 1890; *G.H.* 12 May 1890.

72. Edin.: Comm. Minutes, 21 May 1890, 1 July 1890, 24 June 1891, 3 December 1895; Glasgow: Minutes, 30 April 1890, 14 May 1890, 17 June 1891; Abdn.: Minutes, 13 June 1890.

16

Business on the Scottish Markets

THERE was a growing divergence between the business handled by the stockbroker and that transacted on the local stock exchange in the second half of the nineteenth century. Each local stockbroker handled all the buying and selling requirements of his clients, but this necessitated an increasing resort to stockbrokers in other markets. Only those bargains that could be settled on a local basis, between the local stockbrokers themselves, utilised the services of the local stock exchange. It is impossible to measure what proportion of investment business bypassed the local market, apart from the impression that the volume was significant and growing. Nevertheless, business settled locally remained both substantial and important, though it varied enormously between the five Scottish stock exchanges. For each of these exchanges it is possible to describe, with varying precision, the business being done, and its changes in composition and volume over time.

In 1850 turnover on the Glasgow Stock Exchange[1] was at a very low level, but it increased during 1851/2, before falling back in the course of 1853. Recovery came in 1856, and this was sustained through the rest of the decade. Activity on the market centred on the traditional range of joint-stock company securities, notably railways, banks, insurance companies, and gas and water utilities. Increasingly, the trading in railway shares came to dominate business, especially from 1853 onwards. The majority of transactions were in Scottish, if not local companies, with the only main exceptions being in railways. English railways were quite active on the Glasgow exchange throughout the 1850s, and Canadian railways — Grand Trunk and Great Western — became important from 1855 onwards.

During the 1860s turnover grew steadily in volume, with the only marked upsurge being in 1863. The composition of business was much the same as in the later 1850s, with transactions in Scottish, English and foreign railways dominating the market and complementing dealings in local financial and urban services. Variety was added to activity in foreign railways when the Great Luxembourg Railway was added towards the end of the decade. The only novel feature was the small amount of business in Scottish and foreign mines in 1866/7.

Business continued to expand in the course of the 1870s, with a very substantial increase in 1872/3, sustained during 1874/5, before suffering a relapse in 1876/8, and then recovering slightly in 1879. Railways of all descriptions continued to dominate business, with the securities of U.S. companies becoming increasingly popular. At the same time, activity in local financial and urban services was becoming merely a small sector of the market, despite the addition of transactions in Glasgow tramways. Three new features became important in the 1870s. At the beginning of the 1870s dealings in U.S. government stock were significant, while by the end there was a growing trade in a few local industrial concerns. However, the decade was marked by a great increase of business in every kind of mining share, especially between May 1872 and 1877. These consisted of both local oil, coal, iron ore and mining concerns, such as Merry & Cunninghame, and overseas metal mining companies like the Tharsis Sulphur & Copper Co. In the course of the 1870s transactions in railways and mining companies dominated the business of the Glasgow Stock Exchange, and Glasgow ceased to be a serious market for Scottish financial concerns.[2] With the collapse of the City of Glasgow Bank in 1878, for example, Glasgow possessed only one bank that was truly its own.[3] Even Aberdeen could do better than that, with two. There was much less incentive in Glasgow to develop investment companies, as trade outlets such as shipping, industry and commerce absorbed many of the funds that were lent on a short-term basis to these institutions elsewhere in Scotland.

The volume of turnover during the 1880s increased at the beginning of the decade, began to fall in 1882, and reached a nadir in 1885 when business was at a very low level. It recovered in 1886, fell back again in the course of 1887/8 and then rose slightly in 1889. In June 1884, for example, the Glasgow stockbrokers, Kerr, Anderson, complained that 'our markets for all classes of securities continue very dull and lifeless and the tendency is still downward'.[4] Activity was still concentrated in British and foreign railway and mining securities. During the decade, dealings in U.S., Canadian and Mexican railroads probably equalled those in Scottish and English railways, especially from the mid-1880s onwards. A similar situation prevailed in mining, with overseas concerns coming to attract more attention than domestic ventures. Throughout the period the greatest interest was evinced in Scottish oil companies and Spanish mines, while U.S. silver and Indian gold attracted attention from 1885 onwards. Local industrial enterprises, such as Nobel Explosives, India Rubber and Telegraph Works, and Distillers Co., were all the subject of numerous transactions, although mainly in the first half of the decade. Glasgow continued to be a poor market for financial companies, but it was of major importance for North American railways or speculative stocks, whether they were local industrial concerns or Scottish and overseas mining ventures.[5] Edinburgh stockbrokers, for example, used the Glasgow market for dealings in Canadian railways during the 1880s.[6]

Business began on a high note in 1890/1, fell heavily in 1892/3, recovered strongly in 1894/6, and then declined for the rest of the decade. Although domestic and foreign railways continued to be the most important overall, the middle years of the decade were characterised by rampant speculation in mining and allied shares, especially those involved in South African gold. In the years 1895 and 1896 (until May), activity in mining outweighed all other business, with few dealings in other sectors. Throughout, however, there were many transactions in local industrial concerns, with Nobel's continuing to be a favourite, while Lipton's was popular towards the end of the decade.

Until the mid-1870s the business on the Glasgow Stock Exchange was that of any local stock exchange, namely transactions in the securities of 'local' companies. The only exception to that was the dealing in the shares of English and foreign railways. However, from the mid-1870s onwards Glasgow emerged as a specialist market in railways and mining companies. These were not only Glasgow-based concerns such as the Caledonian Railway or the Tharsis Copper but, increasingly, enterprises formed elsewhere, especially English, U.S. and Canadian railways and overseas mining ventures, with London head offices. This specialisation partly resulted from Glasgow's weakness as a financial centre and the failure of local companies to present sufficiently large and attractive openings, such as in urban utilities or industrial and commercial enterprise. Many of those firms that did offer public participation were popular with investors, such as Nobel's, Lipton's, Distillers, or the State Steamship Line. Specialisation, however, was not merely a product of Glasgow's weakness but far more a result of its strength. The wealth of its investors was directed into both safe and risky opportunities at home and abroad. This led to a large and active market, not only in British and foreign railways but also in Scottish and overseas mining. This, in turn, attracted investors from outside the area, further enhancing the appeal of the exchange. What created the particular business of the Glasgow Stock Exchange more than anything else was the fact that by the late nineteenth century Glasgow contained numerous very, and numerous moderately, rich people who had made their fortunes in industry, trade, shipping and mining and were now realising and diversifying part of their wealth. This led them into railways as secure investments and also into mining companies and novel industrial and commercial ventures, for they could afford to take a gamble on success.

During the 1850s and 1860s dealings in railways gradually revived on the Edinburgh Stock Exchange[7] as funds for investment became more plentiful and confidence in the prospects of railways returned, with some beginning to pay regular dividends. Robert Allan, an Edinburgh stockbroker, observed, in 1860, that:

> A different class of purchasers appear to be now in the market for railway stocks, the higher grades of which are looked upon as good permanent investments . . . the buying of late has been decidedly of a substantial character . . .[8]

While most of the activity was in Scottish lines, especially the Edinburgh-based North British Railway, substantial business was done in both English and foreign railways. In 1862, for example, there was a large number of transactions in such companies as the Great Western of Canada, and the Erie and Illinois of the United States. By 1872 railways dominated business on the Edinburgh Stock Exchange.[9] However, railway securities were never as important as in Glasgow, for Edinburgh maintained considerable activity in other sectors. This was partly because dealings in railways occurred less in Edinburgh than in Glasgow and were more confined to local lines. Yet, of greater importance was the fact that Edinburgh retained a far larger banking and insurance sector than Glasgow, and this generated much business for the local market.

During the 1870s Edinburgh also became heavily involved in domestic and foreign mining concerns, and there was an active market in these securities on the stock exchange. At the same time, however, the financial component of business was substantially strengthened with the addition of numerous investment companies which channelled their funds into either Scottish property or overseas railways and mortgages. This began a divergence between the business of the Glasgow and Edinburgh stock exchanges which continued into the following decades. In the 1880s transactions in railways on the Edinburgh stock exchange remained the most important component of business, with Scottish, English, Canadian and U.S. railways being of major interest. Speculative activity focused on overseas copper mines and Scottish shale oil, although U.S. cattle ranches had absorbed much attention in the first half of the decade. There remained, however, a heavy volume of trading in established financial concerns, especially banks, insurance companies, and overseas investment enterprises.

As in Glasgow, the major burst of activity on the Edinburgh Stock Exchange in the 1890s was the speculation in South African and Australian gold-mining and allied shares, in the middle years of the decade. Bell, Begg & Cowan reported in October 1895 that:

> The dealings in South African and West Australian Mining, Land and Finance Companies continue on a very large scale, and further advances of a sensational description have taken place in many instances.[10]

Although Edinburgh was also smitten by the gold fever, the level of activity in mining securities was much less than in Glasgow. At the same time, transactions in the shares of local industrial and commercial enterprises were becoming of greater importance on the Edinburgh Stock Exchange, while the financial sector continued to attract a large volume of business. In a parallel fashion to Glasgow, urban utilities had become of very minor significance.

In the second half of the nineteenth century there was a growing divergence between the business of the Edinburgh and Glasgow stock exchanges, with the split coming during the 1870s. There was a quadruple foundation to business on the Edinburgh Stock Exchange, as compared with the triple basis at Glasgow. Edinburgh was an important market for railway securities, including those of Scottish, English and North American companies, but was never so committed to the stocks of Canadian and U.S. railroads as was Glasgow. Home and foreign mining securities also became of major importance on the Edinburgh Stock Exchange, with involvement in the whole range of Scottish oil, coal, and iron ore and overseas copper and gold. Again, however, the level of activity in Edinburgh was much lower than in Glasgow, which developed as a specialist mining market. The stocks and shares of enterprises operating in the Edinburgh region continued to occupy the interest of investors, although, as with Glasgow, the composition changed considerably. Urban utilities declined steadily in relative importance, while industrial and commercial concerns became of major significance. In each city, large numbers of firms in manufacturing and distribution were converted into public joint-stock concerns and were actively traded on their local stock exchanges. Although these conversions reflected the economy of each region, such as engineering and textiles in Glasgow, and paper and printing in Edinburgh, the overall effect was the same. The real difference between the two came in the financial field, for this largely disappeared in Glasgow but remained a major component of the Edinburgh market. In composition the markets differed only in the role played by the securities of financial institutions, but there was also an important difference in orientation, for the main business of the Edinburgh Stock Exchange remained transactions in 'local' securities, while Glasgow developed as a specialist market serving a much wider public than the investors of its own locality and seeking to do more than create a market in purely 'local' securities.

Turnover on the Aberdeen Stock Exchange[11] had declined steadily from 1846 to reach a low of only £37,274 in 1851, when it was less than a third of its 1846 total. A short recovery came in 1852/3, but business was back to a lower level in 1854, though it grew from then on, apart from a relapse in 1857, to reach a peak of £111,196 in 1858. With the exception of 1852/3, when dealing on the Aberdeen Stock Exchange was dominated by the city's Australian and North American investment companies, the decade showed a marked rehabilitation of railways at the relative expense of the financial sector. In 1850/1, only 6 per cent of the value of transactions was in railways compared to 63 per cent in banking, insurance and investment, while in 1858, 48 per cent was in railways — their peak year — compared with 27 per cent in financial institutions. Shipping and gas were of declining importance, though still significant, as interest switched to railways. There were only occasional flurries of activity in commercial service or mining enterprises which, in aggregate, were of limited importance. Again, with the exception of the overseas investment companies, most of the business was in the stocks and shares of companies operating in the locality. The only 'non-local' concerns that were regularly traded on the Aberdeen Stock Exchange in the 1850s were other Scottish and English railways. Scottish banks were of occasional importance, and Canadian railroads appeared towards the end of the decade. If 1853 is excluded from the decade, 86 per cent of business is British (80% — local; 5% — rest of Scotland; 1% — English).

Turnover showed much less variation in the 1860s compared to the 1850s. There was a growing amount of business up to and including 1863, followed by a steady but lower level from 1864 to 1866, and then recovery in 1867/9. The nadir was reached in 1865, with £93,402, and the zenith in 1863, with £147,311. Business was dominated by railways and financial institutions which, between them, provided almost 80 per cent of the value of turnover. Railways were now the biggest sector, having ousted the traditional leader, banks. Decline in the activity in shipping and gas continued, with gas of little significance. The only new features were a steady stream of transactions in the local agricultural commercial companies which provided 5 per cent of business over the decade, and a flurry of speculation in Australian mining shares in the early 1860s, peaking in 1862 when they provided 18 per cent of the turnover. Transactions were overwhelmingly in 'local' securities, especially those which operated in North-East Scotland, apart from the regular dealing in other British railways and Scottish banks, and the fluctuating interest in Canadian railways, African agriculture or Australian mines. Altogether 89 per cent of business was in the securities of companies operating in Britain (77% — local; 7% — rest of Scotland; 4% — English). The remaining 11 per cent was provided by Aberdeen's own overseas investment companies, with the small addition of a few London-based mining and agricultural enterprises, and Canadian, U.S. and Indian railways.

The value of turnover on the Aberdeen Stock Exchange expanded steadily in the course of the 1870s, rising from a low of £124,920 in 1870 to a peak of £351,572 in 1879. The only minor relapses were 1873 and 1878. As in the 1860s, railways and financial institutions provided 80 per cent of business between them. However, although the railways remained the largest sector, with 36 per cent of turnover, financial transactions grew afresh, spurred on by insurance shares, which became the second largest component of business. As the proportion of dealings in railways declined in the course of the decade, from a peak of 67 per cent in 1871 to a low of 18 per cent in 1877, the relative importance of insurance grew, from only 4 per cent in 1871 to 39 per cent in 1877. While most of the transactions in railways were in local concerns (83%), a growing proportion of the activity in insurance centred upon the securities of English companies (24%), as opposed to the local enterprises (71%), large and successful as these were. Elsewhere in the market there were few signs of substantial change, though a few local industrial and property ventures generated a little variety. As a whole, business remained concentrated upon companies operating locally (76% — local; 7% — rest of Scotland; 9% — English), despite the importance of English insurance and the introduction of additional overseas enterprises such as investment companies and Indian tea plantations.

Growth in turnover was more erratic in the 1880s but still substantial, being almost £1m up on the total for the 1870s. The decade opened with a steady decline from the high of £386,127 in 1880 to £290,897 in 1883, recovered in 1886 to reach £437,044, and then followed a lower but steady level of business which averaged £390,000 in 1887/9. During the 1880s railways dropped from the premier position which they had held since the late 1850s, being surpassed not only by the growing volume of business in insurance (25%), but also by banking (18%). Altogether, the financial sector provided 52 per cent of the turnover, compared with the 17 per cent of railways. The novel features of business were the revival of activity in shipping (8%), with the addition of fleets of tramp steamers to the coastal lines; the growing business in overseas agricultural concerns (5%), which comprised U.S. cattle ranches and Indian plantations; and the increasing number of industrial concerns whose securities were publicly dealt in (8%), especially local paper manufacturing companies. During the 1880s there was an expansion of activity in the growing variety of securities of companies operating overseas, but the proportion of business done in concerns operating locally remained constant at 77 per cent of the total. The doubling of transactions in 'foreign' securities (1870s — 8%; 1880s — 16%) was at the relative expense of turnover in those belonging to England and the rest of Scotland (1870s — 16%; 1880s — 7%), leaving the local proportion untouched. Of course the nature of this local enterprise was changing as the banks, insurance companies and shipping ventures extended their operations beyond the confines of North-East Scotland.

The 1890s were a poor decade for turnover on the Aberdeen Stock Exchange, as its overall value was £0.6m down on the previous decade. Business declined until 1893, when it stood at £239,195 compared to £356,618 in 1890. It recovered in 1894/8 but reached only £312,273 in 1898 before falling back to £254,000 in both 1899 and 1900. The Aberdeen Stock Exchange did not participate to any great extent in the speculative mania in the gold and allied shares that occurred in the middle years of the decade, as this was centred elsewhere, especially in Glasgow, and it was there that Aberdeen stockbrokers directed their orders. The composition of business did not differ greatly from the 1880s, with banking and insurance dominating (Insurance — 24%; Banking — 23%), and the decline in railways continuing (Railways — 15%). Financial institutions still provided 56 per cent of turnover. The major changes were the decline of activity in overseas agricultural enterprises (1%), owing to the collapse of interest in U.S. cattle ranches, and the growing importance of industrial enterprises, whose shares provided 12 per cent of turnover in the 1890s and 19 per cent in 1900. Prominent amongst these were local papermakers, and food and drink manufacturers. The proportion of business in locally operating concerns remained at 77 per cent and the movement took place entirely within the other locations, with the rest of Scotland gaining at the expense of overseas. North-East investors became more involved with the securities issued by other Scottish insurance companies in particular, especially the Edinburgh-based North British and Mercantile which took over the Aberdeen-based Scottish Provincial. At the same time the speculative interest in overseas agricultural enterprises had switched to mining concerns and Aberdeen was directly involved in very few of these. As a consequence, dealings in companies operating outside Britain fell to 11 per cent of the total, as compared with the 13 per cent provided by English and non-local Scottish concerns.

Over the whole period the value of business transacted on the Aberdeen Stock Exchange rose from an average of £87,000 per annum in the late 1840s to £350,000 per annum in the 1880s before falling back to £290,000 per annum in the 1890s. Unlike Glasgow, Aberdeen especially remained almost wholly a market in 'local' companies. Concerns operating in the locality regularly provided three-quarters of all business, and much of the remainder took the form of Aberdeen-based, or linked, enterprises operating overseas, such as the investment companies, cattle ranches or tea plantations. There was, certainly, extensive dealing on the Aberdeen Stock Exchange in the stocks of other Scottish, English and foreign railways, but this was never a major part of business. Between 1846 and 1900, for example, only 1 per cent of the value of transactions was in overseas railways, mostly those of the United States and Canada. This contrasted with 83 per cent in local railways, mainly the Great North of Scotland and its branch lines, 11 per cent in other Scottish lines, and 5 per cent in English companies. The same situation prevailed in most other sectors such as banking, where the North of Scotland

Bank, and Aberdeen Town and County Bank, dominated the market. Only in insurance was there extensive activity in the shares of companies based in other British towns, especially Edinburgh, London and Liverpool. The success of Aberdeen's own insurance ventures, especially the North of Scotland (or Northern), both encouraged local investors to purchase the stocks and shares of other insurance companies and made the Aberdeen Stock Exchange a good market in these securities, thus attracting business from elsewhere.

In composition, the period 1846-1900 was dominated by activity in three main areas. Up to the mid-1870s railways were of growing importance and occupied a premier position but then declined substantially. From the 1870s banking and insurance, aided by additional overseas investment companies, displaced railways to put financial institutions in the forefront of stock exchange business. At the same time local commercial and industrial companies further eroded the position of railways, as their combined proportion of turnover rose from a mere 5 per cent in the 1870s to 16 per cent in the 1890s and 22 per cent in 1900. Local urban utilities, services and property witnessed momentary periods of interest, when new concerns were formed, but occupied a very small part of the market. Overseas agricultural enterprises were slightly more successful, although only in the 1880s, but, apart from the 1860s, Aberdeen never developed into anything of a market for mining securities. Transactions in any of the major companies based in, or associated with, Aberdeen, such as Great North of Scotland Railway, North of Scotland Bank, Northern Assurance, Texas Land and Mortgage Co., or Alex. Pirie & Sons, were directed to the Aberdeen Stock Exchange, whether by the great number of local holders of their stock, or those from a distance who were also shareholders. The Edinburgh publisher, Thomas Nelson, for example, had a holding of 2,721 shares in the North of Scotland Canadian Mortgage Co. in 1891.[12] Conversely, local interest in the securities of, for instance, U.S. railroads or overseas mining ventures, was channelled by the Aberdeen stockbrokers to other stock exchanges. Apart from its 'local' securities, the Aberdeen Stock Exchange's only area of specialisation lay in insurance shares, for it became a major market in this field. Turnover in the stocks and shares of insurance companies rose from £107,684 in the 1860s, when 99 per cent was in local concerns, to £604,251 in the 1870s, when 24 per cent was in English companies, reaching a peak of £886,299 in the 1880s when the share of local companies had recovered to 89 per cent, but then fell back to £697,335 in the 1890s, by which time only 66 per cent was local compared to 8 per cent English and 26 per cent other Scottish companies. However, insurance was an exception, for Aberdeen was a local' market, whether it was railways in the early years, industrial and commercial concerns in the later years, or banking, insurance or investment throughout.[13]

Although the Dundee Stock Exchange[14] was not formed until 1879, there existed an active local market long before that. During the 1850s and 1860s Dundee was a purely local market, but the business it transacted was of steadily diminishing importance as the city's railway, banking and insurance enterprises were taken over by outside concerns. This left only a few local shipping, whaling, gas and water companies whose stocks and shares required a local market. Revival came with the formation of Dundee's own overseas investment companies, and these provided most of the business transacted on the Dundee Stock Exchange when it was formed in 1879. In that year, 63 per cent of all deals were in investment, trust, and mortgage companies, while a further 21 per cent were in local shipping enterprise, especially the Dundee, Perth and London Shipping Co. There were no transactions in banks, while only 1 per cent of the total was in insurance, and 2 per cent in railways. Local urban utilities and services and municipal securities provided the rest. Because of the role played by these investment companies, two-thirds of the bargains made on the Dundee Stock Exchange in 1879 were in overseas companies, especially those operating in the United States, while the remainder was almost all local.

In the 1880s activity on the Dundee market rose to a peak of 1,332 bargains in 1883, fell to only 547 in 1886, and then recovered slightly, reaching 690 in 1889. Business was again concentrated in investment companies with 44 per cent of the deals, but U.S. cattle ranches came a close second, especially in the mid-1880s. In 1884, for example, 47 per cent, by number, of all transactions were in cattle ranches, while, over the decade, their share of business was 30 per cent. Activity in railways revived momentarily, providing 8 per cent of business overall, and 24 per cent in 1881, as a result of Dundee's involvement in U.S. railroad investment, especially its own company, the Oregonian. When this failed, most U.S. railroad business again bypassed the local market, being transacted in Glasgow, Edinburgh or London. With the interest in investment companies continuing and being supplemented by specific overseas ventures, notably cattle ranches and a railroad, the proportion of deals which were in companies operating locally was small, averaging only 15 per cent over the decade, as compared with 82 per cent in concerns operating abroad.

The number of transactions during the 1890s was not far short of the 1880s total, but it never reached the same peaks. Activity was low and erratic in the early 1890s but began to rise steadily from 1894 onwards, reaching a peak of 954 deals in 1899, as compared with 646 in 1894 or 506 in 1891. The dominance of investment companies was even greater (59%), as the challenge of cattle ranches (8%) and railroads (3%) had largely disappeared. There continued to be a steady and substantial business in shipping companies (10%) and municipal securities (5%), but other areas such as banking, insurance, property and urban utilities and services were of minimal importance. The real growth in the 1890s took place in industrial and commercial enterprises as local firms were converted into public companies, especially those operating in textiles and food and drink, while the issues of the Dundee-based Indian jute textile mills became more actively traded. A total of 13 per cent of transactions in the 1890s was in the securities of companies engaged in manufacturing and distribution, and that rose to 23 per cent in 1900. As a consequence, the proportion of bargains struck in the shares of companies operating locally rose to 25 per cent in the 1890s, but those concerns operating overseas continued to dominate, with 71 per cent of business.

Until the 1870s Dundee was a local market of steadily declining importance, with the disappearance of the companies which had provided the bulk of activity.

A new role was discovered in the 1870s with the investment companies, for not only was a market necessary to handle the transactions of local investors in these concerns, but also the degree of activity in Dundee attracted business from outside the area. This was reinforced in the 1880s with the formation of the stock exchange in 1879 and the creation of additional companies operating overseas, especially cattle ranches and a railway. Once the initial excitement declined, the Dundee Stock Exchange developed into a market for a limited range of 'local' companies. These were either investment concerns channelling funds to North America and Australasia, India jute mills, and U.S. cattle ranches or shipping, or industrial and commercial enterprises operating in the Dundee area itself. Although Dundee, like Aberdeen, was also a 'local' stock exchange, its range of business was therefore very much more limited. Its involvement in such major areas as railways, banking and insurance was negligible. The one area of specialisation it possessed was as a market for U.S. orientated investment companies and, for a few years, cattle ranches.

Business on the Greenock Stock Exchange[15] was of little significance in the Scottish context, with the exception of 1888 when it was the main market for Greenock Harbour Bonds. After that date it continued to carry on a limited business in the Harbour Bonds, and that dominated the market, but most of the activity switched to the Glasgow Stock Exchange. Almost all of the local investment in railways, banks, insurance companies or utilities found its way to other exchanges, particularly Glasgow. A few firms did convert into public companies, such as R. Thorne & Sons, distillers, Brown Stewart & Co., papermakers, and Fleming Reid & Co., textiles, but they were small enterprises and provided little in the way of activity for the Greenock Stock Exchange, though transactions were settled there. Similarly, a tramway company and a shipping association were formed and their issues were traded locally, but the level of business was very low. Altogether, the Greenock Stock Exchange was a local market of little significance beyond that of supplementing some of the business done on the Glasgow Stock Exchange. Most of the transactions could have been handled informally by the brokers themselves without recourse to a stock exchange at all.

Each of the four main Scottish stock exchanges began in the 1850s with a similar, but particular, role to play, for each provided a local market for the securities of 'local' companies. Additional stocks and shares were also dealt in, especially non-local railways and banks, reflecting the interest of the investors in the respective catchment areas. However, in the course of the half century there was an increasing divergence between these stock exchanges. The transformation was greatest in Glasgow, which developed from the 1870s onwards into a specialist market in speculative stocks, especially those of mining and industrial companies, and in North American railroads. In this role it served the British investing public as well as that of Scotland. Lipton's, for example, had 70,000 shareholders when it was formed.[16] Glasgow continued to provide a service for 'local' enterprise and local investors, but this became subsidiary to its specialist business, such as in the 1890s when an additional and separate market had been set up to cater for mining stocks. Dundee also underwent a similar metamorphosis, as it lost much of its original local business, to be replaced in the 1870s by a specialisation in U.S. orientated investment companies, supplemented in the 1880s by cattle ranches. Conversions of industrial, commercial and shipping companies somewhat restored the importance of locally operating concerns, but the role of the Dundee Stock Exchange remained that of a market for a particular group of investment companies, and it attracted business in these from throughout Scotland.

For both Edinburgh and Aberdeen, their original function of being markets for 'local' securities and local investors remained of prime importance. This was especially the case in Edinburgh, which could offer a full range of joint-stock enterprise to the investing public, including Scottish and overseas mining ventures, as well as a large enough turnover to make it feasible for local investors to transact a substantial and regular business in such non-local securities as those of English and foreign railways, and indulge in speculative buying and selling. In contrast, Aberdeen was too small a market to support much in the way of speculation, while it did not develop certain branches of enterprise, especially mining, though it had representatives in most other fields. The business in these 'local' securities of Edinburgh and Aberdeen increasingly gravitated to these markets, no matter its origin. In terms of specialisation, Edinburgh developed as a major market for all forms of financial concerns, while Aberdeen was a much paler imitation, with only insurance being of non-local significance.

As the interests of investors widened and the inter-connections of markets improved through advances in communications and the corresponding-broker system, all the Scottish stock exchanges saw their local role diminish, especially in Glasgow and Dundee, but also in Edinburgh and Aberdeen. The most self-contained was Edinburgh, but even it lost business in such speculative stocks as mines and railroads to Glasgow, and attracted transactions in both 'local' concerns and financial institutions. Losses were greater at Aberdeen, with the disappearance of almost all speculative activity by the mid 1860s and the failure to develop much of a market in non-local securities apart from insurance. Unless local investors were interested in the companies with which Aberdeen and its area had particular attachments, the likelihood was that their orders would be passed to another market. Conversely, Aberdeen attracted business in these concerns. Glasgow did retain an important market in 'local' securities, but this was increasingly dwarfed by its activity in non-local securities like overseas railways and mines, in which it became the largest market outside London. The size, wealth and nature of the investing public in West Central Scotland underlay the creation of this specialism but, once begun, its growth was further enhanced by its attractions as a large and active market in these stocks. Of all the stock exchanges apart from Greenock, Dundee was the most imperfect, having lost almost all business in the local securities that dominated the other exchanges, namely railways, banking and insurance, and not being of a size to develop as a market in non-local enterprise. It was saved from oblivion by becoming a specialist market in overseas investment companies and by catering for the growing number of other types of local company. However, though it was a useful market in 'local' securities, its position as a market for the financial sector was confined solely to a limited range of investment companies. In this, it was much on a par with Aberdeen and Glasgow and considerably inferior to Edinburgh.

Thus the business done on the Scottish stock exchanges presented an increasingly distorted picture of the interests of investors in each particular region, as the exchanges were moulded into a regional and national network by the strengths and weaknesses of both their joint-stock enterprise and their investors. Each retained a base of 'local' transactions, but all lost a part of the business of their local investors and gained some from outside the region. Undoubtedly Glasgow gained and Dundee lost most, with Edinburgh and Aberdeen somewhere in the middle. Even before 1900 there was a discernible movement of business towards the larger exchanges that could offer a high volume of turnover and a wide variety of investment opportunities. However, none were now purely regional segments of a national market, for each was either more or less than that. Together they represented a Scottish Stock Exchange, but not a self-contained one, for much business emanated from, and was transacted in, England, especially London. The Scottish stock exchanges complemented each other and the other British exchanges, not only geographically but also in the specialisms that they developed, and this latter role was of growing importance.

Table 6
Value and Proportion of Aberdeen Stock Exchange Turnover: by Location, 1846–1900

| Year | Scotland | | | Eng % | Brit % | Foreign % | North Am % | Aus & N.Z. % | Lat Am % | Eu % | I & C % | Africa % | Total Value % |
	Local %	Rest of Sc %	Total Sc %										
1846	72	4	77	9	85	15	8	92	—	—	—	—	134,409
1847	69	3	72	4	75	25	6	94	—	—	—	—	86,411
1848	83	1	84	—	84	16	3	97	—	—	—	—	70,376
1849	82	3	85	1	86	14	3	97	—	—	—	—	58,349
1846–9	75	3	78	4	83	17	6	94	—	—	—	—	349,545
1850	70	6	76	—	76	24	—	100	—	—	—	—	41,287
1851	60	23	83	—	83	17	5	95	—	—	—	—	37,274
1852	65	2	66	—	66	34	3	97	—	—	—	—	51,024
1853	18	—	18	—	18	82	16	84	—	—	—	—	409,071
1854	59	1	60	6	66	34	5	95	—	—	—	—	64,003
1855	90	—	90	1	91	9	2	98	—	—	—	—	68,421
1856	94	1	94	—	94	6	9	91	—	—	—	—	78,411
1857	94	—	94	—	94	6	—	100	—	—	—	—	53,895
1858	78	16	94	1	95	5	8	92	—	—	—	—	111,196
1859	86	1	88	—	88	12	12	88	—	—	—	—	72,062
1850–9	54	3	57	1	58	42	13	87	—	—	—	—	986,644
1860	66	10	76	15	91	9	20	80	—	—	—	—	107,227
1861	84	3	88	1	88	12	—	100	—	—	—	—	97,059
1862	74	5	79	1	80	20	—	99	—	—	—	—	126,870
1863	76	13	89	4	93	7	—	71	—	2	—	—	147,311
1864	78	4	82	2	84	16	—	97	—	—	—	27	98,343
1865	85	1	86	1	87	13	10	89	—	—	—	3	93,402
1866	83	1	85	8	93	7	—	100	—	—	—	—	96,700
1867	80	11	90	2	93	7	—	95	—	—	5	—	119,412
1868	78	6	85	5	90	10	—	97	3	—	—	—	133,111
1869	73	14	87	4	92	8	15	85	—	—	—	—	127,606
1860–9	77	7	85	4	89	11	4	92	—	—	—	3	1,147,041

Year	Scotland Local %	Scotland Rest of Sc %	Total Sc %	Eng %	Brit %	Foreign %	North Am %	Aus & N.Z. %	Lat Am %	Eu %	I & C %	Africa %	Total Value %
1870	70	10	80	17	97	3	—	100	—	—	—	—	124,920
1871	85	4	89	8	97	3	22	44	—	—	34	—	215,772
1872	72	20	92	1	93	7	33	54	—	2	11	—	229,239
1873	86	4	90	1	91	9	37	45	—	—	18	—	154,575
1874	85	5	90	3	93	7	40	46	—	—	14	—	250,125
1875	85	3	88	8	96	4	26	21	—	—	52	1	297,465
1876	75	5	80	14	94	6	45	11	—	—	44	—	314,858
1877	63	7	70	20	91	9	38	8	—	—	47	6	343,920
1878	71	7	77	9	87	13	48	24	—	1	25	3	333,643
1879	79	6	85	3	89	11	55	23	—	1	21	1	351,572
1870-9	76	7	83	9	92	8	42	28	—	—	28	2	2,616,089
1880	79	3	81	5	86	14	79	11	—	1	8	1	386,127
1881	81	3	84	2	87	13	59	13	1	4	23	—	346,478
1882	78	1	79	4	83	17	81	13	—	—	5	1	321,065
1883	70	5	75	2	76	24	87	12	—	—	1	—	290,897
1884	75	2	77	3	79	21	77	20	—	—	3	—	267,468
1885	74	4	78	3	80	20	76	14	—	—	10	—	316,920
1886	84	3	86	2	88	12	73	13	—	—	14	—	437,044
1887	76	6	81	3	85	15	74	8	—	—	16	2	382,247
1888	76	6	82	2	84	16	70	15	—	—	15	—	396,747
1889	79	4	83	2	85	15	81	9	—	—	9	—	392,022
1880-9	77	4	81	3	84	16	76	13	—	—	10	—	3,537,015
1890	71	13	84	1	85	15	88	8	—	—	4	—	356,618
1891	71	12	83	3	86	14	90	5	—	—	5	—	285,107
1892	74	11	84	4	89	11	84	3	—	1	11	2	303,287
1893	75	12	87	2	89	11	95	—	—	—	4	—	239,195
1894	83	8	91	3	94	6	87	2	—	—	6	5	278,306
1895	80	7	87	2	89	11	84	3	—	—	4	9	296,674
1896	81	8	89	3	92	8	82	7	—	—	11	—	303,598
1897	76	10	86	4	90	10	97	1	—	—	1	1	281,869
1898	78	10	88	2	91	9	95	5	—	—	—	—	312,273
1899	80	8	88	2	90	10	96	3	—	—	1	—	254,027
1890-9	77	10	87	3	89	11	89	4	—	—	5	2	2,910,954
1900	77	8	85	3	88	12	97	—	—	2	1	—	254,396
1846-1900	75	6	81	4	85	15	52	39	—	—	8	1	11,801,684

Table 7
Value and Proportion of Aberdeen Stock Exchange Turnover: by Sector, 1846-1890

Year	Rail%	Ship%	Bank%	Ins%	Inv%	Gas%	Comm%	Ind%	Ser%	Prop%	Min%	Ag%	Gov%	Total Value
1846	24	11	26	5	18	15	1	—	1	—	—	—	—	134,409
1847	11	21	26	8	26	7	1	—	—	—	—	—	—	86,411
1848	4	17	50	9	16	3	1	—	—	—	—	—	—	70,376
1849	9	19	46	6	14	5	—	—	1	—	—	—	—	58,349
1846-9	14	16	34	7	19	9	—	—	1	—	—	—	—	349,545
1850	6	24	27	11	24	7	1	—	1	—	—	—	—	41,287
1851	6	17	39	8	17	11	1	—	—	—	—	—	—	37,274
1852	4	8	24	13	34	15	1	—	1	—	—	—	—	51,024
1853	1	3	7	2	82	3	—	—	3	—	—	—	—	409,071
1854	12	11	14	16	34	4	3	—	6	—	—	—	—	64,003
1855	34	14	23	8	9	7	1	—	3	—	—	—	—	68,421
1856	45	12	19	10	6	6	1	—	1	—	—	—	—	78,411
1857	20	15	25	18	6	11	4	—	—	—	—	—	—	53,895
1858	48	4	20	5	2	15	3	—	—	1	3	—	—	111,196
1859	24	7	29	6	2	15	5	—	1	—	9	—	—	72,062
1850-9	16	8	16	7	41	7	2	—	2	—	1	—	—	986,644
1860	54	4	17	7	4	9	2	—	1	—	3	—	—	107,227
1861	33	6	25	13	3	6	4	—	1	—	9	—	—	97,059
1862	35	9	19	7	2	4	5	—	1	1	18	—	—	126,870
1863	48	2	23	8	3	5	5	—	1	1	2	2	—	147,311
1864	26	4	34	11	13	4	4	—	—	—	3	1	—	98,343
1865	32	6	24	14	10	6	3	—	1	2	2	—	—	93,402
1866	34	5	33	11	6	5	3	—	—	1	1	—	2	96,700
1867	32	6	35	9	6	4	4	—	2	1	1	—	—	119,412
1868	40	5	25	8	4	3	7	—	1	—	2	—	5	133,111
1869	39	7	26	9	5	3	7	—	1	—	1	—	2	127,606
1860-9	38	6	26	9	5	5	5	—	1	—	4	—	1	1,147,041

Year	Rail%	Ship%	Bank%	Ins%	Inv%	Gas%	Comm%	Ind%	Ser%	Prop%	Min%	Ag%	Gov%	Total Value
1870	52	5	26	5	2	3	5	—	1	—	—	—	—	124,920
1871	67	3	14	4	2	5	3	—	1	—	—	1	—	215,772
1872	58	5	13	9	3	4	4	—	—	—	—	1	4	229,239
1873	46	6	18	14	6	3	5	—	—	—	1	1	—	154,575
1874	39	7	17	19	6	5	5	—	1	—	1	1	—	250,125
1875	37	7	18	28	2	3	2	1	—	—	—	2	—	297,465
1876	30	9	17	29	3	2	3	1	1	2	—	3	—	314,858
1877	18	8	14	39	5	2	2	2	1	4	—	4	—	343,920
1878	19	7	18	30	9	1	5	1	2	2	—	3	—	333,643
1879	26	4	19	26	9	2	6	3	2	1	—	2	—	351,572
1870-9	36	6	17	23	5	3	4	1	1	1	—	2	—	2,616,089
1880	31	8	15	24	8	2	4	2	1	2	1	2	—	386,127
1881	24	7	18	26	7	1	4	3	2	2	—	4	—	346,478
1882	21	8	21	24	9	1	4	2	2	4	1	4	—	321,065
1883	13	10	22	16	16	1	7	6	2	1	2	6	—	290,897
1884	10	5	15	24	9	1	6	15	2	1	1	10	—	367,468
1885	18	9	19	21	10	1	2	8	1	1	1	8	—	316,920
1886	10	10	15	37	7	1	2	11	2	1	1	4	—	437,044
1887	12	6	20	31	10	1	2	10	1	2	1	4	—	382,247
1888	15	9	21	21	10	2	3	10	1	2	2	4	—	396,747
1889	16	12	19	22	10	1	1	11	2	2	1	4	—	392,022
1880-9	17	8	18	25	9	1	3	8	2	2	1	5	—	3,537,015
1890	18	7	15	30	12	3	3	7	1	1	1	1	1	356,718
1891	17	7	18	23	11	2	4	11	2	1	1	2	—	285,107
1892	17	5	21	27	9	3	3	11	2	1	1	1	—	303,287
1893	17	8	26	19	10	2	2	12	1	—	2	1	—	239,195
1894	14	8	27	27	6	1	4	8	1	1	1	—	—	278,306
1895	17	7	27	20	8	1	5	11	2	—	2	1	—	296,674
1896	14	7	27	23	7	1	3	11	2	3	—	1	—	303,598
1897	14	6	24	22	10	—	5	15	1	2	1	—	—	281,869
1898	12	6	27	22	8	2	3	16	1	2	1	1	—	312,273
1899	11	8	23	24	8	1	3	15	1	2	2	1	1	254,027
1890-9	15	7	23	24	9	2	4	12	2	1	1	1	—	2,911,054
1900	12	9	21	16	10	1	2	19	2	2	2	2	—	254,396
1846-1900	22	7	20	21	11	3	3	6	1	1	1	2	—	11,801,784

Table 8
Number and Proportion of Transactions on the Dundee Stock Exchange: by Location, 1879-1900

Year	Scotland Local %	Scotland Rest of Sc %	Total Sc %	Eng %	Brit %	Foreign %	North Am %	Aus & N.Z. %	South Am %	Africa %	Europe %	India & Ceylon %	Total Number
1879	34	2	36	—	36	64	90	6	—	—	—	4	285
1880	13	2	15	—	15	85	87	11	—	—	—	3	625
1881	14	3	17	—	17	83	91	9	—	—	—	—	629
1882	13	1	14	—	14	86	94	4	—	—	—	1	1,235
1883	17	4	21	—	21	79	94	6	—	—	—	—	1,332
1884	8	3	11	—	11	89	91	9	—	—	—	—	1,043
1885	16	4	19	—	19	81	91	9	—	—	—	—	651
1886	10	3	13	—	13	87	91	9	—	—	—	—	547
1887	16	3	19	—	19	81	87	12	—	—	1	—	571
1888	23	2	25	1	26	74	85	14	—	—	—	1	589
1889	27	1	28	—	28	72	90	10	—	—	—	1	690
1880-9	15	3	18	—	18	82	91	8	—	—	—	1	7,912
1890	24	1	25	—	25	75	93	7	—	—	—	1	555
1891	31	1	32	—	33	67	92	6	—	—	—	1	506
1892	27	2	29	—	29	71	94	5	—	—	—	1	648
1893	21	2	24	—	24	76	87	3	—	—	—	10	761
1894	23	2	25	—	25	75	90	3	—	—	—	7	646
1895	22	3	25	1	25	75	86	6	—	—	—	8	702
1896	28	3	31	—	31	69	86	4	—	—	—	10	902
1897	22	3	25	1	26	74	92	1	—	—	—	7	939
1898	28	6	33	4	37	63	92	1	—	—	—	7	936
1899	26	2	28	2	29	71	86	2	—	—	—	12	954
1890-9	25	3	28	1	29	71	89	3	—	—	—	7	7,549
1900	29	3	32	1	34	66	85	1	—	—	—	13	764
1880-1900	20	3	23	1	24	76	90	6	—	—	—	4	16,225

Table 9
Number and Proportion of Transactions on the Dundee Stock Exchange: by Sector, 1879-1900

Year	Rail %	Ship %	Bank %	Ins. %	Inv. %	Gas %	Services & Prpty %	Muni-cipal %	Comm. %	Ind. %	Ag. %	Min. %	Total No.
1879	2	21	—	1	63	4	1	4	—	—	4	1	285
1880	10	6	—	1	76	2	1	3	—	—	1	—	625
1881	24	10	—	2	54	2	—	1	—	—	6	—	629
1882	10	8	—	1	32	1	1	1	—	—	42	6	1,235
1883	5	14	—	—	26	1	—	1	—	—	45	8	1,332
1884	3	5	—	1	40	1	1	1	—	—	47	2	1,043
1885	5	8	—	1	43	2	2	2	—	—	34	3	651
1886	8	6	—	1	49	1	—	2	—	—	32	1	547
1887	4	11	—	2	53	1	1	2	—	—	25	1	571
1888	5	11	—	—	51	2	1	6	—	3	22	—	589
1889	10	14	—	—	52	1	—	6	—	4	12	—	690
1880-9	8	9	—	1	44	1	1	2	—	1	30	3	7,912
1890	1	12	—	—	58	1	1	8	—	2	17	—	555
1891	3	11	1	—	62	2	1	9	1	2	8	—	506
1892	2	10	—	1	65	1	1	5	—	5	8	—	648
1893	3	11	1	1	60	1	—	4	—	12	9	—	761
1894	4	10	—	1	68	1	—	3	—	8	4	—	646
1895	4	11	—	1	60	—	2	3	1	9	8	1	702
1896	2	9	—	—	56	—	1	6	—	17	7	1	902
1897	3	6	—	—	62	1	1	4	1	14	8	—	939
1898	2	11	—	1	52	1	—	4	4	18	7	1	936
1899	1	8	—	—	55	1	1	7	1	18	7	1	954
1890-9	3	10	—	1	59	1	1	5	1	12	8	—	7,549
1900	1	11	—	—	50	—	—	5	2	21	8	—	764
1880-1900	5	10	—	1	51	1	1	4	1	7	19	2	16,229

R

NOTES

1. Glasgow Daily Share List, 2 January 1850 – 31 December 1900. On the Glasgow Stock Exchange transactions were largely unrecorded, apart from marking changing prices against the issue being traded in. Stocks with volatile share prices thus gave the impression of dominating the market, and allowance had to be made for that when trying to assess, visually, trends in volume and composition of business. For a statement regarding the categories of transactions marked, see the Daily List, 3 March 1846.

2. Cf. the business of defaulting brokers, Glasgow Stock Exchange Association: Minutes, 13 November 1873, 9 December 1873.

3. S. G. Checkland, *Scottish Banking: A History, 1695-1973* (Glasgow 1975) pp. 485, 497.

4. Kerr, Anderson to A. Nobel, 16 June 1884.

5. Glasgow: Minutes, 28 February 1883, 16 January 1884, 15 May 1884, 12 June 1884, 16 April 1890; *Econ.*, 19 April 1884, 19 December 1885, 2 October 1886; W. A. Thomas, *The Provincial Stock Exchanges* (Lon. 1973) p. 304.

6. Edinburgh Stock Exchange Association: Minutes, 12 April 1881; *Edinburgh Courant* 17 May 1884.

7. Information concerning business on the Edinburgh Stock Exchange was gleaned from the following: Robert Allan, *Monthly Circular* (Edin. 1850-1868); *S.R.G.* 1850-1; *S.B. & I.M.* 1879-1886; *B.E.* 1886-8; *N.B.E.* 1889-1895; *B. & I.M.* 1896-7; Bell, Begg & Cowan, Monthly Market Report (Edin. 1882-1897); W. R. Lawson, *The Scottish Investor's Manual* (Edin. 1884); *Econ.*, 19 April 1884, 2 October 1886.

8. Allan, op. cit., February 1860.

9. W. Vamplew, Railways and the Transformation of the Scottish Economy (Ph.D. Edin. 1970) p. 46.

10. Bell, Begg & Cowan, October 1895.

11. Aberdeen Stock Exchange: Record & Ledger, January 1850 – December 1900. On the Aberdeen Stock Exchange every transaction made was recorded with regard to the security involved, the number transferred, and the price agreed upon. According to Rule 27 of the Aberdeen Stock Exchange Association (Abdn. 1847):

> In order to obtain a correct list of prices, all transactions betwixt members of this association shall be daily reported in the list provided for that purpose in the Stock Exchange.

By classifying these deals according to the nature and location of the company whose securities were involved, an accurate measure of the value and composition of business was obtained.

12. P. D. Holcombe, Scottish Investment in Canada, 1870-1914 (M.Litt. Strathclyde 1975) p. 312.

13. *Econ.*, 19 April 1884; Aberdeen Stock Exchange Association: Minutes, 19 February 1901.

14. Dundee Stock Exchange Association: Concerns Quoted, May 1879 – December 1900. Against each quotation a 'mark' was placed each time a transfer of shares was made, or a bargain struck. Unlike Glasgow, this was not limited to when prices changed, but attempted to record every deal, even those done after hours. Companies were classified as with the Aberdeen data. However, these statistics give no more than the vaguest impression of business, and overstate the importance of securities with low values, such as U.S. cattle ranching companies in the 1880s.

15. *G.T.* 1888, 1889, 1895, 1900.

16. E. T. Powell, *The Mechanism of the City* (Lon. 1910) p. 134.

PART V:

INVESTMENT AND THE SCOTTISH SHARE MARKET, 1820-1914

... it is the class of persons who will, with the chance of obtaining a prize, venture their money, knowing that they may, instead of the prize, get a blank, that send forth from this mighty and beating heart of commerce and enterprise those currents of wealth which set and keep the industry of the world in motion, and give it, in place of the mere animal enjoyments of barbarism, the comforts and luxuries of civilised life.

W. Bartlett & H. Chapman, *A Handy-Book for Investors* (London 1869) p. 340.

... the market performs an act of magic, for it permits long-term investments to be financed by funds provided by individuals, many of whom wish to make them available for only a very limited period, or who wish to be able to withdraw them at will. Thus it imparts a measure of liquidity to long-term investments that permits their instruments to be sold at a lower rate of return than would otherwise be required.

W. J. Baumol, *The Stock Market and Economic Efficiency* (New York 1965) p. 3.

17

The Functions of the Market

THE share market served two distinct functions, as there existed separate markets for both newly issued stocks and shares, and for securities already in circulation. The former, or primary market, was served mainly by such intermediaries and entrepreneurs as stockbrokers, solicitors, accountants, bankers, and numerous well connected amateurs. These people employed various means to obtain subscriptions for their share issues, ranging from the public prospectus, which was widely advertised in the national press and handled by a merchant bank or firm of stockbrokers, to the private circulation of a proposal amongst the members of a small and closely connected syndicate.[1] There did not exist one means by which capital was raised in the way of share subscription, and these unco-ordinated and informal methods remained important throughout the nineteenth century. This was even true in an area that needed a degree of expertise and management, such as investment abroad.[2]

Financial institutions and professional company promoters were becoming more in evidence and played a larger role in the capital market. In 1887, for example, it was felt that:

> An entirely new class of Financiers, known as promoters, has sprung into existence. The end and aim of the existence of these gentlemen is to form or promote companies for the purchase or working of undertakings, and to look for their remuneration in the form of commission upon the amount of capital obtained, or the profit difference between the price at which they themselves acquire a business and the price at which they can effect its sale to a company. Promoters, as such, are undoubtedly necessary intermediaries between vendors and the public.[3]

A number of Scottish companies were promoted by these itinerant professionals or by specialised institutions. In 1864, the London Financial Association converted the established Glasgow firm of Smith & Rodger into the Clyde Engineering & Iron Shipbuilding Co., and floated the concern as a joint-stock company. Similarly, the London promoter, H. O. O'Hagan, was instrumental in the amalgamation of four Edinburgh breweries and the promotion of the combination as the Edinburgh United Breweries in 1889.[4]

However, these were not common occurrences, for most Scottish joint-stock companies appear to have been promoted by Scots themselves, especially lawyers and amateurs, and to have obtained subscriptions through informal contacts, often at a regional level.[5] This was also true for the whole of Britain.[6] Evidence of the success of this primary market is available from Aberdeen. Between 1845 and 1895, 1,650 different companies appealed for capital from the Aberdeen public, as gauged by the appearance of a prospectus in the local press. Their success in obtaining finance was judged by whether or not the company's shares ever made even a single appearance on the Aberdeen Stock Exchange. If shares were acquired in any number by people resident in the area, they could expect to be traded locally. Where the majority of shares were held elsewhere, the transactions settled locally would be limited, but at least an occasional transfer would have appeared. Certainly, transactions took place in the securities of two companies in which Aberdonians were known to have invested, namely the North Staffordshire Railway and the West Hartlepool Harbour and Railway.[7] Similarly, although Aberdeen was a poor market for government stock, mining companies and foreign railways, there were intermittent deals as stockbrokers continued to test the local market and, at times, found receptive buyers and sellers.

Of the 1,650 companies, 1,484 were unsuccessful in obtaining any support in the North-East of Scotland. Only 166 concerns, or 10 per cent of the total, did attract finance. The rate of success ranged from 30 per cent of insurance and 20 per cent of investment companies to only 4 per cent of mines and 3 per cent of gas undertakings. While these figures apparently damn the primary capital market, further investigation presents a different picture. Of the 111 companies which proposed to operate in North-East Scotland itself, and which looked for local finance, a total of 65 — or 59 per cent — were successful. Similarly, of the 73 companies operating outside the region, but in whose promotion well-known local figures were involved, a total of 31 — or 42 per cent — were successful in obtaining local subscriptions. Overall, a 'local' company had a 52 per cent chance of attracting investment funds from North-East Scotland, while a non-local concern had only a 4 per cent chance.

The main support for a new issue was to be found in either the locality where the company was to operate or already operated, or where the promoters were known and respected. For most enterprises there was no real need to indulge in costly national advertising and the use of specialist institutions and intermediaries, for the insertion of the prospectus in the local press, the marshalling of support by the promoters themselves, and the enlistment of the aid of local stockbrokers, solicitors and bankers were usually sufficient to provide a wide range of potential support. All such means were used to promote the City of Aberdeen Land Association in 1874/5, for example, and were commonplace throughout Scotland.[8] However, this did not guarantee success, for every company still had to prove its worth to the local investing public. Many of the 'local' ventures which failed to find sufficient financial support from the area were either speculative enterprises, such as overseas mining and ranching companies, or dubious domestic property and industrial concerns.

The importance of local connections gave new companies the opportunity to raise the capital they required, but their success in so doing remained dependent upon the intrinsic merit of the venture, or the appearance which it gave, and the prevailing market conditions. Although the means of arranging new issues were usually regional and informal, that did not make them immune either to outside forces or to investment criteria. It did, however, allow all manner and size of companies to be easily and cheaply promoted, with a reasonable prospect of success. Between 1850 and 1900, for example, the number of industrial and commercial companies quoted on the Glasgow Stock Exchange rose from 2 to 117, and their paid-up capital went as low as £25,000. Similarly, on the Aberdeen Stock Exchange the number of industrial and commercial concerns listed increased from 7 in 1878 to 25 in 1900, and their paid-up capital reached down to £3,500, with many being under £15,000. Consequently, there is little evidence from Scotland that the costs of a new issue for a small industrial or commercial concern were prohibitive.[9]

London-based financial institutions were not geared to the handling of such promotions, but that did not mean that these concerns lacked the means of obtaining finance from the public. Depending on the path chosen, a company could be formed, and subscriptions obtained, for an almost negligible sum. Even advertising costs and commissions could be dispensed with if the promoters cared to canvass potential investors themselves. All that was required was a handwritten list of names on which could be inserted the number of shares which each agreed to take. Institutions and specialists were necessary only in the case of large national or international issues, when the size of the capital to be raised could justify the cost of expertise and coverage. The new issue market in Scotland, in all its forms, was sufficiently flexible to accommodate every level of enterprise that wished to raise capital publicly, but it did discriminate between different enterprises and its willingness to provide the funds for which a company asked did vary from time to time.

The importance of the new issue market is readily apparent. Without the ability to raise capital by the issue of shares to the investing public, economic development could have been severely and increasingly curtailed, as the capital requirements of the economy grew in the nineteenth century. It was through joint-stock companies that most of the advances in public facilities and services were provided, such as railways, shipping, gas, water, banking and insurance. Many branches of industry and commerce also came to rely upon public share issues in order to obtain the finance necessary for growth. As the scale of enterprise grew, it became more and more difficult for the individual to finance development, while in some areas it never really had been possible. Thomson observed in 1886, that:

> . . . a vast number of undertakings either from their magnitude, or the risk that attends them, . . . could not be carried on, unless some means were devised by which a large number of individuals could unite their capitals together into a common fund. Such a work as a railway, for instance, is beyond the power of any capitalist to carry on.[10]

Joint-stock enterprise was not the only way by which this could have been organised. Social overhead capital could have been provided by national or local government through taxation and rates, for much came to be financed in that way.[11] Similarly, the growing scale of industrial, commercial and financial enterprise could have been funded through continued reinvestment and by outside borrowing, as was a substantial proportion of existing business, although banks were very unwilling to provide long-term finance.[12] Property development was still largely supplied with capital without the aid of joint-stock companies, through either savings or loans. Building societies, for example, were of growing importance.[13] Many of the joint-stock companies that did appear, and sought funds from the public, were only conversions of established private firms and represented a change of ownership rather than an addition to the capital of the economy.[14]

Nevertheless, despite the importance of these alternatives in certain spheres of economic life, the fact remains that it was the joint-stock form that offered both the easiest and most flexible means of mobilising available funds for productive investment and managing the enterprise so created. The joint-stock company was not indispensable, but it was the method best suited to the conditions of the nineteenth century. Therefore the successful functioning of the new issue market provided the stream of funds required by the ever-widening scope of joint-stock enterprise, and that enterprise was of vital importance in nineteenth century economic growth.

The more organised and institutional part of the share market was that which provided a means by which issued shares could be bought and sold, and this was served by the stockbroker, again, and the stock exchange. While the stockbroker played a role of increasing importance in both aspects of the share market, the stock exchange's function was almost entirely limited to this secondary market. Occasionally, if a company had a number of unissued shares of which it needed to dispose, it might unload them gradually on the stock exchange through a broker, but this was neither normal practice nor a commonplace occurrence.[15] The value of this market in issued securities is less immediately obvious than the primary market, for it did not raise any capital for economic development. Investment on the secondary market was neither capital formation nor the provision of funds for capital formation. Sales and purchases of stocks and shares by brokers on the stock exchanges had, therefore, no immediate effect upon the financing of joint-stock enterprise and, through them, upon the economy.[16] There was a tendency for many contemporaries to dismiss much of stock exchange business as gambling on the rise and fall of share prices, and as of little value to the community as a whole.[17]

Although an element in the transactions was little more than that, even speculation had a vital use, while the provision of a secondary market was of central importance in raising fresh capital and imparting flexibility to investment. The essential role played by the stock exchange was long recognised in Scotland, such as by this author in the *Edinburgh Review* in 1819:

> . . . as the debts thus contracted by government are not usually paid for a long period of time, it is requisite that any creditor of the public should have the power of obtaining money for what is thereby due to him, by the disposal of his share of the funds to any other person.[18]

The existence of a market for issued securities considerably reduced the risk involved in providing funds for capital formation, as it meant that investment was not of indefinite length but readily realisable by sale of the shares. Although the actual investment itself could not be liquidated, the claim to the return on that investment was transferable to another. Thus, to the individual investor his commitment was a short-term one, but to the company issuing the shares the capital was available on a long-term basis.[19]

This had the dual effect of reducing the cost of capital and maximising available savings. Moreover, as investments in stocks and shares were readily realisable, and became more and more so with improvements in the market, the investor did not demand a high rate of interest by way of compensation for the long-term alienation of his savings. His funds remained liquid and so the return could be low. The better the secondary market for the securities of specific companies, the lower was their yield and the easier it was for these enterprises to raise additional capital. Conversely, the lack of marketability lowered the price of a security and increased the return it had to offer, in order to attract support.[20] Therefore the existence of the secondary market ensured that the cost of long-term investment was substantially lower than it would have been otherwise.

At the same time, the ability to buy and sell stocks and shares quickly and to speculate on short-term price fluctuations allowed the employment of funds that were only temporarily idle and would be shortly required for other purposes. A substantial proportion of stock exchange operations was undertaken by borrowing the money which was continually being made available and absorbed in the everyday business of trade as goods were sold and bills paid, but new stock was not yet acquired. Each individual tranche of this money could not be used to buy and hold stock exchange securities but, by continually renewing and replacing these funds with others as they became available, it was possible to use finance of the shortest of terms to purchase long-term investments. The returns lay in both the differential between the low interest paid on short-term funds and the higher rate paid on longer-term investments, and any capital gain made on buying at one price and selling at another. These types of operation were continually being conducted on the market and, while they gave the appearance of gambling, they represented an effective mobilisation of idle funds and an expansion of the supply of capital available for productive enterprise. It was no longer necessary for individuals and institutions to keep much money in the form of currency, as this could be invested but still remain readily available. This could be done either through direct purchases of stocks and shares, or through lending to those buying securities.[21]

If the economy had had to rely only upon those savings which could be spared indefinitely in order to finance large projects with a long gestation period, not only would very few of these have been implemented, but the cost of the capital used would have been almost prohibitive. The secondary market played a dynamic role in the economy by generating an increasing supply of cheap capital which could be tapped for all manner of enterprise. Without the secondary market, the pace of economic progress in the nineteenth century would have been much slower, the scale of development would have been much less, and the nature of the economy would have been very different.

The changing seasonal nature of investment illustrates the growing integration of the stock exchange into the capital market and the economy. The buying and selling of shares did not occur evenly throughout the year, but took place in certain months more than others. In the late 1840s, by January/February turnover on the Aberdeen Stock Exchange was twice the level of that of August/September. Even by the late nineteenth century, monthly variations in investment remained, although they were more moderate, and during the 1890s an average of 7 per cent of the yearly investment was done in July, August and September, as compared with 10 per cent in April and May.[22] In Edinburgh the stockbrokers Bell, Begg & Cowan noted in 1887 that:

> As is not unusual in August there has been a very small amount of business doing on the Stock Exchange, . . .[23]

Similarly, in Glasgow, the stockbrokers Kerr, Anderson continued to observe seasonal variations in stock exchange activity.[24]

Nevertheless, investment on the stock exchange did become more evenly distributed over the year, in the course of the nineteenth century. This was especially so after 1850, with the relative decline of the speculative manias that had characterised the earlier period. These manias usually began at the end of the year, particularly November, and gained momentum until May or June of the following year, before they collapsed in October or November.[25] The domination of these manias can be seen in the events in Aberdeen in 1852/3, when the Stock Exchange was caught up in the frenzy of speculation in Australian gold mining through its Australian investment companies:

> The excitement in our share market during the last three months has, if possible, exceeded that of 1845-6. Our local stocks have all experienced a considerable improvement, and one after another of the distant Investment Companies has sprung from a state of collapse into the most buoyant activity,

reported the *Aberdeen Herald* in March 1853.[26] Under the influence of this mania, almost half of all investment done, in 1852, took place in the last quarter of the year, especially the month of December, while almost 60 per cent of investment in 1853 was concentrated in the first quarter. In contrast, during the 1860s, the maximum investment done in any quarter was 42 per cent, and this fell to 38 per cent in the 1870s, 34 per cent in the 1880s, and 32 per cent in the 1890s.[27] Fluctuations continued to occur, but their impact was progressively more moderate.

The causes of this seasonal pattern of investment lay in the changing consequences of the weather for an economy that became less and less agrarian. Certainly, in the first half of the century the economic state of the country was heavily reliant upon the state of the harvest, and this in turn was largely conditioned by the weather. 'The Harvest is an object of great and general interest,' reported the *Bankers' Circular* in August 1830.[28] The weather, through its effect on crops, produced considerable uncertainty among investors. A poor harvest would absorb available funds, both in financing costly purchases of domestic and foreign grain, and in providing credit for those domestic farmers suffering from reduced income because their own crops had failed. This would severely reduce the amount of short-term funds seeking investments on the stock exchange. At the same time the longer-term demand for stocks and shares would be curtailed by the increase in the cost of living which resulted from higher food costs. This would directly diminish savings in general and reduce profits in the non-agricultural sector owing to falling real incomes. Thus, investors had every reason to be wary of the weather when investing and to hold back until future conditions were better known.

The comments made in June 1847 by the Edinburgh Stock Exchange correspondent of the *Scottish Railway Gazette* illustrate the effects of these uncertain circumstances upon investment:

> If the weather continues warm and fair, there is every reason to believe that we shall soon have a large demand, and much higher prices given for good Railway Shares. The value of the Government securities and Railway stocks, alike depend on the state of the weather and the price of grain. A shower of rain raises the price of wheat, and a corresponding fall takes place in the funds as well as in shares — while a warm, sunny day produces an exactly opposite effect.[29]

Thus, the uncertainty which existed until the harvest was known discouraged investment among the cautious, as a bad harvest would drive share prices down.

However, the very pattern of agricultural production produced a counter-cyclical trend in investment. From October to January there was a strong temporary demand for currency as production in agriculture was concentrated into a few months, but consumption was spread, fairly evenly, over the year. Thus, the harvest and the resulting stocks of agricultural produce had to be financed while awaiting consumption. Much of this required the use of specie, especially the payment of harvest labour and small farmers, and this was withdrawn from the financial system and only slowly filtered back, so reducing the basis of credit in the economy. An indication of this seasonal pressure on the money supply was that, over the period 1845-1900, the rate of discount was usually at its highest in winter. In the months which followed harvest, stocks were gradually sold, and funds were released which would not be required until the next harvest. These could be left idle or employed for any return which they could produce. One use that was open to them was to lend to those who wished to purchase and hold stock exchange securities.

This growing supply of funds, temporarily released by trade, was held in check by uncertainty regarding the state of the next harvest, which discouraged investment. However, this self-regulating mechanism could be unbalanced by a sequence of exceptionally good harvests. Through falling unit prices, good harvests led to a growth in disposable income and, with greater aggregate farm income, made agriculture more profitable. This stimulated savings, while the series of good harvests generated an air of confidence that encouraged investors to commit their funds to stock exchange investments. When the harvest turned out to be a failure, confidence evaporated, currency was required to finance crisis imports, and credit collapsed, bringing the boom to an end, as in 1825 and 1845.[30]

However, this seasonal influence was steadily diminishing. The very nature of the British economy was changing with the expansion of manufacturing industry, the growth of the urban population, and the integration into a world system of production and trade. Instead of being dependent upon the cycle of one dominant activity — agriculture — and one that was very prone to seasonal influences, fluctuations in the economy became more affected by the varying trends within numerous industries, many of which were only slightly influenced by the seasons. The importance of the seasons was never completely removed, although the need to use the expensive fixed plant increasingly installed in many sectors ensured that they were kept to a minimum. As Chiozza Money observed in 1912:

> By no process of law can we make it as convenient to build a house in the winter as in the summer, or cause as great a demand for artificial light in the summer as in the winter in northern latitudes.[31]

Major activities such as construction, gas production, textile manufacture or coalmining all continued to be strongly affected by the weather, especially winter.[32] In building, for example, frost and generally inclement conditions brought house-building to a near standstill in winter, while gas production reached a peak due to the need for heat and light.[33] Even within agriculture, the ever-widening sources of production which regularly supplied the British market helped to minimise the consequences of adverse or beneficial weather.[34] Improvements in transportation, communications and marketing also combined to reduce fluctuations over the year. Nevertheless, despite these developments and the natural balances between certain sectors, such as building and gas, variations over the year remained, and they continued to affect the capital market. As the builder, for instance, completed and sold property towards the end of the year and did not commence new projects, his supplies of funds rose. Conversely, when he began to be active again in March/April, he had need of outside finance. Therefore, between November and March the builder was looking for suitable investments for his idle funds, while between April and August he was realising these and seeking outside support.[35]

These natural forces which conditioned investment were also being supplemented by the entirely artificial cycles of an industrial/urban society. Holidays, for example, could lead to marked downturns in activity, while the timing of dividend receipts, house-lettings and tax payments all affected the inclination and ability to invest and determined the length of investment. If payments had to be made in the near future, only short-term loans or the purchase of easily liquidated securities could be contemplated. However, these variations over the year did not have the uniformity of timing imposed by the harvest, with trends in one neutralising another, such as bank holdings of bills of exchange and advances to customers.[36] In these seasonal variations, the secondary share market played an increasingly vital role as it constantly made available securities which could be easily bought and sold, so that idle balances were directly or indirectly absorbed and put to some use rather than creating conditions leading to a speculative mania.

The very size of this secondary market also diminished the importance of these fluctuations, for the value of the securities in circulation rose year by year, not just absolutely but also relative to any new creations. Thus, the impact of any speculative craze was considerably diluted by the prior existence of a great amount of existing investments. The growing sophistication of the secondary market made it more and more capable of fulfilling this role. Therefore by helping to even out the effects of the seasons and providing employment for otherwise idle funds, the stockbrokers and the stock exchange showed themselves to be a central part of the capital market and occupied a position of growing importance. This was not just due to the obvious role that they played in obtaining funds for new enterprises, but owed more to their pervasive, but indirect, influence upon the supply and use of capital.

NOTES

1. Cf. R. C. Michie, 'Options, Concessions, Syndicates and the Provision of Venture Capital, 1880-1913' *Business History* (forthcoming); R. C. Michie, 'The Social Web of Investment in the Nineteenth Century' *International Review of the History of Banking* (forthcoming).

2. P. D. Holcombe, Scottish Investment in Canada, 1870-1914 (M.Litt. Strathclyde 1975) p. 42; D. G. Paterson, *British Direct Investment in Canada, 1890-1914* (Toronto 1976) p. 41.

3. *Phillips' Investors' Manual* (Lon. 1887) p. 30.

4. P. L. Cottrell, Investment Banking in England, 1856-1882 (Ph.D. Hull 1974) pp. 407-8; H. O. O'Hagan, *Leaves from my life* (Lon. 1929) I, pp. 204, 254.

5. J. Scott & M. Hughes, *The Anatomy of Scottish Capital* (Lon. 1980) pp. 44-6.

6. Cottrell, op. cit., pp. 421-4, 442; S. F. Van Oss & F. C. Mathieson, *Stock Exchange Values: A Decade of Finance, 1885-1895* (Lon. 1895) LIX; H. Lowenfeld, *All About Investment* (Lon. 1909) pp. 163-197; F. Lavington, *The English Capital Market* (Lon. 1921) p. 122; O'Hagan, op. cit., I, pp. 29, 32, 87, 257; A. J. Merret, et al, *Equity Issues and the London Capital Market* (Lon. 1967) pp. 5-10; F. W. Paish, 'The London New Issue Market' *Ec.* 28 (1951) p. 13.

7. *A.F.P.* 21 February 1863, 13 May 1865.

8. City of Aberdeen Land Association: Minutes, 9 February 1875, 18 March 1875; A. Anderson to A. Edmond, 14 December 1874; A. Edmond to A. Anderson, 28 January 1875; A. Anderson, Circular to Aberdeen Solicitors, 3 February 1875; M. Gray, *The Fishing Industries of Scotland, 1790-1914* (Abdn. 1978) pp. 168, 179; *Memoirs and Portraits of One Hundred Glasgow Men* (Glasgow 1886) p. 247; J. A. Hassan, The Development of the Coal Industry in Mid and West Lothian, 1815-1873 (Ph.D. Strathclyde 1976) p. 187; N. Crathorne, *Tennant's Stalk* (Lon. 1973) pp. 138-141.

9. Cf. M. Edelstein, 'Rigidity and Bias in the British Capital Market, 1870-1913' in D. N. McCloskey (ed.), *Essays on a Mature Economy: Britain after 1840* (Lon. 1971); W. P. Kennedy, 'Institutional Response to Economic Growth: Capital Markets in Britain to 1914' in L. Hannah (ed.), *Management Strategy and Business Development* (Lon. 1976).

10. T. Thomson, 'The Effect on Commerce of the Law of Limited Liability' *J.I.B.* 7 (1886) p. 501.

11. G. Clare, 'Stock Exchange Securities: Their Nature and Characteristics', *J.I.B.* 15 (1894) p. 59.

12. C. W. Munn, The Scottish Provincial Banking Companies, 1747-1864 (Ph.D. Glasgow 1976) p. 325; Thomson, op. cit., p. 501.

13. I. H. Adams, *The Making of Urban Scotland* (Lon. 1978) p. 194; J. Lyon, *Jubilee Souvenir of Dumbarton Building Society, 1873-1923* (Dumbarton 1923).

14. A. K. Cairncross, 'The English Capital Market before 1914' *Ec.* 25 (1958) p. 143.

15. O'Hagan, op. cit., p. 266; Lavington, op. cit., p. 203.

16. C. W. J. Grainger & O. Morgenstern, *Predictability of Stock Market Prices* (Lexington 1970) p. 1.

17. *The Bank — The Stock Exchange — The Bankers — The Bankers' Clearing House — The Minister, and the public: An Exposé*, (Lon. 1821) pp. 1-20; *Exposure of the Stock Exchange and Bubble Companies* (Lon. 1854) pp. 3, 13; *On the Analogy between the Stock Exchange and the Turf* (Lon. 1885) pp. 9, 14; W. R. Lawson, *The Scottish Investors' Manual* (Edin. 1884) p. 35.

18. *E.R.* April 1819; cf. J. M. Stone, 'Financial Panics: Their Implications for Mix of Domestic and Foreign Investments of Great Britain, 1880-1913' *Q.J.E.* 85 (1971) p. 323.

19. W. J. Baumol, *The Stock Market and Economic Efficiency* (N.Y. 1965) p. 3; Merrett, op. cit., p. 2; Lavington, op. cit., pp. 122, 224-5, 229; J. H. Murchison, *British Mines considered as a means of Investment* (Lon. 1854) pp. 15, 77; M. S. Rix, *Stock Market Economics* (Lon. 1954) pp. 27, 36-7.

20. G. F. Gibson, *The Stock Exchanges of London, Paris and New York* (Lon. 1889) p. 11; *How to Commence Investing* (Lon. 1901) p. 14.

21. H. S. Muller, *Scientific Speculation* (Lon. 1901) pp. 38, 90-4; *One Hundred Problems Solved* (Lon. 1901) p. 14; Cottrell, op. cit., pp. 749, 801-2.

22. Aberdeen Stock Exchange Monthly Value of Turnover, 1845-1900.

23. Bell, Begg & Cowan: Circular, September 1887, January 1893.

24. Kerr, Anderson to A. Nobel, 14 December 1886.

25. Cf. Chs. 7 & 8.

26. *A.H.* 12 March 1853.

27. Abdn. St. Ex. Turnover, 1845-1900.

28. *B.C.* 22 August 1828, 24 October 1828, 15 May 1829, 6 August 1830.

29. *S.R.G.* 28 June 1847.

30. R. H. Inglis Palgrave, *Bank Rate and the Money Market, 1844-1900* (Lon. 1903) pp. 107, 135, 139; W. S. Jevons, *Investigations in Currency and Finance* (Lon. 1884) pp. 3, 7, 8, 171; J. P. Lewis, *Building Cycles and Britain's Growth* (Lon. 1965) p. 25; W. A. Steel, 'Periodic Commercial and Financial Fluctuations considered in their relationship to the business of banking' *J.I.B.* 6 (1885) pp. 374-6; Munn, op. cit., p. 309.

31. L. G. Chiozza Money, *Insurance versus Poverty* (Lon. 1912) p. 301.

32. J. H. Treble, 'The seasonal demand for adult labour in Glasgow, 1890-1914' *S.H.* 3 (1978) pp. 44-7, 54; Chiozza Money, op. cit., p. 301.

33. R. G. Rodger, Scottish Urban Housebuilding, 1870-1914 (Ph.D. Edinburgh 1975) p. 426; Cotterill, op. cit., p. 760.

34. D. H. Robertson, *A Study of Industrial Fluctuation* (Lon. 1915) pp. 15-25, 138, 143, 150.

35. Rodger, op. cit., pp. 426-8.

36. S. Kuznets, *Seasonal Variations in Industry and Trade* (N.Y. 1933) p. 197; Bell, Begg & Cowan, Circular, August 1890; P. Holcombe, Scottish Investment in Canada, 1870-1914 (M.Litt. Strathclyde 1975) p. 316; Steel, op. cit., p. 371; Munn, op. cit., p. 309; C. A. E. Goodhart, *The Business of Banking, 1891-1914* (Lon. 1912) pp. 150, 160.

18

The Nature of Investment

THE secondary market was of vital importance to the individual investor as it allowed him to alter his portfolio according to his changing personal circumstances and the opportunities for investment available to him:[1]

> Most investments, however bad they may be, can, as a rule, be sold, and the proceeds invested in the very stocks which an Investor should hold

was the opinion of Lowenfeld in 1909.[2] The flexibility imparted by the stock exchange was important in attracting investors to stocks and shares rather than other forms of investment. In addition, the secondary market opened up to the investor the possibility of purchasing any of the securities ever issued and did not leave him confined to whichever new issue was currently on offer. As the amount and variety of stock in the market grew, so securities became a much more popular investment, for they were able to cater for the varied needs of each individual investor.

Many individual and institutional investors had no desire to trust their savings to some untried venture or, like trustees, were unable to do so, but were keen to purchase the securities of some proven enterprise. The secondary market made this available to them and, at the same time, released the capital of those investors who were willing to risk part of their funds on a novel venture. Through the secondary market, maximum use was made of risk capital, for, once the enterprise was established, it could be replaced by risk-averting finance, which paid for its caution in the price at which it acquired the stock or share. Thus, the secondary market was more and more able to match investors and investments to the benefit of both, and it did this continuously in the buying and selling of issued securities.[3]

Of course, not all investment was directed to stocks and shares, for much remained within enterprises or was directed into bank deposits, mortgages, land or property.[4] The terminable debentures issued in Scotland by many investment companies, for example, were redeemable but not transferable and so were not traded on the stock exchanges.[5] The proportion invested in stocks and shares was growing as they became more attractive in terms of security, yield, potential and marketability.[6] Nevertheless, there continued to be times when investors were disillusioned with the stock exchange and directed their attention to other fields. The resurgence of property in the 1890s was one example of this, for it coincided with a decline in stock exchange turnover, apart from that in speculative mining stocks.

Consequently, stock exchange investment was one of a group of alternatives available to the investor. Firstly, he was faced with securities as opposed to property, deposits, trade investments, etc. If he chose stocks and shares, he then had the option of subscribing to a new issue or of purchasing a security which was already in the market. Finally, if he did enter the secondary market, he had the whole range of stocks and shares to choose from. The options open to any investor were thus quite varied and becoming more so as the market improved and the popularity of joint-stock enterprise grew. In contrast, new issues were very much a momentary and limited reflection of current investment interest, tempered by what it was possible to promote at any one time.[7] They did not represent the whole range of opportunities available to any one investor. It took progressively longer to shift, fundamentally, the composition of the secondary market, as the value of issued securities became larger every year, both through new additions and rising prices for established concerns such as banks and insurance companies.

The secondary market added a substantial measure of stability to the share market as a whole by diluting any changes to what was already in existence. Thus, for example, cattle ranching companies appear to have dominated the attention of all investors during the 1880s, but the maximum reached on the Aberdeen Stock Exchange, one of the most affected markets, was 10 per cent of turnover in 1884. Business in the securities of long-established banks, railways and insurance companies was, individually, of equivalent or greater importance. Therefore the statistics of the secondary market can reveal much about the behaviour of investors which the measurement of new issues completely omits, especially as many investors did not participate in these new issues but waited until a company was established before purchasing its securities.[8] The investing public were not a homogeneous group but varied considerably in the risks each was willing to take and the type of investments which interested them.[9] Without an understanding of the wider picture of investment, it is impossible to understand the motivation of investors and the factors that conditioned their choices.

There are two main components to any investment decision — when to invest and what to invest in — and decisions were conditioned by the multitude of factors which influenced every individual investor. With regard to the level of investment and its timing, general economic forces and investment criteria appear to have operated fairly strongly. As interest rates rose, stock exchange investment fell, and vice versa, which indicates that the popularity of stocks and shares was dependent upon the attractions of rival investments, such as trade credit or bank deposits. Between 1846 and 1896, for example, the fluctuations in the rate of interest paid by Scottish banks upon money deposited with them was inversely related to the level of turnover on the Aberdeen Stock Exchange.[10] The inverse relationship was not perfect, but it was sufficient to suggest a strong direct link. Certainly, contemporaries saw a causal connection between cheap money and a rising tide of investment.[11] In Edinburgh, in February 1891, Bell, Begg & Cowan observed that:

> Money has continuously declined in value during the month of January, and appears likely to cheapen still further, and, as a consequence, a steady stream of investment buying has manifested itself on the Stock Exchange.[12]

It was the accumulation of savings requiring profitable outlets that stimulated stock exchange investment, rather than new demands from the economy.

However, the relationship was not automatic, for investors had to be reasonably confident about the future before purchasing stocks and shares. After the collapse of an investment boom, for instance, interest rates could be low and still falling at a time when investment itself continued to decline. The late 1840s was one such time, with the aftermath of the 'Railway Mania'. Such a paradox often perplexed contemporaries who ignored the lasting shock to confidence occasioned by a period of rapidly declining security prices, unsaleable assets, and the collapse of unsound ventures:

> The continued fall in the value of money, combined with the increasing difficulty of employing capital profitably, while at the same time stocks of every description are quoted at ruinous depreciation — all this presents an anomaly in the commercial and industrial condition of the country entirely without precedent,

ran an editorial in the *Scottish Railway Gazette* in 1849.[13]

It took time for the confidence of investors to return, and, in the meantime, they restricted themselves to securities with an established reputation, bank deposits or property:[14]

> Here (Edinburgh) for a long time deposits and debentures in Trust and Investment companies and Colonial Banks were the favourite class of investment; but these having now been so thoroughly discredited, people were at a loss how to place their money so as to bring them a return of something like four per cent with fairly good security, and have been investing largely in Scottish Banks,

reported the *Banking and Insurance Magazine* in 1896.[15] At these times speculative stocks of all hues were shunned by most investors, and safer securities were sought.[16] Trends in investment were also not merely a reflection upon what was available. On the Aberdeen Stock Exchange joint-stock companies could appear as the focus of interest for the first time long after they had been promoted, while others were immediately popular. Stock exchange activity seems to have been able to generate its own securities rather than vice versa. Thus, the timing and level of investment in stocks and shares were largely determined by prevailing economic conditions as manifested in the current rate of interest and the confidence of the investor in an improving investment environment. It was the coincidence of confidence and a low rate of interest that created a rising tide of investment.

However, this only explains the overall pattern of investment and not its geographical or sectoral composition. In a broad way, trends in investment reflected the growing needs of the economy for financial services, urban facilities, communications, and a larger scale of industrial and commercial enterprise, as well as an increasing involvement with the world outside the immediate locality. None of these categories, however, appear to have been in direct competition with each other. In an analysis[17] of the monthly data of the Aberdeen Stock Exchange, from 1846 to 1900, no systematic relationship between any of the individual variables was discovered. Obviously, in relative terms, as one component of investment rose another fell but, in absolute terms, all tended to rise and fall together, although at different rates. The changes in total investment were closely matched, for example, by the alterations in each of the geographical components, not only local or Scottish, but also English and foreign. A similar situation existed for the different sectoral components. Consequently, purchases of railway or foreign stocks were not directly at the expense of any other sector, or region, in the realm of activity on the stock exchange, although stocks and shares as a whole may have been. The intrinsic merits of each security were far less important than general external factors — in the ratio of 1 to 7 according to the *Financial Review of Reviews* in 1905.[18] Endogenous forces were not insignificant in themselves but they were of little consequence compared with exogenous influences.[19] Activity in the various components of the secondary market waxed and waned along with the total, illustrating the fact that there were alternatives to stocks and shares, such as bank deposits, property, cash or even consumption, while income and savings did not pursue a path of steady growth.

The actual characteristics of stock exchange investment were governed by a variety of factors, of which the pursuit of the highest rate of interest with the greatest security was only one, albeit an important one.[20] With many investments it was impossible to measure either the potential yield or the risk involved, and some form of subjective criteria had to be substituted for mathematical accuracy.[21] At the same time, the motivation of the investor was not entirely financial and this was an important influence upon his investment behaviour.[22]

What is immediately obvious concerning the nature of Scottish investment is the early influence of the investor's own locality in determining what he invested in. Much investment was directed into the securities of companies that had been formed to operate not just in Scotland but in the investor's own part of the country. In the mid-1830s, 91 per cent of the turnover of John Robertson, the Edinburgh stockbroker, was in the stocks and shares serving the Edinburgh region, as compared with only 8 per cent for concerns located in the rest of Scotland and 1 per cent each for England and abroad. This position also existed in other parts of Scotland, such as Aberdeen and Glasgow.[23] The influence of locality continued to exercise a lasting, though diminishing, influence throughout the nineteenth century. Approximately three-quarters of the value of turnover on the Aberdeen Stock Exchange, for example, was in the securities of locally operating companies in each decade from 1860 to 1900, although of course the nature of stock exchange business over-emphasised the local proportion.[24] However, there is other evidence to suggest that the locality remained a potent force.

Joint-stock enterprise continued to draw much of its support from specific areas, while the portfolios of some investors consisted largely of the stocks and shares of companies operating in their own area.[25] Most iron, steel and colliery companies, for instance, drew their financial support from their own regions, especially Glasgow and Central Scotland.[26] Reflecting the continued partial immobility of capital in Scotland was the variation in the state of housing, for its level and quality was much better in the relatively wealthier cities of Aberdeen and Edinburgh than in Dundee and Glasgow.[27]

It is not surprising that local investment should be so dominant when one considers the non-financial benefits that any local investor derived from the facilities provided by the joint-stock enterprise of his own area. The investor at a distance received only his dividends, and any capital gain on realisation, while the local investor obtained all the advantages of a gas and water supply, improved transportation, a friendly bank and insurance company, and a boost to his own business.[28] For much of the nineteenth century the concerns operating locally were such as to offer numerous inducements to a wide spectrum of investors. In the mid-1830s, 97 per cent of John Robertson's turnover in companies operating locally was in banking, insurance, gas and water, railways, shipping and canals, while in Aberdeen these categories still provided 77 per cent of turnover in the local sector in the 1890s. Manufacturing, distribution and property did grow in importance, and their benefits for the investor were much less than those of services or social overhead capital, but they were still dwarfed by the traditional components of local investment.[29] Therefore there remained a strong but declining compromise between financial, business and general self-interest which helped to determine the choices made by investors. In addition, locality also meant familiarity and, even where the investor received nothing beyond the dividend, his tendency would be to hold that security with which he was personally acquainted, rather than one which was unknown.[30]

A number of developments eroded the dominance of locality as a major influence upon investment. Of prime importance was the changing nature of local enterprise, with not only the move towards companies with fewer direct linkages, but also the altered character of the local company. Many concerns were either extending their operations beyond the original town or region that spawned them or were themselves being absorbed into larger units. The London-based British Electric Traction Co., for instance, operated tramways in Airdrie, Coatbridge, Greenock and Rothesay, as well as in numerous other locations.[31] There did remain many concerns which confined their business to one area and drew their financial support from it, especially with the conversion into joint-stock companies of established local firms, but their overall importance was declining and this led to a gradual disappearance of the regional characteristics of investment. In addition, the facility for investing at a distance was steadily improving with better communications and the growing sophistication of financial intermediaries such as banks, insurance, or the stockbroking profession itself. Consequently, it was easy for an investor to include in his portfolio the securities of more remote ventures such as English or U.S. railways. This was especially so as investment experts such as stockbrokers increasingly recommended them to their clients because of their combination of good security and reasonable yield. Judging from the portfolios of individuals and the activity on the Scottish stock exchanges, especially Glasgow and Edinburgh, these unattached securities became a major component of investment in the course of the second half of the century.[32]

The contacts of investors were also extending beyond the confines of their own locality through business, marriage, education and travel. Families such as the Bairds and the Tennants, who had made fortunes in coal and iron and in chemicals, respectively, were gradually absorbed into the British upper classes through marriage, and this opened up a wider perspective of investment for them.[33] Increasingly, the separate identity of Scottish investors was disappearing as inter-connection led them to participate at a national or international level. Nevertheless, local contacts and identification remained important, even on the wider scale, for they were also utilised to channel investment outside the locality. Both the Tennants and the Coats depended heavily on their circle of wealthy contacts in West Central Scotland to mobilise capital finance for their various schemes, whether it was explosives or coal mining within Scotland, or mining and other enterprises outside the country.[34] Increasingly, the web of contacts that had been used to create local enterprise of benefit to the community was tapped so as to provide funds for a variety of overseas ventures, ranging from the fairly secure financial trusts to the more speculative mining, ranching, plantation, and industrial concerns.[35]

Investment outside Scotland was not just a general response to the greater opportunities but was strongly influenced by personal and business links. Whether they were army officers or colonial administrators in India and Ceylon, or settlers in North America, Australasia or South Africa, expatriate Scots could not help but take notice of profitable investment opportunities.[36] Most did little more than that, but a few made an effort to obtain the necessary development finance — and where better than through their contacts back in Scotland? Robert Burnett of Kincardineshire emigrated to the United States in the 1860s and, through the ownership of a cattle ranch, saw the opportunities for large profits to be made if capital was available. He returned to Britain and became closely involved in a number of companies formed to invest in the agricultural resources of the western United States, including the Espuela Land and Cattle Company and the Texas Land and Mortgage Company. Both these concerns derived much of their financial support from North-East Scotland, where Robert Burnett was a well-respected member of a local landed family.[37] Similar examples abound throughout Scotland, which indicates that these international contacts played a major role in directing Scottish capital to specific destinations, especially the Empire and areas of recent settlement.[38]

William Hector, for example, was a resident in Rio de Janeiro and was involved, in 1898, in proposals to build a railway in Brazil. He approached William Anderson, a Glasgow stockbroker and a personal friend, about arranging the finance for the project. Anderson was somewhat reluctant to take up the enterprise but replied positively:

What I propose is to put the matter before a few wealthy people and see whether they would not take the whole thing up. I would propose forming in the first place a small company or syndicate with a capital of a few thousand pounds and to send out a competent engineer to go over the present railway and the proposed extension to the hill and generally to look into the whole scheme and if satisfied to obtain through you the option from Senor Vieira to take over the concession on certain distinct terms within a specified period . .

Should my friends be prepared to go in for it I should like to have the negotiations conducted through you, as it is entirely on your recommendation and relying upon you that I would think of bringing the matter forward at all.[39]

Exactly the same approaches and methods led to the formation of the Scottish African Corporation in 1895.[40]

It was not so much the blind pursuit of the highest interest and the greatest security that drew Scottish capital to the furthest corners of the world, but an intricate network of local, personal and business relationships which channelled available funds from particular localities into the profitable opportunities recognised by expatriate Scots. Investors felt a sense of kin with these expatriates and so were willing to trust them with a part of their wealth which would not have been readily released to an unknown foreigner, no matter the inducements promised. Again, judging by the activity on the various Scottish stock exchanges, Scottish investment abroad went, overwhelmingly, to North America, Australasia, or India and Ceylon, with the rest of the world being relatively ignored.

Corresponding to the changes in the destination of investment were alterations in the activities that attracted the interest of investors. Stock exchange investment was dominated by the tertiary sector of the economy with financial, urban and transportation services being of paramount importance. These provided 97 per cent of John Robertson's turnover in the mid-1830s, and 82 per cent of the Aberdeen Stock Exchange's turnover in the 1890s.[41] Many Scottish investors continued to place the bulk of their investments in the securities of such enterprises. William Stirling, for instance, who was a Glasgow merchant, had 65 per cent of his portfolio of £264,000 in railways, tramways, insurance and financial companies, while all of Peter Brough's funds were in railways by 1882.[42] The great attractions of this type of investment were that the security rested upon the economic performance of a whole town or region rather than upon one trade or a few individuals. In recommending British railway stock to a client, the Glasgow stockbrokers J. & G. Moffat gave their opinion, in 1889, that:

All these stocks are quite safe, their Dividends being thoroughly reliable, and the principal not likely to decline in value unless the value of everything declines from some unlooked for and unlikely cause which cannot be foreseen, such as Invasion from abroad, or the Socialists getting the upper hand at home, or some similarly disturbing but unlikely cause!!![43]

This opinion was commonplace among the investing public, and therefore those seeking security sought the stocks and shares of governments, railways, urban utilities, banks, insurance companies, investment trusts, and other like enterprises.[44] As specific joint-stock companies and the sectors in which they operated came to be regarded as safe, so they attracted those investors who sought security above all else, such as trustees and widows. In 1832, only 3.5 per cent of the shareholders in the Western Bank of Scotland were female, but the proportion was 25 per cent in 1858. Similarly, the Glasgow City and Suburban Gas Co. had a large number of its shares held by ladies and trustees in 1869, because gas companies were regarded as a safe haven for capital and returned a reasonable dividend. Differential interest rates largely determined the flow of funds between these safe sectors, conditioned by the market's assessment of their relative security.[45]

However, the range of joint-stock enterprise gradually widened in the course of the nineteenth century and came to include numerous companies operating directly in agriculture, fishing and mining and in manufacturing and distribution. By the 1890s, 18 per cent of the value of turnover on the Aberdeen Stock Exchange was in these sectors as compared with 3 per cent in the 1850s, and Aberdeen did not possess an active mining market as did Glasgow and Edinburgh. Despite the appearance of safe overseas securities in the form of railway and government bonds, investors in stocks and shares were also willing to risk substantial sums on investments that were both risky and of a fluctuating character:

> ... even the best of such securities must rise and fall as the trade they are interested in is prosperous or depressed ...

was the view, in 1884, of the Glasgow stockbroker, W. J. Anderson, regarding the securities of such concerns as Railway and Electrical Appliances Co., Sugar Refiners Appliances Co., Mysore Gold Mining Co., and Tharsis Sulphur and Copper Co.[46] Again, this was universally accepted, but there appears to have been no lack of investors willing to accept this risk for the promised gains.[47]

Mining securities, for example, appear to have become increasingly popular amongst investors, with some specialising in their buying and selling, while others added them to their existing portfolio to improve its yield and growth potential. It was the very gamble that mining or any other risky enterprise involved that attracted the investor.[48] The *Aberdeen Free Press* observed in 1889 that:

> It has become quite the fashion for everybody to have a little excitement out of a transaction in a Gold Mine, ... The charm about this kind of speculation is its uncertainty. There is no necessity to make any calculation about what a purchase will yield in interest. The great bulk of the South African Mines have never paid sixpence of interest or dividend, and it is safe to say that at least half of them never will ...[49]

Throughout the nineteenth century, especially during the second half, investors were attracted in growing numbers to speculative ventures at home and abroad, culminating in the 1910 mania which centred on domestic skating rink enterprises and tropical rubber companies. At that time the Glasgow printer and publisher, W. F. Maclaren, invested substantial amounts in at least 18 different rubber companies whose capital totalled £3m.[50] Thus, while the majority of investors sought security for the funds they had to invest, with the dividend or capital gain a secondary consideration, there were also many who had the reverse view or sought to combine the two.[51] Stock exchange investment was one medium that could accommodate all, for what one sold another purchased at a price. Investment was not a simple matter of buying a new security and holding it but involved the continuous turnover of stock as individuals adjusted their portfolios to take account of their own changing circumstances, alterations in the securities they held, and developments in the capital market and the economy.[52]

The existence of this large and important secondary market in securities destroys the illusion of simplicity when investigating the behaviour of the investor. Certainly, in general terms, the level, timing, and even broad composition of stock exchange investments reflected trends in interest rates and the needs of the economy. However, within the components of investment, there were no easy inverse relationships, while the motivation of the investor cannot be reduced to mere calculation of return and risk. For many investors, especially in the earlier years, the non-financial benefits of any purchase were of crucial importance, while family, business or other contacts were significant influences upon the composition and direction of investment. As these waned with the growth of impersonal investment, professional expertise and arithmetic measurement, a major element of stock exchange investment continued to be immune to these forces. Risky securities, especially those of mining companies, appealed to the investor through the lure of incalculable gain, not by the offer of a steady return and a secure capital. At the same time, there continued to be those, such as trustees, widows, or the reserves of institutions, that had no alternative but to be ultra-cautious, as losses would endanger their very existence. The decisions made by the nineteenth century investor need to be explained before they can be criticised. Even the briefest of investigations into the secondary market shows the investor to be a complex animal, well able to consider the overall consequences of any purchase or sale for his particular position.

NOTES

1. R. Giffen, *Stock Exchange Securities* (Lon. 1877) p. 98.

2. Lowenfeld, op. cit., p. 57.

3. Lowenfeld, op. cit., pp. 167, 185-6, 188, 196; H. Withers, *Stocks and Shares* (Lon. 1914) p. 101; *Stock Exchange Investments: Their History, Practice, and Results* (Lon. 1897) p. 57; R. L. Nash, *A Short Inquiry into the Profitable Nature of our Investments* (Lon. 1881) p. 124.

4. R. Giffen, *The Growth of Capital* (Lon. 1889) pp. 4, 153; Paish, op. cit., p. 12; Rix, op. cit., p. 184.

5. Holcombe, op. cit., p. 216.

6. *S.P.G.* 4 March 1892.

7. Lawson, op. cit., p. 16.

8. W. Bartlett & H. Chapman, *A Handy-Book for Investors* (Lon. 1869) p. 340.

9. E. T. Powell, *The Mechanism of the City* (Lon. 1910) pp. 141-2.

10. Aberdeen Stock Exchange: Value of Turnover, 1846-1896. The Scottish bank deposit rate of interest was obtained from Boase, op. cit., p. 550; *S.B. & I.M.* 1879-1886; *B.E.* 1886-8; *N.B.E.* 1889-1895; *B. & I.M.* 1896-7.

11. W. W. Wall, *How to Invest in Railways* (Lon. 1903) p. 50.

12. Bell, Begg & Cowan, February 1891; cf. March 1886.

13. *S.R.G.* 26 May 1849.

14. E. Seyd, 'Our Wealth in Relation to Imports and Exports, and the causes of Decline in the Latter' *Journal of the Society of Arts*, 5 April 1878; Lawson, op. cit., p. 1; Robertson, op. cit., pp. 26, 181.

15. *B. & I.M.* January 1896.

16. *S.B. & I.M.* 14 February 1883; *D.Y.B.* (1892) p. 52, (1894) p. 48; *I.R.* (1892) p. 264, (1896) p. 1.

17. Carried out by Adrian Darnell of the Dept. of Economics, University of Durham, utilising simple techniques of correlation and regression analysis.

18. *F.R.* October 1905.

19. Bell, Begg & Cowan, op. cit., July 1895; S. F. Van Oss & F. C. Mathieson, *Stock Exchange Values: A Decade of Finance, 1885-1895* (Lon. 1895) LXXXVIII.

20. Cf. R. C. Michie, 'The Social Web of Investment in the Nineteenth Century' *Revue Internationale d'Histoire de la Banque* (forthcoming).

21. R. J. Briston, *The Stock Exchange and Investment Analysis* (Lon. 1970) p. 457; *Stock and Share Review*, February 1884.

22. E. T. Powell, *The Mechanism of the City* (Lon. 1910) pp. 116, 141.

23. John Robertson & Co.: Value of Turnover, January 1833 – April 1836; Aberdeen Stock Exchange: Value of Turnover, 1845-9; J. R. Kellett, 'The Private Investments of Glasgow's Lord Provosts' *A.M.* (November 1968) p. 602; J. B. Sturrock, *Peter Brough: A Paisley Philanthropist* (Paisley 1890) pp. 234-254.

24. Abdn. St. Ex.: Value of Turnover, 1860-1900.

25. *A.F.P.* 11 June 1864, 7 September 1893; P. L. Payne, *The Early Scottish Limited Companies, 1856-1895: An Historical and Analytical Survey* (Pasadena 1978) p. 92.

26. C. McLaren, 'Prospects of Iron and Steel Investments' *F.R.* October 1906 pp. 248-253; M. M. Mason, 'Dangers of Colliery Investments' *F.R.* November 1913, p. 903.

27. T. J. Byres, The Scottish Economy during the 'Great Depression' 1873-1896 (Glasgow B.Litt. 1963) p. 175; R. G. Rodger, Scottish Urban Housebuilding 1870-1914 (Ph.D. Edin. 1975) p. 445; Lowenfeld, op. cit., p. 99.

28. M. A. Whitehead, The Western Bank and the Crisis of 1857 (M.Litt.Strathclyde 1978) p. 104; H. H. Bassett (ed.), *Business Men at Home and Abroad, 1912-13* (Lon. 1912) e.g. 'W. Ainslie', 'R. Gray', 'J. Inglis'; *A.F.P.* 16 July 1895; P. L. Payne, *The Early Scottish Limited Companies, 1856-1895: An Historical and Analytical Survey* (Pasadena 1978) p. 26.

29. Robertson, loc. cit.; Abdn., loc. cit.

30. Lowenfeld, op. cit., p. 100; C. K. Hobson, *The Export of Capital* (Lon. 1914) XIX.

31. B.E.T.: Annual Report, 18 June 1914.

32. Bartlett & Chapman, op. cit., pp. 1-5; Powell, op. cit., p. 156; Holcombe, op. cit., pp. 38-40; W. H. Fisher, *Investing at its Best and Safeguarding Invested Capital* (Lon. 1912); Sturrock, loc. cit.; R. D. Corrins, William Baird & Co.: Coal & Iron Masters, 1830-1914 (Ph.D. Strathclyde 1974) p. 86; B. Lenman & K. Donaldson, 'Partners' Incomes, Investment and Diversification in the Scottish Linen Area, 1850-1921' *B.H.* 13 (1971) pp. 12-17; J. A. Wenley, 'On the History and Development of Banking in Scotland' *J.I.B.* 3 (1882) pp. 142-3 (cf. Part VI, Chap. 6).

33. Corrins, op.cit., p. 282; N. Crathorne, *Tennants' stalk: The Story of the Tennants of the Glen* (Lon. 1973) p. 166; R. Perren, *John Fleming & Co. Ltd., 1877-1977* (Abdn. 1978) p. 40; D.I.A. Steel, The Linen Industry in Fife in the later Eighteenth and Nineteenth Centuries (Ph.D. St. Andrews 1975) p. 405; P. L. Cottrell, Investment Banking in England, 1856-1882 (Ph.D. Hull 1974) p. 694; J. Scott & M. Hughes, *The Anatomy of Scottish Capital* (Lon. 1980) pp. 49, 53.

34. J. A. Hassan, The Development of the Coal Industry in Mid & West Lothian, 1815-1873 (Ph.D. Strathclyde 1976) pp. 187-9; *Memoirs & Portraits of One Hundred Glasgow Men* (Glasgow 1886) p. 247; Crathorne, op. cit., pp. 136-141; M. Gray, *The Fishing Industries of Scotland, 1790-1914: A Study in Regional Adaptation* (Abdn. 1978) pp. 168, 179; Payne, op. cit., pp. 34A, 40, 92.

35. W. G. Kerr, *Scottish Capital on the American Credit Frontier* (Austin 1976) pp. 50, 64-5, 69; D. McCallan, 'Peter Buchanan, London Agent for the Great Western Railway of Canada' in D. S. MacMillan (ed.), *Canadian Business History* (Toronto 1972) pp. 203, 197-8; *D.Y.B.* (1892) p. 65.

36. Eg. L. M. Homsher (ed.), *South Pass, 1868: James Chisholm's Journal of the Wyoming Gold Rush* (Nebraska 1960) p. 83.

37. *A.F.P.* 16 January 1894; W. C. Holden, *The Espuela Land and Cattle Company* (Austin 1970) pp. 44, 52; W. G. Kerr, *Scottish Capital on the American Credit Frontier* (Austin 1976) pp. 50, 54, 64, 65, 69.

38. Byres, op. cit., p. 296; Holcombe, op. cit., pp. 238, 262, 287, 301-2, 359; D. G. Paterson, *British Direct Investment in Canada, 1890-1914* (Toronto 1976) p. 42; M. G. Mulhall, *The English in South America* (Buenos Aires 1878) pp. 345-6, 350; Crathorne, op. cit., pp. 104, 138.

39. W. J. Anderson to W. Hector, 5 June 1898.

40. *A.F.P.* 25 November 1895.

41. Robertson, loc. cit.; Abdn., loc. cit.

42. W. J. Anderson to W. Stirling, 4 December 1884; Sturrock, loc. cit.; Bassett (ed.), op. cit., 'A. Cross', 'W. Duff', 'R. Gray', 'J. Inglis', 'A. Sinclair'.

43. J. & G. Moffat to W. N. Neilson, 14 February 1889.

44. *A Guide to the Unprotected in every-day matters relating to Property and Income* (Lon. 1891) p. 2; Holcombe, op. cit., pp. 38-40, 190; R. B. Weir, The Distilling Industry in Scotland in the Nineteenth and early Twentieth Centuries (Ph.D. Edin. 1974) pp. 478, 487; Powell, op. cit., pp. 146-151; M. S. Cotterill, The Scottish Gas Industry up to 1914 (Ph.D. Strathclyde 1976) p. 828.

45. Whitehead, op. cit., pp. 58-9; Cotterill, op. cit., pp. 741, 1006; cf. M. Edelstein, 'The Determinants of U.K. Investment Abroad, 1870-1913: The U.S. Case' *J.Ec.H.* 24 (1974); M. Edelstein, 'Realized Rates of Return on U.K. Home and Overseas Portfolio Investment in the Age of High Imperialism' *E.C.H.* 13 (1976).

46. W. J. Anderson to W. Stirling, 4 December 1884.

47. *A Guide,* op. cit., p. 3; Powell, op. cit., p. 155.

48. *A New Dictionary of Mining Terms* (Lon. 1901) p. 14; K. Robinson, *The Mining Market* (Lon. 1907) V.

49. *A.F.P.* 26 October 1889.

50. W. R. Lawson & T. H. Reid, 'The Rubber Madness in the City' *F.R.* June 1910; Bassett (ed.), op. cit., 'W. F. Maclaren'; Powell, op. cit., p. 95.

51. H. Lowenfeld, 'The Investor's Mind' *F.R.* November 1907, pp. 16-18; Powell, op. cit., pp. 142, 155.

52. Lowenfeld, op. cit., p. 236; R. H. I. Palgrave (ed.), *Dictionary of Political Economy* (Lon. 1894-1901) p. 215; R. Griffen, *The Growth of Capital* (Lon. 1889) p. 154; N. Withers, *Stocks and Shares* (Lon. 1914) p. 295.

19

London and Scotland

THE London Stock Exchange has been the subject of intensive study ever since its foundation two centuries ago. Even by 1911 Day was able to note that:

> The history of the Exchange has been written time and time again, from the Change Alley and Jonathan's Coffee House days to times comparatively recent ...[1]

Within this work on London, very little space has been devoted to investigating the specific function which was actually performed by the London Stock Exchange, and even less to the relationship of London with the other stock exchanges. The impression that emerges from the work on London is that the other stock exchanges occupied a purely local position of very minor significance and that their activities were co-ordinated by and completely subordinate to those of the London Stock Exchange.[2] However, it has been increasingly recognised that this is only a partial picture of the relationship, and that there were important differences of function between London and the other British stock exchanges.[3] Together, these stock exchanges comprised the British share market, for all were interdependent.

It was, perhaps, perverse that it was at a time of increasing communication within Britain, in the 1830s and 1840s, that stock exchanges were appearing outside London, rather than the established central market growing to accommodate the additional needs. The time taken for a journey between Edinburgh and London was being progressively reduced, so that it could be done in 26 hours by 1840. At the same time postal communications were being both improved and cheapened, with the introduction of the penny post in 1840.[4] As early as the end of the eighteenth century these transportation improvements were allowing London, the administrative capital of a unified country, to influence developments in the remoter areas such as Scotland, and centralising forces became progressively stronger.[5] The Scottish newspapers, for example, relied on the London press for much of the material that they printed.[6]

There were many Scots who had migrated to London, and they retained strong links with those friends, relatives, and associates who remained behind, while other Scots had spent some time in business in London before returning home. Also, it became customary for the Scottish gentry to acquire houses in London as winter residences, with their Scottish homes being retained for the summer and autumn.[7] Events in London came to be considered important by many in Scotland, and were closely followed. The arrival of the London newspapers and business correspondence was eagerly awaited, and any delays or interruptions quickly gave rise to complaints. In 1816 Dundee merchants were often doing business in the coffee houses, or the Exchange, until midnight as they did not receive the London mail until eight o'clock at night.[8] Altogether, in political, social and business affairs, events in London had a bearing of growing importance upon Scottish life, and so attention was increasingly focused upon London.

This growing communication with London, and interest in London affairs, included an increasing Scottish awareness of the activities on the London stock market. As early as May 1720, the Edinburgh newspaper, the *Caledonian Mercury*, began to quote the current London prices of government and associated stocks. This became a regular feature in the newspaper and was taken up by most other major Scottish newspapers and journals. Some Scottish newspapers, such as the *Edinburgh Advertiser* or *Aberdeen Star,* even included a regular article on the state of the market on the London Stock Exchange.[9] Such was the Scottish interest in the London stock market that a number of London stockbrokers extended their activities to cover Scotland. Brooksbank and Ruddle, London brokers, advertised in the Scottish Press in 1778 that:

> All letters post paid duly answered, and every branch of business in the Lottery and in the public funds, is legally and faithfully transacted.[10]

Nicholson & Co., Hazard & Co., and Hornsby & Co. were among the other London stockbrokers who advertised their business extensively in Scotland. A number of these firms went so far as to appoint Scottish agents through whom business was conducted. Hornsby & Co., for instance, had James Morison, bookseller in Perth, as one of their agents.[11]

Certainly, most interested Scots were fully aware of the nature of the public stocks and the means by which they were bought and sold. Numerous Scots wrote treatises on the subject, while newspapers and journals included brief descriptions for the benefit of their readers.[12] Some Scotsmen, such as Alexander Fordyce, an Aberdeen hosier, had actually gone to London and speculated in government stocks, while others had become stockbrokers there.[13] Thus, Scottish investors were well acquainted with the services which were offered by London stockbrokers and the London Stock Exchange, and the nature of the stocks and shares in which they dealt. In addition, there is evidence to show that Scots in Scotland did make use of London facilities, mainly the very wealthy and well connected, such as the landed classes or the banks:[14]

> The wealth of the Bankers of Scotland is great, and they have always been in the practice of resorting to the British funds for the employment of a large portion of their surplus capital,

was the opinion of the *Bankers' Circular* in 1829.[15]

Those living at a distance from London were enabled to deal on the stock exchange there, either by having an agent who acted for them, as with the Scottish banks, or by corresponding directly with a London stockbroker, who was given a great deal of discretion as to when to buy and sell.[16] London was the central market for all government stocks, not only because most of the holders lived in and around

London — this was less true after the Napoleonic wars — but also as a result of legal restrictions which confined deals to the vicinity of the Bank of England, where the transfer books were kept and dividends paid.[17] These factors allowed London to monopolise dealings in the National Debt which was by far the largest component of transferable securities in existence. With the substantial Scottish holdings of the funds in the immediate post-war years, there were suggestions that a secondary market be set up, such as in Edinburgh:

> Why might not a Stock Exchange, and a proportion of the funded property, be transacted in Edinburgh, and dividends be received there also, without the Scotch capitalist, etc. coming through the impediments of power of attorney, postage, agency, brokerage, commission, Stock Exchange turn etc. etc. etc., . . .

wrote one London observer in 1821.[18] However, these moves came to nought and Scottish investors had to continue to suffer the inconveniences of distance, although these were lessening over time.

Although the London Stock Exchange monopolised dealings in government and allied stocks, its participation in other areas of the market was often very limited. Even within London, alternative exchanges existed from time to time which catered for the securities which were ignored by the London Stock Exchange, such as the shares of joint-stock companies or mining enterprises.[19] One illustration of the domination of the London Stock Exchange and its members by business in government securities comes from the transactions handled by the firm of Marjoribanks, Capel & Co. Between June and November 1830 the value of their total business came to £3m, of which 87 per cent was in British Government securities, 7 per cent in foreign government securities, mainly of France, Denmark and the United States, while the remainder was in colonial issues. Almost no business was done in British non-government securities.[20]

The few joint-stock company shares that were dealt in on the London Stock Exchange in the first half of the nineteenth century tended to be those of London concerns, as those from the rest of the country were traded locally.[21] Included in the London Stock Exchange list was a section of Scottish stocks and shares and their current prices, but this was supplied by Edinburgh stockbrokers and was often omitted if additional news had to be given, such as the current interest being paid on the funds.[22] Scotland and the Scots were aware of the current state of the London Stock Exchange, but that market was largely unaware of the joint-stock companies that occupied the attention of Scottish investors.[23] The shares of these companies were locally owned and transactions were locally settled, and so there was no need for a central institution that would match buying and selling orders at a national level, as was required for government stocks.[24]

However, even if London stockbrokers and the London Stock Exchange had wished to handle dealings in joint-stock enterprise from throughout the country, they would have been ill-equipped to do so. The unique jobbing system of the London Stock Exchange evolved to cater for a substantial turnover in a small number of standard securities, such as 3 per cent consols. Under this system brokers did not deal directly with each other but through the jobbers who were always ready to buy and sell, at a price, whatever stock the broker wanted. Playford, a broker on the Exchange, explained the benefits of the practice in 1856

> ... without the mediation of the Jobber (who is really the middleman in the transaction) the public business to its present extent could not possibly be transacted; for it may be easily understood, that, if a Broker, employed to purchase for his Principal a certain amount of stock, were compelled to wait till he met with another Broker having a commission to sell an amount exactly corresponding with that he had to purchase, the same business, which now — to the great convenience of the public — only occupies a few minutes, might very possibly require many days, or even weeks, for its transaction, owing to the difficulty of finding a buyer, who wants precisely the same amount of stock.[25]

Where there was a large volume of business, as in government stock, the margin between the buying and selling prices, upon which the jobbers operated and which provided their income, could be very low. As a consequence, the cost of providing this ready market was either minute or non-existent, with the greater volume of business and keener prices generated by the active market, which the jobbers had created, itself paying for the provision of market intermediaries. Conversely, in securities where there was not a high volume of turnover, the difference between the buying and selling prices quoted by the jobber, in order to justify his effort, made the London Stock Exchange a poor market for the shares of anything but the largest enterprises or the most active of stocks.[26] The Glasgow stockbroker, James Watson, recognised in 1834 the advantages and disadvantages of the system operating on the London Stock Exchange:

> Every description of English (Government) Stock is at all times saleable at the prices of the day, as there are numerous dealers or Jobbers, all eagerly competing for business, ... In many descriptions of Foreign or share security, the transactions are infrequent, and the business often gets wholly into the hands of a few, sometimes of only one dealer ... where there is much business, or many dealers, the Broker is enabled to deal at what are termed close or near prices, i.e. near to the true value; and on the contrary, where there are few transactions or dealers, he is often obliged to deal at much wider prices, i.e. wide of the true value.[27]

Consequently, the London Stock Exchange was an excellent market for individual stocks in which there was a large volume of business, as the jobbing system provided a ready market at negligible cost, but where turnover was low the jobbing system was a disadvantage as it made transactions too costly. Not only had the broker's commission to be paid, but also the jobber's turn, or difference between his buying and selling price. In these low-volume securities, the non-London markets were far superior, as broker dealt directly with broker and so there was no jobber's turn to pay.

Therefore, because of the very nature of its method of dealing, as well as its limited knowledge and involvement with joint-stock enterprise outside London, the London Stock Exchange was in no position to provide an alternative to the local stock exchanges which were appearing. The London and provincial markets evolved to meet differing needs. The London Stock Exchange developed to provide a market for government securities — large issues, substantial turnover, little differentiation — while the local stock exchanges met the needs of joint-stock enterprise — small issues, limited turnover, great variety. Neither could do the job of the other, and each was designed to meet a specific requirement. At mid-century the London Stock Exchange could only have monopolised the securities market if the nature of joint-stock company formation had been very different, namely large national concerns rather than small local or regional ventures.

The method of business on the London Stock Exchange remained unchanged throughout the second half of the century and continued to possess the same merits and defects. It continued to afford the best market for securities with a substantial turnover and was weak in the area of small or medium-sized joint-stock companies.[28] Moreover, the London Stock Exchange itself recognised the deficiencies of its market and normally refused to quote companies with a paid-up capital of less than £50,000 and even, at times, £100,000.[29] Many small London-based concerns, such as the Beariz Tin Streaming Co. and the Medway Paper Mills Co., sought quotations on other stock exchanges with which they could claim a connection, as they could not get a market on the London Stock Exchange.[30] For these enterprises London could not compete with the other exchanges, as their methods of dealing allowed both the quotation of very small companies, and business to be done in their shares not only intermittently but at a low cost to buyer and seller.[31] There was, thus, a separation between London and the local stock exchanges, not only geographically, but also in the type of securities in which they traded.

Most of the historical literature gives the impression that, with the improvement in communication through the telegraph, the London Stock Exchange was enabled to dominate transactions in stocks and shares in Britain from 1850 onwards, so relegating the provincial exchanges to small corners of the national market.[32] Certainly London was by far and away the largest stock exchange and would still have been so if it had merely catered for its own local enterprise and local investors. In 1885, for example, London had 2,500 members compared with 121 in Glasgow.[33] However, London did far more than act as a local exchange, for it dominated transactions in extensive national and international stocks, especially those of British and foreign governments and railways, for which its jobbing system was ideally suited. In these, London attracted business not only from all over Britain, but from all over the world. There were numerous instances, for example, of French and German capital being invested in Canadian and American securities through the medium of London brokers and the London Stock Exchange.[34] The active market provided by London attracted investors from the world as a whole, whether to internationally traded stocks such as the Canadian Pacific Railway, or current speculative counters like South African gold mining shares in 1895 or Malayan rubber companies in 1910.[35]

Increasingly, it was easier to transfer stocks and shares between countries in response to the varying demands from investors. The type of stocks for which this could be done was also steadily growing. U.S. railroads, for instance, were held by investors throughout Europe and North America, and ownership could be switched from one country to another without difficulty. By 1911, telegrams between London and New York took only 3 minutes for actual transmission, and a telegram between the two stock exchanges could be sent and a reply received within 20 minutes. Increasingly, all parts of the world were linked by the telegraph, with the London-Paris link coming in 1851.[36] Therefore the London Stock Exchange came to occupy a world role as the central arbiter of the growing volume of international stocks, which moved in response to changing interest and exchange rates and the fluctuating fortunes and obsessions of investors. It was the movement of these international stocks that facilitated the smooth operation of the international economy.[37]

An integral part of this function of the London Stock Exchange was the role played by London as a home for temporary funds. The institutions of London attracted substantial amounts of short-term capital from almost every world centre. Within Britain it was traditional for Scottish financial institutions to funnel much of their surplus cash into the London capital market, where it would obtain some return and be immediately available, thus reducing the amount of money that had to be kept idle in order to meet any sudden crisis.[38] Increasingly, banks and financial institutions in other countries adopted this practice, and they were enabled to do so by the size and nature of the London Stock Exchange. Thus, by lending to jobbers, brokers, and other professional and amateur speculators on the security of stocks and shares, this continually revolving volume of short-term funds could be remuneratively employed in long-term investments. Moreover, the large turnover on the London Stock Exchange and the ready market provided by the jobbers ensured that stocks and shares could be easily and quickly bought and sold without any violent fluctuations in price. Naturally, this limited transactions to large issues of fixed interest securities, such as those of government, railways, or very large corporations, as these would alter least in value.[39]

The development of London as a world financial centre, and the benefits which that brought, had repercussions on the network of stock exchanges, for the concentration of London upon international transactions and large issues left gaps which the provincial markets were able to fill. London, for example, was a poor market for small but speculative mining stocks, and a market the size of Glasgow was able to develop a speciality as a mining exchange which attracted business from throughout the country.[40] The same was true for industrial and commercial ventures. However, this did not mean that these were particularly at a disadvantage, because the British share market was an increasingly integrated one and, although there were few openings in London for small joint-stock enterprises of whatever description, they abounded elsewhere. As Powell noted in 1910:

> The telegraph, the telephone, and the express train have carried the destruction of time and space far enough for this island to be practically one market area.[41]

In isolation, the London Stock Exchange gives the impression of an obsession with overseas investment and large corporations but, when its function is examined, it is seen to be a part of a wider market in which the areas it neglected were looked after in other locations. The integration of the brokers and exchanges ensured that all investors could participate if they so wished. Thus it is a gross oversimplification to see the period after 1850 as one in which London gradually engrossed the stock exchange business of the country. This was not true, for the other stock exchanges themselves grew, though not nearly so much as London.

The London Stock Exchange was 'primus inter pares' in the realm of local stock exchanges. As such, it attracted business in its own local stocks and, through the corresponding system, sent out buying and selling orders to other centres. However, it did not act as a central market for securities, for brokers throughout the country sent their orders to the most appropriate markets, and that need not be, and often was not, London.[42] In this role London was the most important because it was the largest, not because it acted as a national stock exchange which matched deals in all securities from the whole country. Joint-stock enterprise was not yet organised in that way and company formation at a local level was still a dynamic element in the capital market. The London Stock Exchange was the most important part of the national web, but still only a part, for this web had no real centre, only more or less important components. Secondly, the London Stock Exchange was the market for British government securities and, directly or indirectly, received all the buying and selling orders in this stock. Here it had no challengers. Thirdly, London was the major market for dealings in international stocks, and so it attracted business from throughout Britain and the world in such securities as foreign governments and railways, especially the former. Yet, despite its importance in this field, it was not the sole market with, for example, Glasgow being a major force in North American railroads. Finally, London was the prime speculative market, as befitted its role as the largest exchange and national and international home for a growing volume of short-term funds. Nevertheless, even here London was not unchallenged for Glasgow, again, was an important centre for transactions in mining securities, the most speculative of all joint-stock enterprises.

Therefore, in an analysis of the functions of the London Stock Exchange and its links with the other British exchanges, especially those in Scotland, the important but specialist nature of London becomes clear, as does the vital role played by the provincial stock exchanges, including the Scottish ones. Each was the main centre for certain types of enterprise and share activity, but each was also part of a unified market, which forced and allowed them all to play particular roles:

> Their relation to the London Stock Exchange is somewhat like that of the provincial banks to the Bank of England,

was an observation made in 1899.[43] To contemporaries, the London and provincial stock exchanges were both useful and necessary, but different, in the functions they performed.

By the end of the nineteenth century Scotland possessed a mature, formal share market. Although centred on the four major Scottish cities, this market served the whole of Scotland, with either stockbrokers, or their contacts, accessible to all.

This market was as independent as any could be in the modern world economy. Internally, stocks and shares had become an important, distinct and separate form of property, served by their own intermediaries and institutions in a fashion that met their special needs. This had not been the case at the beginning of the century. Externally, while individual brokers had numerous links with brokers outside Scotland, these were for mutual convenience. Scottish stockbrokers were not the country agents of a central share market, but a professional group independently handling the affairs of their clients. This did, however, increasingly necessitate the active use of contacts outside the region. Similarly, the relationship between stock exchanges, within and without Scotland, was that of institutions which complemented rather than competed with each other while becoming more and more closely interdependent. Each stock exchange fulfilled a unique geographical and often sectoral role in the share market, even London, though its scope was far wider than that of any other.

Maintaining the independence of the Scottish share market was the fact that each stock exchange did a substantial business in securities peculiar to itself. A national market existed only to the extent that there were securities whose appeal was more than local, and whose ownership could change from area to area, and that each stockbroker took note of what was happening elsewhere and acted accordingly in the pricing and buying and selling of stocks and shares. There were only a limited number of securities that could be shifted from one market to another through arbitrage, nationally or internationally, in order to equalise changing conditions of supply and demand, but they were essential to the operation of the whole system. Apart from these, each market was largely dominated by transactions in its own 'local' securities, which were not universally or readily acceptable outside the area.

However, in the course of the twentieth century the number and importance of these local or regional joint-stock ventures were greatly reduced and so the existence of the Scottish and provincial stock exchanges was undermined. The general expansion of government spending, owing to wars and the welfare state, ensured that the relative importance of the National Debt grew instead of declining, as it had done in the century between 1815 and 1914. Moreover, part of this growth was at the expense of local enterprise. Local or regionally operating services, such as railways, gas and electricity, or companies in industries like coal, steel and shipbuilding, were nationalised and their geographically limited shareholdings were replaced by undifferentiated government stock that could command a national market.[44] Similarly the merging or growth of local industrial, commercial and financial companies with head offices in London submerged the support of investors from a specific area in a nationwide investing public.[45]

The securities issued by these national, or multi-national, corporations were ideally suited to the facilities provided by the London Stock Exchange. It was designed to act as a central market for the buying and selling of large individual issues of stocks and shares, which were widely held and which enjoyed a high volume of turnover. These developments removed much of the need to provide local settling facilities and therefore made the decline of all but the London Stock

Exchange inevitable. A local stockbroker, channelling business to and from a central market in London, could do all that was necessary for his clients without the aid of a local stock exchange. However, the disappearance of the local markets and the accompanying centralisation removed more than the separate geographical components of a national capital market. It also destroyed the personnel and the institutions that had been important in encouraging small joint-stock enterprise and in providing a market for their securities. This the London Stock Exchange was not designed to do and the British capital market was, consequently, poorer as a result.[46]

NOTES

1. J. A. Day, *Stockbroker's Office Organisation, Management and Accounts* (Lon. 1911) p. 77.

2. E. V. Morgan & W. A. Thomas, *The Stock Exchange* (Lon. 1962) pp. 141-2.

3. M. Edelstein, 'Rigidity and bias in the British Capital Market, 1870-1913' in D. N. McCloskey (ed.), *Essays on a Mature Economy: Britain after 1840* (Lon. 1871).

4. A. C. O'Dell, 'A Geographical Examination of the Development of Scottish Railways' *S.G.M.* 55 (1939) p. 147; *The New Picture of Edinburgh* (Edin. 1816) p. 259.

5. R. Price, *Observations on Reversionary Payments* (Lon. 1783) II, p. 251; *Journal of Henry Cockburn, 1831-54* (Edin. 1874) I, p. 115 (23 April 1836), II, p. 89 (11 August 1844).

6. *The Periodical Press of Great Britain and Ireland* (Lon. 1824) p. 164; R. M. W. Cowan, *The Newspaper in Scotland* (Glasgow 1946) pp. 7-8.

7. 'Scotsmen in London' in C. Knight (ed.), *London* (Lon. 1842) II, pp. 335-6; H. Miller, *Memoir of William Forsyth: A Scotch Merchant of the 18th Century* (Lon. 1839); A. Allardyce (ed.), *Scotland and Scotsmen in the Eighteenth Century: from the manuscript of John Ramsay of Ochtertyre* (Edin. 1888) I, ix; A. J. Youngson, *The Making of Classical Edinburgh, 1750-1840* (Edin. 1966) pp. 10, 237; H. Cockburn, *Memorials of His Time* (Edin. 1856) p. 264.

8. A. R. B. Haldane, *Three Centuries of Scottish Posts* (Edin. 1971) p. 58; W. J. Couper, 'Old Glasgow Coffee-Houses' in *Old Glasgow Club*, March 1911, p. 17.

9. Cowan, op. cit., p. 5; *E.A.* 20 April 1779 et seq.; *S.M.* 1739 et seq.; *Aberdeen Star*, 1827 et seq.

10. *E.A.* 29 October 1778.

11. *E.A.* 1781/2; *E.W.J.* 1801; *A.C.* 1816.

12. W. Gordon, *The Universal Accountant and Complete Merchant* (Edin. 1763) I, pp. 218, 221; H. Hamilton, *An Inquiry Concerning the Rise and Progress, the redemption and present state and management of the National Debt* (Edin. 1818) pp. 313-4; *Aberdeen Magazine*, May 1761; *E.A.* 27 October 1778; *E.R.* April 1819; *Chambers Edinburgh Journal* 4 August 1832.

13. H. A. Meredith, *The Drama of Money Making* (Lon. 1931) p. 41; M. C. Reed, *A History of James Capel & Co.* (Lon. 1975) p. 20; *The Bank — The Stock Exchange — The Bankers — The Bankers' Clearing House — The Minister, and the Public: An Exposé* (Lon. 1821) p. 25.

14. Reed, op. cit., p. 31; Law Case between Archibald Farquharson of Finzean and Miss Francis Barstow, residing in Aberdeen (H. of L., May 1826); C. W. Munn, The Scottish Provincial Banking Companies, 1747-1864 (Ph.D. Glasgow 1976) p. 207.

15. *B.C.* 27 November 1829.

16. *The Calumnious Aspersions contained in the Report of the Sub-Committee of the Stock Exchange, exposed and refuted* (Lon. 1814) p. 31; Hamilton, op. cit., p. 314.

17. J. Lowe, *Present State of England in regard to Agriculture, Trade and Finance* (Lon. 1823) p. 364.

18. *The Bank*, op.cit., p. 94.

T

19. C. Duguid, *The Story of the Stock Exchange* (Lon. 1901) p. 162; G. W. Edwards, *The Evolution of Finance Capitalism* (N.Y. 1938) pp. 10, 19; A. D. Gayer, et al, *The Growth and Fluctuation of the British Economy, 1790-1850* (Oxford 1953) pp. 407-8; R. Burt, 'The London Mining Exchange, 1850-1900' *B.H.* 14 (1972); *London: A Complete Guide to the British Capital* (Lon. 1810) pp. 451-3; P. Cunningham *Hand-Book of London* (Lon. 1850) p. 24; *Picture of London* (Lon. 1815, 1816, 1819, 1820, 1824, 1826).

20. Reed, op. cit., pp. 28, 30, 65.

21. Gayer, op. cit., p. 426; A. B. Dubois, *The English Business Company after the Bubble Act, 1720-1800* (N.Y. 1938) p. 409; J. P. McCulloch, *Dictionary of Commerce* (Lon. 1832) p. 555; C. Fenn, *A Compendium of the English and Foreign Funds and the Principal Joint-Stock Companies* (Lon. 1838) pp. 121, 137.

22. J. Wetenhall, *Course of the Exchange* (Lon. 1835-1845); M. C. Burdett, *Official Intelligence* (Lon. 1882) xvi.

23. Allardyce, op. cit., I, p. 432; J. H. A. MacDonald, *Life Jottings of an Old Edinburgh Citizen* (Edin. 1915) pp. 185-6.

24. G. Evans, *British Corporation Finance, 1775-1850* (Baltimore 1936); S. Broadbridge, *Studies in Railway Expansion and the Capital Market in England, 1825-1873* (Lon. 1970) p. 113.

25. F. Playford, *Practical Hints for Investing Money: with an explanation of the mode of transacting business on the Stock Exchange* (Lon. 1856) p. 10.

26. Playford, op. cit., pp. 11, 49; *The Bank*, op. cit., p. 96; *Exposure of the Stock Exchange and Bubble Companies* (Lon. 1854) p. 9.

27. *G.H.* 4 August 1834.

28. E. T. Powell, *The Mechanism of the City* (Lon. 1910) pp. 43, 45; Report from the Commissioners on the London Stock Exchange (*B.P.P.* C.2157-1 (1878)) 206 (Q5187) 214 (Q5358) 126-130 (Q3353-4, 3440).

29. Report, op. cit., 150 (Q3898-3900); Powell, op. cit., p. 95; F. Gore-Browne & W. Jordan, *A Handy Book on the Formation Management and Winding-up of Joint-Stock Companies* (Lon. 1902) p. 454.

30. H. Burdett, London St. Ex., to Sec., Abdn. St. Ex., 12 September 1884; Note concerning Beariz Tin Streaming Co., January 1863 (Abdn. St. Ex.); *Econ.* 19 April 1884; J. R. Killick & W. A. Thomas, 'The Provincial Stock Exchanges, 1830-1870' *Ec.H.R.* 22 (1970) p. 105.

31. R. H. I. Palgrave (ed.), *Dictionary of Political Economy* (Lon. 1894-1901) I, p. 770.

32. Edwards, op. cit., pp. 31-2; M. C. Reed, 'Railways and the Growth of the Capital Market' in M. C. Reed (ed.), *Railways in the Victorian Economy* (Newton Abbot 1969) pp. 181-2; G. R. Hawke, *Railways and Economic Growth in England and Wales, 1840-70* (Lon. 1970) p. 388; B. L. Anderson, 'Law, Finance and economic growth in England: some long-term influences' in B. M. Ratcliffe (ed.), *Great Britain and her world, 1750-1914* (Man. 1975).

33. *Econ.* 3 January 1885; *Records of the Glasgow Stock Exchange Association, 1844-1926* (Glasgow 1927) p. 11.

34. F. W. Field, *Capital Investments in Canada* (Toronto 1911) pp. 43, 51; P. L. Cottrell, Investment Banking in England, 1856-1882 (Ph.D. Hull 1974) pp. 702-3; W. F. Spalding, 'The Establishment and Growth of Foreign Branch Banks in London' *J.I.B.* 32 (1922) p. 448; O. Haupt *The London Arbitrageur* (Lon. 1870) IV; W. J. Greenwood, *Foreign Stock Exchange Practice and Company Laws* (Lon. 1911) iii; T. Skinner (ed.), *The Stock Exchange Year-Book* (Lon. 1874) iii.

35. Field, op. cit., pp. 84, 88; A. E. Davies, *Investments Abroad* (Chicago 1927) pp. 93-4; Spalding, op. cit., p. 437; L. H. Jenks, *The Migration of British Capital to 1875* (N.Y. 1927) p. 279; *Econ.* 3 July 1880; *Encyclopaedia Britannica*, (1902) p. 864.

36. G. Withers, 'English Investors and American Securities' *F.R.* (1907) p. 34; Greenwood, op. cit., p. 204; P. Ripley, *A Short History of Investment* (Lon. 1934) p. 88.

37. C. P. Kindleberger, *Manias, Panics and Crashes: A History of Financial Crises* (Lon. 1978) pp. 119, 190-2; F. Schuster, 'Foreign Trade and the Money Market' *J.I.B.* 25 (1904) pp. 58, 101; W. A. Cole & E. E. Gellender, 'The Relations between Banks and Stock Exchanges' *J.I.B.* 20 (1899) p. 411.

38. P. D. Holcombe, Scottish Investment in Canada, 1870-1914 (M.Litt. Strathclyde 1975); D. P. O'Brien (ed.), *The Correspondence of Lord Overstone* (Cam. 1971) p. 769; Munn, op. cit., pp. 305-311; B. Lenman, *An Economic History of Modern Scotland* (Lon. 1977) p. 189; J. S. Fleming, 'On the Theory and Practice of Banking in Scotland' *J.I.B.* 4 (1883) p. 144.

39. O'Brien, op. cit., p. 769; W. P. Kennedy, 'Institutional Response to Economic Growth: Capital Markets in Britain to 1914' in L. Hannah (ed.), *Management Strategy and Business Development* (Lon. 1976) p. 155; Cottrell, op. cit., pp. 593, 638, 749, 801-2; *I.R.* (1892) pp. 263, 434, (1895) p. 41; D. Williams, 'The Evolution of the Sterling System' in C. R. Whittlesey & J. S. G. Wilson (ed.), *Essays in Money and Banking* (Oxford 1968) pp. 267, 272-4, 286; C. A. E. Goodhart, *The Business of Banking, 1891-1914* (Lon. 1972) pp. 122-4, 128; Playford, op. cit., pp. 3, 30, 62; A. C. Cole, 'Notes on the London Money Market' *J.I.B.* 25 (1904) p. 134; Spalding, op. cit., pp. 444, 453; F. E. Steele, 'On changes in the Bank Rate of Discount' *J.I.B.* 12 (1891) pp. 496-7; Cole & Gellender, op. cit., pp. 408-9; C. A. Conant, *Wall Street and the Country: A Study of Recent Financial Tendencies* (N.Y. 1904) p. 147; Jenks, op. cit., p. 335; A. S. J. Baster, *The International Banks* (Lon. 1935) pp. 234, 245.

40. D. G. Paterson, *British Direct Investment in Canada, 1890-1914* (Toronto 1976) p. 97; cf. 'Business on the Scottish Markets'.

41. Powell, op. cit., pp. 63-4.

42. Glasgow Stock Exchange Association: Minutes, 5 April 1888.

43. Cole & Gellender, op. cit., p. 490.

44. J. Scott & M. Hughes, *The Anatomy of Scottish Capital* (Lon. 1980) pp. 66, 82, 126, 135, 189, 202.

45. Scott & Hughes, op. cit., pp. 72-3, 107, 131, 135, 183, 190.

46. R. F. Henderson, *The New Issue Market and the Finance of Industry* (Cam. 1951) p. 154; F. Machlup, *The Stock Market, Credit and Capital Formation* (Lon. 1940) pp. 20, 33, 250, 272.

CONCLUSION

All men, with few exceptions, whether of exalted or of humble station, ardently endeavour to obtain wealth, as the means of securing happiness and escaping misery.
A Monetary Manual for the Million (London 1861) p. 5.

Now, that gambling-houses have been swept from our land, and those transitory institutions of vice (the lottery betting clubs on horse racing) that for a while perverted every principle of honesty in our working classes, have been extinguished, it is time the Legislature should turn its attention to an evil worse than these, to gambling more ruinous, to demoralisation more extensive than all the Hells ever could produce: as now carried on in the heart of this City, and not only there, but through the length and breadth of the land, by the medium of Time Bargains on the Stock Exchange.
Exposure of the Stock Exchange and Bubble Companies (London 1854) p. 3.

Let the intending investor weigh well the relative advantages of America and the colonies as fields for investment, and let him have the courage of his convictions. It is in the growing values of one or other, or both, that future wealth for him is to be found, and not in this country.
J. S. Tait, *The Cattle Fields of the Far West* (Edinburgh 1884) p. 64.

Conclusion

FROM at least the late seventeenth century there existed in Scotland the ability to transfer the shares of joint-stock ventures, particularly banks, insurance companies, and shipping concerns. The means generally employed for arranging transfers was the Scottish legal profession with its long-established expertise in handling the sale and purchase of all forms of property, with shares being treated no differently from houses, land, ships or annuities. If a transfer could not be arranged by the lawyer through professional contacts, shares were disposed of through newspaper advertisements or public auctions. The use of such methods was facilitated by the small number of existing and potential investors and their preference for the securities of local companies. Nevertheless, a number of serious problems stemmed from the inclusion of shares within the general property market. To lawyers, the business in shares was of very minor importance, being subsidiary to the practice of law itself or the disposal of houses and estates, and the heavy fees charged for handling transfers were not justified by the limited service given. No lists of current prices for Scottish shares were compiled and published, though such prices were informally known by the late eighteenth century. This lack of specialisation, and the existence of numerous lawyers who were willing to handle transfers, made it difficult to arrange deals at a professional level and necessitated the additional use of costly advertisements and auctions. The unsatisfactory service offered by the legal profession, and the financial rewards available, encouraged other groups to add share dealing to their own activities. Accountants and bank and insurance agents were among the professional groups who found it easy to become involved in the kindred activity of buying and selling securities on commission. However, that only served to fragment further an already strained share market.

In the nineteenth century two fundamental developments forced changes in the established methods of handling share transfers. The number of joint-stock companies, and consequently the number and variety of shares, expanded greatly from the mid-1820s onwards. Investors and shareholders also became much more numerous, and less confined to a single locality and a few social classes, while there was a growing volume of business at the same time as transfers were becoming more complex. However, the events which made change imperative were the recurring periods of speculative activity when capital for investment became particularly abundant and new openings appeared. One avenue of investment taken up with great enthusiasm at these times was the shares of joint-stock companies, for many new ventures were promoted and there was much dealing in the shares of both new and established concerns. The expansion of share business, at such times, meant that it became practicable for individuals to specialise in the arrangement of transfers. Stockbrokers appeared first in Scotland in 1824, being initially confined to Edinburgh and Glasgow, although they had agents throughout Scotland who channelled business to them. With the collapse of the 1820s speculation in 1825-6, the number of stockbrokers fell. None remained in business in Glasgow. However, the independent and regular means of share transfer created by the appearance of these brokers remained and were centred on Edinburgh throughout the 1820s. Recovery from the collapse of the mania, and a period of mild speculation in the 1830s, led to a growth in the numbers of stockbrokers with their re-appearance in Glasgow and their establishment in Aberdeen and Dundee. The independent Scottish share market came into being through these brokers and their regular communication, contacts and clients.

The speculative mania of the mid-1840s did more than increase the numbers of stockbrokers and their locational spread; it also led to the establishment of the first Scottish stock exchanges. Before the boom, the share market had existed and operated on an informal level without any institutional framework. The speculation led to a greatly increased volume of business and a larger number of people involved in handling it, so placing existing methods of business under considerable strain and making it necessary for stockbrokers to create a formal organisation to facilitate transactions. It was agreed to establish a meeting place, regular hours of attendance, uniform charges and a code of business practice and conduct. These were embodied in a stock exchange association and its rules, and the meeting place was to be known as the Stock Exchange. Stock exchanges were formed in Glasgow and Edinburgh in 1844, and in Aberdeen in 1845. Important as the speculations were that produced these developments, without a basis of regular business neither the specialists nor the institutions would have survived. With the collapse of the 'Railway Mania', stockbrokers declined in number, disappearing entirely for a time from the smaller Scottish towns. Also, the rival stock exchanges formed in both Edinburgh and Glasgow were reduced to one in each city by the mid-1850s.

Two further stock exchanges were formed in Scotland in the nineteenth century. Dundee had a local market in shares long before the formation of the stock exchanges. What forced the institutionalisation of this market was the promotion of a number of substantial Dundee companies in the 1870s which were mainly orientated towards overseas investment. The shares of these concerns were held largely in the Dundee region and this created an increased demand for better local settling facilities, hence the stock exchange was established in 1879. In Greenock it was the financial difficulties of the Harbour Trust that led to the formation of a local stock exchange in 1888. Without the existence of heavily capitalised local concerns whose shares were locally held, there was no need for a local stock exchange. Bargains in a diverse collection of widely held shares were unlikely to be readily matched in one restricted locality. In these cases it was easier for the stockbroker to transact business through his contacts on the most appropriate exchange rather than have recourse to other local brokers and their clients.

The nature of the business transacted by the Scottish stockbrokers changed little once the stock exchanges were established. Transactions were mainly in financial institutions such as banks and insurance companies, and such facilities as gas works, railway lines, and shipping companies. There was very little direct involvement in either the primary or secondary sectors of the economy until the late nineteenth century. It was from about 1875 onwards that an increasing number of industrial and commercial companies issued transferable securities to the investing public with the purpose of raising new funds or of releasing the capital of the existing owners. At the same time established domestic mining concerns were being converted into joint-stock companies while, from the outset, overseas mining and agricultural ventures raised capital through public subscription. Whatever the nature of the enterprise, however, 'local' joint-stock companies dominated stock exchange activity in Scotland as a whole. Investors were attracted to the shares of companies operating or formed in their own localities. The individuals involved in such companies were usually known to the investors by reputation, if not personally, while the progress of the concerns could be readily observed. Indirect benefits might also accrue to the investors through increased employment and prosperity, or improved services, such as with a local railway or bank. Nevertheless, an increasing proportion of investment was attracted into the stocks and shares of distant enterprises, owing either to the security offered, as with governments or railroads, or to the submerging of 'local' identity through the creation of regional or national corporations.

The Scottish stockbrokers and stock exchanges were essential components of a national market in stocks and shares, serving the needs of the investors and companies resident and/or operating in their own respective areas. Specialisation could develop, and certain stock exchanges were regarded as more than a local market in certain activities. The Glasgow Stock Exchange, as the second largest share market in Britain, became a major centre for speculative transactions focusing on overseas mining and railway companies, and this attracted investors from all over Britain. Similarly, the Dundee Stock Exchange was mainly a market in the stocks and shares of companies formed to invest in the United States. Although this national share market existed, it was by no means centralised. Certainly, the sale and purchase of domestic and foreign government securities were confined almost entirely to the London Stock Exchange. As London was also the largest market by far, most of the speculative investment undertaken in Britain was done there. However, the general transactions in the securities of joint-stock companies were not dominated by London but by the markets in the towns and cities where these companies were formed and where their shareholders lived. These markets also offered a home to the smaller enterprises unsuited to the conditions of the London Stock Exchange.

Over a period of two centuries the Scottish share market evolved to meet the needs of both investors and the economy. Increasingly, investors were attracted to stocks and shares as a destination for their savings. Transferable securities could be easily realised in whole or part and were capable of producing both an acceptable return and capital gains. Progress in the economy required growing amounts of capital in large aggregate sums, often for long periods. It was by the device of transferable securities that the necessary capital was obtained. Without the ability to transfer, investors would have been unlikely to part with their savings in the amounts which were required for such indefinite lengths of time. The issue of stocks and shares was convenient for both the investor and the company, and increasingly became the principal means by which both risk capital and long-term funds were obtained for economic development. The growing popularity and importance of transferable securities forced the share market to become better organised and more sophisticated, and its personnel to become more professional and knowledgeable. In the long run, this is what happened in Scotland between 1700 and 1900, although temporary factors were of great importance in precipitating events and altering aspects of the market.

Bibliography

RATHER than present an exhaustive listing of all the works consulted that have been relevant to this study, I have selected the material that was found to be the most useful. General texts on finance, economic history and Scottish history have been omitted in the expectation that they would be familiar to most readers. Most of the contemporary printed material is to be found in the local and Scottish collections of the main Scottish university and public libraries. The King/Thomson/Herald pamphlet collection at Aberdeen University is a particularly valuable source of works that might otherwise have disappeared, such as company prospectuses, while that same library's O'Dell Transport Collection is an excellent repository of miscellaneous works concerning Scottish canals and railways.

A. Manuscript Sources

1. *Aberdeen: University Library*
   Aberdeen Stock Exchange Association: Record of Transactions, Correspondence, Stock and Share Lists
   Macdonald Collection: *City of Aberdeen Land Association*
   Davidson & Garden Collection: *Forbes & Co., Col. D. Forbes, Bruce Shand, Stewart & Co., W. Shand*
   Correspondence of William Leslie of Warthill
2. *Aberdeen: Horne & Mackinnon*
   Aberdeen Stock Exchange Association: Minutes
3. *Dundee: University Library*
   Dundee Stock Exchange Association: Record of Transactions
4. *Dundee: Public Library*
   Highest and Lowest Prices of Dundee Stocks, compiled by Stephen Ower
5. *Dundee: Chalmers, Ogilvie & Co.*
   Dundee Stock Exchange Association: Minutes
6. *Edinburgh: Public Library*
   Edinburgh Sugar House Company: Minutes
   Journal of an Edinburgh Resident (in manuscript)
7. *Edinburgh: Register House*
   The records of Scottish companies registered under the Companies' Acts
   Letter and Stock books of Thomas Kennedy (unextracted processes of the Court of Session)

8. *Edinburgh: Bell, Lawrie, Macgregor & Co.*
   Sale Book of John Robertson & Co.
   Circular of Robert Allan
   Circular of Bell, Begg & Cowan
9. *Edinburgh: Scottish Stock Exchange*
   Edinburgh Stock Exchange Association: Minutes & Committee Minutes
10. *Glasgow: Department of Economic History*
    Circulars and Papers of Hardie & Rowan
11. *Glasgow: Strathclyde University*
    Glasgow Stock Exchange: Stock and Share List
12. *Glasgow: Strathclyde Regional Archives*
    Kerr, Anderson, Miller, Stevenson & Co.
    Bannatyne, Kirkwood & France; Hill, Brown; Hill & Hogan; Mitchells,
    Johnston & Co.; MacKenzie, Robertson & Co. (solicitors' deposits)
13. *Glasgow: Scottish Stock Exchange*
    Glasgow Stock Exchange Association: Minutes

B. Directories (abbreviations in brackets)

Aberdeen Directory, 1824-1900   (A.D.)
Dundee Directory, 1824-1900   (D.D.)
Edinburgh Directory, 1824-1900   (E.D.)
Glasgow Directory, 1824-1900   (G.D.)
Greenock Directory, 1866-1900   (Gr.D.)
Inverness Directory, 1875-1900   (I.D.)
The British and Foreign Stock Exchange and Joint-Stock Companies Directory
(London 1836)
National Commercial Directory of the Whole of Scotland (Pigot & Co. London,
1825-6, 1837)
Royal National Directory of Scotland (Edinburgh 1899)
Slater's Commercial Directory of Scotland (London 1852, 1861, 1878, 1882)
The Stockbrokers' Directory of Great Britain and Ireland (London 1873-4)
Stubb's Directory (London 1892, 1896)
United Kingdom Stock and Sharebrokers' Directory (London 1900-1)

C. Newspapers and Magazines (abbreviations in brackets)

Aberdeen Chronicle, 1816-1821   (A.C.)
Aberdeen Free Press, 1853-5, 1876-1896   (A.F.P.)
Aberdeen Herald, 1832-1876   (A.H.)
Aberdeen Journal, 1823-5, 1835-6, 1838-9, 1845, 1853   (A.J.)
Dundee Courier and Argus, 1879   (D.C.)
Dundee, Perth and Cupar Advertiser, 1823-5, 1834-6, 1843-5, 1850, 1860,
1870, 1879   (D.P. & C.A.)

Dundee Year Book, 1878-1900   *(D.Y.B.)*
Edinburgh Advertiser, 1778-1783, 1817   *(E.A.)*
Edinburgh Evening Courant, 1795   *(E.E.C.)*
Edinburgh Weekly Journal, 1824-6, 1836-7, 1844-5   *(E.W.J.)*
Glasgow Chronicle, 1825   *(G.C.)*
Glasgow Herald, 1824-5, 1834-6, 1844-5   *(G.H.)*
Greenock Telegraph and Clyde Shipping Gazette, 1888-1900   *(G.T.)*
Inverness Journal and Northern Advertiser, 1822-5   *(I.J.)*
The Scots Magazine, 1823-6   *(S.M.)*
The Scotsman, 1844-5   *(Sc.M.)*

D. *Periodicals* (abbreviations in brackets)

Accountants' Magazine, 1897-1900   *(A.M.)*
Bankers' Magazine, 1844-1850   *(B.M.)*
Banking and Insurance Magazine, 1896-7   *(B. & I.M.)*
British Economist, 1886-8   *(B.E.)*
Burdett's Official Intelligence, 1882-1898   *(S.E.O.I.)*
Economist, 1843-1914 (selected years)   *(Econ.)*
Edinburgh Property Review, 1879   *(E.P.R.)*
Financial Review of Reviews, 1904-1914   *(F.R.)*
Journal of the Institute of Bankers, 1882-1914   *(J.I.B.)*
North British Economist, 1889-1895   *(N.B.E.)*
Scottish Banking and Insurance Magazine, 1879-1886   *(S.B. & I.M.)*
Scottish Property Gazette, 1892   *(S.P.G.)*
Scottish Critic of Finance and Insurance, 1898-1900   *(S.C.F.I.)*
Scottish Financier, 1883   *(S.F.)*
Scottish Railway Gazette, 1845-1851   *(S.R.G.)*
Stock Exchange Official Intelligence, 1899-1914   *(S.E.O.I.)*
J. Wetenhall, *Course of the Exchange, 1835-45*

E. *Parliamentary Papers*

'An Account of the Number of Banks established in Scotland', *B.P.P.* 23 (1826)
'Report on the Law of Partnership', (H. B. Ker) *B.P.P.* 44 (1837)
'Banks of Issue (Scotland): A Return, 1815-1845', *B.P.P.* 28 (1845)
Report from the Commissioners on the London Stock Exchange with Minutes of Evidence, Appendix, Index and Analysis', *B.P.P.* c. 2157-61 (1878)

F. *Contemporary Printed Works*
(The place of publication is London unless otherwise stated)

W. M. Acworth, *The Railways of Scotland* (1890)
A. Alison, *England in 1815 and 1845* (Edin. 1845)

A. Allardyce (ed.), *Scotland and Scotsmen in the Eighteenth Century: From the Mss. of John Ramsay of Ochtertyre* (Edin. 1888)

On the Analogy between the Stock Exchange and the Turf (1885)

W. Bagehot, *Lombard Street: A Description of the Money Market* (1873, repr. 1896)

The Bank — The Stock Exchange — The Bankers — The Bankers' Clearing House — The Minister, and the public: An Exposé (1821)

W. Bartlett & H. Chapman, *A Handy-Book for Investors* (1869)

H. H. Bassett (ed.), *Men of Note in Finance and Commerce* (1900-1)

H. H. Bassett (ed.), *Business Men at Home and Abroad, 1912-13* (1912)

C. W. Boase, *A Century of Banking in Dundee* (Edin. 1867)

D. Bremner, *The Industries of Scotland: Their rise, progress and present condition* (Edin. 1869)

J. Burnet, *History of the Water Supply to Glasgow* (Glasgow 1869)

W. Chambers, *The Book of Scotland* (Edin. 1830)

L. G. Chiozza Money, *Riches and Poverty* (1910)

G. Clare, *A Money-Market Primer and Key to the Exchanges* (1900)

J. Cleland, *Annals of Glasgow* (Glasgow 1816)

J. Cleland, *The Rise and Progress of the City of Glasgow* (Glasgow 1820)

H. Cockburn, *Journal of Henry Cockburn, 1831-1854* (Edin. 1874)

H. Cockburn, *Memorials of His Time* (Edin. 1856)

P. Colquhoun, *A Treatise on the Wealth, Power and Resources of the British Empire* (1815)

Commerce in Consternation (1826)

Counsel for Emigrants (Abdn. 1834)

J. Craig, *Remarks on some Financial Doctrines in Political Economy illustrated: A Brief Inquiry into the Commercial State of Britain since the year 1815* (Edin. 1821)

E. Crammond, 'The Economic Position of Scotland and her Financial Relations with England and Ireland', *J.R.S.S.* 75 (1912)

W. Creech, *Edinburgh Fugitive Pieces* (Edin. 1792, repr. 1815)

The Curious and Remarkable History of the Royal British Bank (1850)

The Currency Question from a Mercantile Point of View by a member of the Edinburgh Chamber of Commerce (Edin. 1856)

T. Doubleday, *A Financial, Monetary and Statistical History of England from the Revolution of 1688* (1859)

C. Duguid, *The Story of the Stock Exchange* (1901)

H. English, *A Complete View of the Joint-Stock Companies formed during the years 1824 and 1825* (1827)

H. English, *A Compendium of the Companies formed for working British Mines* (1826)

D. M. Evans, *The Commercial Crisis, 1847-8* (1848)

D. M. Evans, *The History of the Commercial Crisis, 1857-8* (1859)

Exposure of the Stock Exchange and Bubble Companies (1854)

J. Exter, *Causes of the Present Depression in Our Money Market* (1825)

C. Fenn, *A Compendium of the English and Foreign Companies* (1838, 1860, 1867, 1869)

F. W. Field, *Capital Investments in Canada* (Toronto 1911)

J. S. Fleming, *Scottish Banking* (Edin. 1877)

J. Francis, *Chronicles and Characters of the Stock Exchange* (1849)

W. Fraser, 'Fluctuations of the Building Trade, and Glasgow's House Accommodation', *P.R.P.S.G.* 39 (1907-8)

General Observations on the Principal Railways, written by a Liverpool Resident (1838)

G. F. Gibson, *The Stock Exchanges of London, Paris and New York* (1889)

R. Giffen, *Stock Exchange Securities* (1877)

R. Giffen, *The Growth of Capital* (1889)

W. Gordon, *The Universal Accountant and Complete Merchant* (1763)

F. Gore-Browne & W. Jordan, *A Handy Book on the Formation, Management and Winding-up of Joint-Stock Companies* (1902)

G. Graham, *The Caledonian Railway: Accounts of its Origin and Completion* (Glasgow 1888)

W. B. Grohman, 'Cattle Ranches in the Far West', *Fortnightly Review* 28 (1880)

W. B. Grohman, *Camps in the Rockies* (1882)

A Guide to the Unprotected in every-day matters relating to Property and Income (1891)

R. Hamilton, *An Inquiry Concerning the rise and progress, the redemption and present state and management of the National Debt* (Edin. 1818)

R. Hamilton, *Observations upon the causes of Distress in the Country* (Glasgow 1822)

D. Hardcastle, *Banks and Bankers* (1842)

J. Harley, *The Currency: Its Influences on the Internal Trade of the Country* (Glasgow 1839)

D. O. Hill & G. Buchanan, *Views of the Opening of the Glasgow and Garnkirk Railway: Also an account of that and other Railways in Lanarkshire* (Edin. 1832)

C. K. Hobson, *The Export of Capital* (1914)

J. Hopkirk, *Account of the Forth and Clyde Canal Navigation from its origin to the present time* (Glasgow 1816)

G. D. Ingall & G. Withers, *The Stock Exchange* (1904)

J. S. Jeans, *Western Worthies* (Glasgow 1872)

W. S. Jevons, *Investigations into Currency and Finance* (1884)

A. Johnston, *Sketch etc. of the Illinois Investment Company* (Edin. 1857)

A. W. Kerr, *Scottish Banking during the period of published Accounts, 1865-1896* (1898)

G. Kinnear, *A History of the Rise of Exchange Companies in Scotland* (Glasgow 1848)

The Land: The Report of the Land Enquiry Committee (1914)

The Late Commercial Crisis; being a retrospect of the years 1836 to 1838, by a Glasgow Manufacturer (Glasgow 1839)

W. R. Lawson, *The Scottish Investors' Manual* (Edin. 1884)

A Letter to the inhabitants of Edinburgh on Joint-Stock Companies by a Citizen (Edin. 1824)

Letters from Edinburgh, 1774-5 (1776)

L. Levi, 'Joint-Stock Companies', *J.R.S.S.* 33 (1870)

W. H. Logan, *The Scottish Banker* (Edin. 1838, repr. 1844)

J. Lowe, *The Present State of England in regard to Agriculture, Trade and Finance* (1823)

H. Lowenfeld, *All about Investment* (1909)

J. R. McCulloch, *Dictionary of Commerce* (1832, 1846, 1875)

J. R. McCulloch, *A Descriptive and Statistical Account of the British Empire* (1854)

J. R. McCulloch, *A Treatise on the Succession to Property* (1848)

J. MacDonald, *Food from the Far West* (Edin. 1878)

W. M. M'Ilwraith, *The Glasgow and South Western Railway* (Glasgow 1880)

C. MacLaren, *Railways Compared with Canals and Common Roads and their uses and advantages explained* (1825)

A. McLean (ed.), *Local Industries of Glasgow and the West of Scotland* (Glasgow 1901)

C. H. Marshall, 'Dundee as a centre of Investment', *British Association* (Dundee 1912)

J. Meetwell, *Incidents, Errors and Experiences in the Life of a Scottish Merchant* (Edin. 1866)

J. Mitchell, *Reminiscences of my life in the Highlands* (1883, 1887, repr. Newton Abbot 1971)

W. Mitchell, *Our Scotch Banks* (Edin. 1879)

A. Moffat, *Scottish Railways: Their Present and Future Value considered as an Investment for Capital* (Edin. 1849)

R. Z. Mudge, *Observations on Railways* (1837)

M. G. Mulhall, *Fifty Years of National Progress, 1837-1887* (1887)

A. Mundell, *A Comparative View of the Industrial Situation of Great Britain, 1775-1832* (1832)

J. H. Murchison, *British Mines considered as a means of Investment* (1854)

R. L. Nash, *A Short Inquiry into the Profitable Nature of our Investments* (1881)

J. Nicol, *Vital, Social, and Economic Statistics of the City of Glasgow, 1885-1891* (Glasgow 1891)

R. R. Notman, *The Deeside Railway: A Letter to the landed proprietors of Deeside* (Abdn. 1850)

R. H. I. Palgrave, *Notes on Banking* (1873)

R. H. I. Palgrave, *Bank Rate and the Money Market in England, France, Germany, Holland and Belgium, 1844-1900* (1903)

R. H. I. Palgrave (ed.), *Dictionary of Political Economy* (1894-1901)

Philanthropos, *Everyman his own broker* (1761)

Phillips' Investors' Manual (1887)

F. Playford, *Practical Hints for Investing Money, with an Explanation of the Mode of Transacting Business on the Stock Exchange* (1856)

E. T. Powell, *The Mechanism of the City* (1910)

R. Price, *Observations on Reversionary Payments* (1783)

J. Priestley, *Historical Account of the Navigable Rivers, Canals and Railways of Great Britain* (1831)

Proposals for carrying on certain public works in the City of Edinburgh (Edin. 1752)

G. Purves, *All Classes Productive of National Wealth* (1817)

Records of the Glasgow Stock Exchange Association, 1844-1898 (Glasgow 1898)

J. Reid, *Manual of the Scottish Stocks and British Funds* (Edin. 1842)

K. Robinson, *The Mining Market* (1907)

A. Romney, *Three Letters on the Speculative Schemes of the Present Times and the Projected Banks* (Edin. 1825)

W. R. Scott (ed.), *The Records of a Scottish Cloth Manufactory at New Mills, Haddingtonshire, 1681-1703* (Edin. 1905)

Scottish Land: The Report of the Scottish Land Enquiry Committee (1914)

The Scottish Railway Shareholder's Manual (Edin. 1849)

H. Scrivenor, *The Railways of the United Kingdom Statistically Considered* (1849)

Sequel to the Counsel for Emigrants (Abdn. 1834)

J. Sinclair, *Analysis of the Statistical Account of Scotland* (Edin. 1825)

Sketch of the Affairs of the Treasury of Aberdeen under the Administration of the Trustees — By one of their number (Abdn. 1821)

T. Skinner (ed.), *The Stock Exchange Year Book* (1874, 1881)

R. Somers, *The Scotch Banks and Systems of Issue* (Edin. 1873)

Statistical Illustrations of the British Empire (1827)

Stock Exchange Investments: Their History; Practice; and Results (1897)

J. S. Tait, *The Cattle Fields of the Far West* (Edin. 1884)

Thoughts on Trade and Public Spirit (1716)

T. Tooke, *A History of Prices* (1838-1857)

'On the Transfer of British Capital to the United States', *Scottish Monthly Magazine* 1 (1836)

H. Tuck, *Railway Shareholders' Manual* (1847)

S. F. Van Oss, *American Railroads and British Investors* (1893)

S. F. Van Oss & V. G. Mathieson, *Stock Exchange Values: A Decade of Finance, 1885-1895* (1895)

W. W. Wall, *How to Invest in Railways* (1903)

R. A. Ward, *A Treatise on Investments* (1852)

W. Watt, 'Fifty Years' Progress in Aberdeen', *T.A.P.S.* 4 (1900-1910)

E. Wishaw, *The Railways of Great Britain and Ireland* (1840)

H. Withers, *Stocks and Shares* (1914)

N. Wood, *A Practical Treatise on Railroads* (1825, repr. 1831)

Words of Warning to the People of Scotland on Sir Robert Peel's Scotch Currency Scheme (Edin. 1844)

G. *Secondary Printed Works*

I. H. Adams, *The Making of Urban Scotland* (1978)

B. L. Anderson, 'Provincial Aspects of the Financial Revolution of the eighteenth century', *B.H.* 11 (1969)

B. L. Anderson, 'The Attorney and the Early Capital Market in Lancashire', in J. R. Harris (ed.), *Liverpool and Merseyside* (1969)

B. L. Anderson, 'Law, finance and economic growth in England: some long-term influences', in B. M. Ratcliffe (ed.), *Great Britain and her World, 1750-1914* (Man. 1975)

J. L. Anderson, *The Story of the Commercial Bank of Scotland, 1810-1910* (Edin. 1910)

J. D. Bailey, 'Australian Borrowing in Scotland in the Nineteenth Century', *Ec.H.R.* 12 (1959-60)

T. Binnie, *Memoir of Thomas Binnie, Builder in Glasgow, 1792-1867* (Glasgow 1882)

S. Broadbridge, *Studies in Railway Expansion, and the Capital Market in England, 1825-1873* (1970)

R. Brown, *History of Accounting and Accountants* (Edin. 1905)

R. Brown, 'The Genesis of Company Law in England and Scotland', *Juridical Review* 13 (1901)

R. Brown, 'Early Scottish Joint-Stock Companies', *P.R.P.S.G.* 34 (1902-3)

R. Burt, 'The London Mining Exchange, 1850-1900', *B.H.* 14 (1972)

J. Butt, 'Capital and Enterprise in the Scottish Iron Industry, 1780-1840', in J. Butt & J. T. Ward (ed.), *Scottish Themes* (Edin. 1976)

A. K. Cairncross, *Home and Foreign Investment, 1870-1913* (Cam. 1953)

A. K. Cairncross, 'The English Capital Market before 1914', *Economica* 25 (1958)

A. K. Cairncross & B. Weber, 'Fluctuations in Building in Great Britain, 1785-1849', *Ec.H.R.* 9 (1957)

R. Cameron (ed.), *Banking in the early stages of Industrialisation* (N.Y. 1967)

R. H. Campbell, 'Investment in the Scottish pig iron trade, 1830-1843', *S.J.P.E.* 1 (1954)

R. H. Campbell, 'Edinburgh Bankers and the Western Bank of Scotland', *S.J.P.E.* 2 (1955)

R. H. Campbell, 'Fluctuations in Stocks: A Nineteenth Century Case Study', *O.E.P.* 9 (1957)

R. H. Campbell, 'The Financing of Carron Company', *B.H.* 1 (1958)

R. H. Campbell, *Carron Company* (Edin. 1961)

R. H. Campbell, 'Early Malleable Iron Production in Scotland', *B.H.* 4 (1961-2)

R. H. Campbell, 'The Law and the Joint-Stock Company in Scotland', in P. L. Payne (ed.), *Studies in Scottish Business History* (1967)

S. D. Chapman, 'Working Capital in the British Cotton Industry, 1770-1850', *E.B.H.C.P.* 1975

S. G. Checkland, *The Mines of Tharsis* (1967)

S. G. Checkland, *Scottish Banking: A History, 1695-1973* (Glasgow 1975)

J. R. Christie, 'Joint-Stock Enterprise in Scotland before the Companies Acts', *Juridical Review* 21 (1909-10)

J. Clapham, *The Bank of England: A History* (Cam. 1944)

E. W. Cooney, 'Long waves in building in the British Economy of the nineteenth century', *Ec.H.R.* 13 (1960-1)

P. L. Cottrell, *Industrial Finance, 1830-1914: The Finance and Organisation of English Manufacturing Industry* (1980)

R. S. Craig, 'Some Aspects of Capital Formation in Shipping in the Age of Sail and Steam', *E.B.H.C.P.* 1975

N. Crathorne, *Tennants' Stalk: The Story of the Tennants of the Glen* (1973)

L. Davis, 'The Capital Market and industrial concentration, the U.S. and U.K.: A Comparative Study', *Ec.H.R.* 19 (1966)

T. M. Devine, *The Tobacco Lords: A Study of the Tobacco Merchants of Glasgow and their Trading Activities, 1740-90* (Edin. 1975)

I. Donnachie, *A History of the Brewing Industry in Scotland* (Edin. 1979)

A. B. Dubois, *The English Business Company after the Bubble Act, 1720-1800* (N.Y. 1938)

B. Duckham, *A History of the Scottish Coal Industry, 1700-1815* (Newton Abbot 1970)

'Early Scottish Railways', *T.B.R.* 74 (1967)

M. Edelstein, 'Rigidity and bias in the British capital market, 1870-1913', in D. McCloskey (ed.), *Essays on a Mature Economy: Britain after 1840* (1971)

M. Edelstein, 'The Determinants of U.K. Investment Abroad, 1870-1913: The U.S. Case', *J.Ec.H.* 34 (1974)

M. Edelstein, 'Realized Rates of Return on U.K. Home and Overseas Portfolio Investment in the Age of High Imperialism', *E.E.H.* 13 (1976)

The Edinburgh Stock Exchange, 1844-1944 (Edin. 1944)

G. W. Edwards, *The Evolution of Finance Capitalism* (N.Y. 1938)

P. M. Edwards, 'Scottish Investments in the American West', *Scottish Colloquium Proceedings,* Guelph 4-5 (1972)

G. H. Evans, *British Corporation Finance, 1775-1850: A Study of Preference Shares* (Baltimore 1936)

R. N. Forbes, 'Early Banking Excursions', *T.B.R.* 10 (1974)

A. D. Gayer, et al, *The Growth and Fluctuation of the British Economy, 1790-1850* (Oxford 1953)

I. F. Gibson, 'The Establishment of the Scottish Steel Industry', *S.J.P.E.* 5 (1958)

J. C. Gilbert, *A History of Investment Trusts in Dundee, 1873-1938* (1949)

G. Glasgow, *The Scottish Investment Trust Companies* (1932)

C. A. E. Goodhart, *The Business of Banking 1891-1914* (1912)

T. B. Gourvish & M. C. Reed, 'The Financing of Scottish Railways before 1860: A Comment', *S.J.P.E.* 18 (1971)

W. Graham, *The One Pound Note in the History of Banking in Great Britain* (Edin. 1911)

M. Gray, *The Fishing Industries of Scotland, 1790-1914: A Study in Regional Adaptation* (Abdn. 1978)

C. Gulvin, *The Tweedmakers: A History of the Scottish Fancy Woollen Industry, 1600-1914* (Newton Abbot 1973)

H. J. Habakkuk, 'Fluctuations and Growth in the Nineteenth Century', in M. Kooy (ed.), *Studies in Economics and Economic History* (1972)

A. R. Hall, *The London Capital Market and Australia, 1870-1914* (Canberra 1963)

A. R. Hall, 'A Note on the English Capital Market as a source of Funds for Home Investment before 1914', *Economica* 24 (1957) & 25 (1958)

G. R. Hawke, *Railways and Economic Growth in England and Wales, 1840-70* (1970)

G. R. Hawke & M. C. Reed, 'Railway Capital in the United Kingdom in the Nineteenth Century', *Ec.H.R.* 22 (1969)

F. W. Hirst, *The Stock Exchange* (1948)

History of the Chartered Accountants of Scotland (Edin. 1954)

J. R. T. Hughes, *Fluctuations in Trade, Industry, and Finance: A Study of British Economic Development, 1850-60* (Oxford 1960)

B. C. Hunt, *The Development of the Business Corporation in England, 1800-1867* (Cam., Mass., 1936)

W. T. Jackson, *The Enterprising Scot: Investors in the American West after 1873* (Edin. 1968)

J. B. Jeffreys, 'The Denomination and Character of Shares, 1855-1885', *Ec.H.R.* 16 (1946)

L. H. Jenks, *The Migration of British Capital to 1875* (N.Y. 1927)

A. Keith, *The North of Scotland Bank Ltd., 1836-1936* (Abdn. 1936)

W. P. Kennedy, 'Foreign Investment, Trade and Growth in the United Kingdom, 1870-1913', *E.E.H.* 11 (1974)

W. P. Kennedy, 'Institutional Response to Economic Growth: Capital Markets in Britain to 1914', in L. Hannah (ed.), *Management Strategy and Business Development* (1976)

A. G. Kenwood, 'Railway Investment in Britain, 1825-75', *Economica* 32 (1965)

A. W. Kerr, *History of Banking in Scotland* (1918)

W. G. Kerr, 'Scotland and the Texas Mortgage Business', *Ec.H.R.* 16 (1963-4)

W. G. Kerr, 'Scottish Investment and Enterprise in Texas', in P. L. Payne (ed.), *Studies in Scottish Business History* (1967)

W. G. Kerr, *Scottish Capital on the American Credit Frontier* (Austin 1976)

J. R. Killick & W. A. Thomas, 'The Provincial Stock Exchanges, 1830-1870', *Ec.H.R.* 23 (1970)

J. R. Killick & W. A. Thomas, 'The Stock Exchanges of the North of England, 1836-1850', *Northern History* 5 (1970)

C. P. Kindleberger, *Manias, Panics and Crashes: A History of Financial Crises* (1978)

D. Laird, *Paddy Henderson* (Glasgow 1961)

F. Lavington, *The English Capital Market* (1921)

B. Lenman, *From Esk to Tweed; Harbours, Ships and Men of the East Coast of Scotland* (Glasgow 1975)

B. Lenman, et al, *Dundee and its Textile Industry* (Dundee 1969)

B. Lenman & K. Donaldson, 'Partners' Incomes, Investment and Diversification in the Scottish Linen Area, 1850-1921', *B.H.* 13 (1971)

H. G. Lewin, *Early British Railways, 1801-1844* (1925)

H. G. Lewin, *The Railway Mania and its Aftermath, 1845-1852* (1936)

J. Lindsay, *The Canals of Scotland* (Newton Abbot 1968)

S. G. E. Lythe, 'The Canal Mania in East Scotland', *The Scots Magazine* 33 (1940)

S. G. E. Lythe, 'The Dundee and Newtyle Railway', *Railway Magazine* 97 (1951)

S. G. E. Lythe, 'The Early Days of the Arbroath and Forfar Railway', *Railway Magazine* 99 (1953)

D. Macallan, 'Peter Buchanan, London Agent for the Great Western Railway of Canada', in D. S. MacMillan (ed.), *Canadian Business History* (Toronto 1972)

D. S. MacMillan, *The Debtor's War — Scottish Capitalists and the Economic Crisis in Australia, 1841-6* (Melbourne 1960)

D. S. MacMillan, 'The Scottish Australian Company, 1840-80', *Scottish Historical Review* 39 (1960)

D. S. MacMillan, 'Scottish Enterprise in Australia, 1798-1879' in P. L. Payne (ed.), *Studies in Scottish Business History* (1967)

D. S. MacMillan, 'The Transfer of Company Control from Scotland to London in the nineteenth century: The Case of the Scottish Australian Company, 1853', *B.H.* 12 (1970)

D. S. MacMillan, *Scotland and Australia, 1788-1850: Emigration, Commerce and Investment* (1967)

C. A. Malcolm, *The Bank of Scotland, 1695-1945* (Edin. 1948)

C. A. Malcolm, *The History of the British Linen Bank* (Edin. 1950)

J. Mann, 'Glimpses of Early Accountancy in Glasgow', *A.M.* 58 (1954)

W. H. Marwick, 'The Limited Company in Scottish Economic Development', *Ec.H.R.* 3 (1934-7)

W. H. Marwick, 'Scottish Overseas Investment in the Nineteenth Century', *Scottish Bankers' Magazine* 27 (1935-6)

R. C. O. Matthews, *A Study in Trade-Cycle History: Economic Fluctuations in Great Britain, 1833-1842* (Cam. 1954)

Memoirs and Portraits of One Hundred Glasgow Men (Glasgow 1886)

R. C. Michie, 'North-East Scotland and the Northern Whale Fishing, 1752-1893', *Northern Scotland* 3 (1977-8)

R. C. Michie, 'The Transfer of Shares in Scotland, 1700-1820', *B.H.* 20 (1978)

R. N. Millman, *The Making of the Scottish Landscape* (1975)

A. Mitchell, *Political and Social Movements in Dalkeith, 1831-1882* (Dalkeith 1882)

E. V. Morgan & W. A. Thomas, *The Stock Exchange: Its History and Functions* (1962)

H. R. Mothershead, *The Swan Land and Cattle Company* (Norman 1971)

N. Munro, *The History of the Union Bank of Scotland* (Glasgow 1930)

T. B. Napier, 'The History of Joint-Stock and Limited Liability Companies', in *A Century of Law Reform* (1901)

North British and Mercantile Insurance Company, 1809-1909 (Edin. 1909)

A. C. O'Dell, 'A Geographical Examination of the Development of Scottish Railways', *Scottish Geographical Magazine* 55 (1939)

H. O. O'Hagan, *Leaves from my Life* (1929)

P. L. Payne (ed.), *Studies in Scottish Business History* (1967)

P. L. Payne, 'The Early Scottish Limited Companies, 1856-1895: An Historical and Analytical Survey', *California Institute of Technology: Social Science Working Paper* 222 (1978)

D. G. Paterson, *British Direct Investment in Canada, 1890-1914* (Toronto 1976)

W. M. Pearce, *The Matador Land and Cattle Company* (Norman 1964)

H. Pollins, 'The Marketing of Railway Shares in the first half of the nineteenth century', *Ec.H.R.* 7 (1954-5)

H. Pollins, 'Railway contractors and the finance of railway development in Britain', *Journal of Transport History* 3 (1957-8)

E. T. Powell, *The Evolution of the Money Market, 1385-1915* (1916)

E. A. Pratt, *Scottish Canals and Waterways* (1922)

R. S. Rait, *The History of the Union Bank of Scotland* (Glasgow 1930)

Records of the Glasgow Stock Exchange Association, 1844-1926 (Glasgow 1927)

M. C. Reed, 'George Stephenson and W. T. Salvin: The early capital market at work', *T.H.* 1 (1968)

M. C. Reed, 'Railways and the growth of the capital market', in M. C. Reed (ed.), *Railways in the Victorian Economy* (Newton Abbot 1969)

M. C. Reed, *Investment in Railways in Britain, 1820-44: A study in the development of the capital market* (Oxford 1975)

M. C. Reed, *A History of James Capel & Co.* (1975)

M. C. Reed (ed.), *Railways in the Victorian Economy* (Newton Abbot 1969)

J. M. Reid, *The History of the Clydesdale Bank, 1838-1938* (Glasgow 1938)

M. Robbins, 'Sir Walter Scott and two early railway schemes', *Railway Magazine* (1951)

C. J. A. Robertson, 'The cheap railway movement in Scotland: The St. Andrews Railway Company', *T.H.* 7 (1974)

D. H. Robertson, *A Study of Industrial Fluctuation* (1915)

R. G. Rodger, 'Speculative Builders and the Structure of the Scottish Building Industry, 1860-1914', *B.H.* 21 (1979)

Salas 150: A History of the Scottish Amicable Life Assurance Society, 1826-1976 (Glasgow 1976)

S. B. Saul, 'House Building in England, 1890-1914', *Ec.H.R.* 15 (1962-3)

L. J. Saunders, *Scottish Democracy, 1815-1840* (Edin. 1950)

J. Scott & M. Hughes, *The Anatomy of Scottish Capital* (1980)

W. R. Scott, *The Constitution and Finance of English, Scottish and Irish Joint-Stock Companies to 1720* (Cam. 1910-12)

A. E. Smith, *George Smith's Money: A Scottish Investor in America* (Madison 1966)

J. B. Sturrock, *Peter Brough: A Paisley Philanthropist* (Paisley 1890)

W. A. Thomas, *The Provincial Stock Exchanges* (1973)

F. M. L. Thompson, 'The Land market in the nineteenth century', *O.E.P.* 9 (1957)

G. Todd, 'Some aspects of joint-stock companies, 1844-1900', *Ec.H.R.* 4 (1932-4)

'Tontines and the Royal Bank', *T.B.R.* 57 (1963)

R. E. Tyson, 'Scottish investment in American Railways: The Case of the City of Glasgow Bank, 1856-1881', in P. L. Payne (ed.), *Studies in Scottish Business History* (1967)

W. Vamplew, 'Sources of Scottish Railway Share Capital before 1860', *S.J.P.E.* 17 (1970)

W. Vamplew, 'Banks and Railway Finance: A note on the Scottish experience', *T.H.* 4 (1971)

C. N. Ward-Perkins, 'The Commercial Crisis of 1847', *O.E.P.* 2 (1950)

R. B. Weir, *A History of the Scottish American Investment Company, Ltd., 1873-1973* (Edin. 1973)

A. J. Youngson, *The Making of Classical Edinburgh, 1750-1840* (Edin. 1966)

H. Theses

H. W. Bull, Working-Class Housing in Glasgow, 1862-1902 *(M.Litt. Strathclyde 1973)*

T. J. Byres, The Scottish Economy during the 'Great Depression', 1873-1896 *(B.Litt. Glasgow 1963)*

R. D. Corrins, William Baird and Company: Coal and Iron Masters, 1830-1914 *(Ph.D. Strathclyde 1974)*

M. S. Cotterill, The Scottish Gas Industry up to 1914 *(Ph.D. Strathclyde 1976)*

P. L. Cottrell, Investment Banking in England, 1856-1882 *(Ph.D. Hull 1974)*

M. J. Fenn, British Investment in South America and the Financial Crisis of 1825-6 *(M.A. Durham 1969)*

I. F. Gibson, The Economic History of the Scottish Iron and Steel Industry *(Ph.D. London 1955)*

J. A. Hassan, The Development of the Coal Industry in Mid and West Lothian, 1815-1873 *(Ph.D. Strathclyde 1976)*

P. D. Holcombe, Scottish Investment in Canada, 1870-1914 *(M.Litt. Strathclyde 1975)*

J. B. Jeffreys, Trends in Business Organisation in Great Britain since 1856 *(Ph.D. London 1938)*

J. C. Logan, The Dumbarton Glass Works Company, c.1777-c.1850 *(M.Litt. Strathclyde 1970)*

A. M. C. MacEwan, The Shotts Iron Company, 1800-1850 *(M.Litt. Strathclyde 1972)*

J. McKee, Glasgow Working Class Housing between the Wars, 1919-1939 *(M.Litt. Strathclyde 1977)*

R. C. Michie, The Scottish Stock Exchange in the Nineteenth Century *(Ph.D. Aberdeen 1979)*

H. V. Mulligan, Early Railway Development in Angus *(M.A. St. Andrews 1952)*

C. W. Munn, The Scottish Provincial Banking Companies, 1747-1864 *(Ph.D. Glasgow 1976)*

R. G. Rodger, Scottish Urban Housebuilding, 1870-1914 *(Ph.D. Edinburgh 1975)*

D. I. A. Steel, The Linen Industry of Fife in the Later Eighteenth and Nineteenth Centuries *(Ph.D. St. Andrews 1975)*

W. Vamplew, Railways and the Transformation of the Scottish Economy *(Ph.D. Edinburgh 1970)*

R. B. Weir, The Distilling Industry in Scotland in the Nineteenth and early Twentieth Centuries *(Ph.D. Edinburgh 1974)*

C. A. Whatley, The Process of Industrialisation in Ayrshire, c.1707-1871 *(Ph.D. Strathclyde 1975)*

M. A. Whitehead, The Western Bank and the Crisis of 1857 *(M.Litt. Strathclyde 1978)*

Index